'AGRARIANS' AND 'ARISTOCRATS'

Party Political Ideology in the
United States, 1837-1846

TO MARIA

'Agrarians' and 'Aristocrats'

Party Political Ideology in the United States, 1837-1846

JOHN ASHWORTH

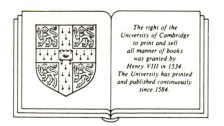

The right of the
University of Cambridge
to print and sell
all manner of books
was granted by
Henry VIII in 1534.
The University has printed
and published continuously
since 1584.

CAMBRIDGE UNIVERSITY PRESS

CAMBRIDGE

LONDON   NEW YORK   NEW ROCHELLE

MELBOURNE   SYDNEY

Published by the Press Syndicate of the University of Cambridge
The Pitt Building, Trumpington Street, Cambridge CB2 1RP
32 East 57th Street, New York, NY 10022, USA
10 Stamford Road, Oakleigh, Melbourne 3166, Australia

First published in Great Britian in 1983 by Swift Printers (Publishing) Ltd., London EC1
for The Royal Historical Society
and in the U.S.A. by Humanities Press Inc., Atlantic Highlands, NJ 07716

First paperback edition 1987

Printed in the United States of America

British Library Cataloguing in Publication Data
Ashworth, John
'Agrarians' & 'aristocrats': party political ideology in the
United States, 1837-1846.
(Royal Historical Society studies in history series; no. 37)
1. United States–Politics and government–1837-1841
2. United States–Politics and government–1841-1845
3. United States–Politics and government–1845-1849
I. Title   II. Series
973.5   E381
ISBN 0-521-33567-1

PREFACE TO THE PAPERBACK EDITION

The decision by Cambridge University Press to republish this book in paperback form gives me the opportunity, first and foremost, to thank Frank Smith of CUP for his help and encouragement, second, to correct some typoographical errors and third, to state more clearly one of the premises on which the study rests.

Historians of the revolutionary period have, since the appearance of Bernard Bailyn's work on the intellectual origins of the struggle, subjected the ideas of the revolutionaries to the closest scrutiny. Somewhat more recently, the ideas of the Jeffersonians and Federalists have been analysed in great depth and, in the best works, with considerable sensitivity to tone and nuance. Jacksonian historiography, however, is rather different. Whilst there have been some excellent surveys of Democratic and Whig ideology, there remains on the part of many historians a reluctance to take these ideas seriously.

This reluctance is explained, perhaps, by the resemblance between politics in contemporary America and in the Jacksonian era. Many of the campaigning techniques and the political practices which we associate with modern America have their origins in the Jacksonian period. It is therefore tempting to assume that the role of ideology in Jacksonian politics is comparable to its function in modern American politics and that the ideological gap between the parties is comparable to that between Democrats and Republicans in the 1980s.

This is not my view of Jacksonian politics. I have tried to take the utterances of statesmen seriously, believing in their sincerity except when I have specific cause to doubt it. The result is that when I find evidence of, for example, Democratic hostility to capitalism, I have generally taken it to denote precisely that. This perhaps runs counter to what some readers will take to be "common sense"; an age which has lived through the Watergate scandal, to name only the most notorious example of modern political chicanery, has little confidence in the veracity of the politician. The problem with this approach, however, is that "common sense" is not a single transhistorical category which remains constant at all times and in all places. The reader who rejects evidence of Democratic hostility to capitalism because it violates his notion of "common sense" is in danger of projecting into the past the values of the present, of imposing contemporary America's consensus on democracy and capitalism on to an era which is fundamentally and irretrievably different. This does not, of course, constitute an *a priori* argument for Democratic radicalism or for a wide divergence of opinion between Democrat and Whig. These propositions can only be established by a full presentation of the evidence. Such is my task in the pages that follow.

ACKNOWLEDGEMENTS

During the past eight years I have been greatly assisted by two scholars. It was Michael J. Heale of the University of Lancaster who first introduced me to Jacksonian politics. I am moreover greatly indebted to him for reading the present manuscript in its entirety and for making important criticisms. Thanks also to Duncan J. MacLeod of St. Catherine's College, Oxford who supervised this work as a doctoral dissertation. He was quite simply the ideal supervisor and much of the credit for whatever is original in this work belongs to him. I am grateful also to Richard Crockatt of the University of East Anglia for reading the manuscript and suggesting some important alterations and revisions, to Helen Butler for reading the proofs, and to Mrs Janet Godden, executive editor to the Royal Historical Society's *Studies In History* series. I should like to express my gratitude to those who assisted me at the Library of Congress, where most of the research for this work was done: Bob Gross of the microform division was especially helpful. Finally I wish to thank my parents for all their help and support.

CONTENTS

ABBREVIATIONS

A.B.S.	American Behavioral Scientist
A.E.J.	Albany Evening Journal
A.H.R.	American Historical Review
A.J.S.	American Journal of Sociology
A.M.M.	American Monthly Magazine
A.Q.	American Quarterly
A.Q.R.	American Quarterly Review
Ark.H.Q.	Arkansas Historical Quarterly
A.R.	Alabama Review
Bo.Q.R.	Boston Quarterly Review
Br.Q.R.	Brownson's Quarterly Review
B.S.D	Bay State Democrat
Cong. Gl.	Congressional Globe
Dem. Exp.	Democratic Expositor
Dem. Rev.	Democratic Review
Ga.H.Q.	Georgia Historical Quarterly
Hill's Pat.	Hill's New Hampshire Patriot
H.J.	Journal of the United States House of Representatives
H.N.H.	Historical New Hampshire
H.P.S.O.	Historical and Philosophical Society of Ohio
I.J.H.P.	Iowa Journal of History and Politics
Ind.MH.	Indiana Magazine of History
Iowa C.C.	Fragments of the Debates of the Iowa Constitutional Conventions of 1844 and 1846 ed. Benjamin F. Shambaugh (Iowa City, 1900)
I.S.R.	Illinois State Register
J.A.H.	Journal of American History
J.E.H.	Journal of Economic History
J.S.H.	Journal of Southern History
J.S.H.P.	James Sprunt Historical Publications
La. C.C.	Proceedings and Debates of the Convention of Louisiana (New Orleans, 1845)
M.H.	Michigan History
Mich. C.C.	The Michigan Constitutional Conventions of 1835-1836 ed. Harold M. Dorr (Ann Arbor, 1940)

Mo. H.R.	Missouri Historical Review
M.V.H.R.	Mississippi Valley Historical Review
Nat. Am.	Native American (Washington)
Nat. Int.	National Intelligencer
N.C.S. & H.J.	North Carolina Senate and House Journal
N.E.Q.	New England Quarterly
N.H.P.	New Hampshire Patriot
N.Y.H.	New York History
N.Y.H.S.Q.	New York Historical Society Quarterly
N.Y.R.	New York Review
O.H.	Ohio History
O.S.A.H.Q.	Ohio State Archaeological and Historical Quarterly
Pa. C.C.	Proceedings of the Convention of Pennsylvania to Propose Amendments to the Constitution, 14 vols. (Harrisburg, 1837-9)
P.S.Q.	Political Science Quarterly
R.A.H.	Reviews in American History
R.I.H.	Rhode Island History
R.P.	Review of Politics
S.A.Q.	South Atlantic Quarterly
S.J.	Journal of the United States Senate
S.L.	Studies on the Left
S.S.	Science and Society
T.H.M.	Tennessee Historical Magazine
T.H.Q.	Tennessee Historical Quarterly
Vt. H.	Vermont History
Whig Rev.	Whig Review
W.M.A.	Working Man's Advocate

INTRODUCTION

Almost a decade ago I began research into American political ideology in the Jacksonian era. At the outset I intended to study the differing attitudes of the major parties to business and commerce. I soon found, however, that this was scarcely a feasible project. The problem was not that distinctive party attitudes could not be discerned; rather it was the reverse. The differing responses of statesmen were rooted in conflicting perceptions of human nature. What was at issue, it seemed, were full blown ideologies, that is to say world views comprised of beliefs, fears and hopes, a series of assumptions about government, society and the economy. None of these constituent parts, it was at once apparent, was fully intelligible without the others. It was thus not possible clearly to understand Democratic or Whig attitudes towards business and commerce without examining their philosophies of government or their assumptions about human nature. Hence the present work.

Although much has been written on Jacksonian Democracy historians have not given adequate consideration to the Democratic conception of equality. This seems to me to be an unfortunate omission. For I shall suggest that Jacksonian Democracy contained a clear levelling thrust. The clash between the two parties was therefore in good part a debate over the Democratic proposition that one (white) man was approximately the equivalent of another. This was not, of course, of merely theoretical significance for it involved a fundamental disagreement about the kind of society Americans had created and the kind of government under which they wished to live. Essentially Democratic levelling theory implied an agrarian, pre-capitalist society. The meritocratic outlook of the Whigs, on the other hand, implied a welcoming response to the quickening pace of commercial change which the economy was now experiencing. Moreover, it involved (for most Whigs at least) a profound suspicion of the claims now being made for the common man and for the democratic form of government. As a nation the United States in modern times has become associated with a political economy based upon liberal capitalism. The claim advanced in this work is that during the Jacksonian era at least, there was a collision between democratic politics and capitalist economics.

The modern controversy over the Jacksonian era dates from 1945, the year in which Arthur M. Schlesinger's *Age of Jackson* appeared. Although Schlesinger's book was an extraordinary achievement it was open to damaging criticisms which it will not be necessary to repeat here. Suffice it to say that Schlesinger undoubtedly found too many parallels between the 1830s and the 1930s and perhaps missed the essentially pre-capitalist nature of Democratic ideology (and hence its levelling tendencies). For the next twenty years or so that Jacksonian era like the American past generally was perceived in terms of a 'consensus' upon the fundamentals of liberal capitalism. As I have already implied I find this view highly unsatisfactory. More recently, some historians have emphasised the role of ethnocultural and institutional factors in politics. In the third part of this work I consider these (and other) alternative interpretations. Similarly, in recent times a number of scholars have re-emphasised the agrarian foundation of Jacksonian Democracy; others have surveyed important aspects of political ideology. I have found many of these works invaluable. It remains true, however, that no one has drawn attention to what I believe to be the levelling offensive of Jacksonian Democracy. I hope that it may be possible to construct a new synthesis of Jacksonian politics around this notion. The present work represents a first step in that direction.[1]

In this analysis of Democratic and Whig ideology I have focused almost exclusively upon the decade between 1837 and 1846. The concluding date requires little comment : by the mid-1840s the spread of the nation westwards was beginning to deprive the great issues of the Jacksonian era of much of their force and the 1850s would witness a series of political upheavals culminating in the Civil War. It may, however, be appropriate to explain the choice of 1837 as a starting point.

When the Jacksonian coalition came to power in 1829 it was not at all clear what its guiding principles would be. But gradually, under the pressure of events a distinctive programme was elaborated. In the nullification crisis (when the single state of South Carolina attempted to nullify a federal tariff law) Jackson acted with vigour and resolution. Although sympathetic to the idea of a reduction in tariff rates (the Democrats were to become the low tariff or free trade party), Jackson was enraged at what he took to be a threat to the integrity of the Union. The President obtained a Force Bill from Congress which provided for military action against those resisting federal laws. Many former Jacksonians, including John C. Calhoun of South Carolina (who had held no less an office than Vice President in Jackson's first

---

[1] For works dealing with Jacksonian historiography see below Chapter 1 note 1.

term) left the Jackson party during the controversy and rallied under the banner of 'states rights'.[2]

Other steps taken by Old Hickory alienated many of his former supporters and at the same time deepened the ideological commitment of his party. Although never entirely consistent on the subject of internal improvements Jackson nonetheless was quite prepared to veto some measures which had passed Congress. Most prominent here was the veto of the Maysville Road. Jackson increasingly identified his party with the limited government philosophy of Thomas Jefferson. Once again many erstwhile supporters defected.

But of greater importance than the issue of internal improvements was the question of banking. Motivated, it would seem, primarily by the agrarian's dislike of banks Andrew Jackson in 1832 vetoed the bill rechartering the Bank of the United States. In his veto message Jackson went far towards inscribing on the Democratic flag the principles for which it would do battle for more than a decade. Jackson charged that the bank represented privilege: it took from the poor in order to give to the rich. The message was a direct appeal to the people and in the election of 1832 the President won a decisive victory. Jackson then removed from the bank the government's deposits. Now increasingly the Democratic party began to voice opposition to paper money. This implied a hostility towards the nation's financial system and it raised fundamental questions about the kind of society Americans desired to live in. In 1836 with the Specie Circular the Democratic administration attempted to check an inflationary boom by insisting that public lands could only be paid for in gold and silver.

By this time an effective opposition was beginning to emerge. At its centre were the National Republicans who, under Henry Clay's leadership, had contested the election of 1832. But the new party was much more broadly based than its predecessor. Announcing its eternal hostility to 'executive tyranny' (the tyrant being, of course, Andrew Jackson), the new party took a name redolent of the revolutionary era. Into the Whig party came men antagonised by Jackson's nullification policy, by the Maysville veto, by the war on the bank and by the populistic appeals of the Democrats. In 1836 three candidates were run against Martin Van Buren, heir to Jackson and the Jacksonian policies.

---

[2]Good surveys of Jacksonian politics in these years include Glyndon G. Van Deusen, *The Jacksonian Era* (N.Y., 1963) and Richard B. Latner, *The Presidency of Andrew Jackson* (Athens, Ga., 1979).

Van Buren won the election but it was clear that the days of easy Democratic victories were over. Moreover in his first year of office the nation was struck by a financial Panic. Prices fell, banks suspended specie payments and subsequently a recession began from which the nation would not recover until the mid-1840s.

It is with the politics of these years that the present work deals. The effect of the Panic was to accelerate the process by which Jacksonian Democracy was being defined. It exposed the divisions within the party and helped drive out many of those who could not accept the agrarian philosophy to which the party was now increasingly committed. Similarly, within the Whig party a greater agreement upon principle and policy began to appear. Thus even though complete unanimity was never achieved each party became less a coalition of interests, more a union of like-minded individuals. Each party became indentified with a coherent ideology. These ideologies are my main concern in the pages that follow.

PART ONE

PARTY IDEOLOGY

1

DEMOCRATS

The debate over Jacksonian Democracy has produced a welter of conflicting interpretations. Probably because of the widely acknowledged importance of the Jacksonian era as a phase in the development of the liberal tradition, historians, in search of the meaning of American democracy, have differed for over a century in their judgments of the ideas and principles with which the Democratic party of Andrew Jackson, Martin Van Buren and James K. Polk was associated.[1] It is therefore surprising that the Jacksonian concept of equality has never been adequately studied. For it is this which gives coherence and consistency to the ideology of Democracy in the antebellum era.[2] It will be convenient, however, to begin this analysis of the Democratic world view with an examination of Jacksonian ideas on government.

Government

The Democratic party was not inappropriately named. For unlike their Whig opponents the Jacksonians seized every opportunity to proclaim their dedication to the principles of popular government. In 1841 New York Democrat Benjamin F. Butler reviewed the progress of American democracy and concluded that 'the great experiment' had

[1] On Jacksonian historiography see Alfred A. Cave, *Jacksonian Democracy and the Historians* (Gainesville, 1964); Edward Pessen, *Jacksonian America: Society, Personality and Politics* rev. ed. (Homewood, Ill., 1978), 351-67; Charles G. Sellers Jr., 'Andrew Jackson *versus* the Historians,' *M.V.H.R.* (March 1958), 615-34; John W. Ward, 'The Age of the Common Man', in John Higham (ed.), *The Reconstruction of American History* (N.Y., 1962), 82-97; Don F. Flatt, 'Historians View Jacksonian Democracy: A Historiographical Study,' (Ph.D. thesis. University of Kentucky, 1974); Ronald P. Formisano., 'Toward a Reorientation of Jacksonian Politics: A Review of the Literature, 1959-1975,' *J.A.H.,* LX II (June 1976), 42-65.

[2] A very different interpretation from that offered here is to be found in Marvin Meyers's influential work *The Jacksonian Persuasion* (Stanford, 1957). Meyers assumed that the Jacksonian agrarian rhetoric was merely a front for entrepreneurial activities. Hence he examined the psychic basis of the rhetoric rather than Democratic ideology itself. The assumption itself is questionable – see Michael A. Lebowitz, 'The Jacksonians: Paradox Lost?' in Barton J. Bernstein (ed.), *Towards a New Past* (London, 1968), 65-89. In addition to the 'genuflection to indices of economic growth', noted by Lebowitz, there was also genuflection to the standards of psychological 'normality' which prevailed in the 1950s. Thus dissent was psychologised out of existence. More commanding is Rush Welter, *The Mind of America, 1820-1860* (N.Y., 1975). However, even Welter does not perceive the true nature of Democratic egalitarianism and without this recognition the politics of the era, it seems to me, are ultimately incomprehensible.

been 'gloriously successful'. Francis P. Blair, editor of the party newspaper, *The Globe*, credited democracy with developing the 'resources, both moral and physical' of Americans 'in a degree and with a rapidity which are almost incredible'. Did 'the history of the world', he wondered, 'present a similar example'? Blair saw a spectacle of improvement which was 'almost too vast for contemplation, too marvellous for belief'.[3]

For the Jacksonian Democrats the nation's identity derived from its democratic institutions; national triumphs, in whatever sphere, redounded to the credit of democracy. The economic and territorial expansion which had taken place since 1776, in addition to the successful wars undertaken against foreign powers, had completed, in the Jacksonian mind, the union of democracy and nationalism. In the Jacksonian era, the Democrats, with a greater faith in democracy than most of their opponents, were also more aggressively nationalistic.[4]

Democrats were aware that the success of their government had overturned many of the axioms of political theory with which their ancestors had set out in 1776 and which the rest of the world had shared. A republic had been established and sustained upon 'so grand a scale' and over 'so wide a surface'. This was a government 'without a regal capital and aristocratic pillars', and established 'of the democratic element exclusively'. It effectively repudiated previous political systems; it was a successful translation into reality of theories which the most 'advanced' writers of the revolutionary generation had hardly even dared to advance. Because American democracy had 'done more, in fifty years, to elevate the moral and political condition of man, than has been achieved by any other civil institutions since the Christian era', it was 'perhaps the greatest achievement of modern times'.[5]

In repudiating so much of the pessimism with which most European writers had treated democracy, Jacksonians also repudiated and reversed the traditionally accepted explanations for the failure of popular governments. All former republics, it was noted, had contained other ingredients besides democracy. But the mixture had

[3] Benjamin F. Butler, *Representative Democracy in the United States* (Albany, 1841), 16; *Globe*, 15 Dec. 1837

[4] Jackson's policy towards England and France was generally more aggressive than most of his opponents would have liked – see Glyndon G. Van Deusen, *The Jacksonian Era 1828-1848* (N.Y., 1959), 100-103. Democracy and nationalism were, of course, fused in the 'Manifest Destiny' crusade of the 1840s, pursued most vigorously by the Democrats.

[5] *Globe*, 5 July, 1837; Samuel McRoberts, *To the Members of the General Assembly of Illinois* (n.p., n.d.), 7.

failed. This was not, as had traditionally been assumed, because of the democratic ingredient but because of the others which 'became too strong in the mixture'. In any case, it was 'a mixture which naturally destroys itself' since 'those foreign ingredients are at enmity with the genius of free institutions'. Again reversing the traditional theory Democrats claimed that a popular government was inherently more stable and tranquil than one based upon the monarchical principle. Democracy, it was now argued, brought stability.[6]

Democracy to the Jacksonians was thus linked not merely with the success of the American nation but with the concept of progess itself. George Bancroft was wont to argue that the two were virtually synonymous while Hugh A. Garland of Virginia delivered an Oration entitled 'The Principles of Democracy Identical with the Moral Improvement of Mankind'. The *Democratic Review,* knowing of 'no limit to the advantages which belong to the habit of self-government', wondered whether 'we may not originate improvements in like manner, which shall be as substantial as those which have already distinguished ours from the Governments of the Old World'. More democracy would thus bring more progress. And the democratic progress already achieved in effect rendered obsolete the arguments that had traditionally been employed against reforms and innovations suggested for the American government. Referring to a proposal for the election of the judiciary, Louisiana Democrat James A. Brent explained that 'the fact that this principle is not to be found in any of the ancient constitutions of the confederacy is no argument against its adoption now'. For, Brent pointed out, 'the capacity of man for self-government was then an unsolved problem. The republican principle was then in its infancy.' But since that time it had 'grown and expanded into the full vigor of maturity' and was 'now in the strong and lusty prime of its golden manhood'. Other Democrats explicitly rejected the force of precedent 'relative to the creation or charter of governments'. For the Democrats, the success of the democratic principle in America was thus an indication that it might be capable of a wider application.[7]

It was Brent's conviction that 'the American people' were 'capable of self-government on its widest and most extended signification'. This was a belief that was widely shared within the Democratic party. For the triumphs of the American Republic had nourished a belief in a

[6]*Iowa C.C.,* 327.

[7]George Bancroft, *The Principles of Democracy* (Hartford, 1840), 9; Hugh A. Garland, *The Principles of Democracy Identical with the Moral Improvement of Mankind* (N.Y., n.d.); *Dem. Rev.* XVII (Sept. 1845), 172; *La. C.C.,* 757; *Iowa C.C.,* 272-3.

populistic democracy which emphasised the virtue and goodness of the people. Had not 'the capacity of this people for self-government . . . stood tests and trials probably as rude as any to which it may again be subjected'? Martin Van Buren told Andrew Jackson that 'every day convinces me more of the perfect reliance that may, under all circumstances, be placed on the intelligence, patriotism, and fortitude of the people'. Jackson himself declared, in a letter written in 1841, that 'a long and intimate acquaintance with the character of the American people inspired me with the most implicit faith in their disposition to pursue and maintain truth, virtue, patriotism and independence with a single purpose'. 'And', he added, 'at this late day of my life, it gives me joy to say that this faith is unabated'. The 'imperishable basis of Democratic faith', according to *The Globe*, was 'that the mass of the people are honest and capable of self-government'.[8]

Even though this faith had existed in America even prior to the separation from England, it is safe to say that with the Jacksonians it reached new proportions. Jefferson had believed in 'the cherishment of the people' and, as he himself noted, this had distinguished his party from its opponents. By the Jacksonian era, however, just as democracy had been sanctified so the Jeffersonian faith in the people had been intensified to the point where George Bancroft could argue that 'truth is a social spirit; her home is in the heart of the people, in the breast of the race; she rests her head serenely on the bosom of humanity'. From this Bancroft concluded that by giving 'power to the whole people . . . you gain the nearest expression of the law of God, the voice of conscience, the oracle of universal reason'. This was a large step beyond the mild condescension implied in Jefferson's 'cherishment of the people' and it signified the enormous shift which had taken place in American political thought since 1776. It was now possible to argue that the elective principle was superior to the appointive since 'public opinion is the only test of the character of a public man'. Democracy was now definable as 'the unrestrained, direct, and active influence of the public will upon Government'.[9]

As the populistic tendencies of American democracy became more pronounced, so also, in the Jacksonian era, did its egalitarian

[8]*Globe,* 5 July, 1837; Van Buren to Jackson, 17 Oct. 1837, in John S. Bassett (ed.), *Correspondence of Andrew Jackson,* 7 vols. (Washington, D.C., 1926-37) V,516; Jackson to J.P. Hardwicke *et al.,* 20 Oct. 1841, *Niles Register* LXI, 151; *Globe,* 24 Aug. 1840.

[9]Jefferson in Charles A. Beard, *The Economic Origins of Jeffersonian Democracy* (N.Y., 1915), 420; Bancroft, *An Oration delivered before the Democracy of Springfield and Neighboring Towns, July 4 1836* (Springfield, 1836), 17; Bancroft, *Principles of Democracy,* 4; *Iowa C.C.,* 325; *Globe,* 28 June 1840.

content. It was a favourite and often repeated Whig charge – though one to which historians have given little attention – that the Jacksonians were paying little heed to the natural differences among men. And Jacksonian political theory did indeed represent an assault upon traditional – and some not so traditional – views of the distribution of political power and influence within the state. The political theory which provoked and stimulated the Revolution was based upon the assumption that government should be in the hands of an élite who would have attained a unitary superiority – in wealth, influence, wisdom, education and culture. Political leadership would thus be provided by the natural leaders of society, the social élite. Conversely, there would be, at the bottom of the scale, an order whose inferiority in wealth, knowledge and social status would be visible in the political system. This order would perhaps be disfranchised or excluded from officeholding by means of a property qualification. At the minimum it was expected to display a deferential respect for the ruling élite. Thus the entire system was based upon the translation into politics of social inequalities; it presupposed a large degree of political inequality.[10]

The Democrats rejected this theory at almost every point. They rejected especially its assumptions of inequality in politics: 'The Democratic principle', according to one group of Democrats, 'teaches the perfect civil and political equality of mankind'. Samuel Young of New York called for 'a perfect equality among mankind of legal, social, civic and political privileges' while the *Bay State Democrat*, a leading party newspaper in New England, spoke of democracy as 'a principle at the heart of which lies EQUALITY'. In Louisiana Isaac T. Preston urged his fellow delegates at the state's Constitutional Convention to 'place all your citizens upon a footing of perfect equality as to their political rights' in order to 'promote the well-being and happiness of all'. Other Democrats were similarly explicit in their utterances. Thus William Allen of Ohio informed the Senate that 'every law of nature' was 'a law of equality'. This, he argued, was the 'basis' upon which 'this government' was 'formed', and 'by its fundamental laws each citizen stands upon a political level'. It was a level which 'he never leaves'. Allen's colleague, Alexander Duncan, went so far as to claim that it was the mechanisms of political inequality, the restrictions on voting and officeholding, that were responsible for the decline of the ancient republics of Greece, Rome

---

[10] Bernard Bailyn, *The Ideological Origins of the American Revolution* (Camb., Mass., 1967), 302. These generalisations apply, of course, to the mainstream of Revolutionary thought rather than to its minor currents.

and Carthage. Democracy, the Democrats clearly believed, was virtually synonymous with political equality.[11]

In denying the political significance of social inequalities, Democrats emphasised the irrelevance of the traditional qualifications for office and the franchise. Wealth was an obvious target. One Southerner believed it 'repugnant to the true principles of democracy to say that a farmer without slaves, working on his own farm, should have less weight in the government than the rich proprietor adjoining his little farm, who had a hundred negroes'. The rich and the poor were 'all citizens alike'. It was equally intolerable that poverty sould be 'punished by exclusion from stations of honor and responsible trust'. Thus property did not bring with it any political entitlement; the lack of it was no grounds for political exclusion. Orthodox Democrats invariably rejected the traditional stake-in-society theory upon which so much of American republicanism had been based. A conflict had been perceived by the Tories of the revolutionary era between a government based upon the rights of property and one based upon the rights of men. Jeffersonians and the most progressive revolutionary Whigs had tended to deny the antithesis, affirming that all men could become property-holders. But the Democrats of the Jacksonian era reintroduced it and claimed for the rights of man an existence separate from, independent of, and superior to, the rights of property. American democracy did not rest upon, or express the needs of, men in their capacity as property-holders; it could not since 'if property be everything, it must be protected under a despotism, at the point of the bayonet'. Other Democrats nominally retained the stake-in-society theory but distorted it out of all recognition when they argued that the propertyless had their personal rights to defend. This stake would secure their loyalty to a democratic government which, better than any other, would preserve those rights. Economic inequality, the Democrats thus believed, should find no expression in politics.[12]

Instead, they urged, the political system should reflect all that was egalitarian in American society. Those who were set apart from the broad mass of the community should not be entrusted with the reins of government. Andrew Johnson, in an electioneering address in 1845, expressed his hope that 'the time may come when the offices of this

[11]*Address of the Democratic Republic Young Men's Central Committee of the City of New York* ... (N.Y., 1840), 3; Samuel Young, *Oration at New York, 4 July 1840* (N.Y., 1841), 5; *B. S. D.* in *Frankfort (Ky.) Democrat,* 25 Oct. 1838; *La. C. C.,* 315; *Cong. Gl* 26 i App., 178, 59.

[12]*La. C. C.,* 315, 118; *N.H.P.,* 17 Oct. 1844; *Globe,* 8 Sept., 1838, 19 March 1841. See also the Address in *Mississippian,* 16 Aug. 1844; Arthur M. Schlesinger Jr., *The Age of Jackson* (Boston, 1945), 311-2.

nation, both State and Federal, profitable and honorable, from the President down to the lowest in the gift of the people, will be filled with the farmers and mechanics of the country'. Other Democrats insisted that the rich were particularly unsuited to government in a democratic state. This was the old theory not simply set aside, but stood upon its head.[13]

Yet in their desire for political equality the Democrats did not merely cast doubt upon those distinguished by their wealth or occupational prestige. The same process that was shaking the traditional assumptions about wealth was also undermining previous ideas on the role of talents and intellect. As with property, it was not talents or intellect *per se* that were under assault; it was rather their role in politics that was being challenged. This involved a sharp break with Jeffersonian as well as with more conservative traditions. For previous political theory had believed it almost self-evident that government should be in the hands of the natural aristocracy. Jefferson had believed that this aristocracy, 'the grounds' of which were 'virtue and talents', was no less than 'the most precious gift of nature for the instruction, the trusts and government of society'. But this idea was not enthusiastically received by most Democrats. The party took its cue from Andrew Jackson himself who had told Congress that the duties of officeholders could be made 'so plain and simple that men of intelligence may readily qualify themselves for their performance'. According to Governor John Barry of Michigan 'plain men of sound heads and honest hearts are found adequate to the highest and most responsible duties of government'. Similarly the *Cincinnati Daily Enquirer* affirmed that 'it is not great talents that we admire most in public men, but sterling public integrity, disinterestedness of purpose, and purity of moral character'.[14]

[13] Leroy P. Graf and Ralph W. Haskins (eds.), *The Papers of Andrew Johnson* (Knoxville, Tennessee, 1967-), I, 270. See also *Globe*, 19 March 1841; *Old Dominion*, 31 Aug. 1839; *Evening Post*, 21 Jan. 1835.

[14] Jefferson to John Adams, 28 Oct. 1813 in e.g. Albert Fried, *The Essential Jefferson* (New York, 1963), 517; James D. Richardson, *A Compilation of the Messages and Papers of the Presidents, 1789-1907* (Washington D.C., 1908), II, 448-9; George N. Fuller (ed.), *Messages of the Governors of Michigan* (Lansing, 1925), I, 430; *Cincinnati Daily Enquirer and Message*, 18 April 1846. John W. Ward argues that the Jacksonians retained the Jefferson veneration for the national aristocracy. Yet both the society and the government which the Jacksonians desired offered little scope for the talents of the natural aristocrat. Ward's evidence, it should be noted, is extremely limited – see Ward, 'Jacksonian Democratic Thought: A Natural Charter of Privilege', in Stanley Coben and Lorman Ratner (eds.), *The Development of an American Culture* (Englewood Cliffs, 1970), 44-63. Merrill D. Peterson reaches the same conclusion as that reached here – Peterson, *The Jefferson Image in the American Mind* (N.Y., 1962), 83. (It is, however, possible that Jefferson with his emphasis upon the natural aristocracy was rather an atypical Jeffersonian).

Thus where previous republican theory had sought to facilitate the emergence, and guarantee the retention, of a superior governing élite, many Democrats now wished to place in office men whose chief personal characteristic was their similarity to the people whom they represented. As a result men who were distinguished by their learning fell under suspicion. George Bancroft (himself in this category) acknowledged that 'men of learning' were 'excellent... in their place'. But, he added, they were politically suspect since 'learning has a pride and arrogance of its own'. Bancroft was therefore 'loathe to resign the government of the country into the hands of college professors or the learned of the land'. A Democrat in Louisiana displayed similar suspicions when, advocating the popular election of more officeholders, he asserted that 'the people will never unite upon a candidate merely because of his learning, his talents, or his family influence'. 'Mere' learning and talents were apparently inadequate. In 1844 Thomas L. Nichols, editing a newspaper that was dedicated to the election of James K. Polk, praised the party's Presidential candidate as 'a man whose virtues are more conspicuous than his talents'. (Previous generations might have thought this an argument in favour of his oponents.) Similarly, George Sidney Camp, a Democratic theorist, acknowledged that in the United States men 'of the most shining abilities' were not chosen for office. Yet this was 'a subject for congratulation rather than for chagrin to the friends of popular government'. Likewise Isaac C. Preston, the Attorney General of Louisiana, desired a judiciary comprised of men whose life-style would not distinguish them from the rest of the community. Opposing a suggested increase in judicial salaries, Preston called for 'men of simple lives, of frugal habits, of great economy in their families'. If required in the 'extravagant city' of New Orleans, the judges should not stay at a 'splendid and extravagant' hotel but at one of 'the neat, quiet and excellent but moderate boarding houses of the hundreds of widows who follow that occupation'. This was a direct assault upon the accepted view of the judiciary for in effect Preston sought to make the Chief Justices of the state, traditionally a much revered élite, socially and intellectually indistinguishable from the people. But Preston at least assumed that lawyers would continue to hold a monopoly on judicial offices. John P. Tarbell of Massachusetts, on the other hand, believed 'that plain farmers are as capable of judging as lawyers'. Here then was the egalitarian thrust of Jacksonian Democracy. Democrats could now castigate their opponents for believing that 'the common people could be better ruled by those that are a little uncommon than by themselves'.[15]

[15] Bancroft, *Principles of Democracy*, 3; *La. C.C.*, 743; *Young Hickory Banner*, 17

If government did not require the selection of an élite class, whether social, administrative, or intellectual, neither should its offices confer élite status. Amos Kendall held that public officers 'should be considered [as] having nothing of dignity, or power, or splendor about them, beyond that which belongs to honest men representing others in the private walks of life'. Kendall attacked the idea that government and its officers should command prestige automatically and receive deferential treatment:

> The world will not be governed as it ought to be, until government shall be stripped of the majesty with which the arts and errors of ages have clothed it, and come to be considered as a part of the ordinary business of society, nor until those who administer it can travel abroad without other attentions than those bestowed on respectable gentlemen engaged in other concerns.

It was a view which many other Democrats would have endorsed.[16]

Yet if the generation of 1776 had been able to observe the Democrats as they challenged or ignored the traditional assumptions about deference and élitism, wealth and talent, they would, after the initial shock and horror, have wondered how the stability of the state and the cohesion of society were to be maintained. How, for example, was the obedience of the people to government and to law to be secured in a society which had so undermined the claims, and therefore weakened the grip, of authority? With the devaluation of talent and intellect in politics and the erosion of the stake-in-society theory, what force could counter that of self-interest? The latter question was particularly significant for the social and political relations that were patterned upon authority and respect, upon unitary superiority and unitary inferiority, had been visualised as a means of subduing and restraining the all-destructive force of self-interest. Faith in the people had previously been checked by a vivid awareness of their potential power which, when mobilised at the command of self-interest, could, it was assumed, shatter the social and political structures and replace them with anarchy, disorder and ruin. John Taylor of Caroline, the great theorist of Jeffersonian Democracy, had, in his famous 'Inquiry into the Principles and Policy of the Government of the United States', attempted the most direct refutation

---

Aug. 1844; George Sidney Camp, *Democracy* (N.Y., 1845), 139; *La. C.C.,* 719-20; John P. Tarbell, *An Oration delivered before the Democratic Citizens of the North Part of Middlesex County, at Groton, July 4, 1839* (Lowell, 1839), 27-8; *Cong. Gl.,* 25 i App., 21.

[16]*Kendall's Expositor* II (20 Jan. 1842), 18, III (25 July 1843), 241.

of these theories. In the Jacksonian era his views became Democratic orthodoxy.[17]

Like Taylor, the Jacksonians reversed the traditional formulation and pronounced self-interest to be not the major threat to social and political order but instead their major support. Thus political power need not reflect intellectual ability or educational attainment since even though 'the theory of government' might be 'an abstruse matter', yet its operation was 'felt by every one'. For – and the juxtaposition and assumed relevance of this remark is highly significant – 'every man knows whether he enjoys more or less liberty, or is exposed to few or greater burdens'. It was 'unnecessary to be profoundly versed in government to appreciate all this' since 'one man feels results as well as another, although he may not clearly understand how these results are effected'. This was the sense in which there was 'an instinct of liberty' and in which it could be said that 'liberty springs spontaneous in the human breast'. Since the political expression of this liberty was democracy, it followed that the suffrage was 'a right which is implanted in the human soul'. And did not 'all history' teach 'that when men are deprived of what they conceive to be a right, they hate the instrument by which it is effected'? If this injustice were 'persisted in' then 'opposition' would 'ripen into deadly hostility'. Once again the force of self-interest was injected into the political debate. It was a force which cut across all distinctions that were founded on wealth, talent or intellectual capacity. It was a highly egalitarian force and it had unmistakable levelling tendencies.[18]

In fact it was self-interest which for the Democrats occupied the central position in political theory that had formerly been held by the supposedly higher qualities. The Democratic view of man was essentially ambivalent and dualistic for while the ordinary man was naturally good and virtuous he was also potentially greedy and grasping. Was not 'the desire of wealth a universal propensity of mankind'? Was not 'the love of money' one of 'the strongest passions of the human heart'? To a Democrat these propositions were unchallengeable. For the force of self-interest did not operate only upon the vicious and the depraved; it operated almost equally upon the virtuous. Thus if a banker were able to print as much money as he chose, and if he stood to gain more by printing more, then 'the chances' were 'ten, ay, a hundred to one against the man so situated'. There were to be sure 'those who might withstand the united

---

[17] Taylor's thought has not received the attention it deserves. He was probably the most important theorist of American Democracy in the ante-bellum period.

[18] *La. C.C.*, 175; Bancroft, *Oration at Springfield*, 18; *La. C.C.*, 191, 321.

temptation of opportunity and impunity' but such men 'come like angel visits – few and far between'. Yet the same writer assured his readers that he was 'not among those who profess to have little or no reliance on the integrity of mankind'. It was rather that the staunchest integrity could, on certain occasions, fall victim to greed.[19]

The force of self-interest was responsible not only for the greed for wealth that was all but endemic in the human race but also for the love of power. This was likewise one of 'the strongest passions of the human heart'. It was also self-nourishing in that 'instead of satisfying the desire it creates an insatiable craving for more'. There was of course in the English and American Whig traditions an acute awareness of the dangers of power and an assumption that in politics and in society, power and liberty were in perpetual conflict. Yet the pre-occupation with power was in some respects even more marked in the Jacksonian era than in the revolutionary age. It was according to Samuel Young 'a fact exemplified by all history, that human power is ever at war with its boundaries'. Andrew Johnson reminded a colleague that 'vigilance eternal' was 'the price of liberty'. These beliefs were perhaps universal among Democrats. For 'the rights of a free people are never secure without the most untiring vigilance, the sternest determination to maintain them at every hazard'. Man 'must continually work out his liberty, like his salvation, with fear and trembling'.[20]

To the Democrats history exhibited a long, continuous struggle on the part of the masses – the many – to restrain the holders of power – usually the few. Again and again they reviewed the history of the past in order to demonstrate that 'the legislation of every age and country' had resulted in 'a vast and continual sacrifice of human rights to the mercenary exactions and the capricious ebullitions of power'. '*All past history*', it was argued, presented the same dismal spectacle: governments 'taking some of the rights of the Many and giving them to the Few.' 'An order or class of men', it was claimed, had 'ever existed, in almost every nation of the civilised world', that had 'lived in idleness, and been supported in their luxury from the industry and labor of the great mass of the working people.' There was 'an eternal struggle' in society; 'a portion of mankind' constantly sought to 'pervert the laws and institutions of society to their own temporary aggrandize-ment, and to the permanent oppression of the mass of their fellow

[19] *Globe*, 9 Dec. 1840; *Cong. Gl*, 25 ii App., 123.

[20] *Cong. Gl*, 25 ii App., 123; Robert Rantoul, *An Oration delivered before the Democrats and Antimasons of the County of Plymouth, 4 July, 1836* (Boston, 1836), 7; Young, *Oration at New York*, 6 14; *Papers of Johnson*, I, 158; *Globe*, 18 Oct., 1838.

creatures'. This danger was no less real in a democratic government than in any other. For 'in proportion as freedom exists, the workings of ambition, and the aspirations for power, for wealth and for distinction are developed'. *The Globe* told its readers that it was 'of little consequence whether the sole exercise of authority is derived from popular elections, or hereditary right, if it is left unrestrained by a counterbalancing power, or by some constitutional provision'. The force of self-interest, upon which democracy rested, was also, 'when it passes its true and natural bounds and urges man to encroach upon the rights and immunities of man', democracy's greatest threat.[21]

The danger was to be eliminated by mobilising the self-interest, and therefore the power, of the majority. For it was a cardinal tenet of Democratic ideology that 'a majority cannot subsist upon a minority'.[22] The interest of the majority could therefore only be employed defensively; there was no danger of any permanent majority tyranny. It would thus balance the self-interest of the powerful minority. This was the sense in which Edmund Burke of New Hampshire hailed the nation's democratic institutions for placing the common man 'upon the platform of equality with the proudest and the most powerful'. The ballot was thus a 'potent weapon' which he could use 'to protect and defend himself from the encroachments of power and wealth'. It was the task of the majority to ensure that the control of government did not fall into the hands of the powerful minority.[23]

This meant, in effect, the near annihilation of political power. Where previous generations had often concluded that the dangers of power necessitated a careful selection process that would secure the emergence of the natural aristocracy, the Democrats insisted that no adequate selection process could be devised. Instead political power had to be curbed and restricted to the point where government exercised only administrative duties. 'The best government', according to the *Democratic Review*, 'is that which governs least.' Martin Van Buren publicly complained that 'all communities are apt to look to government for too much', while William Roane of Virginia told the Senate that the opposing view – that it was 'the duty of the *Government* to take care of the people' – was 'much better suited' to England than to the United States. 'The main office of government'

---

[21] Young, *Oration at New York,* 5, 9; *The Crisis Met* (n.p., n.d.), 2; *Cong. Gl.,* 25 ii App., 423; *Globe,* 16 Sept. 13 Jan. 1842; Ely Moore, *Trades' Unions: An Address...* (N.Y., 1833), 3.

[22] It was assumed that the gains potentially available to the majority would be slight in comparison with those which a grasping minority could obtain.

[23] *Dem. Rev.,* I (Oct. 1837), 4; *Cong. Gl.,* 26 i App., 574.

was, in the words of one New York Congressman, to protect 'the citizen in the pursuit of his honest industry'. For the Democrats were convinced that an active government would inevitably further the interests of the powerful minority at the expense of the majority. Such was the force of self-interest that those who held power would almost inevitably, unless checked, abuse it. Hence 'as a general rule, the tendency of all legislative bodies is to excess of legislation'.[24]

The urgent need in politics was thus to curb the power of government, to ensure that it became and remained inactive and impartial. How was this to be done? The first and most obvious tactic was to bring its officers closer to the people. Democrats insisted that all elected officers were merely delegates. The representative was an employee who, in the words of the *Democratic Review*, 'should have no will of his own which is independent of that of his constituents'. Similarly, the legislative system was 'but a set of convenient labor-saving machinery, to supersede the necessity for the assemblage of the great masses of the people themselves'. Consequently, Democrats consistently defended the right of instruction. According to one Ohio newspaper, this was 'the only safeguard of the people against the encroachments of power'. Governor Henry Hubbard of New Hampshire believed that it was the circumscribed role of public servants, their obligation to 'become the exponents' of the people's 'opinions', which raised the American system of government 'high above all forms and political compacts which have hitherto been devised'. To deny the right of instruction was, according to George Bancroft, to 'surrender the government for the time to the arbitrary caprice, the bigotry or the selfishness of an individual'.[25]

The Democrats thus endeavoured to set the interest of the people against the greed and cupidity of the men with power. To guard against the evils of power 'the people should delegate authority sparingly, resume it, and invest it again in the most frequent intervals, consistent with the stability of governmnent'. In order to secure 'swift responsibility', 'frequent elections' were needed. Similarly more offices should be made elective. Lyman Evans of Iowa bluntly stated that 'the

---

[24] *Dem. Rev.,* Motto; *Messages of Presidents,* III, 344; *Cong. Gl,* 25 iii App., 186, 26 i App., 326 *Messages of Govs. of Michigan,* I, 259. See also Bancroft, *Principles of Democracy,* 7; Theodore Sedgwick Jr. (ed.), *A Collection of the Political Writings of William Leggett,* 2 vols. (N.Y., 1840), II, 273.

[25] *Dem. Rev.,* IX (Nov. 1841), 435, XXIX (Dec. 1851), 520; *Lancaster Eagle* in *Globe,* 9 Sept. 1837; *N. H. Senate Journal* (1842), 4; Bancroft, *Oration at Springfield,* 4. See also *I. S. R.,* 29 Sept. 1839; *La. C. C.,* 150; Iowa State Democratic Convention quoted in Louis Pelzer, 'The History and Principles of the Democratic party of the Territory of Iowa', *L.J.H.P.,* VI (Jan. 1908), 51.

20

people should elect everything, from Constable to President'. The mass of democratic citizens, seeking no advantage from government, would exert their influence through frequent elections and their right of instruction to control and supervise the branches of government, and to check the tendency towards partial legislation.[26]

A second restraint upon government was found to lie in the traditional separation of powers. 'You advance from monarchy to republicanism', the *Democratic Review* argued, 'just in proportion as you divide and separate' the power of government. A system of checks and balances would thus allow ambition or greed in one department to neutralise ambition or greed in another. Moreover although Democrats believed that the government should rest squarely on majority opinion, they recognised that the majority might err or even (temporarily) encroach upon the rights of the minority. Here too a system of checks and balances, by preventing the passage of 'immature, unwise and unequal legislation' which a majority might sanction, would help preserve the equal rights of all. Every department would, of course, 'be dependent with equal directness and promptness on the influence of public opinion', but democracy required that each be separated from the rest.[27]

By harnessing the self-interest of the people and that of the representatives themselves, Democrats expected to preserve a limited, inactive government. This opened up the prospect of a truly breathtaking degree of freedom for every citizen. Every American, his rights guaranteed by the power of his vote, his liberty secure in the absence of governmental intervention, would be able to 'rove free, as the free air which he breathes'. Freedom, like democracy itself, was a function of self-interest.[28]

The Democratic view of politics thus emphasised self-interest as the basis of liberty and democracy. Government was no longer the instrument by which the talented élite regulated society and derived harmony and cohesion from the anarchy of self-interest. Instead political power, whether in the form of officeholding or voting, was to be essentially independent of wealth, talent, intellect or prestige. Inequality would find no expression in politics; politics would promote no further inequality. A political system that was explicitly and avowedly based upon the qualities common to all men – this was the levelling thrust of Jacksonian Democracy.

[26]*Iowa C.C.*, 222-3, 120; Bancroft, *Principles of Democracy*, 6.

[27]*Dem. Rev.*, XXII(March 1848), 204, XXIV(Jan. 1844), 16, I(Oct. 1837), 2. See Michael J. Heale, *The Making of American Politics* (London, 1977), 173-4.

[28]Rantoul, *Oration . . . 4 July 1836*, 42.

Society

Although they insisted that government relinquish its control over the economy, the Democrats were nevertheless confident about the society which would emerge. It would be a society marked by ever-increasing prosperity and economic progress. For 'nothing is so favorable to the progress of society, and the development of national wealth, as this self-depending energy'. Rather than 'interference and regulation' what was needed was 'the truly healthful action of the free voluntary principle'. Government, by its very inactivity, would promote prosperity.[29]

Yet this was only one of the claims made for a society free from governmental intervention. The influence of Adam Smith, whose 'discoveries on the earth were like those of Newton in the heavens', was pervasive among Democrats. For 'the monetary laws, the laws of trade, and indeed all the laws which appertain to national, civic and social intercommunication among men, are as determinate and fixed in their general results as the laws of light, heat and gravitation.' The 'natural order' in society was one of harmony and by following the 'natural laws' a society would inevitably remain just and harmonious.[30]

Smith's economics accorded easily with Democratic theory. Both assumed that the individual almost invariably identified and pursued his self-interest; both sought to derive from the pursuit of self-interest a just and equitable social order. There was, however, a significant difference between the application of Smith's doctrines in England and in the United States. In England the free trade theory was directed primarily against the often reactionary landed interest; it was a potent weapon in the hands of those representing the newer forms of wealth. In the United States, on the other hand, free trade and the 'natural laws' were cited in defence of agriculture and an agrarian society. Again following Jefferson and John Taylor of Caroline, the Democrats asserted the superiority of the farmer.

Assuming, on the basis of their own experience, a natural compatibility between democratic government and urban, industrial society, many historians have overlooked or underestimated the Democratic commitment to agriculture. Jacksonian America was, of course, an overwhelmingly rural society. Agriculture, when Andrew Jackson left office, employed over 80 per cent of the nation's

---

[29]*Globe,* 8 Dec. 1837; *Dem. Rev.,* I (Oct. 1837), 9.

[30]Theodore Sedgwick, *Public and Private Economy,* 2 vols. (N.Y., 1836), II, 119; Young, *Oration at New York,* 10; *Dem. Rev.,* I (Oct. 1837), 7. On Smith's influence see Schlesinger, *Age of Jackson,* 314-17.

labour force and accounted for almost 70 per cent of commodity output. Despite the conspicuous growth of some major urban centres, only one man in ten lived in a community of over 2,500 inhabitants. Hence it was natural for the Democrats to heap praise upon the farmer. Some went so far as to endorse the principles of the Physiocrats in claiming that 'the entire riches of a country come from its soil'. Others were content to claim for agriculture the major role in creating national wealth.[31]

Yet the primacy of agriculture was not merely a consequence of the numerical superiority of the farmers. When Governor John H. Steele of New Hampshire noted that the American people were 'in fact essentially, and I sincerely hope will always continue to be, an agricultural people', he was not simply applauding the farmer as the creator of national wealth. For 'the landed interest' was, in the words of *The Globe*, 'the backbone of the country'. The farmer's superiority was complete; he was no less than the man around whom democracy revolved and upon whom its survival depended. According to Silas Wright, 'a well educated, industrious and independent yeomanry are the safest repository of freedom and free institutions'.[32]

Democrats often explained why the farmer was the ideal citizen. In the many eulogies which they offered no attribute was given more consideration than that of independence. For the farmer was 'less dependent on the hourly aid of others, in the regular routine of his life, as likewise on their opinions, their example, their influence'. Hence it was not only because of 'the vast superiority of their numbers' but also because of 'the peculiar adaptation of their occupation to the cultivation of the independent spirit of man' that 'the cultivators of the earth must be looked upon as the great and perennial fountain of that Republican Spirit which is to maintain and perpetuate our free institutions'. 'A virtuous and *independent* yeomanry' was thus 'the richest boast which any country can make'.[33]

The way in which the farmer secured and preserved his independence was the key to his superiority. In Jacksonian America farming was still practised on a relatively small scale and since the

[31] Douglass C. North, *Growth and Welfare in the American Past* (Englewood Cliffs, N.J., 1966), 19-22; *Globe,* 18 June 1838.

[32] *N.H. Senate Journal* (1844), 21; *Globe,* 1 July 1839; Silas Wright, 'Address to the New State Agricultural Society', in Ransom H. Gillett, *The Life and Times of Silas Wright,* 2 vols. (Albany, 1874), II, 1961.

[33] My Italics. *Dem. Rev.,* VI (Dec. 1839), 500-2; *Cong. Gl,* 25 ii App., 292; Edmund Burke, *An Address delivered before the Democratic Republican Citizens of Lempster, N.H., 8 Jan. 1839* (Newport, N.H., 1839), 17.

availability of cheap land made it difficult to find agricultural workers, the vast majority of farmers worked their own holdings. These were the farmers whom the Democrats most esteemed. For while 'tenantry is unfavorable to freedom, the freeholder', by contrast, 'is the natural supporter of a free government'. His interest was to improve the land upon which he lived and which he owned. Hence it could be said that 'to live' the farmer 'must labor', and 'hence does he better appreciate the true worth and dignity of labor'. Here was a quality the importance of which could hardly be exaggerated. Labour, in addition to being the source of all wealth, was a fount of moral virtue; indeed individual morality, some Democrats seemed to assume, was safe in a society which respected the dignity of labour. Productive labour gave rise to such commendable qualities as steadiness, simplicity, frugality, sternness and endurance. Isolated upon his lands, the yeoman farmer was impelled to labour in order to retain his independence. His moral welfare was therefore assured.[34]

Even this, however, did not exhaust the farmer's claims to pre-eminence. Most Democrats believed that 'all the wealth of the world is the product of labour'. From this, the labour theory of value, it followed that in a just and fair society, the individual should himself receive the benefits brought by his labour. Here was a cardinal tenet of the Democratic faith. 'The interest of every man in every nation and clime' is, wrote Amos Kendall, 'in one respect alike: *It is in the full enjoyment of the fruits of his own labor.'* There could be no exploitation, it was believed, no utilisation of some men as means to secure the ends of others, if a true reward for labour were everywhere received. Such a reward was readily attainable – in the agrarian society. The Democrats pictured a society of yeoman farmers, whose labour, when applied to the soil, would yield enough produce both to meet their own needs and also to permit them to exchange their surplus for those necessities they could not themselves produce. This exchange would be a series of simple operations, regulated by the 'unchanging' laws of supply and demand. Since he would not be in the power of those with whom he traded, the farmer's independence would be essentially unimpaired. The role of the government was, of course, merely negative: it should refuse to intervene. Thus the farmer, insulated both geographically and morally from the corrupting sources of power, would channel his self-interest into productive and

---

[34] *Cong., Gl.,* 29 i 727-8; *Dem. Rev.,* VI (Dec. 1839), 500-2, XIII (Nov. 1843), 460. On farming in Jacksonian American see Paul W. Gates, *The Farmer's Age, 1815-1860* (N.Y., 1960), 98, 197.

rewarding activities. Hence he would be the ideal citizen of the limited, democratic government.[35]

For the Democrats, power was based upon, and grew out of, the just reward for labour to which Kendall referred. Power over oneself, or liberty, was the right to enjoy the fruits of one's own labour; power over another was the appropriation of the rewards of his labour. There was thus an aggregate, a total mass of power within the entire community, to be shared between people and government. If government remained inactive, then power would be divided among the people; if all received the fruits of their labour, the division would be an equal one. The Democratic demand that every citizen have 'the full enjoyment of the fruits of his own labor' was thus a claim for equal social power. Here was the economic base upon which the equality of political power would rest.

Although it has hardly been recognised by historians, the drive for equal and atomised power lay at the core of Jacksonian Democracy. Amos Kendall believed that if a measure would 'necessarily subject one man to the power or influence of another' then this was 'a conclusive argument against it'. Again and again Democrats insisted upon the 'equal rights' of every citizen; this was no less than a demand for an equality of social power.[36]

It was not, of course, a demand for equal wealth. 'Equality of . . . wealth', as Andrew Jackson told Congress, 'cannot be produced by human institutions.' No Democrat every challenged this belief. For 'God has made some men superior to others in physical and mental power' and 'to the advantages of superior strength, intelligence and skill . . . we hold every man to be entitled.' 'Nature's own endowment' meant that a perfect equality of wealth was 'a palpable absurdity'.[37]

Yet it would be a grave error to conclude that this denotes a 'classic bourgeois ideal' or typifies 'the philosophy of a rising middle class', as some scholars have maintained. It is important to consider the extent of economic inequality that Democrats would sanction. For democracy – a system of equal social and political power – both required and created an equality of conditions, an approximate equality of wealth. The agrarian society would bring a fair and just reward to those who were prepared to labour. In the absence of

[35] *Dem. Rev.*, XVI (Jan. 1845), 20; *Kendall's Expositor*, I (2 Dec. 1841), 389.

[36] *Kendall's Expositor*, II (17 March 1842), 82.

[37] *Messages of Presidents*, II, 590; *Globe*, 24 Sept. 1840; *Dem. Rev.*, IX (Oct. 1841), 319, XIX (Sept. 1846), 218.

governmental intervention the basic force of self-interest would operate without impediment upon the farmer and would propel him directly towards honest labour. Wealth would depend, to a considerable extent, therefore, upon the individual's personal exertion. The result would be a society in which the similarities among men were reflected in the distribution of wealth. In 1838 Senator William Allen of Ohio, an ardent Van Burenite, explained how political equality necessarily resulted in an egalitarian society. Although Allen's view of the Founding Fathers was probably erroneous, his speech brilliantly exposes one of the now hidden assumptions of Democratic theory:

> The framers of the Constitution knew that political power was neither more nor less than the control of one man over another; that, amidst the necessities of human life, control over the labor, the property and the subsistence of man, was control over the man himself. They knew, too, that *the natural disparity in the capacities, energies, and dispositions of men, unaided by political discriminations, was insufficient to destroy that equality of conditions so essential to the safety of each, and to the common happiness of all.* [My italics][38]

Because men *were* similar a 'natural order' would create a society of approximately equal units. Again and again Democrats drew attention to what they believed was a common nature among men, a set of characteristics that was all but universal and which should be reflected in the social structure. In an 'Address to the Workingmen of the United States' (published in *The Globe*) a group of Democrats (one of whom was Amos Kendall) emphasised these shared qualities and traits:

> What makes one man better than another? Are not all made of the same earth? Do not all breathe the same air, eat similar food and drink the same water? Are not all alike endued [sic] with the same immortal mind, all alike created in the image of their maker?... Are not all, in a degree, alike improveable [sic] in their physical powers and mental faculties? Are they not alike in their hopes and fears, their joys and sorrows, their passions, appetites, and aspirations?

The *Western Review*, a staunchly Democratic magazine, likewise drew attention to the similarities among men:

> We are but equals, if we would regard our condition with a philosophic eye. Our points of difference are all artificial – those

---

[38] Richard Hofstadter, *The American Political Tradition* (N.Y., 1948), 61; *Cong. Gl.*, 25 ii, 251.

of resemblance are all from nature. We are bound together by our common wants and our common frailties, – by our hopes, fears, aspirations, and aims, – by our lofty ambitions, our grovelling desires, and our general pursuit of the vainest of vanities – by our manner of entering upon life, by our mode of spending it, by the way in which it ends.

The *Democratic Review* related this general outlook to the distribution of wealth when it proclaimed that 'as far as the conditions of animal existence go, there is very little difference in the ability of all men to provide for themselves and family'. Clearly the journal considered this statement to have contemporary social relevance for it was used as a premise on which to base an argument for the equality of conditions. According to Governor Marcus Morton of Massachusetts the excellence of a society was directly related to the extent of equality between its members. For 'that state of civil society which approximates the nearest to general equality among its members, is most promotive of contentment and happiness, while that which departs most widely from it, is most productive of evil passions and wretchedness.' How was this equality to be achieved? Morton's answer presupposed the basic similarity among men and assumed that without the obstruction of government, the 'natural laws' would convert that similarity into an approximate equality of wealth. Thus, in order to furnish 'the most effectual guaranty against that gross inequality of social condition' it was necessary to secure 'to everyone the fruits of his own industry, with an equal division of *intestate* property among *heirs*'. Morton was convinced that if the *acquisitions* of individuals' were 'limited to the value of their *contributions*', there could be 'little danger of those extremes which are alike unfavorable to the Christian, moral and political well-being of society'. Morton's sentiments were explicitly egalitarian but the equality which he took for granted was no less significant than that which he demanded. The natural equality was the link between equality of opportunity and equality of condition. It was a levelling equality – and it suffused Democratic thought and theory.[39]

Democrats were not content, however, to insist that democracy created an essentially equal society. They also warned that an unequal society would ultimately destroy any popular government. What was needed was a society in which 'inequalities both of property and of power' were 'comparatively trifling'. For 'there and only there can the experiment of self-government be successful.' 'A democratic

---

[39]*Globe,* 24 Sept. 1840; *Western Review,* I (April 1846), 18; *Dem. Rev.,* XXI (March 1847), 202; Morton quoted in *Providence Daily Journal,* 25 Jan. 1843.

government', it was claimed, was 'the natural expression of a general equality of condition and especially of property among the people.' It followed that 'where this equality . . . exists, a democratic government is real, substantial, and of course, permanent'. Why was this so? John Bigelow, in the *Democratic Review,* effectively argued that severe social inequalities would subvert the political equality that democracy promised:

> where a great diversity of condition exists, where the comforts of life and the means of happiness are very unequally distributed, the wealth and intelligence of the superior class will both enable and dispose them to take advantage of the ignorance and necessities of the inferior class, and to disfranchise them actually or by indirection.

'To secure the enjoyment of *equal laws*', it was, according to an official resolution agreed by the Democrats of Vermont and Massachusetts, 'essential that the people from whom they emanate, should be on an equallity [sic] in their social and political condition'. Democracy was thus inseparable from the equality of conditions. Some men would always be richer than others; this was inevitable. But if the distance between rich and poor became too great, then democracy itself would perish. This belief formed a cornerstone of Democratic ideology.[40]

In asserting the pre-eminence of agriculture and the superiority of the farmer, Democrats were continuing a tradition which pre-dated the Revolution. For by the Jacksonian era the image of the virtuous farmer possessed a hold upon the American mind which would prove strong enough to resist decades of urban and commercial expansion. It was a vision of moral excellence, acquired from proximity to, and harmony with, nature. The idea of moral regeneration and rebirth, from which the Revolution had in part sprung, had its roots in nature and in an image of pristine simplicity in the agrarian republic. This image had been fortified by those Europeans who had told the revolutionaries that their nation and populace were ideally placed to enjoy the moral health necessary to support a republic. The post-revolutionary epoch had only served to strengthen the symbolic appeal of the agrarian republic. For with Jefferson's formulation of what would be for several generations the American democratic creed, the farmer and the democrat were merged finally into one. Jefferson had claimed

---

[40] Rantoul, *Oration delivered before the Democratic Citizens of the County of Worcester, July 4, 1837* (Worcester, 1837), 6; *Dem. Rev.,* II (July 1838), 344-50, XIII (Dec. 1843), 566; Democratic State Convention (of Vermont) in Danville (Vt.) *North Star,* 3 July 1837. See also *Dem. Rev.,* VI (Nov. 1839), 374.

that 'the proportion which the aggregate of other classes of citizens bears in any State to that of its husbandmen' was 'generally speaking', 'the proportion of its unsound to its healthy parts'. Similarly he had maintained that by abolishing primogeniture and entails he had 'broke[n] up the hereditary and high-handed aristocracy, which, by accumulating immense masses of property in single lines of families, had divided our country into two distant orders, of nobles and plebeians'. The effect was 'to complete the equality among our citizens so essential to the maintenance of republican government'. A generation later Alexander Everett of Massachusetts argued that the aristocratic spirit 'in the country . . . encounters its natural antidote in the equal diffusion of intelligence and property which form the basis of a democratic state of society'. Henceforth the land would be beyond the reach of grasping aristocrats; it would be the haven of democracy.[41]

Jefferson's triumph over the 'undemocratic' Federalists, secured by the votes of the agricultural interest, had left an agrarian legacy to all who would espouse the democratic cause. The failure of the urban interest to find a competing or countervailing democratic creed, and the onward march of democracy itself, had created an ideological universe in which to be enthusiastically democratic – and to be unequivocally egalitarian – was, almost inevitably, to share the agrarian preference. The countryside, Jefferson, John Taylor, and virtually all other prominent democrats had taught, was safe. It was perhaps inevitable that despite, or rather explicitly in opposition to, capitalist and urban expansion, Jacksonian Democracy found its inspiration in the pastoral, agrarian ideal.[42]

Although Democrats were lavish in their praise of farming, there were certain claims for the agrarian society that were conspicuously absent. The society of yeoman farmers would encourage industry; it would hardly promote talent or specialised abilities. It would not offer scope to the differing and diverse qualities which particular individuals or groups might possess. Instead the Democrats envisaged an essentially undifferentiated society in which the farmer laboured almost in isolation for his wealth and then sold his produce in a series of straightforward, undemanding operations. Talent would be lacking in economic significance.

This did not mean, of course, that the agrarian society would

[41] Jefferson, 'Notes on Virginia', in Fried, *Essential Jefferson*, 217-18; A.A. Lipscombe and A.E. Bergh (eds.), *The Writings of Thomas Jefferson*, 20 vols. (Washington, D.C., 1903), XVII, 461 (see also XIII, 398); Alexander E. Everett, *An Oration delivered at Holloston, July 4, 1839* (Boston, 1839), 37.

[42] See Peterson, *Jefferson Image*, 69-70, 217-18.

contain no other occupational groups. Rather it meant that other pursuits should be regarded as subordinate to that of farming and, moreover, that the personal and social qualities that were promoted on the farm should be displayed throughout society. Democrats recognised that the craftsman and the artisan would be needed to serve the wants of the agricultural producers; in bestowing their approval upon these occupations, they employed the familiar terms that were used to describe the farmer. Once again independence was stressed. *The Globe* referred to

> the healthy mechanic or artisan, who works for himself at his own shop, or if he goes abroad, returns home to his meals every day, and sleeps under his own roof every night; whose earnings are regulated by the wants of the community at large, not by the discretion of a pernicious master; whose hours of labor depend on universal custom; who, when the sun goes down, is a freeman until he rises again; who can eat his meals in comfort, and sleep as long as nature requires.

The mechanic and labourer comprised, together with the farmer, the 'producing classes' to which the Democratic rhetoric constantly referred. Logically, moreover, if the agrarian society were to trade its agricultural surplus in return for manufactured goods, then merchants would be needed. Few Democrats were able to enthuse over this profession. Nevertheless the manner in which the merchant should conduct his business bore a clear resemblance to the way in which the farmer operated. What was desired were 'the slow, sure, and silent gains of a business prudently conducted, requiring years of cautious sagacity, and, above all, a character as clear as the sun, to build up an independency'. The slight social differentiation which Democrats recognised as inevitable should not, however, result in any maldistribution of wealth and power. For provided that government did not intervene, the natural laws of supply and demand would direct men's labour into productive and rewarding activities and 'would tend to equalize the distribution of wealth'. The *Democratic Review* argued that 'among a free and enterprising people, the rates of profit, realised by individuals engaged in the various employments of life, have a constant tendency to the same level'. Once again Democratic theory refused to emphasise the natural differences among men. The idea of specialised talents being catered for by some occupational pursuits and meeting with a financial reward commensurate with their inherent exclusiveness was absent. Democratic egalitarianism was once more reaffirmed.[43]

[43] *Globe*, 11 Jan. 1842, 1 July 1839; *Dem. Rev.*, VI (Sept. 1839), 215, 1 March 1838), 389.

Democrats thus associated democracy with an undifferentiated atomised society. Such a society was, of course, threatened by the process of growth which the economy was then undergoing. The agrarian society of Democratic rhetoric was under assault not merely because of the ever-increasing size of the non-agricultural sector but also because of a general decline in the social virtues that were associated with the yeoman farmer. Thus Democrats were bitter in their attacks upon the mercantile interest; they resented especially the manner in which merchants acquired their wealth. 'The profession of a merchant', was, according to *The Globe*, 'with many honorable exceptions, a succession of throws of the die.' Too willing to contract large debts, the merchant too often lived on credit and was therefore a likely candidate for bankruptcy. If, instead, high-risk endeavours were successful, the result would be great wealth – an obvious threat to democracy. For merchants were 'accustomed to handle large sums of money, which they accumulate without much bodily toil' and were able to live 'in ease, and splendour not enjoyed by any other large class or community'. Hence 'the common principles of human nature incline them to aristocratic feelings.' It was the conclusion of Senator Robert Strange of North Carolina that 'from the beginning of history to the present day, merchants have become princes, and constituted the aristocracy of their respective countries'. One Democratic Congressman referred contemptuously to

> the Whig merchants in Boston, New York, Philadelphia, and other large cities, who ride in their carriages, drawn by gay horses, surrounded by rich equipage, who live in marble palaces, furnished in the most splendid and magnificent style, who fare sumptuously every day, sitting down at tables which groan under the weight of the luxuries and the dainties of the season.

Far better, Democrats believed, to retain the republican simplicity of the farmer.[44]

If the activities of contemporary merchants alarmed many Democrats, the growth of manufacturing industry disturbed them still further. The factory system, which had sprung into a healthy existence after the War of 1812, was an obvious threat to the agrarian society. Silas Wright warned Congress that since the factory labourer lacked skills and was unfitted for other occupations, he was necessarily too dependent upon his employer. Hence, Wright noted, 'the great power which the manufacturing capitalist must hold over the employee, and, by necessary consequence, over the living, the comfort, and the

[44] *Globe,* 1 July 1839; *Cong. Gl,* 25 i App., 46, 26 i App., 494.

independence of the laborer'. This compared unfavourably, he added, with 'the more free, and equally comfortable and respectable employments of agriculture and commerce'. Other Democrats claimed that the factory system resulted in a labour force that was 'bound hand and foot by a system of petty despotism as galling as ever oppressed the subjects of a tyranny in the old world'. It was a system that would bring 'ignorance, degradation, immorality, and slavery'. Amos Kendall urged the sons and daughters of farmers to remain on the farm, rather than to seek employment in the factories; he expressed his hope that the nation's *principal* and *governing* population' would 'long' remain either freehold farmers or 'independent mechanics'. For such a mechanic, unlike the factory labourer, could refuse 'to sell [his] services to any man on other conditions than those of perfect equality – both as citizens and men.' The factory worker, Democrats thus believed, would almost inevitably be deprived of that equality to which he was entitled.[45]

It was also frequently claimed that manufacturing resulted in the degradation of labour. This was 'exemplified in processions of hundreds of girls, separated from home and from parental guardianship, marching in long rows to and from their meals and their work, two by two, like yokes of oxen'. Already there was in America a class – the factory workers of Massachusetts – who lived like 'serfs and slaves', going to their dinners 'at the tap of the bell' and returning 'at the tap of the bell'. Such workers were 'not like free American citizens'. The factory system thus threatened to put an end to republican equality. While the labourers were enslaved, the owners formed an 'aristocracy' that was 'more haughty and farther removed from the rest of the population, than is ever seen in any other portion of American society'. 'Manufacturing', Aaron Brown of Tennessee declared in 1841, 'has been overdone'. 'Many establishments', he added ominously, probably 'will have to go down'. The factory system, according to one Democrat, was 'a national curse'.[46]

The development of manufacturing was being accompanied, in Jacksonian America, by urban expansion upon a hitherto unprecedented scale. Although the urban population was still tiny in comparison with the whole, the larger cities were experiencing a rate of growth which both made them increasingly conspicuous and gave them what was perhaps a disproportionate amount of social power

[45] Gillett, *Wright*, II, 1487-8; *Democratic Statesman*, 10 May 1845; *Young Hickory Banner*, 24 Aug. 1844; *Kendall's Expositor*, II (31 May 1842), 163.

[46] *Globe*, 11 Jan. 1842; *Iowa C.C.*, 146; *Young Hickory Banner*, 24 Aug. 1844; *Cong. Gl.*, 27 App., 484.

and influence. Although some Democrats accepted the urban centres, many more viewed them with the traditional agrarian hostility or suspicion. According to John Wentworth, editor of the *Chicago Democrat*, cities were 'festering in corruption'; they were 'supported entirely at the expense of the country'. More specifically, Democrats objected to the cities on two grounds. Firstly, they destroyed individual autonomy. This idea was developed by the *Democratic Review:*

> In the city men move in masses. They catch the current opinion of the hour from their class, and from those public organs of the press on which they are accustomed to depend for their daily supply of superficial thought – for their morning dose of mental stimulus, in those flaming appeals to their passions, their interests or their vanity, which it is the vocation of the latter daily to administer. They have little leisure to reflect calmly and independently for themselves. They are like men in a troubled crowd, swept hither and thither by the current of the huge mass, with a force which the individual can rarely nerve himself to stem. Individuality in fact loses itself, almost of necessity, in the constant pressure of surrounding example, of the general habit and tone of society, and in the contagious excitements which rapidly chase each other in their successive sway over the multitudinous aggregate of minds.

Secondly, the city was the home of inequality. Again the *Democratic Review* enunciated the criticism clearly:

> In the city, too, men live more for artificial, deceptive 'appearances' – for a petty pride of silly fashion – for a mean ostentation of wealth and luxury, in all its relative degrees – in a constant state of jealous sensitiveness to their position in those classifications which naturally arise out of the dense, heterogeneous mass of men that compose the population of a city – in a perpetual, even though unconscious, habit of self-comparison, of an upward looking envy and a downward looking contempt. And how injurious must be the influence of the all-pervading social atmosphere thus generated, to all true independence and elevation of character – to all mental freedom and fearlessness – to that proud democratic dignity of manhood, to that noble love and respect for the *equal human nature and human rights* of the humblest of our fellow men, alone worthy of the American citizen – it cannot be necessary for us to expatiate upon. [My italics]

The Democratic social ethos has often been described as 'bourgeois'. If this word has any meaning to distinguish it from the terms 'capitalist', 'middleclass', or 'entrepreneurial', it is in its traditional connotation of 'town dweller'. A less suitable label for Jacksonian Democracy would be difficult to find.[47]

Yet Democratic hostility to cities, to merchants, and to manufacturing was only the more obvious manifestation of a widespread disenchantment with commercial practices in general.[48] For the sound morality, the individual autonomy, and the social equality which Democrats prized so dearly were under severe threat. Even the agricultural interest, it was feared, was being infected by an essentially alien virus. Although in no way opposed to economic growth, Democrats in effect insisted that it be achieved on their own terms.

As a direct consequence, debt fell under immediate suspicion. Democrats feared that indebtedness destroyed independence and undermined equality. A group of partisans from the state of New York declared that 'individual debts, State debts, and national debts, are productive of a condition of dependence destructive of equality among men and freedom of action among States and nations'. In addition, however, Democrats believed that the individual who conducted business using borrowed capital would be more inclined to embark upon high risk ventures. Because he would not himself have laboured for the wealth that was being employed, the debtor would be insufficiently chastened by the prospect of failure. High risk ventures were, of course, anathema to Democrats since large gains or losses violated the relationship between labour and wealth upon which democratic equality depended. As a result Democrats were often bitterly opposed to lenient terms for bankruptcy. For 'the restraint upon the creation of debt' was 'the obligation to pay it'; without this indebtedness would become rife. The same process of reasoning impelled most Democrats to oppose laws granting limited liability. With full liability, it was felt, 'business transactions . . . are likely to be conducted in a more prudent and less hazardous manner'. Any separation between ownership and management was similarly suspect, since the owner might be unwilling or unable to supervise and therefore restrain the company's activities. Debts, speculation, risks,

---

[47] *Chicago Democrat* in William G. Shade, *Banks or No Banks: The Money Issue in Western Politics, 1832-1865* (Detroit, 1972), 148; *Dem. Rev.,* VI (Dec. 1839), 500-2.

[48] A minority of (conservative) Democrats did not share this outlook. See below, Chapter 4. Similarly hostility to cities was displayed by some conservative social reformers – see David J. Rothman, *The Discovery of the Asylum: Social Order and Disorder in the Early Republic* (Boston, 1971). However, these men did not emphasise the exploitative effects upon the urban wage earner nor the assault upon his autonomy.

bankruptcy – a process of growth which brought these evils was clearly unacceptable.[49]

The Democratic response to the prevailing commercial spirit was thus not one of enthusiasm but of dismay. The idea of Jacksonian Democracy as a movement of 'rising entrepreneurs', men 'on the make', and alert to 'the main chance' is at odds with the party's clearly expressed agrarian ideology. Democrats sought to minimise, or even to eliminate, risk from commercial practices so that the simple, direct, almost one-to-one relationship between wealth and labour which was most clearly visible on the farm could be extended into all activities. *The Globe* warned that since 'we are, notoriously, a moving, striving people' there was 'more danger that we should do too much, than that we should do too little'. It would be more accurate to term the Jacksonian social philosophy 'anti-entrepreneurial' than 'entrepreneurial'. Democrats sought to restrain commercial and industrial development, to keep it within the moral, economic and political confines of the agrarian society. 'Enterprise', according to Frank Blair, was 'a good thing'. But, he added, 'prudence and honesty are better'.[50] Without interference from government, society would, Democrats were confident, match their high expectations. The force of self-interest, unimpeded by artificial restraints, and underwritten by the right to acquire and retain private property, would preserve an agrarian society of essentially equal and autonomous units. An undifferentiated, non-exploitative and egalitarian society rooted in self-interest – this was the social base for democracy.

Policy

With the intention of circumscribing the actions of government and of safeguarding the agrarian society, Democrats presented the electorate with a coherent programme. Voters were invited to support measures and proposals that were wholly consistent with Democratic preconceptions about government and society. On every major issue official policy was rooted in principle.

In pursuit of a limited, inactive government, Democrats focused upon the legislature as the major threat.[51] American liberties, it was

[49] *Address to the Democratic Republic Electors of the State of New York* (Washington, D.C., 1840), 19; *Cong. Gl,* 26 i App., 91; *N.H. Senate Journal* (1840), 5. For other examples of Democratic anti-commercialism see *Dem. Rev.,* V (Jan. 1839), 84, VIII (Aug. 1840), 101-2, 105, X (Jan. 1842), 48-50; *Globe,* 18 July 1837; Theophilus Fisk, *A Vindication of the Rights of Man* (Portsmouth, Va., 1838), 14. The suspicion of debt, of course, had roots in the colonial era.

[50] *Globe,* 8 Dec. 1837.

[51] This, of course, represented an important departure from the Jeffersonian tradition.

argued, could be overthrown by corruption; corruption would 'begin and end in the legislative department'. For the legislature threatened the populistic democracy which Democrats favoured. It was essentially irresponsible and oligarchic with clear, unmistakable 'aristocratic tendencies'. It was a body whose members were able to enter into corrupt alliances in order to pass partial legislation. The very fact that the legislative power was distributed among so many individuals rendered it impersonal and 'irresponsible'.[52]

This antagonism was translated into a vigorous defence of presidential power. For the executive embodied 'the great essential principle of this Government – that of direct responsibility of the ruler to the people'. Hence 'responsibility can be fastened upon an executive, but never upon a legislative body'. True to their commitment to the separation of powers, Democrats defended the President's right to veto legislation. Andrew Jackson had used the veto with an unprecedented frequency and the Democratic party, in sustaining the vetoes, made one of its few breaks with the John Taylor tradition. The veto was 'a mere conservative power' which could 'only be exercised in a negative sense'. According to James K. Polk 'it arrests for the time being hasty, inconsiderate,. or unconstitutional legislation, invites reconsideration, and transfers questions at issue between the legislative and executive departments to the tribunal of the people'. A protection against the power of both the members of the legislature themselves and the self-interested majority in whose name they might claim to act, the veto was 'the greatest check that can possibly be put on partial or hasty systems of legislation'. Since 'the very point where the popular will is most potently concentrated' was 'in the first officer of the Republic', it followed that the veto power was a means of exposing proposed legislation to the scrutiny and supervision of the people. Backed by this process of reasoning, Democrats defended the frequency of Jackson's vetoes and generally justified the expanded role of the President.[53]

More contentious even than the defence of the veto was the Democratic assault upon the judiciary. This branch of government was, Democrats charged, almost the last refuge of those unreconstructed conservatives who resented or despised democracy. Martin Van Buren remarked upon judges' 'want of sympathy, as a general rule, for popular rights' while other Democrats argued that

[52]*Cong. Gl,* 25 ii App., 254; Bancroft, *Principles of Democracy,* 8.

[53]*Globe,* 29 Dec. 1840; *Iowa C.C.,* 224; *Papers of Johnson,* I, 93; *Messages of Presidents,* IV, 375; *La. CC.,* 302; *Globe,* 4 March 1841. Similarly in the states the Democrats tended to defend the power of the governor.

'the present Judicial system' was 'anti-republican in its principles and administration', comprising 'the only aristocratic feature in our constitution'. With the Democratic belief in the corrupting tendency of power it was perhaps inevitable that the judges should become objects of deep suspicion. In the words of *The Globe* 'the judiciary... has ever been found the ready instrument of aggressive power'. Many judges were of course appointed during good behaviour and this, in effect a life tenure, was disturbing to many Democrats. When they observed that the judges had attempted to appropriate 'the exclusive right of deciding upon great constitutional questions' their fears were intensified. One Marylander sought to place the judges 'in some measure on an equality with other men', in order to prevent them from looking down 'with contemptuous scorn upon the feelings and opinions of others'. Other Democrats deplored the reverence that was generally accorded to judicial utterances. There was an 'unaccountable sanctity enveloping the judicial ermine as moss covers the time beaten temples of antiquity'. Yet when 'stript of superstitious veneration, it stands out as the rude creation of man – the workmanship of a noble, yet fallible creature'. Nor were some Democrats loathe to criticise the Supreme Court. One Congressman declared that it was 'the stationary political branch of the Government'. 'There', he added, with a barely concealed disdain, 'we can hear the response of the oracles, and see the priests of the Constitution ermined with black gowns, and fixing, by their fiat, the destinies of nations'. Basic Democratic theory thus impelled partisans to view the judiciary as a symbol of social and political inequality.[54]

Democrats did not, however, find a single national policy upon which they could unite and reform the judiciary. Within the states some called for the popular election of judges. James Brent of Louisiana argued that 'our only safety consists in keeping each of the departments [of the government] separate from, and independent of the others'. Upon this premise Brent constructed an argument for an elective judiciary. The dangers to be feared from elections, he explained, were slight in comparison with those inherent in the appointive system. This involved the orthodox Democratic belief that the mass of the people were more trustworthy than any individual, however dignified or illustrious.[55]

[54]Martin Van Buren, *An Inquiry Into the Origins and Course of Political Parties in the United States* (N.Y., 1867), 365-6; Tarbell, *Oration,* 27; *Globe,* 3 Jan., 1844; *Cincinnati Advertiser,* 17 Jan. 1838; *Democrat and Carroll Co. Republican,* 20 Feb. 1840; *La. C.C.,* 741; *Cong. Gl.,* 25 iii App., 154.

[55]*La. C.C.,* 748.

Other Democrats concentrated their reforming energies upon other features of the judicial system. Some called for procedural reforms; some sought a transfer of much of the judge's power to the jury. In the search for a remedy for judicial élitism, the Common Law was often selected for reform. Judges, according to Robert Rantoul,

> are sworn to administer common law as it came down from the dark ages, excepting what has been repealed by the Constitution and the statutes, which exception they are always careful to reduce to the narrowest possible limits. With them, wrong is right, if, wrong has existed from time immemorial: precedents are everything: the spirit of the age is nothing.

The Common Law denied all natural equality since it gave the judiciary 'the absolute power of a despot over the lives, liberties and property of the citizens'. Discretionary power was highly dangerous since 'the discretion of a good man is often nothing better than caprice, while the discretion of a bad man is an odious and irresponsible tyranny'. The solution here was to ensure that the laws were simplified, to create 'a positive and unbending text' in place of the Common Law. Thus by reforming the legal code and by extending popular control over the judges, Democrats sought to curtail judicial power in the interests of the equality and freedom to which they were committed. On the judiciary as on the executive, Democratic policy grew out of Democratic principle.[56]

In other areas of policy Democrats maintained a similar consistency. The defence of the agrarian society, on which so much of their ideology rested, had clear implications for policy when the questions of the acquisition and settlement of new lands arose. Insisting upon both an inactive government and the supervision of that government by the people, Democrats repudiated the traditional notion that a republic was suited only to small territories. The application of the states-rights principle meant that 'the Federal Constitution was wisely adapted in its provisions to any expansion of our limits and population'. Hence Democrats led and inspired the movement for territorial expansion which culminated in the 'Manifest Destiny' crusade of the 1840s. It was the nation's destiny, Democrats proclaimed, to extend the area of freedom. The acquisition of territories in the West, it was argued, would confer incalculable

[56] Rantoul, *Oration . . . 4 July 1836*, 38; Tarbell, *Oration*, 27-8. On the Democratic attempt to codify the laws see Schlesinger, *Age of Jackson*, 332-3.

benefits upon mankind by promoting the power of the United states and therefore the influence of democracy.[57]

Yet there were other compelling reasons for pushing back the nation's frontiers into the sparsely settled West. For it was vital that the agrarian society be perpetuated. 'The great city of Florence', according to one Democratic Senator, 'sank almost as rapidly as it rose, as have the hundred cities whose people have been confined within the narrow circle of a few miles, and where compression causes vice and temptation, and the greatest extremes of wealth and poverty'. What was needed, he continued, was 'a hardy population, honest, industrious and virtuous, spread over a large surface'. Thus the preservation of the agrarian society and hence of democracy itself suggested an extension of the nation's boundaries into the agrarian West, whenever it could be safely achieved.[58]

The same needs also suggested that the lands be opened up to settlers from the East (or even the older West). Democrats favoured the pre-emption policy, by which squatters on unclaimed lands were given priority when the lands were officially disposed of. Similarly they favoured a reduction in the price of Western lands and a graduated scale of prices that would facilitate the settlement of the less attractive areas. This, the graduation scheme, clearly fitted Democratic pre-conceptions. In the words of President Polk, it was 'a wise policy to afford facilities to our citizens to become the owners at low and moderate rates of freeholds of their own instead of being the tenants and dependants of others'. In those Eastern states where economic advancement appeared to be threatened by migration to the West Democrats, responding (as Democratic theory required) to the wishes of their constituents, experienced some difficulty in sustaining the party's liberal land policy. Yet other Eastern Democrats valued Western land as an essential support for a high-wage economy. One Maine newspaper warned that since 'the whole northern legislature is so much in the hands of capitalists', it would be 'the intent of the laws to keep the people at home, by lessening the prospects of emigrants'. For 'the more laborers there are, the lower is the price of labor, and the more means are wielded by rich employers to crush any *insubordination* among the employed.' A liberal land policy would thus reinforce the natural laws and, while strengthening the predominance of the agricultural interest, would indirectly benefit the non-agricultural

[57]*Messages of Presidents,* IV, 465. Major L. Wilson, *Space, Time, and Freedom* (London, 1974), 94–119 is suggestive on this subject.

[58]*Letter of Alexander Anderson, of Tennessee. . .* (n.p., n.d.), 22–3.

sector. Pre-emption and graduation were square in the logic of Democracy.[59]

The issues of land and territorial expansion were not, however, the subjects which aroused greatest concern or controversy in the Jacksonian era. Democratic energies were concentrated instead on the assault upon legislation which could be construed as partial.[60] Jacksonian Democracy came to a focus in the drive for a limited, inactive government and an economy regulated by the laws of nature.

It followed from the labour theory of value (or alternatively from the theories of Physiocracy) that 'the Government has nothing of its own intrinsically'. Hence 'what it bestows upon one, it must wrest from another'. If any 'system of policy' which 'will enable one part of the community to live without labor' were adopted, it would 'tend to throw a greater portion of labor upon those not so favored'. Here was the danger of partial legislation: governmental aid was necessarily unjust. Any advantage that was derived was obtained solely at the expense of the broad mass of the community. Democrats thus sought to eradicate the entire system.[61]

The danger from governmental intervention was not limited, however, to cases in which individuals received some slight financial benefit. For 'when the foundation of the artificial inequality of fortune is once laid . . . all the subsequent operations of society tend to increase the difference in the condition of different classes of the community.' Partial legislation was thus the major threat to that equality without which democracy could not properly function. It would destroy the direct relation between wealth and labour; it would ultimately result in a hierarchical society of ranks, classes and orders.[62]

Again and again Democrats explained the process. Those who received aid from government would lose all desire or motive to labour honestly; 'idleness and dissipation' would thus be encouraged. They would, moreover, come to fear and despise the democratic system itself, resenting, as élitists, its avowed egalitarianism. Those who

---

[59] *Messages of Presidents,* IV, 503; *Belfast Republican Journal,* in Roy M. Robbins, *Our Landed Heritage: The Public Domain 1776-1936* (Princeton, 1942), 85. See also Martin Van Buren in *Messages of Presidents,* III, 389.

[60] 'Partial' legislation was that which benefited a part rather than the whole of the community.

[61] *Cong., Gl.,* 25 ii App., 205, 26 i App., 426.

[62] William M. Gouge, *A Short History of Paper Money and Banking in the United States* (Phil., 1833), 92.

received no benefit, meanwhile, would become demoralised and dejected – 'dejection, poverty and consequent crime' would ensue. As a result the force of self-interest would no longer operate upon men equally. The natural laws would be unable to preserve an equal and harmonious society. The unnatural inequality initiated by government would create a powerful minority which would then seek to obtain further privileges from legislation. A cycle of exploitation and privilege would have been established. The tendency of partial legislation was thus 'in the end, to introduce ranks and classes and family distinctions'. Hence 'if you would have a free country and desire to perpetuate its freedom, you must have equal laws, conferring equal blessings, and imposing equal burdens.'[63]

Particularly objectionable, from the Democratic standpoint, were those items of partial legislation which resulted in the creation of privileged corporations. Charters conferring special privileges were a denial of republican equality. They were 'a compromise of the principle of equality with that of property'. For 'whatever power is given to a corporation is just so much power taken from the State, in derogation of the original power of the mass of the community, and violative of the equality of every individual not incorporated.' If the creation of such corporations were not checked, then 'that system of provident legislation, which guarded against the accumulation and perpetuity of property, by primogeniture and entail', would be 'completely annulled, and the tenure of property carried back to a system not feudal in its military features, but much more strict and lasting than feudal tenure'. One Southern Democrat, acknowledging that 'inequality in wealth will ever exist', nevertheless insisted that 'the policy of all political systems established for the happiness of the mass, and especially of our Republican Government', was 'to diminish these inequalities by guarding against the undue aggregation of capital in the hands of a privileged . . . few and protecting the people in the enjoyment of the fruits of their labor'. 'All monied corporations', he warned, 'are opposed to this policy', since their privileges 'impede the natural tendency of capital to an equal distribution among the people.' Thus it was that, in the words of one New Englander, 'by the aid of acts of incorporation large masses of property are concentrated in one'.[64]

Without such interference, however, the natural equality would remain. 'In the distribution of wealth resulting from the union of labor

---

[63]*Old Dominion,* 20 Oct. 1838; *Cong. Gl.* 27 ii App., 672.
[64]*Pa. C.C.,* I, 366; *Wetumpka Argus,* 21 Aug. 1839; Burke, *Address,* 15.

and capital', it was, according to Martin Van Buren, 'too often the case that an undue proportion falls to the share of the latter'. But 'the discontinuance of partial legislation . . . would be an important step towards correcting this inequality.' The Democratic demand for 'equal rights' was thus a demand for an end to partial legislation. 'The equality of the laws' was 'two-fold; it measurably establishes equality in the fortunes and in the dignity of the citizens'. Equal rights would guarantee an equality of power, an equality of esteem, and an approximate equality of wealth. It was a recognition of the natural equality among men; it was, as Ely Moore argued, an acknowledgement of the basic similarity between citizens:

> Since, then, all men are created equal; since nature has set no difference between her children; since all have the same right to her benefactions; since all possess the same senses, the same organs; since, in her original design, she created neither master nor slave, patrician nor plebeian, wealthy nor poor, how can political laws – which are an absurdity and a curse if they are not the development of natural laws – but establish a glaring and tyrannic difference between the members of a community?

The crusade against partial legislation was thus grounded in the levelling egalitarianism that was the distinguishing feature of Democratic ideology.[65]

An obvious example of partial legislation was the protective tariff, avowedly designed to promote and encourage manufacturing. Most Democrats disliked the factory system; they found in the tariff a convincing explanation for its emergence. A high protective tariff was no less than a device 'to tax labor and aggrandize capital', and its ultimate effect would be to create a society scarred by 'INORDINATE WEALTH, *on the one hand*' and 'SQUALID POVERTY *on the other*'. This view was endorsed at the highest levels. President Polk in an official message complained that the tariff of 1842 had operated 'to swell the profits and overgrown wealth of the comparatively few who had invested their capital in manufactures'. 'It was a system', he continued, whose effect would have been 'to build up immense fortunes in the hands of the few and to reduce the laboring millions to pauperism and misery'. For this had been its tendency in England. Democrats frequently referred to the effects of partial legislation upon English society and insisted that in the United States a similar policy would bring similar results. 'More than any other cause' the protective

---

[65] Martin Van Buren, *Letter to Isaac Lippincott et al. Sept. 14, 1840 in Address to the Workingmen of the United States* (n.p., n.d.), 16; Ely Moore, *Address on Civil Government* (N.Y., 1847), 23, 15.

system had 'introduced the vast disparity of condition among the people of England'. The conclusion was obvious.[65]

It was, however, a conclusion that could be drawn more easily in agricultural areas than in those regions where manufacturing had already taken deep root. Thus in parts of New England and the Middle Atlantic states Democrats were often compelled to defend the interests of those employed in the factories. Hence they moderated or even rejected Democratic demands for free trade. Because all but the most ardent opponents of the tariff acknowledged that some duties were necessary in order to provide revenue, the party officially compromised on the policy of 'incidental protection'. In the different sections of the nation a different emphasis might be given but, in general, Democrats remained the lower tariff party. Even in Pennsylvania, a centre of pro-tariff sentiment, Democratic partisans were often worried about the consequences of protection. Acknowledging that the state needed the tariff, the *Philadelphia Ledger* nevertheless counselled caution:

> Accumulation of wealth is the oligarchy that rules Massachusetts, and through it, New England: and high protection, affording high profits is the instrument of that accumulation. And why do they seek this accumulation? As an instrument of political, as well as social power. . . . The laws of Massachusetts forbidding primogeniture and entails, a substitute is sought in corporations.

Thus Democratic hostility to manufacturing was translated into a preference for a low rate of tariff duties. The tariff met with a principled opposition from the party of limited, inactive government.[67]

Another target for the Democratic crusade against governmental intervention and partial legislation was the internal improvements policy. Both the Federal and the State governments were under considerable pressure to lend their credit or organisational capacity to promote improvements in the nation's transportation system. At national level Democrats in the years following the Panic of 1837 maintained a reasonably consistent opposition to the policy. They resented especially the assumption that the federal government possessed the authority to promote those improvements that were not truly national in scope. Orthodox Democratic theory impelled its exponents to resent the 'combinations of local and sectional interests' which the 'disreputable scramble for the public money' would

[66] *Young Hickory Banner*, 24 Aug. 1844; *N.H. Senate Journal* (1844), 22; *Messages of Presidents*, IV, 499; *Cong. G.*, 27 ii App., 565.

[67] *Philadelphia Ledger* in *Democratic Statesman* , 7 June 1845.

produce. 'The conflict . . . between local and individual interests', on the one hand, and 'the general interests of the whole', on the other, would discredit the democratic process itself. Fearing sectional inequality, Democrats sought to curtail federal power over internal improvements.[68]

Within the states the theory of limited government implied a similar reluctance to embark upon improvements. The minority who secured the unfair advantage of a canal dug or a railroad built in close proximity to their land were able to benefit from the reduced transportation costs. But the benefit was obtained at the expense of the remainder of the community. This, coupled with Democratic hostility to debt creation, drove many partisans to declare their opposition to all state-sponsored improvements. Others, however, exposed to local pressures (to which their theories required them to submit) and mindful of the value to an agrarian economy of a complex transportation network, instead joined the movement for improvements. As a result Democrats responded with less than complete consistency to the internal improvements policy.[69]

Yet the war upon privilege and governmental interference was not confined to the battle for free (or freer) trade on the one hand, and the assault on internal improvements on the other. The major issue of the entire Jacksonian era concerned not these but instead the problems of banking and the currency. According to Thomas Hart Benton, 'the currency question' was 'the greatest question of the age. . . it absorbs and swallows up every other'. For orthodox Democrats found in the nation's banking system a threat to their most cherished values, a fundamental challenge to their social and political ideals, indeed a virtual negation of their entire ideology. The crusade for equal rights and thus the Jacksonian Democratic movement itself culminated in the war against the banks.[70]

It is now widely recognised by historians that Andrew Jackson's destruction of the second Bank of the United States was motivated primarily by an agrarian dislike of banking. Although there were certain entrepreneurial elements within the Democratic party, there can be little doubt that the overriding aim was to restrain, rather than to expand, banking and credit. It was a standard Democratic belief that

[68]*Messages of Presidents,* IV, 464.

[69]See below, Chapter 6, for a further discussion of this and other subjects of financial policy.

[70]Benton quoted in Clarence H. McClaure, *Opposition in Missouri to Thomas Hart Benton* (Nashville, 1927), 81.

'we have too much instead of too little credit' and in every section of the Union the party's spokesmen declared their opposition to the existing banking system. According to Andrew Jackson, it was 'a perfect humbug, an imposition', which 'ought never to have existed' and 'ought to be put down'. In the words of an Alabama Democrat banking was 'in conflict with justice, equity, morality and religion'; there was 'nothing evil that it does not aid – nothing good that it is not averse to'. Senator Bedford Brown of North Carolina expressed grave doubts 'whether banking institutions were at all compatible with the existence of a truly republican government', while one New Englander declared that banking was no less than 'a STUPENDOUS FRAUD upon the people'. Silas Wright was 'not very partial to banks of any description'; to Richard Quinton of Iowa they were 'a set of swindling machines'.[71]

Orthodox Democrats were convinced that their hopes and aspirations for the republic would be frustrated if the banking system were not either reformed or destroyed. In the light of their preconceptions and assumptions this was an entirely logical and rational response. For the banks posed an obvious threat to the society of equalised, atomised power that Democratic theory postulated. In the Jacksonian world-view they symbolised privilege and inequality.

The privileges enjoyed by bankers stemmed from their control over the allocation and expansion of credit. Hence because 'it gives to a particular class the control of the capital as well as the credit of a country' banking was 'the great opponent of equal rights'. Control over credit, moreover, included the right to print paper money and hence alter the price level. This was in effect 'the highest prerogative of sovereignty'; 'a system which commits the currency of the country to the care of a few speculating capitalists, and then shields them from responsibility' was 'monstrous'. Democrats feared that this power would 'be directly wielded. . . to control the people in all our elections'. The ability to determine who should receive loans, to obtain interest not upon real wealth but upon paper money, to alter the real value of all debts as well as all prices and to influence the level of economic activity throughout society – this represented 'a power. . . . more potent than government. . . . and against the overspreading tendency of which written constitutions and the form of government

---

[71] *Cong. Gl,* 25 ii App., 205; Jackson to Dawson, 1 April 1840 in John J. Whalen (ed.), 'The Jackson-Dawson Correspondence', *H.P.S.O.* XVI (Jan. .1958), 3-30; Mace T.P. Brindley in Jonathan M. Thornton, III, 'Politics and Power in a Slave Society; Alabama 1806-1860' (Ph.D. thesis, University of Yale, 1974), 65; *Cong. Gl,* 25 ii App., 167; Burke, *Address,* 7; *Cong. Gl,* 25 i App., 116; *Iowa C.C.,* 70-2.

are but feeble barriers'. It was 'a mass of power' which 'never can be concentrated in any other form than that of paper money'. Who would exercise this authority? 'Do the banks', one Democrat asked, 'choose men who are more honest, faithful and capable than the people? Does a bank stamp upon men as it does upon paper, change their qualities, value, worth and character?' Answering his own question, he declared that 'the history of banks and corporations' was 'the blackest page in the history of fraud and violated trust'. Democratic sensitivity to the dangers of power made the banks an obvious target for condemnation. If government could not be trusted with the financial interests of its citizens then to give this power to a number of irresponsible institutions was the height of folly. The banks represented a conspicuous threat to the agrarian ideal of equalised power and individual autonomy.[72]

Democrats often explained why banking was productive of inequality in society. The 'private interests' of bankers would impel them to 'stimulate extravagance of enterprise by improvidence of credit'. Hence 'proneness to excessive issues has ever been the vice of the banking system.' Eager to loan as much as the community could absorb, the banks would promote high-risk or even purely speculative ventures. These would in turn undermine the direct relationship between wealth and labour that Democratic theory required. Martin Van Buren in 1838 complained that in recent years bank expansions had 'seduced industry from its regular and salutory occupations by the hope of abundance without labor, and deranged the social state by tempting all trades and professions into the vortex of speculation on remote contingencies'. Honest industry would fall into disrepute if the opportunity for easy and rapid gain were presented. A 'sudden increase of currency' and a 'consequent rise of prices', according to the *Democratic Review,* were likely to 'seduce thousands of industrious individuals to abandon their regular employment under the expectation or realising speedy fortunes by speculation'. One Pennsylvania Democrat likewise lamented that as a result of excessive increases in the supply of currency, 'rural occupation, steady habits, moderate living, are cast into such eclipse, that few can endure their lot, contrasted with the glare of sudden fortune'. As agriculture and honest labour were discredited so inequality would emerge.[73]

---

[72]*Address to Working Men, on the Low Price of Wages, by a Mechanic* (n.p., n.d.), 4; *Dem. Rev.,* II (April 1838), 10; *Cong. Gl,* 25 ii App., 46, 158; *Dem. Rev.,* XI (Sept. 1842), 258; *Cong. Gl,* 25 ii App., 251, 228.

[73]*Messages of Presidents,* III, 328, 494; *Dem. Rev.,* IV (Aug. 1839), 97; *Cong. Gl,* 27 i App., 409.

Thus one after another Democrats complained that it was 'the natural operation of our banking system to accumulate wealth in masses'. It has 'already. . . . disturbed the natural order of society' and was 'transferring by strategem and fraud, from A to B, the hard earnings of the latter'. The banks were 'defeating that tendency to equilibrium at which our institutions aim'; they were enabling 'a few to acquire wealth without labor' and 'the necessary consequence' was 'to break up that social equality which is the legitimate foundation of our institutions, and the destruction of which would render our boasted freedom a mere phantom'. Although 'a few banking institutions might be regarded tolerable, as a kind of necessary evil, for commercial purposes', yet 'the natural tendency and undeviating course of such institutions are to make the rich richer and the poor poorer – to create a broad distance between the condition of a few – very rich, and the many – very poor.' Some Democrats believed that the credit system had 'played a major role in the creation of England's mercantile and financial aristocracy'; they insisted that it would produce similar results in America.[74]

From whatever viewpoint they approached the banking system Democrats found inequality in its operations. Having loaned so much that an inflationary cycle was established, the banks would eventually be faced with a demand for specie. An equally severe deflation would then ensue. This cycle of expansion and contraction was 'always. . . . ruinous to those numerous and respectable classes, whose incomes are stationary'. When confidence collapsed those whose savings were invested in the banks would lose them while those who held depreciated or worthless notes would also suffer 'severe losses and great distress'. But the evil effects would extend even beyond this. The working man, unable to wait for prices to rise again, would be compelled to sell his labour for a low return. Or, alternatively, he might easily be thrown out of work. The farmer, in debt as a result of the easy supply of credit, would be unable, in a period of deflation, to meet his debts. Thus, as a result of the banking system the nation would pass from one 'convulsion' to the next. 'And at the end of each convulsion, the chasm between the rich and poor' would be 'wider and deeper'.[75]

[74] *Cong. Gl,* 26 i App., 533, 235; *Milwaukee Courier* in Milo M. Quaife (ed.), The *Struggle over Ratification, 1846-1847* (Madison, 1920), 201; *[Thomas J.] Sutherland's Political Letters, Addressed to Dr. Nelson* (N.Y., 1840), 20.

[75] *Dem. Rev.,* V (May 1839), 455, XVI (June 1845), 607; Edward Barber, *An Oration delivered before the Democrats of Washington County* in Danville (Vt.) *North Star,* 17 Aug. 1839.

It was this process of reasoning which induced even the most august Democrats to make public denunciations of banking and paper money. In Martin Van Buren's Message to Congress for 1839 the banks were roundly criticised for their activities and for the very principles upon which they operated. Three years later, in a letter to the Democratic State Convention of Indiana, the former President passed a similar verdict upon paper money:

> It has in general proved not the handmaid of honest industry and well-regulated enterprise, but the pampered menial of speculation, idleness and fraud. It has corrupted men of the highest standing; almost destroyed the confidence of mankind in each other; and darkened our criminal calendar with names that might otherwise have conferred honor or benefit on the country. There is strong reason for believing that such a system must have some incurable defect of which no legislation can divest it, and against which no human wisdom can guard, or human integrity sustain itself.[76]

Accordingly Martin Van Buren became the accredited leader of the antibank forces within the Democratic party. In the aftermath of the Panic of 1837 the party was controlled by the Van Burenites and both at Washington and in the states strenuous efforts were made to reform, or even to destroy, the banks. Reformers sought to increase the circulation of specie and to check the expansion of credit and paper money. A variety of coercive and restrictive measures were employed against the banks. Desiring to create an uninflated economy in which banknotes would possess a large specie backing, Democrats worked to ensure that the social, political, and moral imperatives of the agrarian society were observed. The problems of banking, credit and the currency were resolved as Democratic theory dictated.[77]

Jacksonian Democracy

Democratic policy on the issues of banking and the currency was the logical application of theory to practice. Indeed, on the entire range of issues with which politicians of the Jacksonian era were concerned Democrats acted largely in accordance with their stated principles. There is no reason, therefore, to deny the basic coherence and consistency of Jacksonian Democracy. Theory by and large was not belied by practice.[78]

---

[76] *Messages of Presidents*, III, 549-54; Van Buren to State Democratic Convention of Indiana in *Globe*, 12 Oct., 1843.

[77] See below, Chapter 6.

[78] *Ibid.*,

How radical were the Democrats? It is essential to recognise that the party was never a monolith. In the post-Panic years a minority of Democrats were disturbed by the hostility to banks and corporations displayed by their colleagues. They supported the party's programme reluctantly, if at all. Such Democrats may properly be termed 'conservative', lacking as they did, any serious reservations about the state of American society. They were, however, a small, unhappy and increasingly incongruous element within the party.[79] At the opposite extreme there was another minority of Democrats who feared that an acute social crisis had already arrived. It was marked by an unacceptable degree of poverty, inequality and exploitation. These partisans urged the leaders of the Democracy to intensify the campaign against the banks and against partial legislation generally. Some called for additional policies and reforms. Like the conservatives within the party, these Democrats were relatively few in number. Unlike the conservatives, however, they were increasingly vocal in their praise for the party's official policies in the years following the Panic.[80]

Between these two groups were the dominant elements within the party. Led by Martin Van Buren, these partisans prosecuted the bank war with vigour. They feared the future consequences of social trends that were already visible. Thus Senator Robert Strange of North Carolina warned that although 'this Republic' was 'but fifty years of age', yet 'if something is not done to arrest the corrupting influences abroad among the people, it will sink into ruin before. . . . those who now fill these halls are gathered to their fathers.' Strange was referring to the effects of banking and paper money. In Vermont, meanwhile, Edward Barber, a candidate for the Lieutenant-Governorship of the state, asked a Fourth of July audience to enquire 'what will be the condition of the country a century or two centuries hence' if the existing 'corporation and paper money system' were 'persevered in'. He then painted a frightening picture of a society in which wealth was steadily 'concentrating in the hands of the few', where the wages of labour had been so reduced that 'the mulititude live only at the beck of the few', where the cities were disfigured by 'squalor, rags and wretchedness. . . .disease. . . .hunger and starvation [and] frenzied crime' and where the land was populated by a 'wretched and degenerate race'. These were the fears which provoked the war against partial legislation.[81]

---

[79]For a discussion of the conservative Democrats see below, Chapter 4.

[80]For a discussion of these extreme radicals see below, Chapter 3.

[81]*Cong. Gl.*, 25 ii App., 153; Barber, *Oration* in *North Star*, 10 Aug. 1839.

Democrats of the Van Buren stamp were wont to encourage a strident politics of conflict. One Pennsylvanian Representative referred to 'the gentlemen in the Opposition' as 'men who can scarcely turn over the leaves in their portfolio without their silk gloves on' while the editor of a campaign sheet in New York described typical Opposition material as 'the drones of society, supported by the labour of the industrious'. This group might include 'the millionaire, with large hereditary estates' or 'the manufacturer, with hundreds of thousands invested in the machinery of cotton mills' or even greedy lawyers, doctors and clergymen, seeking the patronage of the wealthy. Others of the same persuasion denounced as parasites individuals of whose occupation or social power they did not approve. Thus it was argued that 'your bankers and capitalists enrich no part of our country, nor improve no part of its soil, and many of them, as priests of old, with their monks, and their friars at their heels, are mere drones in society, that live upon the labor of the more industrious of the hive'. Many Democrats believed that they were engaged in a war with the wealthy. The last election, a Louisiana newspaper announced in 1841, had been 'a contest between wealth and popular rights'.[82]

Such statements cannot be dismissed as mere rhetorical excesses. For the suspicion of wealth was an integral part of Democratic ideology. Although they expected the natural laws to preserve an approximate equality, Democrats were aware that a minority would always remain richer than the average. Martin Van Buren himself referred to 'the anti-republican tendency of associated wealth' in an official Message to Congress. Similarly a newspaper in Michigan spoke of 'the blighting influence of concentrated wealth and over-shadowing monopolies'. Democrats did not, however, confine their attacks to institutions in which large amounts of wealth were held. They believed that 'to a certain extent, wealth itself is power' and that it must be 'counteracted by constant vigilance on the part of the mass of the community'. Individual wealth was thus suspect. 'Such is the nature of man', declared the *Vermont Statesman*, a prominent Democratic newspaper, 'and such the spirit which inequality of condition engenders, that sleepless vigilance and perpetual conflict, ware the only means by which the DEMOCRACY OF NUMBERS can maintain the ascendency against the power of individual and ASSOCIATED WEALTH'. Governor John H. Steele of New Hampshire likewise warned the people of his state that 'individual as well as associated wealth, rarely, if ever, suffers an opportunity to

[82] *Cong. Gl.*, 26 i App., 588; *Young Hickory Banner*, 14 Sept. 1844; *Cong. Gl*, 25 ii App., 424; *Hebdomadal (Opelousas) Enquirer*, 27 July 1841.

pass without making strenuous efforts to retain, if not to gain, privileges denied to the mass of the community'. Even a Democrat like William Marcy, who inclined towards the conservative wing of the party, admitted that 'it is undoubtedly true as a general abstract proposition that wealth is hostile to democracy'. Many Democrats even speculated upon the causes of this antagonism. They reasoned that because the nation had swept away all hereditary titles and distinctions of rank the desire for superiority had stimulated a craving for great wealth. 'From the pride of wealth to the desire of political ascendancy', it was claimed, 'the transition is easy'. Hence the rich were a constant threat to society. Although they never proposed to strip them of their wealth Democrats urged the electorate to guard against their greed and cupidity.[83]

In view of their suspicion of the social and political power of the wealthy, their hostility to bankers and capitalists, and their fears for the safety of the Republic, the Democrats who dominated the party in the years following the Panic of 1837 may be termed 'radical'. For theirs was a radical critique of the changes taking place in American society as it prepared to enter a period of unprecedented industrial and commercial expansion. The Jacksonian Democrats were heirs of a tradition which emphasised equality and liberty in a society of independent, antonomous farmers. Perhaps because of the success which democracy had already achieved, perhaps because of the inner momentum of the democratic movement itself, the Jacksonian era witnessed an intensification of faith in popular government. Thus at the precise moment when the need for individual autonomy was being reaffirmed, the emergence of a market economy was placing the individual in the grip of external forces that were largely beyond his control. While democracy demanded an equality of power, an uneven, erratic growth rate denied it. Although the democratic tradition postulated an agrarian society, Jacksonian America witnessed urban expansion and an increase in the importance of the non-agricultural sector. The American economy was on a collision course with the American democratic tradition.

Many historians have suggested that Democratic ideology was flawed by an imperfect commitment to equality in its narrowest sense. Yet the main weakness of Democratic theory lay in its entirely

[83] *Messages of Presidents,* III, 483; Marshall (Mich.) *Democratic Expounder,* 30 Oct. 1846; *Cong. Gl.,* 26 i App., 406; *Vermont Statesman,* 30 Aug. 1837; *N.H. Senate Journal* (1845), 19; Marcy to Prosper M. Wetmore in Patricia M. McGee, 'Issues and Factions: New York State Politics from the Panic of 1837 to the Election of 1848' (Ph.D. thesis, St. John's University, 1969), 38-9; William Allen, *Speech . . . at Lancaster, Ohio* (Lancaster, Ohio, 1837), 5.

plausible assumption that society could be readily arranged so as to reflect the basic equivalence in social and political terms of the individual citizens who composed it. Democrats were perhaps too confidently egalitarian but their desire for equality cannot be questioned. More obviously anti-entrepreneurial than entrepreneurial, more nearly anti-capitalist than pro-capitalist, and more overtly radical than conservative, Jacksonian Democracy was an avowedly egalitarian movement which sought to utilise the power that democracy gave to the individual in order to resist those social and political forces which took it away.

2

WHIGS

In the years following the Panic of 1837 the Whig party came to represent a set of principles that were readily distinguishable from the new orthodoxies of Democracy. In the mainstream of the Whig party were men who were repelled by the levelling offensive of the Jacksonians and suspicious of the claims that were now being made for the democratic form of government. These men offered the electorate a world view that was a compelling alternative to that of the Democrats.[1]

Government

At the core of Whig ideology lay a belief, shared by all members of the party, in individuality. The Whigs stressed the dissimilarities among men. They perceived in Democratic egalitarianism a fatal desire to repress nature herself, a vain attempt to deny the diversity which unavoidably existed within the American people. This diversity should be recognised and celebrated; it should be deliberately fostered and encouraged. Thus Henry Clay complained to the Senate that under the Jacksonian régime 'talents and intellectual endowments' were being 'depised'. Many Whig partisans echoed Clay's complaint and may of the policies they advocated were designed to combat the levelling tendencies of Jacksonian Democracy.[2]

In resisting what was felt to be 'too strong a tendency to reduce all the elements of society to a common level', the *Whig Review,* an influential expositor of Whig thought, called instead for a society in which 'each takes the place appointed to him by nature'. Other Whigs appealed to nature as a source of major differences among men and in so doing subscribed whole-heartedly to the idea of a 'natural

[1] Works which deal specifically with Whig ideology include William R. Brock, *Conflict and Transformation: The United States, 1844-1877* (London, 1977); Michael J. Heale, *The Making of American Politics* (London 1977); Robert Kelly, *The Cultural Pattern in American Politics: The First Century* (N.Y., 1979); Rush Welter, *The Mind of America, 1820-1860* (N.Y., 1975) Glyndon G. Van Deusen, 'Some Aspects of Whig Thought and Theory in the Jacksonian Period', *A.H.R.,* LXIII (Jan. 1958), 305-22. This chapter will, I hope, show that it was opposition to the levelling doctrines of Jacksonians which not only united the Whigs but also drove them to adopt a rather more conservative or even reactionary stance than historians have generally allowed.

[2] Calvin Colton (ed.), *The Life and Works of Henry Clay,* 10 vols. (N.Y., 1904), VIII, 101.

aristocracy'. Francis Baylies of Massachusetts expanded upon this theme in a speech given at a party assembly in Taunton:

> I hold to no aristocracy except the aristocracy of nature. To genius, talents, moral worth and public services I render due honor; and I care not whether the claimant to that honor is clad in robes of purple and fine linen, or in the squalid rags of poverty – whether he obtained his education at a district school or at a University – whether he sits in the high places of the nation, or digs the earth for his daily food – whether he be the son of a peasant or the son of a President.

William Seward of New York based a lifelong support for state education on the Jeffersonian belief that 'science and learning always will create an aristocracy in every country where they are cherished'. He was convinced that such an aristocracy was 'the increased power and influence of the most enlightened, and therefore the most useful, members of society'.[3]

The Jeffersonian concept of the 'natural aristocracy' was not in itself anti-democratic. Yet in repudiating Democratic egalitarianism and in pressing the claims of the 'aristocracy of nature', most Whigs were prevented from enthusing about political democracy and were driven instead to point out the inadequacies of the common man. Similarly they were impelled to warn against too strong a faith in the people. In order to defend the 'natural aristocracy', the Whigs often had to emphasise not the glories, but the limitations and the shortcomings of democracy.

It was their insistence that talent and virtue were unevenly distributed that shaped their view of political democracy. Whigs rejected the stark distinction which the Democrats posited between the essential goodness of the 'natural' man and the almost inevitable depravity of the man who wielded power. Although alert to the danger of an unchecked use of authority, they nevertheless refused to condemn political power itself. Instead they conceived of government as an institution through which those of specialised talents and abilities performed functions that were beyond the means or capacities of individual citizens. The *Whig Review* demanded that those elected to office, and particularly to high office, be men of distinction. The qualifications that were necessary were 'of the highest order and the most arduous attainment'. One contributor expressed a view diametrically opposed to Andrew Jackson's when he declared that 'it

---

[3] *Whig Rev.,* IV (July) 1846), 28 I (June 1845), 648; Francis Baylies, *Speech. . . before the Whigs of Taunton* (Taunton, 1837), 6; George E. Baker (ed.), *The Works of William H. Seward,* 5 vols. (Boston, 1884), III, 147.

is doing the people no injustice to say, that the average capacity and intelligence of those whom they elect to high offices are, or should be, greater than their own'. According to one Whig apologist, 'years of study' were 'indispensable to the formation of the sound politician in mixed governments', while to another 'high political morals' and 'proper qualifications' were essential. For 'it was intended that the legislature should be composed of our wisest, best, and most experienced men'. A Whig 'views [government] as the exercise of a trust conferred upon him from above,. . . . the reward for moral and intellectual excellence.' Such a view naturally brought the party into sharp conflict with the Democrats. One Louisiana Congressman complained that 'since the accession of Mr VAN BUREN, the standard of qualification for office has been reduced even lower than it was during the administration of GENERAL JACKSON'. The Whigs believed it to be axiomatic that government required the services of an élite. Hence 'plain men' were not competent to fill important offices. So far as the judiciary, for example, were concerned, learned men were needed. Judges should, of course, be 'conversant with the science of the law'. Law was not, as many Democrats appeared to believe, 'a science to be acquired by intuition'. Instead it 'requires a particular aptitude, great and continued study, and a profound and extended range of knowledge'. Talents were still more important when the officers of the federal government were being chosen. Here 'the skill of legislation' should be 'of a higher order, as combining the concentrated wisdom of the nation'.[4]

The wisdom and talent of the officeholder were, of course, to benefit the nation as a whole. All the Whigs explicitly repudiated the Jeffersonian and Jacksonian ideal of limited government. Employing the terminology of the *Democratic Review*, Horace Greeley told an audience at Hamilton College that 'the best government is' *not* 'that which governs least'. Indeed Greeley believed that the first and most fundamental difference between the parties lay in their conceptions of the role of government. The Whigs held that 'government need not and should not be an institution of purely negative, repressive usefulness and value, but that it should exert a beneficent, paternal, fostering usefulness upon the Industry and Prosperity of the People.' The Democratic assumption that the interests of government and

[4]*Whig Rev.*, III (April 1846), 354, IV (Nov. 1846), 527; [George C. Collins], *Fifty Reasons Why the Honorable Henry Clay Should be Elected President of the United States,* by An Adopted Irish Citizen (Baltimore, 1844), 3; *The Whig Text Book, or Democracy Unmasked* (n.p., n.d.), 29; R. McKinley Ormsby, *A History of the Whig Party* (Boston, 1859), 363, 374; *Letter of Thomas W. Chinn to Hon. Thomas Gibbs Morgan* (Washington, D.C., n.d.), 11-2; *La. C. C.,* 724; 'Junius', *The Currency* (May 1843), 9.

people were in conflict was thus a disastrous error. Instead they were 'identical' and 'ought never to be regarded as diverse'. Government, according to the *Hartford Courant*, was 'a means of aiding and encouraging the pursuits of people'. Whig Governor John Davis of Massachusetts expressed a similar belief when he announced that his party's victory in the Presidential election of 1840 would inaugurate a set of policies designed to 'watch over the great interests of the country, encouraging, protecting, cherishing and harmonizing all of them'. The Whigs thus repudiated the 'laissez-faire' ethos to which Democrats were pledged and advocated instead a positive role for government.[5]

They did not, however, seek to employ the power of government to benefit the weak at the expense of the strong. Rather the Whigs desired a government which would display a paternalist regard for the welfare of the entire society. One of 'the great objects of legislative regard', Governor Thomas Corwin of Ohio announced, was 'the moral and intellectual improvement of the people'. The analogy which was often drawn was with the family. Daniel Webster wanted to mould the nation into a 'family concern' while a New Jersey Congressman declared that 'the attitude which . . . . [government] ought to hold to the people should be. . . . the attitude which a parent holds to a child, or a guardian to a ward'. According to the Whigs 'all' members of society 'ought to be embraced in the same family'.[6]

This view of government and of the relationship between government and society had important implications. From the time of the debate over the Federal Constitution and through the era of Jeffersonian Democracy a strong nexus had existed between the idea of active government, a belief in élite rule and a relative distrust of the people. In the minds of most Whigs the three remained inseparable. For the extravagant claims that Democrats now made for both the people and for popular government were rejected by the Whigs with near unanimity. They disavowed 'the dreamy hope that on the whole, we [are]. . . . a wiser or better people than the countless nations which have gone before us'. In private many Whig leaders expressed grave doubts about the people and their capacity for self-government. Millard Fillmore of New York who was later, of course, to serve as

[5] Horace Greeley, *Hints Towards Reforms* (N.Y., 1850), 126; Greeley, *The Whig Almanac and United States Register for 1843* (N.Y., 1843) 29-30; *Hartford Courant*, 31 Dec. 1842; *Inaugural Address of His Excellency John Davis to the Two Branches of the Legislature of Massachusetts* (Boston 1841), 14.

[6] Josiah Morrow (ed.), *Life and Speeches of Thomas Corwin* (Cincinnati, 1896), 111; J. W. McIntyre (ed.), *The Writings and Speeches of Daniel Webster*, 18 vols. (Boston, 1903), XIII, 184; *Cong. Gl*, 25 i App., 272.

President, referred in his private correspondence to 'the caprice of popular favor' and 'the wild caprice of the ever-changing multitude'. Similarly Rufus Choate of Massachusetts wondered whether the great victory of 1840 owed more to campaign hullabaloo than to the people's ability to appreciate the principles and the policies which the party had put forward. 'Has this people', he asked, 'character enough to carry us through a grand campaign of electioneering on *mere* measures?' Choate then confessed to serious doubts. In public partisans were naturally more cautious. Yet some party spokesmen went so far as to proclaim their suspicion of the populace in clear and unequivocal terms. According to the *Cincinnati Gazette,* history showed 'how frequently in free governments the true patriot has sunk, and the unhallowed demagogue been elevated'. Even more significantly, the *National Intelligencer,* the party's major newspaper, felt it necessary to remind its readers that 'it too often happens, that the multitude acts first, and deliberates afterwards, when inquiry and reasoning are perhaps of no effect but to induce an unavailing repentance'. John Bell of Tennessee, a prominent Whig leader, was still more explicit. In effect addressing the Democrats, he claimed that the primary function of the constitution was to restrain popular power. 'If the people can never err', he asked, 'why have a constitution?' 'If whatever the people may, at any time, approve, must be right', he continued, 'the constitution is an idle piece of mummery.' Bell then pronounced the notion of 'popular government' to be one of the 'most fallacious and insidious doctrines that can be started in a free government'. Suspicious of the people's capacities and sceptical towards Democratic claims for democracy, the Whigs strove to temper the populistic tone of American politics. William Henry Harrison in 1840 dismissed Democratic fears that the Republic might turn into an aristocracy. Rather, he insisted, it might degenerate into a pure democracy.[7]

Whig priorities thus differed sharply from those of the Democrats. Although they did not, for the most part, try to reverse the advancing tide of democracy, the Whigs were nevertheless unsympathetic to many of the changes which it brought. Many of them clung, for

---

[7] John Whipple, *Substance of a Speech Delivered at the Whig Meeting Held at the Town House, Providence, R.I., Aug. 28, 1837* (Providence, 1837), 4; Frank H. Severance (ed.), *The Millard Fillmore Papers,* 2 vols. (Buffalo, 1907), II, 176-7; Rufus Choate to John Davis in Raynor M. Wellington, *The Political and Sectional Influence of the Public Lands 1828-1842* (Cambridge, 1914), 109; *Cincinnati Gazette* in Francis P. Weisenburger, *The Passing of the Frontier, 1825-1850* (Columbus, Ohio, 1941), 388; *Nat. Int.,* 16 July, 1836; Bell quoted in Norman L. Parks, 'The Career of John Bell as Congressman from Tennessee, 1827-1841', *T.H.Q.,* I, (Sept. 1942), 229-49; William Henry Harrison, *Speech at the Dayton Convention, Sept. 10, 1840* (n.p., n.d.), 7-8.

example, to the traditional conception of the suffrage as a privilege rather than, as Democrats maintained, a right. The *Whig Review* declared that it was one of the state's 'most precious privileges' which must not be made 'too cheap'. 'Each individual', it was subsequently argued, 'has an influence, not in the arithmetical ratio of one of the whole mass, but in the moral ratio of his intelligence and virtue'. If the enfranchising of the 'ignorant and vicious' had to be tolerated, it was only because there was 'no safe way' of disfranchising them. Universal suffrage was merely 'a necessary evil'.[8]

Similarly most Whigs sought to retain a significant degree of independence for the representative. While Democratic orthodoxy increasingly required that the power of the representative be curtailed and transferred to the people the Whigs instead desired to utilise the talents of the governing élite to the full. They recognised, of course, that all representatives should remain accountable, but opposed, for example, the doctrine of instruction. Alexander H. Stephens of Georgia insisted that United States Senators retain their discretionary power and freedom of action. The Senate, he argued, should be 'free from the influence and control of sudden changes in popular opinion'. The *National Intelligencer* likewise claimed that the instruction of Senators was 'totally irreconcilable to the first principles of Representative Governments'. 'The true theory of republican government', another Whig subsequently argued, 'should leave the representative entirely free to act after thorough discussion and mature deliberation, as his best judgment shall dictate'. The 'unbiased judgment of the representative', who should be a man of special talent and wisdom and no mere 'specimen of his constituents' would furnish the soundest basis for a republic. Indeed 'the practice of holding members obedient to local views in effect changes our government from a representative republic to a democracy.' Hence the practice must be opposed. For the same reason prominent Whigs refused to give pledges to their constituents. Millard Fillmore in a public letter explained that pledges, like instructions, were inconsistent with true republicanism:

> I am opposed to giving any pledges that shall deprive me hereafter of all discretionary power. My own character must be the guaranty for the general correctness of my legislative deportment. On every important subject I am bound to deliberate before I act, and especially as a legislator, to possess myself of all the information, and listen to every argument that can be adduced by my associates, before I give a final vote. If I stand

[8]*Whig. Rev.*, II (Nov. 1845), 446, IV (July 1846), 29.

> pledged to a particular course of action, I cease to be a
> responsible agent, but I become a mere machine.

This was a highly non-populist view of government. 'There must be no short cut or side path', Daniel D. Barnard warned, 'to the will of the people'. A constant infusion of the popular will would threaten 'that lofty independence and integrity of mind which should characterize the representatives of the people'. Both Whigs and Democrats alike recognised the theoretical dangers of popular and delegated power. Yet Democratic hopes centred on the people, Democratic fears on the respresentative; the Whigs remained anxious about the electorate, optimistic towards the elected.[9]

Yet in rejecting Democratic populism, the Whigs feared for more than the power of the natural aristocracy, for more even than the stability or the rectitude of the body politic. The ultimate evil in the all-conquering ethos of democracy was its enthronement of the individual as an autonomous, self-sufficient unit. The discrepancy between this attitude and the conception of the nation as a family was glaring. Previous generations had commonly believed that a republican government depended upon the people's capacity for self-restraint, their ability to subdue their natural instincts towards self-aggrandisement. The school of thought with which James Madison was identified had seen the government, and especially the federal government, as a harmonising agency, an institution through which the natural aristocrats, whose vision would transcend that of the particular class from which they sprang, would promote the collective good and balance the various competing interests. Whatever their points of difference these two views shared a common assumption: a society composed of individuals acting unchecked as atoms of self-interest could not long survive and would degenerate into anarchy or tyranny. The Democrats had, of course, revised this formulation and had achieved a spectacular reconciliation of self-interest with the old notion of republican virtue. They even pronounced this self-interest to be 'enlightened'. But to the Whigs this was demagoguery of the most blatant sort. It was no less than a threat to the very fabric of society. The *Whig Review's* response was typical:

> An enlightened self-interest indeed! Has not all experience
> shown, that this term is a contradiction, that self-interest is ever

[9]Stephens quoted in Donald A. Debats, 'Elites and Masses: Political Structure, Communication and Behavior in Ante-Bellum Georgia' (Ph. D. thesis, University of Wisconsin, 1973), 226-7; *Nat Int,* 12 Jan. 1836; Ormsby, *History of Whig Party,* 67, 363, 370; *Fillmore Papers,* II, 174; Daniel D. Barnard, *A Discourse delivered before the Senate of Union College* (Albany, 1843), 48; Allen Nevins (ed.) *The Diary of Philip Hone* (N.Y., 1936), 349.

blind, that selfishness is darkness, and has no light, that the present desire will always outweigh the remote good in minds governed solely by the utilitarian principle, and that this is even more apt to be the case with blind and unmeaning masses than with individuals?

The Whigs could see a frightening picture of a society in which the bonds that linked government to people, occupation to occupation, and man to man were broken and where each individual identified in the starkest terms where his self-interest lay, and then relentlessly pursued it, regardless of the social consequences. Thus even a liberal Whig such as William H. Seward was able to detect and deplore a 'spirit of anarchy, that already, ever and anon lifts its horrid front among us'. The conclusion was that restraints were needed. 'For progress in virtue, morality and happiness', Daniel D. Barnard argued, 'there must be a prevalent spirit of subjection and obedience to established law, and constituted authority'. This view was shared by the *Republican Review*, a Whig journal that was modelled on the *Democratic Review*. 'True', the editor acknowledged, 'the people are and ought to be sovereigns'. But 'that sovereignty is to be regulated and restrained by laws and constitutions or it becomes the force of the mob.' For 'isolated man must be restrained by laws human and divine, and when he associates into the body politic, the necessity of that restraint becomes more apparent.' This betrayed an outlook which contrasted sharply with that of the Democrats.[10]

It was, however, difficult for the Whigs to find the necessary restraints and dangerous even to proclaim the need for them in public. As a result many Whigs were reluctant to expound a political philosophy and the Democrats won the debate largely by default. Yet when a minority of spokesmen went out of their way to place their party on record in opposition to some of the major tenets of the emerging Democratic faith, most of their colleagues made no attempt to dissociate themselves from this dissent.

Some of these spokesmen, desiring to check the atomistic tendencies of Democracy, retreated into highly conservative or even reactionary assertions. The Jacksonians had adopted the Jeffersonian concept that 'the earth belongs to the living' and had consequently denied the prescriptive force of both past and future. This, by completing the image of the rootless society whose inhabitants were unattached not only to each other but also in time, merely served to intensify Whig anxieties. Daniel Webster publicly opposed the notion

[10] *Whig Rev.*, II (Sept. 1845), 340; *Works of Seward*, III, 141; Barnard, *Man and the State* (New Haven, 1846), 47-8; *Rep. Rev.*, I (March 1839), 224.

60

that one generation could not bind its descendants. 'The individuals who compose' the political community, he admitted, 'may change' but the community itself 'still exists in its aggregate capacity'. It was in this connection that John Quincy Adams complained that democracy 'looks to no posterity' and that Abraham Lincoln felt constrained to ask every man to 'remember that to violate the law, is to trample on the blood of his father and to tear the charter of his own, and his children's liberty'. James Watson Webb of the New York *Courier and Enquirer* similarly argued that just as 'the Hudson river is as much the Hudson now as it was a hundred years ago (though not a drop of the water which filled its channels then, flows there now)' so the laws and power of the state retained their moral and political authority even though the generation which established them had long since departed.[11] In part the Whigs sought to inculcate a respect for the past as a means of access to 'the collected wisdom of past ages'. But in addition, and perhaps more importantly, they conceived of the past (and of the future) as a unifying influence, opposing the dissolvent force of mere self-interest. 'Human nature', one Whig cautioned, is 'so strongly inclined to go astray that it is safer to rely on the power of habit to keep it on a path approximate to the parallel of rectitude, than to give it unlimited freedom to go right or wrong'. Other Whigs insisted that society was a living organism, whose existence transcended that of any single generation. In this view its eternity was enshrined in the institutions of the state. Society and the state should not, therefore, be regarded as a mere sum of individuals. If they were so regarded then 'the past cannot control the present or the future'. A 'higher theory' was instead advanced: 'that government is a divine institution, and that the state is a moral agent'. Daniel D. Barnard claimed that the state was 'a veritable Entity – a moral Person and Power distinct from the accident of varying numbers' with a 'higher Constitution than such members can give it'. The Whigs strove to identify the state and also the law – which was the expression of its will – with absolute truths that were univeral and timeless and therefore distinct from 'the actual will of the majority'. Law was 'a great Idea enthroned among men, coeval with Eternal Justice' and possessing 'majesty', 'authority', and 'divine force'. If this were not recognised, and if it were regarded instead as 'derived from, and existing by, the uncertain sanctions of the popular will', then, it was feared, the way to anarchy and despotism had been opened.[12]

[11] *Writings . . . of Webster*, III, 79; *The Memoirs of John Quincy Adams*, 12 vols. (Phil., 1874-7), VIII, 519; Roy B. Basler (ed.), *The Collected Works of Abraham Lincoln*, 8 vols. (New Brunswick, N.J., 1953), I, 112; *Courier and Enquirer*, 5 Dec. 1843.

[12] Hubard Winslow, *The Means of the Perpetuity and Prosperity of Our Republic*

Such reminders of the dangers inherent in populistic democracy constantly recur in statements of Whig political philosophy. It is clear that many within the party were uncomfortable with some of the newer facts of political life in the Jacksonian era. Seeking to preserve the traditional republican polity in which a governing élite directed the affairs of state, they viewed the new style and tone of American politics with disdain. Thus Democratic enthusiasm for the spoils system seemed to denote a view of government antithetical to that which a high-minded statesman ought to hold. According to a group of Georgia Whigs 'no rule of political morality can be more dangerous to a republic than that avowed by a leader of the Van Buren party, viz: that 'to the victors belong the spoils'. One Alabama Whig complained that it promoted 'the idolatry of the passions' while a prominent newspaper editor in Tennessee claimed that the election of Jackson had inaugurated 'the long sway of the grossest and vilest demagogueism'. The Whigs cast themselves in the role of defenders of traditional republican values, implacable opponents of the vulgarities of democracy.[13]

It was for this reason that those who did not explicitly challenge Democratic assertions about popular government instead maintained an almost deafening silence on the entire subject of political democracy. For the most part the Whigs were unable to compete with the Democrats in bestowing praise upon the nation's political institutions simply because their ideology did not allow them to. The Democrats thus exposed the basic ambivalence in the Whig attitude to the people. Although dedicated to republican ideals most Whigs could not concede the extreme Democratic claims for the virtue, wisdom and self-sufficiency of the ordinary citizen. Instead they strove to find order, on the one hand by emphasising the transcendental power of government and the laws, and on the other hand, by attempting to secure recognition and respect for the natural aristocracy. It was small wonder that the Whigs felt that they were living in an age of restlessness. 'The nations of Europe', it was noted, 'are restless under the burden of oppression'. But Americans were 'restless under the weight of mere duty and custom'. As the Democrats posited a society of independent equals, so the Whigs stressed both the differences between men and their mutual dependence. The Democrats, in advocating individualism, emphasised the essential similarities among

(Boston, 1838), 18; *Whig Rev.*, I (March 1845), 275, II (Nov. 1845), 446-7; Barnard, *Man and the State*, 37-8; *Whig Rev.*, I (Jan. 1845), 3.

[13] *Address of J. C. Alford [et al.]. . . to their Constituents, May 27, 1840* (n.p., n.d.), 20; John L. Dorsey, *The Spirit of Modern Democracy Explained* (St. Louis, 1840), 9; William G. Brownlow, *A Political Register. . .* (Jonesborough, Tenn., 1844), 9.

62

men; the Whigs, in advocating individuality, emphasised their mutual interdependence.[14]

Society

This fundamental difference is clearly discernible in the parties' different social outlooks. The Whigs' respect for individuality was grounded in the belief that the citizen should be given the widest possible choice of occupational pursuits. For it was, according to Edward Everett of Massachusetts, 'a familiar remark, of which all . . . admit the justice, that a variety of pursuits is a great advantage to a community'. 'It offers', he continued, 'scope to the exercise of the boundless variety of talent and capacity which are bestowed by nature.' Daniel Webster often claimed that unless individuality flourished the progress of civilisation itself would be retarded. He offered a clear statement of this view at Pepperell, Massachusetts in 1844:

> I know of no country far advanced in civilization and happiness, whose people are confined to one single pursuit and I regard a nation much happier, much better refined, much more moral, in proportion as its avenues of industry are multiplied and the modes of its labor varied.

For Webster 'the last twenty or thirty years' had 'had a wonderful effect in producing a variety of employments'. John P. Kennedy of Maryland stated an opinion that was widely held within the Whig party when he declared that 'in truth, no country ever attains to great power or wealth by an exclusive addiction to agriculture'. The Whigs recognised the need for, and sought to promote, a diversified and differentiated society.[15]

In so doing they necessarily came into conflict with the Democratic preference for agriculture. The Whigs resented the constant references to the 'producing classes' and in reply insisted that almost all occupational groups deserved respect or esteem. Was it not self-evident that 'a well-organized community must have the aid of the learned professions, lawyers, doctors, divines, the merchants trades-men, factors, and transporters, embracing the whole of our shipping community, etc., etc.'? They gave special emphasis to the legitimacy

[14] *Whig Rev.*, I (Jan. 1845), 4.

[15] Edward Everett, *Orations and Speeches on Various Occasions*, 4 vols. (Boston, 1850), II, 59; *Writings . . . of Webster*, XIII, 290; Henry T. Tuckerman (ed.), *The Collective Works of John P. Kennedy*, 10 vols. (N.Y., 1871-2), IV, 294.

of manufacturing. Rufus Choate of Massachusetts told the Senate that manufactures helped to 'offer to every faculty and talent and taste, in the community, the specific work best suited to it'. The result was that 'everybody is enabled to be busy on the precise thing the best adapted to his capacity and his inclinations'. Manufactures, Choate concluded, employing a revealing phrase, helped to detect 'the slightest shade of individuality'.[16]

Choate represented a state in which manufacturing was already well established by the 1840s. Elsewhere the Whigs were often vocal in its defence. In New Hampshire, a stronghold of Democratic and free trade sentiment, they sought to convince the electorate that the natural resources of the state demanded a more diversified economy. This was the view of the *New Hampshire Statesman*, the leading Whig newspaper in the state:

> It is absurd and useless in contemplation of the future, to suppose that the people of New England are to be a community of farmers. It cannot, it will not be so. No portion of our country offers less facility to the farming interests or greater to the manufacturing and mechanical. Both of these great branches must be attended to in all coming time.

According to the *Statesman* it had 'ever been the belief of the Whigs that no way is so certain to promote the growth of New Hampshire, as to foster, by reasonably safe enactments, manufacturing enterprise'. Similarly, in sparsely settled Iowa it was argued that 'manufactories' were 'of unquestionable advantage to a country' and that since Iowa was 'excellent wool-growing country' it was in the state's interest to encourage them. Even in the South prominent Whigs declared themselves favourable to manufactures. John J. Berrien, a Senator from Georgia, was one of many who lamented the South's relative industrial backwardness. But in 1844 he reported to the Senate, with unmistakable pride, that 'the march of [the] manufacturing spirit is . . . southward. . . . Georgia is becoming daily more and more convinced of the advantage of a division of labor'. His view was shared by Edward Stanly of North Carolina. In 1841 Stanly expressed the hope that his home state would in future 'turn her attention to manufacturing'.[17]

---

[16] [Robert Mayo], *A Word in Season* (Washington, D.C., 1840), 7; Samuel G. Brown (ed.), *The Life and Writings of Rufus Choate*, 2 vols. (Boston, 1862), II, 213. See also John Quincy Adams, *Parties in the United States* (N.Y., 1941), 39-40.

[17] *New Hampshire Statesman*, 23 Sept. 1842, 18 April 1843; *Iowa C.C.,* 146; John J. Berrien, *Speech on the Tariff* (Washington, D.C., 1844), 16. *Cong. Gl.,* 26 ii App., 356. See below, Chapter 6, for further discussion of these policies.

64

Sympathetic to the manufacturers, the Whigs were, if anything, still more favourable to the merchants. Once again they encountered and rebutted Democratic criticisms. 'Who have done more than they', it was asked, 'to extend the commerce, the wealth, the honor, and the glory of the nation?' The merchants, 'whose sails' had 'whitened every sea' and 'whose vessels' had 'displayed our country's flag in every port', had been since the Revolution 'the most patriotic and enterprising of our citizens'. In a less extravagant vein other Whigs sought to disarm the Democrats by stressing the sheer necessity of mercantile pursuits. Although 'the merchant' was 'nothing more than an agent or factor of the producer', he was nevertheless 'as necessary and as useful a constitutuent part of society as is the producer or laborer'. It was also clear that 'you cannot blast his prosperity without sweeping with it the prosperity of the community with which he is connected'. Still another line of defence was to draw attention to the risks which the merchant was obliged to take and to the social consequences of the wealth which he might obtain. This view in effect praised those features of the occupation which Democrats found most odious:

> it is the merchant who risques his all to bring us the comforts
> and luxuries of foreign climes, and finds a market for our surplus
> produce, who ought to be encouraged – he ought to be eased from
> all duties as much as possible; it is owing to the enterprise and
> liberality of that class of our citizens that so many stupendous
> works of art, of ornament, and of use have sprung up as if by
> magic in this our 'New World'?

In Whig theory the merchant took his place alongside the manufacturer, the labourer, the farmer and the artisan as an eminently desirable citizen of the good society.[18]

From proclaiming the need for individuality in employment, it was a short step to asserting the need for individuality in wealth. Many Whigs believed that a substantial inequality of wealth was inevitable if only because of the inequality of virtue, wisdom and talent that existed in any civilised society. It was suggested that 'a diversity of estate' was 'an unavoidable condition of all social organisation' since 'through all time, some have been rich, and some have been poor'. While Democrats regarded the rich with suspicion the Whigs insisted that they presented no threat to society or to the nation's political institutions. Although it was 'in the nature of wealth to attain *social* power and influence' – indeed it was 'a valuable feature in our system

[18] *Cong. Gl.*, 25 ii App., 513, 25 i App., 284; *New Hampshire Statesman*, 7 Jan. 1837.

that it should do so' – yet 'every man must remark how small is its tendency, how inadequate its efforts to obtain *political* power'. Some Whigs professed themselves unable to understand the logic of Democratic assaults upon the rich. Were they directed against 'those men dispersed everywhere through the country, who, by patient toil and frugal life, have become the artificers of their own fortunes'? Or were the objects of suspicion 'those in our commercial cities, who have amassed wealth in the more hazardous but not less laborious pursuits of trade'? In either case the allegations were unfounded since the members of each group were 'always of the most exemplary life' and would 'yield to none in every virtue that dignifies the man, or ennobles the patriot'. Nor should any hostility be shown to 'the large accumulations of capital which are the source of the enterprise, influence and luxury of our more fortunate and wealthy citizens'. For these were of benefit to the entire community. Thus some Whigs met the charges that Democrats levelled against the rich by claiming that their social and political influence was either benign or so slight as to be negligible.[19]

Perhaps because of the dangers in identifying themselves too closely with wealth, however, a majority of Whigs developed a different line of defence. In essence they claimed that although there might be individuals who possessed considerable wealth they did not constitute a class of the rich. Daniel Webster declared that 'property is everywhere distributed as fast as it is accumulated, and not in more than one case out of a hundred is there an accumulation beyond the earnings of one or two generations'. The Whigs subscribed whole-heartedly to the view that American society was uniquely egalitarian and classless. This was the description of Massachusetts which Webster offered to the Senate in 1838:

> I do not believe there is on earth, in a highly civilized society, a greater equality in the condition of men than exists there. If there be a man in the State who maintains what is called an equipage, or drives four horses in his coach, I am not acquainted with him. On the other hand, there are few who are not able to carry their wives and daughters to church in some decent conveyance. It is no matter of regret or sorrow that few are very rich; but it is our pride and glory that few are very poor.

Similarly John Pope of Kentucky claimed that in the district which he represented there were 'no very wealthy men' and 'but few so poor as not to have the reasonable comforts of life'. His constituents, he

---

[19] *Cong. Gl,* 26 ii App., 261; *New York Express,* 8 Dec. 1846; *Cong. Gl,* 25 ii App., 596, 601; *Works of Kennedy,* IV, 182.

boasted, comprised 'the industrious middle class of society, which, in all countries, is the most virtuous, happy, and independent class – the salt of the earth'. Similarly the fact that 'we all have property, or may have it, if we choose to seek it by honest industry and enterprise' was 'evinced by the general diffusion of compentency and personal independence among all the free inhabitants of the Union'. Some Whigs pushed this argument a little further when they asserted that there was no class of the poor. According to William Cost Johnson of Maryland, 'the only poor, as a class, that we have in this favored nation are the paupers in the various poor-houses throughout the nation'. There was 'no other class that merits the epithet'. The Whigs invited the electorate to share their basic satisfaction with American society; in so doing they stressed its uniquely egalitarian and classless structure.[20]

At the same time as they sought to refute Democratic claims about inequality in society, the Whigs attempted to divert the force of egalitarian sentiment by emphasising the twin ideals of equal opportunity and social mobility. Inequality of results, they often implied, was acceptable provided that equal opportunities existed. Again and again Whig spokesmen insisted that those who were wealthiest were, in general, those who had made best use of their opportunities. In was one of the key articles of their faith that almost all the rich had achieved their success without the advantage of inherited wealth. Francis Baylies was convinced that 'amongst the rich men of New England, nineteen out of every twenty began without a dollar', and Charles Naylor of Pennsylvania explained the process by which the labourer became the capitalist:

> In ninety-nine cases out of a hundred, he who is a capitalist has become so by his own industry and perseverance. He begins as an humble "laborer" – his industry, virtue, and integrity his only capital. He gradually accumulates. Every day of toil increases his means. His means are then united to his labour, and he receives the just and honest profits of them both. Thus he goes on joining his accumulations with his labour, receiving the profits of his capital and his toil . . . and laying up a stock of comfort and enjoyment for his declining years.

This, it was suggested, was the pattern which the careers of 'nearly all the principal shareholders' in the factories of Massachusetts had followed. They had risen 'to competence, and then to affluence' by

---

[20] *Writings . . . of Webster,* XI, 227, VIII, 175; *Cong. Gl,* 25 iii App., 343; *Rep. Rev.,* I (Jan. 1839), 17; *Cong. Gl,* 25 ii App., 547.

virtue of their 'industry, prudence, perseverance, and good economy'. Wealth was thus attributable to merit.[21]

Whatever inequalities of wealth now existed, they had not, the Whigs believed, impaired the mechanisms of mobility for which American society was so justly renowned. The rich might thus suffer a reversal in their fortunes. 'He who is rich to-day', it was argued, 'may be poor tomorrow. We see this constantly occurring all around us.' Large inheritances, it was widely thought, were uncommon as a result of the abolition of the laws of primogeniture and entails. Alternatively it was suggested that inherited wealth was 'enervating' and a curse upon its recipient. One Iowa Whig confessed that he had 'yet to see wealth pass by desent [sic] beyond the third generation'. Yet he could see 'every day the second generation who have squandered the labours of their predecessors or are squandering it, in miserable low degrading dissipation'. So fluid was American society that 'the employer of to-day' was often 'the laborer of to-morrow'.[22]

More importantly, however, 'the laborer' might become 'the employer'. The Whigs understandably placed more emphasis upon upward than downward mobility and they never ceased to exhort the citizen to take advantage of the opportunities for self-advancement that were available to him. These were such that 'no man need be poor if he has a hatchet, and an arm to use it'. Henry Clay was one who claimed that the increasingly diversified economy which was now emerging widened the individual's opportunities still further. For 'in our country, such is the variety of profitable business and pursuits that there is scarcely any in which one can engage with diligence, integrity and ordinary skill, in regular and ordinary times, that he is not sure of being amply rewarded.' The result was that Americans were a uniquely advantaged people. The nation was 'the paradise of the poor man'. Those without capital or significant wealth need never despair. Daniel Webster claimed that 'a wider theatre for useful activity is under their feet, and around them,than was ever spread before the eyes of the young and enterprising generations of men, on any other spot enlightened by the sun'. 'In the state of American society, and in a prosperous condition of the country', 'Junius', the Whig propagandist alleged, 'a comfortable degree of wealth is within the reach

[21] Baylies, *Speech before Whigs of Taunton,* 6; *Cong. Gl.,* 25 i App., 312; John Aiken, *Labor and Wages, At Home and Abroad* (Lowell, 1849), 15.

[22] *The Andover Husking; A Political Tale. . . Dedicated to the Whigs of Massachusetts* (Boston, 1842), 6; John C. Parish (ed.), 'The Autobiography of John Chambers', *I.J.H.P.,* VI 247-86 (April 1908); Sergent S. Prentiss in *Kennebec (Me.) Journal,* 22 Aug. 1840.

of every honest, industrious and enterprising man'. Because of 'the circumstances of this country', there was now 'a condition of society here, never elsewhere seen'. The Whigs constantly reminded the electorate of this elemental fact.[23]

In accounting for the exceptional fluidity of American society, they directed attention to the high wage rates which, they claimed, were the rule throughout the economy. It was because of these unprecedentedly high wages that 'our system is entirely different from that of the Old World'. The American labourer was able to work for himself if he so chose; hence the employer was compelled to pay high wages. As a result, 'among our native population, laborers for hire do not exist as a class'. The labourer could, 'if he be industrious and frugal', set aside a portion of his wages. Thus 'he who five years ago was working for wages, will now be found transacting business for himself; and in a few years hence, will be likely to be found a hirer of the labor of others.' Although the Whigs approved of the factory system and the wage economy, they hoped that the employee who received wages would ultimately establish his own enterprise and thereby achieve independence.[24]

Their outlook was thus thoroughly meritocratic. The individual's progress in society, and the station which he eventually attained would depend almost entirely upon his own abilities, talents and efforts. It was the glory of the nation's institutions that 'they present an open field in which every citizen may labor to advance his fortunes; and in which each workingman, no matter what may be his trade or profession, is sure to obtain, in the end, a reward proportioned to his merit'. According to one Mississippi Whig 'our principles and our institutions' were 'illustrated in the race course, where every horse is put upon his own mettle'. Society resembled a race: 'the slowest cannot win the prize. It belongs to the fleetest.'[25]

Yet Democratic divisiveness threatened the meritocratic and differentiated society which the Whigs desired. Those with talents and merit could not prosper or succeed if the community were taught to resent their success. Thus Van Buren was condemned for failing to 'see but one great family in a nation, having a common interest, as a common country'. Instead he sought 'to array one portion against

[23] Dorsey, *Spirit of Democracy*, 41; *Cong. Gl.*, 26 i App., 727; *Inaugural Address of John Davis*, 7; *Cong. Gl.*, 25 ii App., 633; 'Junius', *Labor and Capital* (March 1844), 14; Aiken, *Labor and Wages*, 16.

[24] *Works of Kennedy*, IV, 292; Aiken, *Labor and Wages*, 16.

[25] *Cong. Gl.*, 26 ii App., 340: Prentiss in *Kennebec Journal*, 22 Aug. 1840. See also *Cong. Gl.*, 25 i App., 312.

another'. Similarly 'Parson' William Brownlow of Tennessee complained about 'the fatal tendency', clearly visible in the years of Andrew Jackson's rule, 'to array the ignorant against the intelligent, the poor against the rich, the wicked against the pious, the vulgar against the decent, the worthless against the worthy, and thieves against honest men'. This was the policy of the demagogue. It was one which no Whig could countenance. One North Carolinian promised, during the campaign of 1840, that Harrison would *not* be 'like an evil spirit seeking to divide the different portions of society and array them against each other'.[26]

The Whigs frequently explained why the politics of conflict which the Democrats pursued would prove ruinous to the nation. 'The fact is', one Maine newspaper declared, 'that the whole body of society is woven together as it were, each individual and each profession being mutually dependent on others and mutually employing each other.' Hence 'an injury to one does not help the others, but affects them injuriously.' More specifically, the Whigs insisted that the different sectors of the economy were mutually dependent. According to Henry Clay, 'nothing could be more erroneous than to suppose the existence of any real incompatibility between the interests of Agriculture, Commerce, and Manufactures.' He added that 'a conflict between them would be just as unnatural and absurd, as between the members of the human body'. Millard Fillmore likewise warned that if one sector of the economy 'languishes', then assuredly 'they all suffer'. Thus in response to Democratic efforts to mobilise the agricultural interest, the Whigs taught the farmer to identify with the merchant and the manufacturer.[27]

With equal certainty they proclaimed the harmony of the different classes within society. The Whigs of Massachusetts contended that 'the interests of all classes' were 'in harmony'. Indeed it was misleading, in view of the equality and mobility which characterised American society, even to speak of 'classes' as though they comprised fixed or unchangeable orders. The Americans were 'one people' and there was neither a class of 'Plebeians' nor one of 'Patricians'. There were, of course, inequalities of wealth in society, yet the poor were in no way oppressed as a consequence. For the wealth of the rich was a

[26]*Address to Democratic Whigs of Westchester County* in *Jeffersonian,* 22 Sept. 1838; Brownlow, *Political Register,* 10; George E. Badger, *Speech delivered at the Great Whig Meeting in the County of Granville (N.C.), 3 March 1840* (Raleigh, 1840), 15.

[27]*Kennebec Journal,* 9 May 1840; *Letter of Henry Clay to Messrs. L. Bradish, Erastus Root etc., 15 April, 1842* in *Kennebec Journal,* 6 May 1842; *Fillmore Papers,* II, 238.

positive benefit to them. 'Large accumulations of capital' were 'centres of reinforcement to the mechanic's thrift; reservoirs from which every class of citizens may find the means of providing against want and gathering independence.' The Whigs asked the electorate to honour 'those enterprising young men, of small capital, who are struggling along in the world' not least because 'they create business – they employ the poor laborer – and pay him well for his services'. Thus the wealth of the capitalist benefited the poor in two ways. Firstly, it provided the essential lubrication for the mechanisms of social mobility which would carry the worthy labourer into the ranks of the employers. Secondly, by increasing the prosperity of the entire nation, it tended to improve the condition of all classes. Hence there was no conflict between the interests of rich and poor or of employer and employee. The Democratic 'attempt to array the rich against the poor' was merely 'a wicked design to appeal to the worst passions of men, their jealousy of one another'. It was the suggestion 'of artful demagogues', 'the vilest imposture ever attempted upon the credulity of the public mind'. The responsible statesman was aware that 'the rich man's prosperity is the poor man's good fortune', that 'any system . . . that benefits the rich, benefits the poor', and that 'both classes' were 'mutually dependant upon each other.' The contrary view, the Whigs warned, 'strikes at the very existence of society'.[28]

Finally, in proclaiming the need for harmony between the various groups which made up American society, the Whigs did not forget the relationship between labour and capital. They insisted that the two 'are, and must be friends'. Again dissociating themselves from the Democrats, Whig spokesmen stressed the tremendous power of the labouring classes and contrasted it with the relative impotence of capital. In the United States, Daniel Webster argued, 'capital cannot say to labor and industry, "Stand ye yonder, while I come up hither"'. Rather 'labor and industry lay hold on capital, break it into parcels, use it, diffuse it widely, and instead of leaving it to repose in its own inertness, compel it to act at once as their own stimulus and their own instrument.' Many Whigs again insisted that any simple division into two categories – in this case of labourers and capitalists – ignored the complexity and the uniqueness of American society. For just as the labourer might easily be transformed into the capitalist so, in the

[28] *Answer of the Whig Members of the Legislature of Massachusetts . . . to the Address of His Excellency Marcus Morton. . .* (Boston, 1840), 29; *Portland (Me.) Advertiser,* 1 July 1842; *Works of Kennedy,* IV, 182; *New Hampshire Statesman,* 20 Jan. 1838; *More than One Hundred Reasons Why William Henry Harrison Should and Will Have the Support of the Democracy. . .* (Boston, 1840), 11; *Answer of the Whig Members,* 29; Harrison, *Speech at Dayton Convention,* 7; *The Essays of Camillus* (Norfolk, 1841), 70; *Cong. Gl.,* 27 i App., 434.

United States, few capitalists ever ceased to be labourers. According to the *New Orleans Bee*, the structure of American society required that all groups and classes be engaged in either manual or mental labour. Hence virtually every citizen was a 'laborer':

> In a republic, whose constitution recognises no distinction between the rich and the poor, in which there are no privileged classes, and whose laws have abolished the system of entails, by which large properties are handed down from generation to generation in the same family, the term workingman embraces, or should embrace every individual member of the community. The merchant is no less a laborer than the mechanic – the attorney is equally indebted to the sweat of his brow for his daily bread as the carpenter or bricklayer. All who employ themselves in useful pursuits to acquire a subsistence or add to their substance are workingmen.

According to Daniel Webster, 'nine tenths of the whole labor of this country is performed by those who cultivate the land they or their fathers own, or who, in their workshops, employ some little capital of their own, and mix it up with their manual toil'. Webster added that 'no such thing exists in other countries'. Hence it could only be an absurdity to claim that the interests of labour and capital were in conflict.[29]

Thus because the distance between the powerful (the rich, the capitalist or the employer) and the weak (the poor, the labourer, the employee) was small, and because the prevailing equality of opportunity enabled the weak to become strong, there could be no reason, the Whigs concluded, to attempt a radical reform of American society. Instead they invited the electorate to share their basic satisfaction with the society in which they lived.

Although this was, in many senses, a frankly and avowedly conservative outlook, the Whigs did not desire a static society. Instead they viewed with pride the changes that were taking place as the pace of economic growth quickened. Whereas Democrats were often dismayed at the effects of commercial and industrial expansion, the Whigs observed the same phenomena with a deep sense of gratification. Their political philosophy allowed them to propose that government intervene in order to supervise the process and thereby check any incidental evils which it might bring. A group of Virginia Whigs complained that the Democratic party of Martin Van Buren

[29]*Address of His Excellency George N. Briggs to the Two Branches of the Legislature of Massachusetts* (Boston, 1846), 3; *Cong. Gl.*, 25 ii App., 633; *New Orleans Bee*, 31 Oct. 1840; *Writings. . . of Webster*, III, 24.

72

was 'anti-credit, anti-commerce'. 'The young, the hardy, and the enterprising', they continued, 'have been struck down.' Similarly the *Republican Review* in 1839 deplored 'the hostility and violence of the ruling party against the commerce and industry of the nation'. For 'he is no friend of the great body of the people of this country, who would curtail the profits of industry by driving away the capital which is its aliment, and diminish enterprise'.[30] The Whigs were bitterly resentful of Democratic attempts to impede capital formation. They welcomed credit and insisted that temporary indebtedness was a necessary and acceptable condition for those involved in commercial and industrial enterprises. They advocated limited liability as a spur to investment and pointedly refrained from endorsing the Jefferson view of cities as 'sores upon the body politic'. Although respectful towards the farmer, they yet sought a more commercialised agricultural sector. In criticising many features of the farmer's life, Horace Greeley in effect condemned what the Democrats most praised:

> [The farmer] is now too nearly an isolated being. His world is a narrow circle of material objects he calls his own, within which he is an autocrat, though out of it little more than a cipher. His associates are few, and these mainly rude dependants and inferiors. His daily discourse savors of beeves and swine, and the death of a sheep on his farm creates more sensation in his circle than the fall of a hero elsewhere. Of the refining, harmonizing, expanding influences of general society, he has little experience. For extensive travel or intercourse with minds which have profited by a large comparison of nations, climates, customs, he has but rare opportunities. The family circle, precious as are its enjoyments, and healthful as are its proper influences, is not alone sufficient to form the noblest character or satisfy all the aspirations of the human heart. The lofty, ingenuous soul revolts at the idea of wearing out its earthly career mainly in the rearing of brutes and the composting of manures, shut out from all free range of congenial associates and obedience to nobler impulses. It feels that a human life is ill spent in the mere production of corn and cattle. . . .

> Not until the solitary farmhouse, with its half-dozen denizens, its mottled array of mere patches of auxiliary acres, its petty flock and herd, its external decorations of piggery, stable-yard, etc., making it the focus of all noisome and villainous odours, shall have been replaced by some arrangement more genial, more expansive, more social in its aspects, affording larger scope to aspiration and a wider field for the infinite capacities of man's nature, may we hope to arrest the tendencies which make the

[30]*Address of the Whig Convention for the Nomination of Electors To the People of Virginia* (n.p., n.d.), 8; *Rep. Rev.*, I, (Jan. 1839), 17.

farmer too often a boor or a clod, and the cultivation of the earth a mindless, repugnant drudgery, when it should be the noblest, the most intellectual, and the most desired of all human employments.

The farmer of the Democratic idyll, the Whigs believed, and indeed the entire Democratic social ethic, presented a serious threat to economic and social progress. The Whigs were the party of enterprise, of 'liberated capitalism', and of commercial progress. According to Daniel Webster, 'we owe more to credit, and to commercial confidence, than any nation which ever existed'. 'Credit and commerce' were, in the words of a Tennessee campaign newspaper, 'the life and spring of the health of a nation'.[31]

Policy

Opposed to the populistic and levelling tendencies of Jacksonian Democracy, the Whigs espoused a set of policies that were, for the most part, in direct conflict with those adopted by the Democrats. Although the party had not, by the time of the Panic of 1837, achieved the degree of unity to which its opponents could lay claim, it was, in the years following, to be successful in rallying its supporters around a coherent and soundly based programme. Whig policy was calculated to preserve an enlightened republican government and an expanding commercial economy.

In accordance with their overtly conservative political philosophy, the Whigs took it upon themselves to defend the judiciary. With few exceptions they were horrified by Democratic assaults upon 'this great bulwark of our institutions – this safest repository of our liberties'. While the Democrats were suspicious of judicial power and influence, many Whigs felt that, of all the branches of government, the judiciary was the best conceived. The *Republican Review* explicitly declared that 'if we were called upon to select that principle in the whole political machinery which is most essential to permanent freedom and which is most conservative of the original design and beauty of our glorious Union, we would unhesitatingly point to the judiciary'. The Whigs even enthused over the judiciary for the very reasons for which Democrats condemned it. Recognising that 'the term of five years is too short to learn to be a judge', they nevertheless embraced the judiciary as an avowedly élitist institution. Hence most Whigs reacted with horror when Democrats proposed that the judges be elected by the people. One Pennsylvanian 'thought that none but those who were

[31] Greeley, *Hints*, 66-8; *Cong. Gl.*, 25 ii App., 606; Nashville *Spirit of '76*, 255.

radicals, and who were prepared for all the horrors that had occurred in France during the French revolution, would go for making the judiciary – the judges of the country – dependant upon the caprice, the whim of the populace.' 'Junius', the Whig pamphleteer, sought to blunt Democratic attacks by arguing that there was 'little or no danger of usurpation or abuse of power' in the judicial department of the government. Hence 'the judiciary ought not to be changeable'. Essentially the Whigs hoped that the power of the judges could be employed to restrain the populistic tendencies of government. The *National Intelligencer* explained that 'we rely upon the Judiciary to correct really illegal constructions of the Constitution, independently of the sense of the People, who may, as indeed we have within our day seen them do, applaud the wrong-doing, instead of condemning it'. Likewise the *Whig Review* insisted that 'of all elements in a government, the judiciary should be left free from external influences'. Instead of being 'subject to periodical revolution by the people', it should be separated 'from popular impression' – and 'by all possible barriers'. Thus many Whigs found in the judiciary a foundation of republican, as opposed to democratic, government.[32]

They were also driven to stress the judges' role as defenders of the Constitution because experience had forced them to question the power of the President. Andrew Jackson had, of course, expanded the role of the Presidency enormously so that, despite their predilection for active government, the Whigs had repeatedly called for a check to be placed upon executive power. Even after Jackson's departure from the White House the Whig party remained committed to a diminished role for the President. Thus in 1840 the editor of the *Ohio Confederate*, a Whig newspaper, claimed that 'at no time since the Declaration of our Independence has the situation of the American people, as a nation, required more vigilance and nerve on the part of the people themselves to resist the encroachments of Executive power on our rights, than is demanded by the present crisis'. In 1837 one Massachusetts Congressman in an address to his constituents warned that executive power was no less than a threat to the entire fabric of American liberties:

> I solemnly warn you against this terrible concentration of power in the hands of the Executive! I see in it a most alarming danger threatening fearfully the liberties of the country! Executive

[32] Balie Payton in *Globe,* 3 Jan. 1844; *Rep. Rev.,* I (April 1839), 322; *Iowa C. C.,* 394; *Pa. C. C.,* I, 124; 'Junius', *One Presidential Term* (N.Y., 1840), 6; *Nat. Int.,* 23 Jan. 1840; *Whig Rev.,* I (Jan. 1845), 2-3. Democrats and Whigs thus refought the battle waged a generation earlier by Republicans and Federalists. See Richard E. Ellis, *The Jeffersonian Crisis* (N.Y., 1971).

power has become a very Colossus, which bestrides the land from one end to the other; and, fellow citizens, if we do not overthrow it, most assuredly it will crush us; and in crushing us, in crushing the people, it will crush liberty, it will crush the Constitution.

Throughout the party's existence the Whigs were virtually unanimous in their suspicion of Presidential power. They therefore demanded restrictions upon the President's right to exercise his veto.[33]

It would be an error to assume, however, that their fears were not, for the most part, genuine and deeply felt. For their anxieties concerning the power to which Democratic Chief Executives now laid claim were a manifestation of their underlying doubts about populistic democracy itself. As Lynn Marshall has observed, Andrew Jackson introduced a new style of Presidential politics in which the President established a direct, almost personal relationship with the people, in whose name he undid the ties with past generations and circumvented the deliberative processes of Congress. It was a head-on assault upon some of the Whigs' most cherished ideals, an attack upon the independence of the representative, a rejection of the claims of the past and the future, and a surrender of the power of government as a moral and harmonising agency. It was no accident that the Whigs instead sought to defend the power of Congress, 'the *home* of American democracy, its theatre, its sacred ground'. In the Jacksonian era, unlike the era of Jeffersonian Democracy, the conservative was impelled to defend the legislature against the alleged encroachments of the executive.[34]

Political conservatism had other important implications for policy. While Democrats announced in ringing tones that the institutions of a popular government were sufficiently well established to permit virtually any extension of the nation's frontiers, the Whigs remained highly sceptical. With few dissenting voices the party placed itself in opposition to the 'Manifest Destiny' crusade of the 1840s. Many Whigs feared that the acquisition of Oregon and Texas would jeopardise the safety of republican institutions. Thus the *Kennebec Journal* restated the traditional belief that a popular government could not preside over an entire continent when it asked rhetorically whether 'any one' believed that the people of California and Oregon 'will compose part of our Republic fifty years hence'? In what was to

[33] John G. Miller, *The Great Convention*. . . (Columbus, n.d.), 11; *Speech of Richard Fletcher to his Constituents*. . . *Nov. 6, 1837* (n.p., n.d.), 9.

[34] Lynn L. Marshall, 'The Strange Stillbirth of the Whig party', *A. H. R.*, LXXII, 445-68 (Jan. 1967); 'Junius', *Democracy* (N.Y., 1844), 6.

prove an ill-fated prediction the newspaper suggested that the inhabitants of these far Western states could scarcely be expected to 'rest content under a government whose central focus must be three thousand miles distant, even though the distance be travelled by steam'. Other Whigs stressed the effects of territorial expansion upon the sectional tensions within the nation. The *National Intelligencer* cited as a 'conclusive reason' against the annexation of Texas the fact that 'the Territory of the United States is already large enough'. It was 'infinitely more important that we should people and improve what we have than grasp after more, especially when its acquisition would be inevitably attended with discord and dissatisfaction'. The Whigs were also troubled by the prospect of 'a want of nationality' if Texas and Oregon were annexed. 'We shall not know ourselves, or know our country', the *Whig Review* lamented. While Democrats welcomed the possibility of extending the area of freedom by protecting the autonomy of the yeoman farmer, the more cosmopolitan outlook of the Whigs resulted in a desire for interdependent ties within a culturally uniform society. 'We want our own Republic and Union', they insisted, 'with a homogeneous people, men of the same general race, blood, education and habits, forming a consolidated nation'. One North Carolina Whig, convinced that the nation 'must have a limit to [its] acquisition of territory', reintroduced the Jeffersonian view of the United States as 'the Mother of Republics' on the North American continent.[35]

The same priorities impelled most Whigs to oppose Democratic efforts to facilitate, and thereby quicken the pace of, land settlement in the West. The party was in effect responding to the widespread Eastern resentment at the effects of Westward expansion. In the Atlantic states it was often felt that 'the vigor of these [Western] States . . . is drawn in part from the life-blood of the parent stock'. The duty of the government was to promote the material and moral improvement of society; its energies and resources should not be diverted and squandered on the West.[36]

Yet it was not merely sectional prejudice which drove most Whigs to denounce the Democratic policies of pre-emption and graduation. Most Democrats supported every proposed reduction in land prices in the belief that they would promote the strength of the agricultural

[35] *Kennebec Journal* in Louis C. Hatch, *Maine: A History*, 4 vols, (N.Y., 1919), II, 331; *Nat. Int.*, 16 March 1844; *Cong. Gl.*, 28 ii App., 56; *Whig Rev.*, VII (May 1848), 440; *Raleigh Register*, 22 Dec. 1843, 17 May 1844.

[36] *Works of Kennedy*, IV, 605; see also 'Report of Whig Minority of the Select Committee of the New York Assembly' in *Tribune*, 18 April 1842.

interest and many Whigs opposed them for the same reason. One Virginian argued that there was 'already, perhaps, too great a portion' of capital and labour 'withdrawn from the mechanic arts'. Hence 'it is not the policy of any of the States further to reduce the price of the public lands.' The lands were not needed as a 'safety-valve' for Eastern discontent since 'a day-laborer or a mechanic can make more profit by continuing his usual occupation, than by clearing and cultivating lands'. Thus the social conservatism of the Whigs permitted them to deny the need for cheap land.[37]

Whig conservatism likewise operated to turn most partisans against pre-emption. Democratic propaganda portrayed the squatters of the West as heroic conquerors of the wilderness; Henry Clay, by contrast, viewed them as 'lawless rabble'. Clay believed that pre-emption was 'a violation of all law' and claimed that the clash over the policy was 'nothing more than a struggle between those who would violate the law and those who would maintain its supremacy'. Consistent with their often avowed concern for the welfare of future generations, the Whigs sought to preserve the nation's landed heritage. This, 'the noblest patrimony ever yet inherited by any people', should be 'husbanded and preserved with care, in such a manner that future generations shall not reproach us with having squandered what was justly theirs, and left them penniless'. Whig land policy thus reflected the party's concern for economic diversification, its basic satisfaction with American society and its regard for the interests of future generations. It was entirely consistent with the party's fundamental philosophy.[38]

The social values which the Whigs most cherished similarly helped determine the party's response to the Free Trade controversy. In 1842, when the Compromise tariff of 1833 expired, the Whigs were able to enact a bill that was overtly protective. One of its goals was 'to invite capital into the establishment of manufactures'. In repudiating the doctrines of Free Trade, the Whigs reminded the electorate that independence in the economic sphere required that America manufacture her own products. Hence 'the protective system nurses in the bosoms of the people' a 'sentiment of national independence'. It was equally evident, the Whigs pointed out, that protection would diversify the nation's economy. Thus Horace Greeley argued that 'protection diverts Labor from non-productive to productive employments'. 'By diversifying industry', he continued, 'it

---

[37] *Cong. Gl.,* 25 iii App., 307.
[38] Roy M. Robbins, *Our Landed Heritage* (Princeton, 1942), 75, 94.

calls into active exercise a wider range of capacities, and develops powers which would otherwise have lain dormant and unsuspected'. Yet the Whigs also claimed that tariffs benefited the farmer by creating a wider home market for his produce. They were consequently able to meet Democratic hostility to the tariff with the assertion that it helped 'bind' the various interests of the community together. Far from being an example of partial legislation it was a measure designed 'to render each branch of labor useful to the rest; to connect them all together; to bind one to another so as to form a perfect chain of mutual dependence.' Finally, in defending the protective policy, the Whigs insisted that without it American labour would be brought into a ruinous competition with the pauper labour of Europe. Tariffs thus guaranteed a high-wage economy and an upwardly mobile society as well as facilitating economic diversification and national independence. They were of obvious value to the Whig party.[39]

Whig partisans were also, and for equally compelling reasons, favourable to internal improvements. Thus Governor William Woodbridge of Michigan declared that 'of all the rights that appertain to a 'sovereign and independent state', he knew 'of none more indisputable than that of uncovering the natural wealth of the country, of facilitating its intercourse, of increasing its commerce, and of encouraging its agriculture by the construction and establishment of roads, canals and railways'. Whig predilections for an active, interventionist government removed the central Democratic objection to internal improvements. Partisans like 'Junius' were wont to emphasise that government must promote these enterprises if only because 'individual capital could not accomplish these great works'. Although some Southern Whigs were reluctant to employ Federal power for this purpose their objections did not extend to state sponsored improvements. Thus one Virginian, although clearly concerned to protect states-rights, yet claimed that 'the example of the New York system has proved incontestably that the general effect of the [internal improvements] policy is to develop the resources of a country, to stimulate its enterprise, and to add to the wealth, comfort and happiness of our species'. Throughout the Union the Whigs were generally recognised as the party that was most favourable to internal improvements. Their support was consonant with their basic perceptions.[40]

[39] *The True Whig Sentiment of Massachusetts* (n.p., n.d.), 5; *Works of Kennedy*, IV, 286; Greeley, *Why I Am A Whig* (n.p.,n.d.), 11; *Writings. . . of Webster*, XIII, 290.

[40] George N. Fuller(ed.), *Messages of the Governors of Michigan* (Lansing, 1925), I, 341; 'Junius', *Labor and Capital* (N.Y., 1844), 5; *Essays of Camillus,* 61-2.

Their enthusiasm for internal improvements impelled the Whigs to proclaim their faith in corporations. In Jacksonian America corporations were chartered by the state and Federal governments for a wide variety of purposes, often (though not always) connected to internal improvements projects. While Democrats objected to corporations largely because they conferred privilege, Whigs hailed them as instruments of commercial expansion. One Maine Whig declared that a corporation was a means 'of forwarding enterprise and industry, and of bringing out the resources and advancing the wellbeing of the State'. The Whigs believed that the nation's chronic shortage of capital required that government intervene to aid its formation. Hence Democratic hostility to corporations was disastrous for the nation's economy. 'Individual capital, enterprise, and powers', Horace Greeley asserted, 'can rarely if ever be equal to the construction of works of the highest public utility.' When the Whigs sought to account for the tremendous expansion which the American economy had achieved in the recent past, they placed a heavy emphasis upon the part played by corporations. The evaluation made by John P. Kennedy of Maryland was typical. What, he asked, were corporations?

> the most signal instruments by which the prosperity of our most prosperous states has been achieved. They are the familiar agencies through which almost every great enterprise has been accomplished. They have given to youthful America all the vigor of a ripe and wealthy nation. They are endeared to us by the richest fruits of our political advancement. What our scant *individual wealth* has been unable to attain, their means of *associated wealth* have brought us in profusion.

While Democrats remained highly suspicious of 'associated wealth' many Whigs praised its influence and power. For this reason alone the two parties were bound to differ in their attitudes to corporations.[41]

Yet the Whigs were not content to argue that corporations promoted economic growth and diversification. In addition they claimed that a corporation permitted men 'of moderate means' to benefit. 'Deprive men of moderate means of this power of association and concentration of their capital', one Indiana Whig warned, 'and all this business must fall into the hands of the wealthy'. By attracting 'the smallest surplus returns of individual enterprise' corporations gave to an ever-increasing section of the population a stake in commercial America. Hence 'an interest is awakened in subjects and modes of

[41]*Kennebec Journal,* 1 May 1841; *Whig Almanac* (1843), 30; *Works of Kennedy,* IV, 138.

human exertion, of which the mass of men would otherwise have no knowledge.' Corporations thus helped to foster the entrepreneurial spirit, and to bind together, in mutual dependence, the otherwise discordant interests of Americans. The Whigs sought to encourage, by offering limited liability, the spread of corporations. In so doing, however, they necessarily encountered Democratic antagonism.[42]

Yet in spite of the obvious importance of corporations they were not, of course, the main area of controversy between the two parties. For the twin issues of banking and the currency were as critically important to the Whigs as to the Democrats. In the years following the Panic of 1837 the energies of both parties were concentrated upon the nation's banks and its credit system. The Democrats led the assault; the Whigs rallied to the defence.

Concerned to preserve the mechanisms of mobility within American society, the Whigs readily proclaimed the need for credit. The Whigs of New York announced that 'every young man whose fortune is yet to be made by industry can have no hope of success through any other means than the credit which his character may enable him to obtain'. Similarly the *Hartford Courant* maintained that the ready availability of credit had permitted the 'poor and friendless young man' to rise into, and indeed to fill, the ranks of the wealthy. Hence it followed that to destroy the credit system was to return to an era in which 'the young man might as well attempt to scale the vault of Heaven, as to raise himself by any exertions from the rank in which he was born'. Credit, according to Whig social theory, was 'the blessing, voluntarily offered to good character and to good conduct . . . the beneficent agent, which assists honesty and enterprise in obtaining comfort and independence'. It was the 'Fulcrum of the American Laborer, by which he lifts himself up to social and pecuniary Equality with the richest Capitalists, and to a superiority above all other Laborers in all other parts of the earth.' The Whigs' commitment to an upwardly mobile society in effect required that they defend the credit system and rebut Democratic criticisms.[43]

In so doing they also stressed the role of credit in promoting economic growth generally. 'Without bank credit', one Indiana Whig claimed, 'it would have been impossible for the new states of the West

---

[42]*Cong., Gl.*, 25 ii App., 589; Barnard in *Jeffersonian*, 17 March 1838. On this subject see Thomas C. Cochran, 'The Business Revolution', *A.H.R.*, LXXIX (Dec. 1974), 1449-66.

[43]*Address of Whig State Convention* [of New York] in *Jeffersonian*, 6 Oct. 1838; *Hartford Courant*, 7 Jan. 1843; *Cong. Gl.*, 25 ii App., 633; James Brooks, 'Address to the Young Men of New York' in *Jeffersonian*, 28 Oct. 1838.

to grow and increase in wealth, population, and business'. Elsewhere prominent Whigs explained that the nation's success in combating poverty and its triumphs in commerce and manufacturing owed much to the operation of her now maligned credit system. Again conscious of the nation's capital shortage, the Whigs relied upon credit to make up for the deficiency.[44]

For this reason they stressed the need for a soundly based and well regulated banking system. Because they were able to issue paper money the banks could, of course, augment the supply of credit. Hence the Whigs claimed for the banks a major role in promoting economic growth. 'Without them', the *Georgia Messenger* suggested, 'one half of our national wealth would never have existed. Without them, the wilds of the South and Southwest would not have been cultivated, as they now are, for a century to come.' Similarly it followed that banks and paper money were indispensable if social mobility were to be maintained. According to William Henry Harrison the Democratic goal of an exclusively specie currency was an idea 'fraught with more fatal consequences than any other scheme, having no relation to the personal rights of the citizens, that has ever been devised'. 'If any scheme', he continued, 'could produce the effect of arresting, at once, that mutation of condition by which thousands of our most indigent fellow-citizens, by their industry and enterprise, are raised to the possession of wealth, that is the one.' Harrison held that 'a properly devised banking system alone possesses the capability of bringing the poor to a level with the rich'. Hence the banking system, by promoting economic advancement and social mobility was a 'proud structure of modern wisdom and civilization', among 'the highest inventions and noblest results of modern civilization'. Noting that banks existed 'in every civilized nation of any commercial or political importance', the Whigs professed themselves unable to comprehend the Democratic demand for hard money. 'What do gentlemen mean?' asked Hugh Lawson White of Tennessee. 'Do they mean to put us back to the year eleven hundred?'[45]

Convinced of the need for banks and paper money, the Whigs nevertheless differed as to whether a national bank was desirable. A minority within the party preferred to rely exclusively upon the state banks in the belief that a national bank represented too large a concentration of power. This view was held in some Northern states

---

[44]*Cong. Gl.,* 25 ii App., 183

[45]*Georgia Messenger,* 20 Sept. 1838; Harrison Inaugural in *Madisonian,* 4 March 1841; Harrison, *Speech at Dayton Convention,* 5; *Essays of Camillus,* 69; William Penn Clark in *Iowa C.C.,* 349; *Cong. Gl.,* 25 ii App., 510.

as well as in the South. Yet in the years following the Panic of 1837 the party united around the proposal for a new national bank. Orthodox Whigs argued that an instrument of national economic management and control was needed, one which could supervise and co-ordinate the actions of the various state banks. In the credit hungry West the bank was especially popular with the Whigs. One Ohio Congressman explained its appeal for Westerners:

> Our want is capital. We want, through the facilities of well-regulated, specie-paying banks, to be able to develop the great resources of our State, to get our produce to market, and anticipate the results of all our labor. This is our want – our only want. . . . We want the facility of making temporary loans, to be repaid out of the sales of the produce of our farms and the manufactures of our shops. This facility was afforded to us in the olden time by the Bank of the United States.

Finally the Whigs were attracted to a national bank because they adopted the Madisonian view that 'the skill of legislation' in the Federal government was 'of a higher order' than that displayed in the State legislatures. Hence 'the power of the General Government over a national institution, to prevent fraud', was 'much more effective than that of the States over their institutions'. A national bank would thus allow the entire financial superstructure of the nation to be regulated by a body which combined 'the concentrated wisdom of the nation'.[46]

Banks, tariffs, internal improvements and corporations – these were the agents of economic progress which the Whigs sought to promote. The financial policies which the party officially advocated were designed to facilitate economic growth and diversification. Equally the political policies to which it was committed represented, in the main, a desire to preserve a republican polity administered by a natural aristocracy. Although some members of the party dissented from specific items which their colleagues proposed,[47] this should not obscure the fact that Whig policies were logically and consistently related to Whig principles.

The Whig party was thus the party of political conservatism and of business dynamism. Contrary to the view advanced by historians of the 'consensus' school, the proponents of 'liberated capitalism' tended to be unsympathetic to the advance of democracy. They

[46] *Cong. Gl.,* 27 iii App., 183: 'Junius', *The Currency,* 9. See also *Richmond (Ind.) Palladium,* 29 May 1841; *Cong. Gl.,* 25 ii App., 183.

[47] See below, Chapter 6.

sensed that Democratic egalitarianism offered a serious threat to a commercial economy and they recoiled from the atomistic society which the most enthusiastic democrats sought to promote. It was these men who joined the Whig party and their views which made up its quasi-official ideology. Although a minority of Whigs had no fears concerning the advance of democracy, their opinions were counter-balanced by another minority to whom the progress of popular government in America since 1776 (or 1800) represented the most melancholy chapter in the nation's history.[48] Between the two lay the majority of Whig partisans, who were frankly sceptical about democracy and who did not seek to conceal it. Their political conservatism was well expressed by Henry Clay, the party's most prominent statesman, in the course of a debate in the Senate in 1840. Clay chastised the Democrats for neglecting the importance of existing social conditions:

> The great error of Senators on the other side is, that they do not sufficiently regard the existing structure of society, the habits and usages which prevail; in short, the actual state of things. All *wise* legislation should be founded upon the condition of society as it is; and even where reform is necessary, it should be introduced slowly, cautiously, and with a careful and vigilant attention to all consequences. But gentlemen seem disposed to consider themselves at liberty to legislate for a new people, just sprung into existence, and commencing its career – one for which they may, without reference to what they see all around them, speculate and theorize at pleasure.[49]

Most Whigs were unable to enthuse about democracy. Like the Democrats they perceived a conflict between the ideology of democracy and that of entrepreneurial capitalism. Driven by élitist preconceptions, however, they almost necessarily plumped for the latter. The Whigs were satisfied with the fundamental structure of their society and with the moral and economic improvement of which it seemed to be capable. They were in effect the apologists for a society based upon commercial agriculture and small-scale industrial capitalism.

Thus the Whigs were the first political party to offer to a mass electorate a viable and appealing conservative programme. Many of the arguments that they employed were to be used, and with considerable success, by later generations. Some retain their force

---

[48] For a discussion of the views of conservative and liberal Whigs see Chapters 3 and 4 respectively.

[49] *Cong. Gl.*, 26 i App., 727.

even to this day. The inegalitarian and meritocratic outlook, the idea of limitless upward mobility, the desire for commercial expansion and diversification – these have passed so completely into the mainstream of American life and culture that it is difficult to appreciate that they could ever have been controversial. Historians have usually assumed that it was the Democrats who left the enduring legacy for American society. The resulting neglect has been unfortunate; the influence of the Whigs was at least as great.

PART TWO
FACTIONS

3

'AGRARIANS' AND 'ARISTOCRATS'

'Agrarians'

Upon entering the White House in March 1837, Martin Van Buren was quickly given the opportunity to fulfil his major campaign promise. Van Buren had been elected as heir to the policies which his illustrious predecessor had pursued, and the financial distress of 1837 was accompanied by a demand for the intensification of the struggle with the banks. In the summer of that year the new President took what was a fateful decision. With the full approval and support of the former President, Van Buren adopted the Independent Treasury proposal. The plan required, of course, the withdrawal and permanent separation of government funds from the banking system. This, it was hoped, would further the Democratic hard money policy since, as one Van Burenite Senator put it, 'the direct tendency of resorting to an independent treasury will be to impress the public with the belief that the Government can manage its affairs without a bank'. Thus 'anti-bank habits' would 'become established'. Similarly, and simultaneously, the banks, now 'deprived of the stimulus which the Government deposites have ministered', would 'gradually diminish in number until they become apportioned to the real commercial demands of the country'. The Independent Treasury was a vote of no confidence in the banks and a possible prelude for later, more direct assaults.[1]

The Congressional majorities which passed the Independent Treasury were composed, in the main, of individuals who feared that current social trends would, if permitted to continue, result in a society as inegalitarian as those in Britain and Europe. A more extreme position was taken, however, by a substantial number of radicals both inside and out of the Democratic party. For these men an acute crisis, signalled most clearly by severe and unacceptable economic inequalities, had already arrived. These two diagnoses were significantly different; yet to a surprising degree the two groups shared a common world view and demanded a common set of policies. The adoption of the Independent Treasury in 1837 signified a victory for these groups and a hardening of the alliance between them. The presence of these radicals in the Democratic ranks was to give a vivid colour to the politics of the next decade.[2]

[1] *Cong. Gl,* 25 i App., 45.

[2] These generalisations apply with extra force to the years of Van Buren's Presidency.

A vocal exponent of the most extreme views that could be found within the Democracy was Theophilus Fisk. As a newspaper editor, public speaker and pamphleteer, Fisk was uncompromising in his denunciations of the inequalities and evils which, he believed, disfigured American society. 'Our present artificial system', he fumed, 'converts nineteen-twentieths of the human species into beasts of burden, annihilating thought, destroying intelligence, and extirpating happiness.' Again and again Fisk railed against 'the plundering, swindling fungi of the social state', 'the pampered parasites of ill-gotten wealth, who consume in sloth what others earn', and 'the blood sucking cormorants of capital, whom heaven's bolt would scorn to crush in their lazy infamy'.[3]

How had this monstrous injustice arisen? Fisk's answer was unmistakably Democratic. He attributed much of the poverty, ignorance and crime to 'special legislation, unequal laws and odious monopolies'. Consequently he demanded the policies which the Democratic party, at both national and state level, was introducing. Implacably opposed to banks and corporate charters, and en-thusiastically in favour of any proposal for extending political democracy, Fisk shared the orthodox party outlook in its essentials. He perceived the world in Jacksonian terms. His role, he clearly believed, was to strengthen the anti-bank wing of the party at the expense of the pro-bank minority. Accordingly he praised Democratic politicians like Thomas Hart Benton, William Allen, Edmund Burke and Jesse Bynum, while at the same time pouring scorn and derision upon those of a more conservative hue. Thus James Buchanan was 'doing more to retard the progress of Democratic principles, than any man here [in Washington]', while it was to the 'unfortunate influence' of no less a Democratic luminary than the quasi-conservative Thomas Ritchie that 'the present ignorance and imbecility of Virginia, in a very great degree is owing'. Nevertheless, Fisk was a staunch Democrat. Believing the Independent Treasury to be 'a question of such paramount importance to the democracy', he remained an ardent partisan into the mid-forties. In 1840 he wrote that the party, though in need of purging, was yet 'the party of Humanity – of Christianity – of truth, duty and universal love'.[4]

Indeed it is often difficult to distinguish between Van Burenite radicals (whose perceptions were discussed in Chapter 2) and the more extreme radicals. A journal such as the *Democratic Review* often adopted what was, according to this definition, an extreme position. It was, however, solidly behind Van Buren and was widely regarded as an administration journal.

[3] *Dem. Exp.*, 2 Aug. 1845; Fisk, *Our Country, Its Dangers and Destiny* (Washington D.C., 1845), 10.

[4] *Dem. Exp.*, 2 Aug.,27 Dec. 1845; *Old Dominion*, 12, 19, 26 Jan., 2 March 1839;

Fisk was not, however, the only Democrat to advance such radical views. The *Western Review* in 1846 warned that there were 'social inequalities, hardly inferior to those which characterize English society beginning to prevail in our midst'. Promising in its prospectus an 'uncompromising advocacy of the views of the Democratic party', the *Review* declared that it was the duty of the 'true democrat' to war 'earnestly against the existing state of society'. Similarly the Washington newspaper *Common Sense* lamented that 'capital has become divorced from Labor and has acquired over it a power too often at war with its interests'. The paper, while criticising conservative Democrats, applauded the Independent Treasury, made the standard demands for a specie currency, and praised party regulars like Van Burenite Congressman George Dromgoole of Virginia. In Philadelphia, the *Spirit of the Times,* one of Pennsylvania's most notable Democratic presses, observed that although the 'theory' of American government was 'based upon the great doctrine of political equality' yet 'we see that, step by step, distinctions are growing up daily in society, grades stepping over grades and a portion of our fellow citizens sinking beneath their merited station in society'. It was solely 'through the possession of wealth' that 'a few. . . contrive to monopolize the gifts of Providence, making the gulf which divides mankind still wider and deeper'. Also in Pennsylvania, at the Constitutional Convention of 1836-9, Charles J. Ingersoll, a Democratic Congressman and one of the leaders of the state party, made what would become a celebrated report upon currency and corporations. Ingersoll argued that all charters should be revocable, a proposal deliberately calculated to impede capital formation. Ingersoll clearly felt that social inequalities justified this radical measure. 'Liberty remains', he acknowledged, 'freedom of speech, of action, of the press, of religion, and of acquiring property.' 'But', he warned, 'equality is rapidly disappearing in the possession, distribution, and transmission of it.' Ingersoll no doubt startled many of his readers when he asserted that 'property is more equally divided, and held in France, than in Pennsylvania'. Some years later, at another Constitutional Convention, this time in Michigan, John S. Bagg, editor of the *Detroit Free Press,* perhaps the foremost Democratic paper in the state, observed that although 'all wealth is the result of labor, yet, strange enough, the man who does the labor never has the wealth'. It was the standard radical protest against the inequality of wealth.[5]

Dem. Exp., 11 Oct., 20 Dec. 13 Sept. 1845. On Fisk's campaign for the Virginia Assembly see *Commercial Chronicle* for 1840.

[5]*Western Review,* I (April 1846), 5, 207 and prospectus; *Common Sense, the Workingman's Advocate,* 2 Oct. 1847 (perhaps the only number to appear); *Spirit of the Times and Daily Keystone,* 14 Aug. 1847; *Pa. C. C.,* I, 367; John S. Bagg quoted in

Much of this radicalism was channelled, of course, into the campaign against the banks. In Wisconsin where the new state constitution had outlawed the banking system entirely, the *Milwaukee Courier,* a Democratic press, expressed a hope that other states would rapidly follow suit. For the people 'have been able to trace the artificial inequality of wealth, much pauperism and crime, the low state of public morals, and many of the other social evils directly to this system'. Similarly, Ohio Democrat B.B. Taylor in the State Senate told his countrymen that they 'now live in a state of vassalage to an order of nobility, the bankers'. For the bankers 'tax your labor, tax your property, and are riding you blindfolded to your own immolation'. Taylor's speech was reported and praised in the Washington *Globe.*[6]

The ideas in it were held by many Democrats. According to Walter Colquitt of Georgia bankers were 'a class of people who have built fine carriages, which they have made out of the labor and industry of the working classes'. This denunciation came in the course of a speech in the House of Representatives favouring the Independent Treasury. The *Cincinnati Advertiser* presumably welcomed the description; two years earlier (in 1838) it had referred to the bankers of New York as a group who 'grind the face of the poor'. The *Ohio Statesman* likewise fulminated against the 'aristocracy of money' which had 'bound' the people 'hand and foot' and which was 'riding "booted and spurred" over them', with 'their rights filched from them'. The *Statesman* and the *Cincinnati Advertiser* were major Democratic newspapers in Ohio. The foremost Democratic newspaper in Mississippi, on the other hand, the *Mississippian,* was preoccupied with the question of the payment of the state's bonds. It nevertheless echoed the sentiments of the Ohio press. Favouring repudiation (a word which was itself sufficient to horrify the commercial community), the *Mississippian* asked whether 'widows and orphans and a people already crushed to the earth' should be 'further oppressed to furnish lucrative salaries' to bankers, 'the most useless classes of the community'.[7]

Throughout the nation there were Democratic radicals convinced

William G. Shade, *Banks or No Banks: The Money Issue in Western Politics, 1832-1864* (Detroit, 1972), 134. Edward Pessen discusses the question of the distribution of wealth in *Riches, Class and Power before the Civil War* (Lexington, 1973).

[6]*Milwaukee Courier* in Milo M. Quaife (ed.), *The Struggle over Ratification, 1846-1847* (Madison, 1920), 200; *Globe,* 28 April 1842.

[7]*Speech of Mr. Colquitt of Georgia. . on the Independent Treasury Bill, June 20, 1840* (Washington D.C., 1840), 15; *Cincinnati Advertiser,* 29 Nov. 1838; *Ohio Statesman,* 14 July 1841; *Mississippian,* 6 Dec. 1843.

that a state of crisis had arisen, convinced that the Democratic party was the instrument through which the social evils could be attacked, and concerned to implement and extend the Democratic programme as set forth by Andrew Jackson and Martin Van Buren. Democratic radicals were vividly class conscious, aware of dramatic differences between occupational groups that grew out of gross economic inequalities. The *Wetumpka Argus,* a major Democratic newspaper in Alabama, drew attention to these inequalities and depicted the class divisions which they spawned:

> The ruffle-shirted counter hopper, rolling in the wealth acquired by driving shrewd bargains with the plain and unassuming farmer, has the high privilege of sauntering through those magnificent halls and of drinking champaign [sic] and other costly wines provided for their delicate palates; while the honest but poor inmate of the log cabin must not enter for fear, it may be, of soiling the polished floor! and of offending the gaze of those princely exclusives.

A still more vivid description of class inequalities and the injustices with which they were accompanied was made in the House of Representatives by Democrat Alexander Duncan of Ohio. Duncan rose to counter the Whig argument that there was no difference between capital and labour. He repudiated the idea utterly:

> Well this is very fine. If it is true, I suppose the capitalist will have no objection to exchanging situations with the laborer; that he will give up his capital to the laborer, and all his lands, and houses, and chattel property, and introduce him into his parlor, upon his soft, brilliant, Turkey carpeting; give him the key to his costly sideboard, and the freehold to his rich wines, gold gobblets, cut glass decanters, and his massy plate, together with his soft sofa to lounge upon; and he, the capitalist will enter the field of toil and sweat, and there labor from morning till night, day after day, week after week, and month after month. . . . When shall such an example as this take place think you? It will be when the lion and the lamb shall sit down in peace.

Duncan concluded that 'it will be found that there is a great difference between labor and capital.' According to the *Cincinnati Enquirer,* it was 'a truism, that, in the past and present organization of society, the pecuniary interests of capital and labor are *antagonist*'.[8]

A deep resentment of economic inequalities between individuals and groups, a conviction that the interests of labour were constantly threatened by capital and a belief that partial legislation was the fundamental cause of society's evils – these were the decisive features

[8]*Wetumpka Argus,* 24 Feb 1841; *Cong. Gl,* 25 ii App., 241; *Cincinnati Enquirer,* 31 Oct. 1845.

of the radical ideology. Because they were never entirely satisfied with the official policy of the party, the most radical Democrats had often dissociated themselves from their more moderate colleagues. There was indeed a continuous debate among some radicals as to whether the fight should be fought from within the party or outside it. The final verdict often depended upon the state of the Democratic party itself so that although the extreme radicals never formed a monolithic block there was nevertheless a general pattern to their behaviour. In the late 1820s and early 1830s they were found in the Workingmen's associations which sprang up in the Eastern cities; they fielded their own candidates for elections and generally severed any links with the Democracy. The radical shift of the Van Buren years, however, and specifically the unfolding of the anti-bank, hard money policy which Andrew Jackson had inaugurated (but not fully established) attracted many (though not all) of them into the party.[9]

Curiously, the radicalism of the Workingmen's parties has often been recognised and then set in contrast to the allegedly pragmatic, non-ideological and assuredly non-radical nature of the Democratic party. It has even been argued that the radicals were as far removed from the Democracy as from the Whig party.[10] In part this reflects a tendency among historians to assume that social radicalism has never existed within the American two party system and even that it somehow cannot. But whatever the explanation the view is clearly untenable. Men like Fisk, Orestes Brownson and Robert Dale Owen were acknowledged leaders of the Workingmen's parties; all became staunch Democrats. Newspapers like the *Boston Weekly Reformer* and *Common Sense* supported radical Democrats and Workingmen alike. In New York there was virtually an apostolic succession from the Workingmen's party to the Locofoco or Equal Rights party. The Locofocos in 1837 returned to the Democratic fold; orthodox Democrats like Van Burenite Preston King were ideologically close to them.[11] There was, moreover, a clear similarity between the policies

[9]Arthur M. Schlesinger, Jr., *The Age of Jackson* (Boston, 1946), Chapter XXI is most helpful on these movements.

[10]The leading advocate of this view is Edward Pessen. See his *Most Uncommon Jacksonians: The Radical Leaders of the Early Labor Movement* (Albany, 1967), 122-3, 172, and his *Jacksonian America, Society, Personality and Politics* rev. ed., (Homewood, Ill., 1978), 270-6 and *passim.*

[11]On Owen see Richard W. Leopold, *Robert Dale Owen, A Biography* (N.Y., 1969), 157. Leopold points out that Owen merely 'toned down' the early radicalism. See also Owen's anonymous article in *Dem. Rev.*, XIV (Feb. 1844), 156-67; Ernest P. Muller, 'Preston King: A Political Biography' (Ph.D. thesis, Columbia, 1957), 183; *Boston Weekly Reformer,* 20 Jan., 24 March, 21 April, 2 June 1837. See also Schlesinger, *Age of Jackson,* 261. Pessen, concerned to dissociate Workingmen from Democrats, has problems with the Locofocos, who were associated with both. On one page they are radical, on another they are not – Pessen, *Jacksonian America,* 279, 186.

favoured by Workingmen and radical Democrats. In 1840 the Workingmen of Charlestown, Massachusetts issued an Address to 'their brethren throughout the Commonwealth and the Union' in which they commented upon the ideas and policies of the Democratic candidate for Governor, Marcus Morton. Morton, a loyal Van Burenite, was opposed by the Whig nominee, John Davis. Although the Workingmen maintained and continued to favour a separate organisation, they nevertheless assessed the two candidates fully. Their conclusions offer a fair indication of their relationship with, and attitude towards, the Democratic party. Praising Morton for his views on banking and the currency and his avowed desire to 'introduce the greatest practicable equality among all the members of the community', the Workingmen declared that 'a more unexceptionable candidate it would not be easy to select'. Clearly Morton's views went 'in the right direction, although they may possibly fall short of our own'. Hence 'when the question comes up, as it now does, whether the workingmen shall vote for him or his whig competitor, it seems to us that no workingman can hesitate a moment to prefer Marcus Morton to John Davis'. More uncompromising than Morton, filled with a greater sense of urgency and, perhaps, more implacable in their demands, these Workingmen yet developed the same ideas and pressed for the same reforms. They were not a breed apart from the Democrats. As far as basic perceptions are concerned, the Workingmen were more Jacksonian than the Jacksonians.[12]

This similarity is visible in their attitude to the city. Although situated in the nation's urban centres, the Workingmen and the radicals in general were far from urban in their ethos. Rather they were thorough-going agrarians. Fisk spoke of 'the mammoth cities of the North – those political and moral sodoms of modern days – those sepulchres of national virtue, liberty and law'. Carl Degler has pointed out that the Locofocos can be described as 'urban agrarians' and this insight can be applied to virtually all the Workingmen's parties.[13] For Workingmen and Democratic radicals alike were evaluating an increasingly urban society in terms of an agricultural,

---

[12] 'Address of the Workingmen of Charlestown, Mass. . . .', in *Bo. Q. R.,* IV (Jan., 1841), 125-6. By far the best analysis of Workingmen's ideology is Robert Geis, 'Liberty, Equality, Fraternity: The Ideology of the American Labor Movement from 1828 to 1848' (Ph.D. thesis, University of Minnesota, 1971) – upon whose evidence this interpretation partly rests. Though he did not consider the Democratic party, Geis' remarks on the Workingmen have, it seems to me, wider application. See also *Atlantic Monthly,* III (April 1859), 393-403.

[13] *Commercial Chronicle,* 10 July 1839; Carl N. Degler, 'The Locofocos: Urban "Agrarians" ', *J.E.H.,* XVI (Sept. 1956), 322-33; Geis, 'Liberty, Equality, Fraternity', 314-18.

94

pastoral idyll. Hence the cities were to many of them what they had been to Jefferson: the home of vice and inequality. Democratic radicals and Workingmen were together in the vanguard of the movement against banks, corporations and manufacturing industry, the harbingers of the nascent industrial and commercial order. Like Andrew Jackson himself they were the heirs of Jefferson; more precisely, they were the heirs of John Taylor of Caroline.[14]

The Democratic radicals sought to combat social evils by the destruction of those institutions which eroded the morals of the community, threatened its political rectitude and created unacceptably harsh economic inequalities. They worked to re-establish the natural order of society by withdrawing governmental aid from the favoured classes and trusted that a limited government, protecting the equal rights of all citizens, would preserve an essentially undifferentiated and truly non-exploitative agrarian society. Perhaps because they expected more of the Democratic programme than the party orthodoxy, or because they pushed Democratic reasoning further, radicals became aware, sometimes dimly but sometimes acutely, of the weaknesses contained within it.

Of those radicals who looked first and foremost to the Democratic party itself, none was more doctrinaire than William Leggett, sometime editor of the New York *Evening Post,* the *Plaindealer,* and the *Truth Teller.*[15] Leggett's radical credentials are scarcely open to serious question. 'A vast disparity of condition', he believed, was opening up in society, with 'vast numbers of men' doomed to 'groan and sweat under a weary life' of 'incessant toil'. Yet these men were 'accumulating nothing around them, to give them hope of respite, and a prospect of comfort in old age'. Leggett emphasised that this inequality was 'to a very great extent artificial'; he attributed it, in sound Jacksonian fashion, to privileges obtained through legislation and at the expense of the equal rights of the people.[16]

Leggett's involvement with the Democratic party was a turbulent

---

[14] For statements that clearly showed the direct influence of Taylor see B.B. Taylor's speech in *Globe,* 28 April 1842, and David Hubbard of Alabama in *Cong. Gl.,* 26 i App., 591.

[15] On Leggett, see Richard Hofstadter, 'William Leggett, Spokesman of Jacksonian Democracy', *P.S.Q.,* X (Dec. 1943), 581-94; Marvin Meyers, *The Jacksonian Persuasion: Politics and Belief* (Stanford, 1957), 141-56; Stanley N. Worton, 'William Leggett, Political Journalist: A Study in Democratic Thought' (Ph.D. thesis, Columbia, 1954). Worton gives a full presentation, if not a full analysis, of Leggett's ideas and the subject matter treated here is drawn in part from his work.

[16] Theodore Sedgwick Jr. (ed.), *A Collection of the Political Writings of William Leggett,* 2 vols. (N.Y., 1840), II, 162-3, 165.

one. On one occasion expelled from the party, he was later reinstated and even received a federal office from President Van Buren. Prominent Democrats like Churchill C. Cambreleng wrote for the *Evening Post* and it was once suggested by Gideon Welles of Connecticut that Leggett should become editor of the Washington *Globe*. Although he never joined the Locofoco party, he nevertheless helped to inspire it and after his death, at an early age in 1839, was virtually canonised by the party regulars.[17]

Leggett drove the principle of limited government and the philosophy of equal rights to their furthest reaches. At one time or another he opposed proposals for free public ferries, projects for asylums for the insane and schemes for pensions to former soldiers. He refused to recognise the need for governmental interference with the exchange rate of gold to silver, for regulation and inspection of merchandise and even for a governmental postal service. His argument in most cases was the same: trust to the 'natural' laws since human legislation almost inevitably violates the principle of equal rights. Yet because of his doctrinal inflexibility and his eagerness to apply Democratic formulations almost universally, Leggett was forced to confront certain key issues.[18]

One of these lurked behind the relatively minor question of copyright. Was a law enforcing copyright a restriction of the equal rights of the people? At first Leggett decided that it was. Like a mechanic's product, he argued, in a telling comparison, a writer's idea or expression could be imitated. Moreover, many individuals might have had a particular thought; the personal characteristics of mental labour could not be conclusively demonstrated. In this light copyright laws were uncomfortably redolent of a monopoly. Leggett at first came down, in the early months of 1837, against them. Within a few months, however, he had changed his mind. A journalist and a poet himself, Leggett had realised that to dispense with copyright would be to stultify the growth of literature and the arts in the nation. It would, moreover, be a clear violation of natural justice; the mental labour of what might have been weeks, months, years or even a lifetime might go unrewarded. Leggett confessed himself uncertain on the issue.[19]

Although in itself a small issue, the copyright question nevertheless illuminates some of the vague and murky areas of the Democratic world view. Leggett's problem was to apply the agrarian conceptions

[17] Worton, 'Leggett', 33, 51, 26, 80; Schlesinger, *Age of Jackson,* 260.
[18] Worton, 'Leggett', 180, 146.
[19] *Ibid.,* 133.

of labour and of a fair reward for that labour to an occupation where they were at best irrelevant. Democratic social philosophy assumed a recognisable product of labour or at least an identifiable service. It assumed, moreover, a direct, or at any rate, a clear relationship between labour and reward. What guarantee was there that this could be obtained when the product was a thought or an idea? Without a copyright law the reward would probably be too low; with one it might well be too high. Democratic theory required that the laws of supply and demand, themselves resting upon and expressing the natural similarity of man with man, preserve the high degree of social equality that was desired. Specialised skills and talents could be accommodated only awkwardly if at all.

The rigour with which Leggett tried to apply the Democratic analysis might here have impelled him to question his fundamental premises. In addition, and almost simultaneously, an episode occurred in New York City which might well have had the same effect. During a bread shortage a group of merchants in the city combined in an effort to raise prices and in so doing, of course, maximise profits. Leggett's first response was to recur to the natural laws; it was impossible, he asserted, for the merchants to maintain prices at an artifically high level. And in the absence of governmental intervention then, according to Democratic theory, this was true. The merchants after all were merely pursuing their self-interest, as Democratic doctrines invited them to do. In the meantime, however, and whilst the natural laws were correcting themselves, people might die of hunger and starvation. Leggett soon realised this and again he reversed himself. If a commodity of undoubted necessity were being withheld, it was fair and just, he now affirmed, for the government to step in and seize it, offering, of course, just compensation to the transgressors.[20]

It was an ironic and peculiar argument for a man who had spent a career delivering warnings about the insidious encroachments of an over-active government. The Democratic matrix of ideas on power, liberty and equality left no room for such positive governmental activities. Nor was this, in reality, so ideologically insignificant an episode as it might have appeared. For once again it laid bare the Democratic assumption that the natural equality among men, when harnessed to the unchanging laws of supply and demand, would create the good society.[21] In this instance, the laws had failed and the natural equality, whether it existed or not, was irrelevant.

[20]*Ibid.*, 293-5.

[21] Similarly, Leggett believed that general incorporation laws, because they would facilitate the operation of 'natural' market forces, would result in the creation of fewer rather than more corporations.

Nevertheless, Leggett's radical stance endeared him to that large section of the Democratic party which shared his commitment to equal rights and applauded his insistent references to the artificial inequalities in American society. Outside the Democratic party too he became a symbol of radicalism. Thus the National Reform Association, although concerned to dissociate itself from the Democracy, honoured his memory and praised his courage. This was not fortuitous. For radicals in Jacksonian America were irresistibly attracted to the Democratic analysis, even as they sought to dispense with the Democratic party.

The National Reform Association in fact presents so clear an illustration of this that it would be only a slight exaggeration to call it 'neo-Jacksonian'. The history of the movement offers significant clues not merely to the character of the Democratic party and its connection with the radical movements of the day, but also to the nature of the party's ideology and the flaws within it. In essence the Reformers perceived a fundamental weakness but ended by retaining far more than they rejected. In so doing they testified to the hegemony of the Democratic world view.

The National Reform Association was set up in 1844 in New York City by George Henry Evans, a veteran of the Workingmen's parties.[22] Throughout its five year history the Association urged a reform of the existing state of society, asking urban workers whether they wished to 'free your country, and the sons of toil everywhere, from the heartless and irresponsible aristocracy of avarice?' The Reformers, in common with other radicals, drew attention to the plight of a large section of the city's population, emphasising the extent of vice and suffering that was attributable to deprivation and social injustice. The *Working Man's Advocate*, official organ of the Association, reminded its readers of 'the haggard, care-worn countenance of the daily laborer, the wasting form of the over tasked seamstress, their contracted and wretched apartments' and 'the squalid children trained to beggary and deceit'.[23]

How then was this poverty and misery to be explained? The Reformers here took a significant step away from orthodox Democratic theory. It was, they argued, primarily attributable to the surplus of labourers (which they estimated to be at one third in every branch of industry) consequent on mechanisation. And the success and

---

[22] On the Reformers see Schlesinger, *Age of Jackson,* 347-8; Helene S. Zahler, *Eastern Workingmen and National Land Policy, 1829-1862* (N.Y., 1941), 19-75; Geis, 'Liberty, Equality, Fraternity', 69-81.

[23] *W.M.A.,* 15 March 1845; 18 May 1844.

ultimate triumph of machine labour, they warned, were inevitable: 'as well might we interfere with the career of the heavenly bodies, or attempt to alter any of nature's fixed laws, as hope to arrest the onward march of science'. The resulting surplus of workers meant unemployment for some and humiliating terms and conditions for others. At present the labourer was 'debased in proportion to his usefulness'; the task was to elevate him 'to his proper rank in society'.[24]

The recognition that mechanisation might threaten the community unless remedial action was taken, marked a significant shift in radical thought. Yet as they devised a remedy – and it was one which involved an equally significant increase in the scope of governmental activity – the Reformers clung to the hallowed Democratic vision of both society and government. For they demanded the opening up of Western lands to actual settlers, with the lands to be given free, to be exempt from suits of debt, and to be inalienable (except to those without land). Evans based his programme upon a theory of a natural right to land and the Association suggested how the holdings might be arranged so as to form small communities. Nowhere is the agrarian character of American radicalism more clearly displayed. According to the Reformers' blueprint, each village or community would comprise 160 farms, each of 160 acres, together with forty smaller allotments of perhaps five acres for those individuals pursuing other occupations. Here was a means of combating the dangerous inequalities of wealth which already scarred American society. For, as the *Advocate* explained, 'in proportion to the inequality of landed possessions among every people, just in the same proportion has there been inequality of condition'. There was 'no truth more clearly developed by history than this'.[25]

By offering free land in the West, the Reformers expected to tempt large numbers of workers to migrate and thus relieve the economic pressure upon those who remained. At one stroke they would have corrected the imbalance in society and cleared the way for the now undisturbed operation of the beneficent natural laws. A healthy relationship between wealth and personal labour would be restored; wealth would now 'consist of the accumulated products of human labor'. It would be 'a changed social element'. Similarly 'the antagonism of capital and labor' would 'forever cease'. And machinery? 'From the formidable rival' it would 'sink into the obedient instrument of our will.' When the Reformers' programme was adopted, in short, the world would drop back upon its axis. This was the prospect which the

[24]*Ibid.*, 13, 30 March 1844.
[25]*Ibid.*, 16 March, 6 April 1844.

Association held out to the workingmen of New York City. The pamphlet which they distributed was entitled simply 'Vote Yourself a Farm'.[26]

Again and again the Reformers insisted that land reform was the key issue and that progress could not be made without the introduction of what they called the 'agrarian' scheme. Apart from this plan, however, and the insight from which it sprang into the role and significance of technological development, the Reformers still embraced Democratic theory. Democratic analysis and Democratic programmes. They favoured free trade and limited government. The second evil, after land monopoly, they affirmed, was the curse of paper money. Although the *Advocate* once concluded that both parties were the same since both condoned the sale of land, the newspaper nevertheless heaped praise on Jefferson and referred to 'the great and good JACKSON'. When faced with the choice between Polk and Clay in the 1844 Presidential election, the editors refused to commit themselves. But their candidate, they declared, had to be against the assumption of state debts by the Federal government, opposed to the establishment of any national bank, and committed against the distribution of land revenues. Since Clay favoured all three measures while Polk opposed them all, the discerning reader who was seeking advice was left in little doubt as to how to cast his vote. Here as elsewhere, it was because of the fundamental ideological similarity between National Reformers and Democrats that the Reformers' attempts to declare their neutrality and independence were not wholly successful.[27]

The Reformers might perceive a fundamental obstacle in the way of a successful implementation of the radical Democratic programme; William Leggett could encounter situations in which that programme was clearly inadequate. Neither, however, significantly questioned the basic Democratic assumptions. The programme was in the one case to be supplemented by a scheme of land reform and in the other to be actually extended into new areas. In both cases the trust in the harmony of the natural order remained essentially unimpaired. It fell to another radical, closely associated with the Democratic party but, as it would finally be seen, sufficiently detached from its ideology, to deliver the most direct and fundamental challenge. This radical was Orestes Brownson.

[26]*Ibid.*, 15 March 1845, 30 March 1844.

[27]*Ibid.*, 16 March, , 18 May, 27 April, 30 March, 8 May, 1844. The Reformers fully shared the atomistic outlook of the Democrats. One contributor, whose words were endorsed by the editors, took issue with the Fourierites precisely because they sought a collectivist society. See *ibid.*, 20 April 1844.

A study of Brownson's thought and career is virtually indispensable to an understanding of Democratic ideology. Closely associated with the Workingmen's party in Boston in the twenties and later converted into an enthusiastic and at first fairly orthodox Democratic partisan, Brownson followed a familiar path. But his career as a radical both culminated and terminated in the publication in July 1840 of his famous article, 'The Laboring Classes', in which he advocated the elimination of inheritance (as well as the abolition of the priesthood). But with the Log Cabin campaign of 1840 and the overthrow of the Democratic party he felt compelled to re-examine his political assumptions. In so doing he delivered what was perhaps the strongest attack upon the American democratic tradition, the tradition of Jefferson, Jackson and John Taylor, that was ever written in the ante-bellum period. Brownson's arguments went unanswered.[28]

But at the time of Van Buren's entry into the White House Brownson was an orthodox radical. 'If we have realised political equality', he told the readers of his *Boston Quarterly Review,* 'we have not yet realised social equality'. The warning came in 1838. Somewhat more than a year later Brownson repeated it. He was not, he avowed, 'satisfied with the inequality in wealth, intelligence and social position' which he saw 'even in this land of equal rights'. In common with other radicals and indeed with those in the mainstream of the Democratic party, Brownson was alert to the danger of aristocracy. This meant 'an aristocracy of wealth', 'the only aristocracy which can amount to any thing in this country'. No-one was more insistent than Brownson that an inescapable fact of American life was the perpetual struggle between the rich and the poor. According to the Whigs, rich and poor were necessary to each other; Brownson concurred and introduced an analogy with the lamb and the wolf – two

[28] On Brownson see Joseph P. Farry, 'Themes of Continuity and Change in the Political Philosophy of Orestes Brownson: A Comparative Study' (Ph.D. thesis, Fordham University, 1968); Nancy C. Hovarter, 'The Social and Political Views of Orestes Augustus Brownson' (Ph.D. thesis, Ball State University, Indiana, 1974); Americo D. Lapati, *Orestes A. Brownson* (N.Y., 1963); Hugh Marshall, *Orestes Brownson and the American Republic* (Washington, D.C., 1971); Theodore Maynard, *Orestes Brownson, Yankee, Radical, Catholic* (N.Y., 1971); Helen S. Mims, 'Early American Democratic Theory and Orestes Brownson', *S.S.,* III (Spring, 1938). 166-98; Robert E. Moffit, 'Metaphysics and Constitutionalism: The Political Theory of Orestes Brownson' (Ph.D. thesis, University of Arizona, 1975); Stanley J. Parry, 'The Premises of Brownson's Political Theory', *R.P.,* XVI (April 1954), 194-211; Lawrence D. Roemer, *Brownson on Democracy and the Trend Towards Socialism* (N.Y., 1953); Thomas R. Ryan, *The Sailor's Snug Harbor, Studies in Brownson's Thought* (Westminister, My., 1953); Arthur M. Schlesinger, Jr., *Orestes A. Brownson, A Pilgrim's Progress* (N.Y., 1963); Doran Whalen, *Granite for God's House: The Life of Orestes Augustus Brownson* (N.Y., 1941).

species which were also necessary to one another. The analogy exemplified the radical mood.[29]

Nevertheless Brownson was as yet optimistic. He was struggling, he announced, 'for a greater degree of equality', and believed that 'it will one day be attained'. What kind of society did he hope to see? Brownson painted a familiar picture. It was the agrarian society of independent, co-equal citizens. He sought a society in which 'all men will be independent proprietors, working on their own capitals, on their own farms, or in their own shops' and was convinced that it would become a reality. 'Business men', he wrote in 1838, 'have had their golden age'; a new age was about to dawn. It would be ushered in by the Democratic party.[30]

For Brownson was now earnestly committed to the Democratic party. In any remotely free country, he asserted, a war was constantly raging between the forces of equality and privilege. It was raging at present in the United States, he wrote in 1839, 'with more fierceness' than at any other time in the nation's history. The Democratic party was now struggling to dethrone the 'Money King'. The events of 1776 and 1800 marked partial successes but a complete triumph had been prevented by the demands of the War of 1812. The party, he wrote in 1839, had needed to fall back on first principles and 'it *has* fallen back on first principles; it has revived the old party lines and brought on virtually the same controversy as that of '98'. Brownson was referring in particular to the adoption of the Independent Treasury scheme with all that it signified. An Independent Treasury or a National Bank? The question was 'one of magnitude, of immense bearings; altogether more so than that which induced our fathers to take up arms against the mother country'. In the United States 'we are in the midst of a revolution which must overthrow the Money King, and inaugurate Humanity'.[31]

Hence Brownson endorsed Democratic policies and eagerly followed the progress of the Democratic assault upon privilege. But his great strength as a writer and commentator lay in his refusal to allow belief to harden into dogma. His mind remained open to the possibility that his ideas might need re-examination and revision. As the 1830s became the 1840s, he began to wonder whether the

---

[29]*Bo. Q. R.,* I (Oct. 1838), 462, III (Jan. 1840), 15, III (April 1840), 212; *Boston Weekly Reformer,* 4 Aug. 1837.

[30]*Bo. Q. R.,* III (Jan. 1840), 16, I (April 1838), 227.

[31]*Bo. Q. R.,* II (Jan. 1839), 123-5, I (April 1838), 227, II (Jan. 1839), 127-31. For Brownson's support for Democratic policy at this time see *ibid.* II (Jan. 1840), 17, 104,

Democratic programme was, after all, capable of creating the society which both he and his fellow radicals within the party desired. The publication of 'The Laboring Classes' in July 1840 with its sequel in October 1840 announced his discovery that it could not.[32]

If Brownson's demand for the abolition of hereditary property was heretical,[33] the social analysis upon which it was based was not. Again the starting point was the artificial inequality in American society. 'There is nothing', he reminded the public, 'in the actual difference of individuals, which accounts for the striking inequalities we discover in their condition.' Indeed, so great was the injustice in society that 'as a general rule, with but few exceptions. . .men are rewarded in an inverse ratio to the amount of actual service they perform.' The problem was essentially that of privilege. The first task was to end the privileges of banks by divorcing the government from them. Next all monopolies had to be destroyed. Finally, the 'greatest of all privileges', that 'of being born rich while others are born poor' had to be removed. This could only be done by abolishing hereditary property.[34]

Like the National Reformers Brownson had reached the conclusion that social evils could not be cured simply by a restoration of the natural order that Democratic theory postulated. Free trade and equal rights were, he acknowledged, excellent principles but they were insufficient if only because 'the competition must start even and with nearly equal chances of success'. It was the conditions in urban America which caused Brownson most concern. Wishing to 'combine labor and capital in the same individual', he claimed that 'to a considerable extent' agriculture did this. Yet even here the situation was deteriorating with the employment of hired hands becoming increasingly common. Hence 'the distance between the owner of the farm, and the men who cultivate it' was 'becoming every day greater and greater'. In the towns and manufacturing villages, however, the problems were far greater. Here 'the distinction between the capitalist and the proletary' was 'as strongly marked as it is in the old world'. Brownson thus focused attention upon the wage system. Here was the ultimate threat to individual autonomy. Wages were 'the cunning device of the devil' and the wage system had to be eliminated 'or else one half of the human race must forever be the virtual slaves of the other'. By abolishing all privileges, including that of inheriting wealth, Brownson hoped to create a truly egalitarian society. No less radical

---

[32] The two articles entitled 'The Laboring Classes' appeared in *ibid.* III (July 1840), 359-93, III (Oct. 1840), 420-510.

[33] The idea had in fact been advanced by Thomas Skidmore in the United States.

[34] *Bo. Q. R.,* III (July 1840), 377, 392-3.

measure, he affirmed, whether it relied upon education or upon the Western lands (which would eventually be exhausted) could accomplish the desired ends.[35]

'Abhorrent doctrines in regard to the rights of property' – the *Globe* reacted strongly to Brownson's articles. The scheme which they proposed was never, of course, adopted by the party; it did not even receive serious consideration. Democrats could not countenance the idea not only because it was so far-reaching as to be virtually revolutionary but because it ran counter to some of their most cherished beliefs. Essentially it denied the natural order as Democrats understood it. As a corollary, it required a tremendous increase in governmental power for which there could be no place in the Democratic world view. Brownson himself never really confronted this problem. His fellow radicals not unnaturally clung to the traditional beliefs.[36]

Yet for all its novelty the abolition of hereditary property was a scheme designed to create a Democratic society. It was the means rather than the ends that were distasteful and unacceptable. 'These doctrines', Brownson insisted at the time of writing, 'are the simple logical results of the acknowledged principles of the democratic party.' A year later, when he had reconsidered and retracted the idea, he remained convinced that 'the equality which many of our democrats are contending for, can be effected by no measure less searching and radical'. Still later (in 1857), when he had utterly renounced all radicalism and no longer professed any faith in democracy as a system of government, he wrote that 'a democratic government that leaves all the social inequalities, or inequalities of condition, which obtain in all countries, always struck me as an absurdity'. He added that he had 'seen no reason to change my opinions on that point'. The abolition of hereditary property, he still believed, was square in the logic of Democracy.[37]

It was designed too to perpetuate the agrarian society that was so vital a concern to radical Democrats. Again looking back upon the famous articles of 1840, Brownson recalled that his plan had been to unite labour and capital:

> Undoubtedly my plan would have broken up the whole modern

[34]*Ibid.* III (Oct 1840), 475, 467-71, III (July 1840), 370, 374.

[36]*Globe.,* 18 Jan. 1841.

[37]*Bo. Q. R.,* III (Oct. 1840), 508, IV (July 1841), 390-1; Brownson, 'The Convert', in Henry F. Brownson (ed.), *The Works of Orestes A. Brownson,* 20 vols. (Detroit, 1882-7), V, 113.

commercial system, prostrated all the great industries, or what I called the factory system, and thrown the mass of the people back on the land to get their living by agricultural and mechanical pursuits. I knew this well enough, but this was one of the results I aimed at.

At the time of writing, Brownson avowed that he sought also to check the acquisitive spirit that was rampant within American society. These were standard Democratic goals. *The Globe* was highly vexed by the schemes; Brownson had run 'all the Democractic doctrines to extremes', it lamented, employing a significant phrase. But other Democrats were less severe. Brownson was still in the October of 1840 'such a powerful champion of Democracy' in the eyes of the *Franklin* (Alabama) *Democrat*, while the *New Hampshire Patriot*, probably the leading Democratic press in New England, believed that 'People must admire Mr. Brownson for his bold original thought and the fearless expression of his views'. William Cullen Bryant, meanwhile, in the New York *Evening Post* praised him for telling 'some home truths' and reserved his censure for those who over-reacted to the articles. Such freedom of enquiry could only be beneficial.[38]

The articles of 1840 thus offer a clue to the kind of society that Brownson and many other Democrats were struggling for. But they also denoted a decisive break with the intellectual tradition to which Democrats were heir. Brownson had perceived a fundamental disorder in the so-called natural order; the experiences of 1840 would enable him to exploit this insight to the full.

The social and political philosophy of American democracy rested, of course, upon a frank recognition of the force of individual self-interest. Self-interest was the motive for labour and labour, in the absence of governmental activity, almost inevitably brought a fair and just reward. It was thus in the interest of those who desired only to live off their own labour to preserve a limited, inactive government; democratic institutions were the only security for such a government. But there were also a powerful few, similarly motivated by self-interest, who constantly sought to enhance their superiority by seizing control of the government. They therefore constituted an ever-present danger. Democrats looked to democratic institutions to check the inegalitarian tendencies, whether natural or artificial, that were at work within society and to ensure that they received no impetus from government. American democracy attempted to balance the self-interest of

---

[38] 'The Convert', *Works of Brownson*, V, 117; *Bo. Q. R.*, (Oct. 1840), 500; *Globe*, 14 Sept. 1843; *Franklin Democrat*, 9 Oct. 1840; *N.H.P.*, 26 Feb. 1841; *Evening Post* in *Nat. Int*, 11 Aug. 1841.

individuals in order to create or perpetuate the good society. John Taylor, its greatest theorist, gave a clear statement of this view in his 'Inquiry into the Principles and Policy of the Government of the United States':

> It was reserved for the United States to discover that by balancing man with man, and by avoiding the artificial combinations of exclusive privileges, no individual of these equipoised millions would be incited by a probability of success, to assail the rest; and that thus the concussions of powerful combinations, and the subversion of liberty and happiness, following a victory on the part of the one, would be avoided.[39]

The Democrats of the Jacksonian era added little to this except perhaps a dynamic element. As democracy advanced so society would become more just and egalitarian.[40] Self-interest, however, would remain as the motive force, allowing the triumph of the majority (whose interest could not be to exploit the minority). This process implied, of course, electoral success for the Democratic party. The election of 1840 checked the process in the most obvious manner.

The great defeat of 1840 both shocked and dismayed the Democratic party. But for most the Democratic faith did not perish. The result came to be seen as an aberration and the popular verdict, it was hoped, would soon be reversed. Only Brownson went beyond the event itself. In the course of his investigations he shattered the Democratic world-view.

Brownson too was dismayed at the result of the election; he too was disgusted by the Whig tactics. But he went on to dissect the Democratic ideology, to expose and challenge its hidden assumptions. 'It was supposed', he wrote, four years after the election, that 'universal suffrage, by admitting the many into the State, would secure a sufficient counterpoise to the wealthy and influential few'. 'But', he added, 'we see now that it does not.' The Democracy's 'overwhelming defeat' had proved 'incontestably' that 'men before property, are as the chaff of the summer threshing-floor before the wind'. 'Free suffrage', he declared, in a sentence which threw the Jacksonian ideological universe into disarray, 'has done very little with us to protect labor against the usurpations of capital'. From this new vantage point, Brownson obtained an entirely different perspective upon the past. Fifty years of struggle by the Democratic party now suddenly seemed

[39] John Taylor, *An Inquiry into the Principles and Policy of the Government of the United States* (London, 1950), 373.

[40] See, for example, *Dem. Exp.*, 20 Sept. 1845.

to prove his point. Property was now, he noted, more unequally divided than at any other era. In a contest like that of 1840 when there was a clear struggle between men and money, money would always triumph. It was a startling conclusion.[41]

Why was the triumph so certain? Brownson now addressed himself to this key problem. The first and in a sense the most obvious answer was that men were naturally unequal. They were different in their physical and intellectual prowess, different in character and personality and different in appearance. Hence the 'perpetual tendency' of 'man's natural inequality' was to 'gross social inequality'. Democracy demanded 'that man always and everywhere, and in all respects, be the exact counterpoise of man'. But men were 'by no means equal' and 'man is never the exact counterpoise of man'. This alone, Brownson believed, 'refuted the pretensions of democracy'.[42]

But Brownson was not content merely to assert the inequality of man. Instead he tried to demonstrate that it was in the motive of self-interest that men were fatally unequal. Once this was recognised, he argued, then existing social evils and inequalities were easily accounted for. In an article for *Brownson's Quarterly Review* for January 1844 he brilliantly exposed what he now believed to be the great fallacy at the heart of Democratic philosophy. He began by restating its assumptions:

> Leave, then free scope to the selfishness of all, and the selfishness of each will neutralize the selfishness of each, and we shall have for the result – Eternal Justice, wise and equitable government, shedding its blessings like the dews of heaven, upon all, without distinction of rank or condition! Assuming the absolute equality of all, and that in all cases the selfishness of one will exactly balance the selfishness of another, the result will be zero, that is to say, absolutely nothing.

If this assumption were wrong, however, the entire philosophy must collapse:

> But, assuming the inequality of the social elements, and that the selfishness of one is not, in all cases, the exact measure of the selfishness of another, then they in whom selfishness predominates will gain the preponderance, and, having the power, must, being governed only by selfishness, wield the government for their own private ends. And this is precisely what has happened, and which

---

[41]*Br. Q. R.,* I (April 1844), 238, 235, 233, 236; *Dem. Rev.,* XII (May 1843), 531.
[42]*Bo. Q. R.,* IV (Jan., 1841), 84-5; *Br. Q. R.,* I (April 1844), 229. See also *Dem. Rev.,* XIII (Aug. 1843), 132.

a little reflection might have enabled anyone to have foretold. The attempt to obtain a wise and equitable government by means of universal competition, then, must always fail.

The root mistake, Brownson warned, lay 'in the attempt, with a mere negative quantity, to obtain a positive, out of selfishness to bring forth virtue'.[43]

Because men were unequal, and in particular, unequal in their 'selfishness', the theory of democracy was hopelessly inadequate and a limited, democratic government could not create or maintain the good society. Where orthodox Democrats looked to democracy to curb the inegalitarian forces at work within society, Brownson insisted that it could only reinforce them. Those individuals, groups or classes whose self-interest was, for whatever reason, strongest or who could, by accident or design, pursue it more avidly, would triumph. The lesson of 1840 was that these groups had always managed to secure control of the government when their power was threatened. Brownson argued that this was inevitable in a democracy where 'diversities of interest' existed:

> The stronger interest by whatever means it is the stronger, whether by numbers, wealth, position, talent, learning, intrigue, fraud, deception, corruption, always possesses itself of the government and taxes all the other interests for its own especial benefit. . . . The democratic theory now under consideration requires for its success a community, in which all the citizens have in all respects one and the same interest, and are all substantially equal in position, wealth and influence. Whether such equality and such identity of interests be or be not attainable, be or be not desirable, neither one nor the other is attained here.

Men and groups were unequal in social power and influence and this inequality would find expression in government, and in a democratic government as much as in any other. Moreover, society, as it became commercialised, would encourage the passion for wealth; government would respond to this and would 'labor especially to promote worldly interests'. Thus instead of an agrarian society in which wealth was obtained slowly and painstakingly by honest industry, an immoral thirst for gain would become increasingly rife. This would enhance the natural inequalities within society (since wealth obtained without labour was at the expense of others) and thus refuel the entire vicious system. A democratic form of government would consequently operate to stimulate the acquisitive, exploitative and inegalitarian

[43]*Br. Q. R.*, I (Jan. 1844), 88-9, 93.

tendencies that it was in fact supposed to check and reverse. Hence 'democracy has a direct tendency to favor inequality and injustice'.[44]

Having undermined the foundation of Democratic theory, Brownson was now able to examine the superstructure. He asked orthodox Democrats how it was that the supposedly wise, virtuous and intelligent people in whom Democracy placed such great faith had ever come to submit to this 'universal misrule and oppression'. To attribute all evils to government, as the Jacksonians often did, was surely to ignore the vice, ignorance and indolence of the people. These were its cause as much as its effect. Hence more democracy 'could only aggravate the disease'; it could not be a cure. Instead what was wanted was a check upon the power of the majority. The people must be prevented from injuring themselves.[45]

Although Brownson had by the mid-forties rejected Democratic theory, he remained as firmly opposed to the Whig party as he had ever been. 'We see personified in the Whig candidates', he wrote, prior to the Presidential election of 1844, 'modern Feudalism, political profligacy, and canting religious bigotry.' They represented 'much the larger portion of the wealth of the community' and spoke for an industrial order which threatened to doom a large section of the populace to ever-increasing misery. Although the Democrats sought to combat these trends, the fatally flawed theory which they embraced vitiated their efforts. What then was to be done? Brownson turned to the power of religion and pinned his faith in moral suasion. 'I wish to see', he told his readers, 'a greater degree of social equality, few factitious distinctions, and a more equitable distribution of the products of labor.' But, he added, 'I hope to effect it, and will effect it, through the aid of the more influential classes themselves.' Religion and moral reform were the only solutions. Wealth must be equalised 'by raising the soul above the love of it'; the poor must be taught 'to count the wealth of this world as mere dross, or dust in the balance'. An appeal to the self-interest of the masses would exacerbate the evils of society, not rectify them. An outside force was required; this could only come from God. And the church was the voice of God upon earth.[46]

---

[44]*Bo.Q.R.,* V (Jan. 1842), 34-5; *Br.Q.R.,* (Oct. 1845), 522.

[45]*Bo.Q.R.,* IV (Oct. 1841), 517, V (Jan. 1842), 37.

[46]*Br.Q.R.,* I (July 1844), 401; *Bo.Q.R.,* V (Jan. 1842), 53; *Br.Q.R.,* I (Jan. 1844), 25. For more criticism of the Whigs see *Bo.Q.R.,* V (Jan. 1842), 92, IV (July 1841), 389.

Brownson had now put together, in a most unusual mixture, a set of ideas taken from radical Democracy and the most reactionary neo-Federalism. His diagnosis of social ills was clearly that of a radical; his desire for more social equality was also close to that of a radical. But his disenchantment with majoritarian democracy was that of an arch-reactionary.[47] Like many conservatives, Brownson saw in the Federal constitution a barrier against popular influence; he came to regard it as almost sacred evidence of the hand of God active in affairs. Hence 'no authority but that of God can absolve a man from his obligation to obey the existing order'. A man must 'show that he has that authority or be convicted of the Satanic spirit'. Democracy could not avert the impending social crisis. The only solution was to foster a humanitarian spirit of brotherly love and concern within society. It was a sign of how far he had moved from the line of Democratic orthodoxy when in 1844 Brownson repudiated virtually the entire tradition of individualism that Americans had inherited from both the Reformation and the Revolution of 1776:

> We are the children of revolution in the State and of dissent in religion. We see nothing sacred in government, we feel nothing binding in ecclesiastical establishments. Our youth are early imbued with a sense of the supremacy of the individual; and those of us, who think seriously at all, grow up with the conviction that our own judgement is in all cases to be our rule of action.

What was needed, he insisted, was instead a religion *over* the people, a religion to control and direct society. By 1844 Brownson had become a Roman Catholic.[48]

Brownson had repudiated Democratic theory; in so doing he had given the most vivid illustration of its power and influence. So complete was the dominance of the Democratic ethic, so basic was it a part of the ideological environment that it was virtually impossible for a radical to reject it and yet seek political action as a remedy for social evils. The categories of thought which it offered virtually monopolised the political radicalism of the age. When Brownson rejected them he was compelled to place himself so far outside the mainstream of American politics as to be almost incomprehensible.

---

[47] In fact Brownson had always been concerned about the theoretical dangers of majoritarianism; 1840 brought home the practical dangers and compelled a re-examination of the theory. See *Dem. Rev.*, XII (May 1843), 531; *Bo. Q. R.*, I (Jan. 1838), 39.

[48] *Bo. Q. R.*, I (July 1844), 376, 379, II (Oct. 1845), 519.

Orthodox radicals could only listen in bewilderment and rage as he passed from a denunciation of contemporary social evils to a rejection of majoritarian democracy to a theory of church and state which seemed astonishingly akin to the Divine Right ideal of the eighteenth century and earlier.[49] Brownson had long been preoccupied with theological controversy; he had been successively a Calvinist, a Universalist, a Unitarian and a Sceptic. But he returned to the Christian faith, and was converted to Roman Catholicism essentially because he had lost the great democratic faith of the era that was in a sense a major competing creed. By 1857, when he wrote 'The Convert', he had been in the Catholic church for more than a decade; the ideas of 1840 were now 'abhorrent doctrines' to him. But he explained that they were the only alternatives to the beliefs which he now held:

> Place me where I stood then; place me outside of the Catholic Church, and make me regard that church as exclusive, as a spiritual tyranny, as all my Protestant countrymen maintain she is, and give me faith only in progress by the natural forces of man, and I would today repeat and endorse every paragraph and every word I then wrote.

The church had been for him, he recognised, his only refuge after he had learnt the lesson of 1840. It had been the 'last Plank of safety'. Brownson had seen the implications and examined the assumptions of Democratic theory. But the manner in which he rejected that theory, and the ideological position to which he was driven are testimony to its commanding position in the intellectual topography of Jacksonian America. The Democratic creed was not merely a set of ideas invoked to give a rationale to the activities of the Democratic party; it was by the 1840s an integral part of the nation's political culture. It was a filter through which large numbers of Americans could not help but see the world.[50]

Convinced that one man was socially and politically more or less the equivalent of another, and that a system rooted in self-interest could express this equivalence, radicals both inside and out of the Democratic party pressed for the programme of Andrew Jackson and

---

[49] See the fascinating debate between Brownson and John L. O'Sullivan which ran through the *Democratic Review* while Brownson was a contributor. O'Sullivan represented the orthodox Democratic viewpoint. He brilliantly satirised Brownson's new conservatism but was unable to meet, perhaps even fully to comprehend, Brownson's equally brilliant attacks on his own position – see *Dem. Rev.*, vols. XII and XIII, especially XIII (Dec. 1843), 656-60.

[50] 'The Convert', *Works of Brownson*, V, 104; Henry F. Brownson, *Brownson's Early Life from 1803 to 1844* (Detroit, 1898), 448-9; 'The Convert', *Works of Brownson*, V, 166.

Martin Van Buren. They might qualify or extend it, modify or adapt it, criticise or condemn Democratic party leaders, but they remained wedded to the fundamental assumptions of Democratic theory. The example of Orestes Brownson suggests that it was difficult to repudiate them and still remain a radical.

Brownson's critique of the Democratic theory was of major significance. Modern critics have chided the Democrats for the shallowness of their commitment to equality.[51] Brownson far more plausibly chided them for their excessive faith in the intensely egalitarian philosophy they had themselves constructed. Can a system of political democracy, he asked, rooted in political equality, rectify the inequalities in society or must it merely reflect them?[52] Democratic radicals assumed the former; Brownson insisted on the latter. He therefore launched a debate which has lasted for over a century – and which remains unresolved.[53]

'Aristocrats'

Although Orestes Brownson turned away from the radicalism of his earlier years, his career as a radical had struck fear and alarm into the hearts of many of his contemporaries who were of a conservative or even reactionary disposition. Such men had responded with horror rather than surprise to Brownson's famous articles of 1840. They found in them a confirmation of their fears for the safety of the Republic and derived only a melancholy satisfaction from the unfolding of events in the pattern they had predicted. Their mood was often one of pessimism approaching despair. Like the radicals to whom they were so implacably opposed, conservatives and reactionaries within and outside the Whig party were convinced that a crisis was at hand. This conviction was also to find a fevered expression in the politics of Jacksonian American.

Conservative Whig utterances should be seen as an essentially rational reaction to the events, activities and proposals of the Jacksonian era. The election of Jackson in 1828 ushered in an era which saw new reforms, new attitudes and new ideological configurations; that some men should have been profoundly shocked

[51] A recent example of such criticism is Rush Welter, *The Mind of America, 1820–1860* (N.Y., 1975), 84.

[52] See *Br. Q. R.,* I (Jan. 1844), 24.

[53] This dispute is at the core of the disagreement on the European left between revolutionary groups and parliamentary reformers.

by them is both understandable and natural. Under the weight of Jackson's pressure, Congress had yielded power to the President; the example of Jackson himself, a man far removed from the traditional ideal of the republican statesman, offered a glimpse of the dubious uses to which that power might be put. For Jackson had forged a new link between President and people. Backed by his army of dedicated partisans, the military chieftain had, it seemed, successfully challenged, and usurped power from, the other branches of government. In the interests of the majority for whom he claimed the exclusive right to speak, he had declared war upon the central banking system, in the process absurdly dubbing its supporters 'aristocrats'. The authority of the Federal government to plan and order the growth of the economy had been challenged; the electorate had, it seemed, sustained the challenge. An excess of democracy, of party spoilsmen, of populistic slogans and of innovating zeal and at the same time a deficiency of true statesmanship, of disinterested leadership and of respect for the time-honoured traditions of the past – this, conservatives lamented, was the legacy of Andrew Jackson's years in the White House.

Events under his successors did little to dispel the gloom. When a Whig finally succeeded in winning a Presidential election the triumph proved short-lived and the party only just escaped dismemberment. When conservatives looked around, they saw convulsions in every corner of the Union. In 1842 the Dorr war shook Rhode Island; conservatives perceived here a blatant attempt by the party of Jackson and Van Buren to risk the safety of the State and its citizens, to invoke the right of revolution against a government which, as all impartial observers agreed, had never acted tyrannically, and to endanger the social fabric merely out of a doctrinaire enthusiasm for equal rights and universal suffrage. In Mississippi the larger portion of the Democratic party officially advocated the repudiation of state debts, a measure which in principle threatened to undermine the entire commercial structure of the nation. In virtually every state Democrats mobilised popular opinion against banks, often trying in the process to excite a frenzied hostility towards wealth and commercial success, and frequently succeeding in penalising or even destroying the offending institutions. In Ohio a bank was sacked and looted; the national Democratic newspaper condemned the bankers, not the mob.[54] Official Democratic spokesmen vented hostility on corporate institutions, on manufacturing industry and on mercantile pursuits. Decrying the influence of wealth and even talent in government,

[54]*Globe*, 21 Jan. 1842. The Democratic *Ohio Statesman* took the same view – see 13 Jan. 1842. For a discussion of the other events alluded to in this paragraph see below, Chapter 7.

Democrats simultaneously spoke the language of class war and demanded for its victims a greater share of social and political power. As they listened, many conservatives could only react with dismay.

The succession of Martin Van Buren in 1837 and the adoption of the Independent Treasury produced analogous responses from both radical Democrats and conservative Whigs. Both groups recognised that the two events showed the direction American politics were now taking. Both recognised that Van Buren was preparing to hew a radical course. The introduction of the Independent Treasury, according to the *National Magazine and Republican Review,* displayed 'the obvious downward tendency of the entire administration to the lowest depths of radicalism'. Van Buren, in the words of the *Boston Atlas,* had emerged 'a champion of the most destructive species of ultraism'. Conservatives in the Whig party thus attached the same significance and importance to the Independent Treasury as the radical Democrats. They perceived it in the same terms. Where the radicals hailed Van Buren, the conservatives reviled him. The salvation of the Republic, according to the radicals, was according to the conservatives, its death-knell. Hence the politics of the Panic and post-Panic years were infused with a double sense of urgency. The chasm between the two opposing groups had deepened; the ideological spectrum contained within the party system had significantly widened.[55]

Whigs in the mainstream of their party were alert to the possibility of an excess or abuse of democracy and popular rule; conservative Whigs were deeply alarmed at the progress which democracy had already made. 'It is to be feared', the Whigs of Chester county, Pennsylvania declared in an official publication, 'that the same tendencies are here developed and developing, which have hurried all former republics to their ruin'. The group referred to the attempt that was being made to array the 'democracy of numbers' against 'the pretended aristocracy of wealth'. Similarily William R. Watson, significantly writing under the pseudonym of 'Hamilton', warned, in apocalyptic terms, of the great dangers to be apprehended from popular rule:

> Whenever popular commotion shall rise so high, and its towering waves dash with such wild fury, that the solid defences of public law shall give way, all our rights, public and private, civil, social, political and religious, will go down – engulfed in one ''submerging Maelstrom'' of anarchy and blood.

[55]*Rep. Rev.,* II (May 1839), 7; *Boston Atlas* in Schlesinger, *Age of Jackson,* 237.

This was of more than theoretical significance. For although the American government was the best and freest ever yet 'the elements of disorganization are everywhere active'. There was a 'wild spirit of insubordination to established authority', a spirit of 'determined disobedience to public law' within the nation. The spirit was 'everywhere so manifest and alarming' that it ought to 'awaken serious misapprehensions in the minds of all considerate and patriotic men'. Watson clearly wished to speak for the Whig party as a whole for his Address bore the title, *The Whig Party; Its Objects – Its Principles – Its Candidates – Its Duties – and Its Prospects.* If this claim was unfounded the remarks were nonetheless representative of the conservative wing. Chancellor Kent of New York was an illustrious and frank exponent of similar opinions. A committed Whig, he too (in 1837) expressed fears of 'destruction from the ascendancy of the democracy of numbers'. The problem as these men saw it was that a populistic political system was instilling false values into the people. Offering inflated estimates of the virtue and wisdom of the masses, Democratic politicians had aroused popular feeling in order to trample on the established institutions of the nation. Representative Ruel Williams of Tennessee conjured up the image of the French revolutionaries 'weltering in human gore, riding over the prostrate religion of the country and all of its hallowed institutions, yet all the time shouting hosannas to the people'. Williams asked his fellow Congressmen to 'compare the equalizing and mobocratic doctrines of the day with the doctrines just alluded to' and promised that they would be 'astonished to find how well they agree'. Some conservative Whigs were irresistibly reminded of the horrors of the French revolution and did not hesitate to deliver the necessary warnings.[56]

That many were fundamentally reactionary is clear from the stance which they sometimes took on the question of universal suffrage. Orthodox Whigs tended to regard the suffrage as a privilege rather than as a right; conservative Whigs did not even concede so much. The *New Haven Herald* argued that since nineteen-twentieths of the laws concerned property, the propertyless should not have an

[56]*Proceedings of the Whigs of Chester County, Favorable to a Distinct Organisation of the Whig Party* (n.p., n.d.), 17-18; [William R. Watson], *The Whig Party; Its Objects – Its Principles – Its Candidates – Its Duties – and Its Prospects, An Address...* by 'Hamilton' (Providence, R.I. 1844), 4; Kent in John T. Horton, *James Kent, A Study in Conservatism 1763-1847* (N.Y., 1939), 318; *Cong. Gl.,* 25 iii App., 372. For other Whig references to the French revolutionaries and their similarities with Democrats see *The Essays of Camillus* (Norfolk, 1841), 90; *Cincinnati Gazette,* 19 March 1841. For other protestations against demagoguery see Theophilus Parsons, *The Duties of Educated Men in a Republic* (Boston, 1835), 19-20; Lyman Beecher, *A Plea for Colleges* (Cincinnati, 1836), 91-2.

equal vote. 'On strict principle, therefore', it concluded, *'universal suffrage* is a violation of equal rights, and a government recognizing such suffrage is founded in injustice'. Similarly in Massachusetts, when Democratic Governor Marcus Morton declared his opposition to the poll tax, the Whig legislators did not seek to conceal their disgust at the idea of universal suffrage:

> Here is the doctrine plainly avowed, of universal suffrage, to be exercised upon the highest occasions, by every vagrant and vagabond in the State, not in a condition of absolute lunacy, no matter how idle or profligate he may be. The lowest receptacles of vice are to be ransacked by party zeal to drag from their obscurity, that they may exercise the highest right of man, creatures who have just enough humanity to be recognized as 'rational beings.'

Although universal suffrage had not yet been attained in Massachusetts, it is clear that Massachusetts Whigs were, as a group, out of sympathy with contemporary developments in other states and indeed in the nation as a whole. This was the conservative Whig standpoint.[57]

Whigs of a more liberal outlook often adopted the prefix 'Democratic' before their party's name; conservative Whigs followed the example with great reluctance, if at all. For them democracy was a system of government to be feared or opposed but not encouraged. One Whig partisan, embittered by President Tyler's break with the party, wrote a tract entitled *John, The Traitor* in which he excoriated not only the President but also the democratic principle. He fulminated against democracy 'with all its great and towering pretensions, its vague delusion, the cabalistic charm and enchantment, which it always exercises over the ignorant mass'. 'There never was', he declared, 'a word so destined to keep a rabble on the hue and cry, and always on a false scent'. The writer's Whiggery was clearly visible as he referred to Henry Clay as 'the very impersonation of the principles contended for' and as 'the manly and consistent champion of them all'.[58]

The principles 'contended for' by this anonymous Whig were essentially those in which conservative Whigs generally placed their faith. They were the principles of republicanism, funda-

---

[57]*New Haven Herald* in *Independent,* 31 May 1841; *Answer of the Whig Members of the Legislature of Massachusetts. . . to the Address of His Excellency Marcus Morton* (Boston 1840), 27-8.

[58]*John, The Traitor; or, The Force of Accident. . .* (N.Y., 1843), 11, 13.

mentally different from, and frequently opposed to, those of democracy. James Watson Webb, whose *Courier and Enquirer* consistently expounded conservative Whig thought, constantly lamented what he saw as the degeneration of the American republic into a democracy. In his view, the task of the Whig party was to form an unbreachable dam against the currents of radicalism that threatened to engulf the nation. The Whig party throughout the country, he noted, was 'the conservative party'; this would be denied by 'no man in his senses'. Equally incontrovertible was the fact that 'the whole tendency' of the American government since 1776 (or 1789) had been 'toward radicalism'. In the process, he explained, the republican framework of government, which had 'suitable guards and checks against the outbursts of popular passion', had been transmuted into a *'Democracy,* in which the majority claim the right to trample down all checks upon their *will'*. Webb's conclusion was representative of conservative Whiggery generally: further constitutional innovations must be resisted, agitation for populistic reforms must cease.[59]

The conservative Whig reading of history thus ironically resembled that of radical Democrats. The two groups perceived the same direct line of development in the American past, representing the triumph of the democratic principle. Each group identified significant phases in the development and, as they retold the history of the nation, they either applauded or condemned the major protagonists. The crucial figure upon which both groups converged was that of Thomas Jefferson.[60] For the radicals (inside or out of the Democratic party), Jefferson had attained the status of a demi-god; as far as the reactionaries were concerned, his was the diabolical influence to which the nation's political decay was attributable. 'The principles of Mr. Jefferson', declared the *Boston Courier,* a prominent conservative Whig newspaper, 'have done more to torment this nation than all the plagues described in the apocalypse could do, if inflicted at one blow'. Thorough-going conservatives like George Gibbs and Theodore Dwight devoted volumes to assaults on Jefferson's character and principles, while Whiggish journals like the *New York Review* and the *American Monthly Magazine* bemoaned his influence and lamented his election to the White House.[61] Even though to question Jefferson

---

[59] *Courier and Enquirer,* 19 May 1845.

[60] See the excellent discussion in Merrill D. Peterson, *The Jefferson Image in the American Mind* (N.Y., 1962), 62-99.

[61] *Boston Courier* in *Cong. Gl.,* 26 i App., 406; George Gibbs, *Memoirs of the Administrations of Washington and John Adams, edited from the Papers of Oliver Wolcott,* 2 vols. (N.Y., 1846), I, 328, II, 487, 515; Theodore Dwight, *The Character of Thomas Jefferson, as Exhibited in His Own Writings* (Boston, 1839), 365-8;

was to question American democracy itself, some Whig sympathisers and activists clearly felt impelled to make the challenge. Often it was delivered in private. When John Quincy Adams described the spectacle of Jefferson as President as 'a slur upon the moral government of the world' he was writing his as yet unpublished memoirs. Similarly, when George Templeton Strong, the New York patrician, suggested that Jefferson shared (with Jackson) the honour of having done as much harm to the nation as any man who had ever lived in it, he was writing only for his diary. But deprecatory remarks were occasionally made in public. Edward Stanly, Whig representative from North Carolina, referred with open contempt to 'the impenetrable bogs of Jeffersonian abstractions', while the *Whig Review* felt it necessary to apologise for the young Joseph Story's Jeffersonian sympathies. 'The explanation of this', the journal suggested, lay in 'his ardent temperament, his want of experience, his consequent over-estimate of the virtue of the mass, and ignorance of the disturbing influences of passion and selfishness'. Conservative Whigs had little respect for Jefferson the democrat. When, after the Whig party's demise, R. McKinly Ormsby, a former partisan, undertook a sympathetic history of the party, he argued that the Jeffersonians had been too zealous for liberty. Ormsby reminded his readers that political wisdom never resides in a majority of the people. It was a judgment which came appropriately from one who had inclined towards the conservative wing of the party.[62]

This distaste for Jefferson was accompanied by a matching warmth towards Hamilton, Adams and the Federalists. Philip Hone, who has been described by a recent biographer as 'one of the Whig party's effective leaders in New York [City]', recorded in his diary (for 1840) his opinion that 'the Federal party, as it was originally constituted, embraced nearly all the great and glorious spirits of the Revolution, and all the real friends of the people'. Charles Miner, in a celebratory Address following the victory of 1840, offered praise for Hamilton and the Federal party. Although in public both parties usually repudiated all connection with the now discredited Federalists, these men were among the conservative Whigs who refused to fall in line. When Ormsby wrote his history of the party he was free from electoral pressures. The Federalists as a group, he declared, had gone into the

N.Y.R., V (Jan, 1842), 15; *A.M.M.,* II (Aug. 1838), 108. (For this journal's Whiggery see new series I (Jan. 1839), introduction).

[62]*Memoirs of John Quincy Adams,* 12 vols. (Phil., 1874-7), IX, 306; Allan Nevins and Milton H. Thomas (eds.), *The Diary of George Templeton Strong,* 4 vols. (N.Y., 1952), I. 262 (see I, 77, 94, 138, 147, 225 for his insistent Whiggery); *Cong. Gl,* 26 ii App., 260; *Whig Rev.,* III (Jan. 1846), 68-9; R. McKinley Ormsby, *A History of the Whig Party* (Boston, 1859), 47-8.

118

Whig party. Although later historians have disputed this, Ormsby was probably right. The essential point is that unreconstructed Federalists could argue their case within the Whig party; they found its conservative wing an attractive home.[63]

Thus the election of 1800, according to the conservatives, marked a watershed in American history. The next date of comparable significance was 1828, the year of Andrew Jackson's election. 'Since 1828', James Watson Webb noted sadly, 'the downward tendency of our government has been more rapid than during any previous period of our political history'. The Jacksonian Democrats, it seemed, had given additional momentum to the destructive forces unleashed by Jefferson. The Sage of Monticello had demanded equal rights, just as the Jacksonians now did. But, as William Slade of Vermont told Congress (in 1839), 'there were Conservative principles in his administration' which 'we shall in vain look for in this'. The Democratic party was now, the *Whig Review* announced in its introductory number, 'in every sense of the word a New Democracy, presenting new issues, new measures of destruction, a new and unexampled spirit of ultra-radicalism of which those whom they claim as their political progenitors had no conception'. 'The doctrines of the new lights', declared the *New Hampshire Statesman*, in reference to the state's Van Burenite Democrats, 'strike at the very root of legislation and of organized society'. The Jacksonians had intensified the politics of conflict which it had been the great disservice of Jefferson to introduce. An emphasis upon conflict between the various groups and social classes, insistent references to the allegedly unnatural inequalities between men, and a demand for a greater degree of popular power and influence – these, according to the conservative Whigs, were the ingredients of Democratic theory. As far as radical Democrats are concerned, it was an accurate description. The fears which conservative and reactionary Whigs experienced were both natural and well-founded.[64]

Virtually all Americans of the Middle Period, it has been said, were

[63] Herbert Kriedman, 'New York's Philip Hone; Businessman– Politician– Patron of Arts and Letters' (Ph.D. thesis, New York University, 1965), 212 and *passim;* Allan Nevins (ed.), *The Diary of Philip Hone, 1828-1851* (N.Y., 1936), 487; Charles Miner, *An Address delivered at the Democratic Whig Festival at Wilkes-Barre, Pennsylvania, Dec 4, 1840* (Wilkes-Barre, 1841), 3-4; Ormsby, *Whig Party,* 187-9. See Frank O. Gatell, 'Beyond Jacksonian Consensus' in Herbert J. Bass (ed.), *The State of American History* (Chicago, 1970), 350-61. Gatell points out that the careers of former Federalists should be examined up to 1840 rather than 1828 or even 1832.

[64] *Courier and Enquirer,* 28 April 1845; *Cong. Gl.,* 25 iii App., 330; *Whig Rev.,* I (Jan. 1845), 19; *New Hampshire Statesman,* 4 Feb. 1842.

egalitarians. If 'egalitarianism' is to be defined in a loose and unspecific fashion, the line appears plausible. If a lowest common denominator of 'egalitarian' sentiment is located (perhaps around the principle of equality before the law) then the great majority of Americans in the Jacksonian era were presumably 'egalitarians'. But the concept of equality is a difficult and elusive one. Without a closer and more exact definition, it can obscure rather than illuminate. In the Jacksonian era the two major parties each asked the question, 'how much equality in government and society?' They gave different answers. Conservatives and reactionaries within the Whig party constructed an ideology that was point by point opposed to the egalitarian system of the radical Democrats. Both groups were on a crusade for freedom. But for the radicals, freedom flourished as the fundamental similarity between men gained social and political recognition. For the reactionaries such a degree of equality was monstrously unnatural; it was a sign not of the enthronement of liberty but of its annihilation.

Conservative Whig theory thus placed a heavy emphasis upon the inequalities among men. Indeed, the more conservative an individual was, and the more he fretted about political democracy, the more frankly he insisted upon this inequality. Journals like the *American Quarterly Review* were wont to carry articles of an unmistakably reactionary nature; writers gave full vent to their fear that democracy would threaten the power of the élite. As they repudiated American democracy and sought a respite from what seemed an inexorable process of change, they almost necessarily emphasised the inequalities among men. Similarly conservative clergymen like the Reverend Hubard Winslow preached that inequality of condition was 'a wise and benevolent ordinance of heaven'. In the Jacksonian era equality was associated with democracy, inequality with traditional republicanism. This was a clustering of ideas that suffused the age.[65]

In their commitment to social inequality, Whig extremists often departed from their more moderate colleagues. Orthodox Whigs normally met the Democratic assault on privilege by emphasising the social and political impotence of the rich, the prosperity of the poor relative to those in other countries and the numerical preponderance of the 'middling classes'. Some conservatives, however, openly

---

[65] Hubard Winslow, *The Means of the Perpetuity and Prosperity of Our Republic* (Boston, 1838), 17. See *A.Q.R.*, XXII (Sept. 1837), 53-76; *N.Y.R.*, X (April 1842), 170-84. See also Jonathan M. Wainwright, *Inequality of Individual Wealth the Ordinance of Providence, and Essential to Civilization* (Boston, 1835), 29-31; Joseph Tuckerman, *The Principles and Results of the Ministry at Large in Boston* (Boston, 1838), 302.

welcomed large accumulations of wealth in society. This was the stance of Francis Lieber in his *Essays on Property and Labour.* Lieber, whose book was approved by Henry Clay, believed that 'a great number of private fortunes' was 'one of the greatest blessings of the people' and he invited his readers to 'rejoice' at the sight of 'an honest accumulation of great wealth'. Similarly the *Whig Review,* always likely to adopt a conservative Whig posture, published an article by George Tucker of Virginia in which extremely large differences in wealth were taken for granted. Tucker spoke without criticism of incomes that were fifty or a hundred times greater than the average. 'The great mass' of any country, on the other hand, he insisted, 'must be poor'; they would remain unrebellious only because they possessed an equal opportunity to grow rich. Tucker was in agreement with his Whig colleagues when he claimed that equality of opportunity was a reality in contemporary America, but in his insistence that such an equality necessarily produced gross inequalities of condition he drove the inegalitarian tendencies of conservative Whiggery to their furthest point. For some Whigs, then, a natural and fair distribution of wealth was an extremely uneven one. Here was the logical underpinning for an inegalitarian political system.[66]

As they openly emphasised the natural inequality among men and appealed for its recognition in government and society, conservative Whigs almost necessarily cut themselves off from the mainstream of American political culture. It was easy to devise an inegalitarian philosophy but difficult to derive a realistic programme from it, and harder still to have it approved by a populace whose power it actually sought to curtail. The problem for these conservatives was that the political reforms they would have liked to introduce were doomed by their intrinsic unpopularity. Nevertheless, they found the Whig party a suprisingly congenial resting place. Reactionary ideas found expression in high quarters within the party and men of a frankly reactionary persuasion remained enthusiastic Whig partisans. Like the radicals in the Democratic party, reactionaries could thrive in the Whig ranks.

One such individual was Calvin Colton, a friend of Henry Clay and the author of the influential (and liberal) *Junius Tracts.* During Andrew Jackson's last years in the White House Colton was absent from the country; when he returned his worst fears for the Republic were confirmed. In 1839 he published anonymously a work entitled *A Voice from America to England* in which he catalogued the sufferings

[66] Francis Lieber, *Essays on Property and Labour* (N.Y., 1841), 96-7; *Whig Rev.,* V (June 1847), 624.

which democracy had inflicted upon the nation. Colton vividly re-counted what was the standard reactionary interpretation of American history, explaining how first Jefferson and then Jackson had perverted the true nature of America's republican institutions so that the nation was now approaching 'the lowest level of democracy'. Colton asserted unequivocally that democracy was antithetical to social order and to civilisation.[67] But the major interest of the work lies in its comments on the Whig party. The Whig espousal of democracy, according to Colton, owed more to necessity than to conviction. For 'no political party' could 'dispense with it'. Any group of partisans, 'whatever their political principles, radical or conservative', needed a passport. And 'their best passport is democracy'. Colton claimed that 'the delicate position of the most elevated statesmen' compelled them to be silent. They could not 'utter all that they fear'. Yet they were 'perfectly aware of the apostacy from these [republican] principles in the actual government of the country'. Colton was referring in particular to Clay and Webster, men 'too high above the people to have their full confidence' but at the same time two individuals upon whom 'in no small measure, in connection with a phalanx of co-adjutors. . . . hang the destinies of republican empire in America'. The Whigs, according to Colton, dared not use the anti-democratic rhetoric of the Federalists. But they shared their principles.[68]

Without doubt Colton stated his case too strongly; the leaders of the Whig party were not the pure blue reactionaries that he described. Nonetheless Colton was close to the men of whom he spoke and his writings cannot be entirely discounted. It is also significant that when in the 1840s Colton wrote under the pseudonym of 'Junius', he affected a commitment to liberal principles that his biographer suggests was less than sincere. The exigencies of democratic politics suppressed reservations about democracy itself. Yet Colton's reactionary works, with their devout respect for, and devotion to the Whig party, suggest that the party could quite comfortably accommodate views that were anything but progressive.[69]

Further support for this hypothesis comes from the life and thought of Charles F. Mercer. Mercer was for several years a National Republican and then a Whig Congressman from Virginia. Unlike Colton he never expounded liberal views. His career in Congress was

---

[67][Calvin Colton], *A Voice from America to England by an American Gentleman* (London, 1839), vii, 347, 57-8, 216-7, 227, 244.

[68][Colton], *Voice,* 3, 220-6, 265.

[69]Alfred A. Cave, *An American Conservative in the Age of Jackson: the Political and Social Thought of Calvin Colton* (Fort Worth, 1969), 57.

unspectacular in the extreme. In 1845, however, he wrote an extraordinary and anonymous work (that would not be published until 1863) entitled *The Weakness and Inefficiency of the Government of the United States of North America*. Almost the entire work took the form of a Jeremiad as Mercer exposed, one after another, the evils of the American democratic polity. 'Nothing but a property qualification', he concluded, 'can save us, or keep our institutions in safe hands.' Mercer predictably had little respect for his fellow Virginian, Thomas Jefferson. 'No matter what evil invades the land,' he exploded, 'what dreadful ruin breaks up our institutions, what disgrace attacks and leaves its foul spots on our character, all may be traced to the damnable policy of Thomas Jefferson and his party.' Mercer thought even less of Andrew Jackson. 'We are rotten to the core', he asserted, as the Jacksonian era neared its end, 'and will fester in our own corruption, until anarchy and disunion shall close the scene.' American politics now displayed 'the lowest level of political corruption'; it was the scene of a 'rule of vagabondism'. In essence Mercer deplored Democratic atomism, the Democratic demand for a society of independent (and therefore equal) citizens and he fought instead for a society bound together by chains of interdependence linking the different (and unequal) individuals and groups. The Democratic conception of liberty effectively prevented 'those thousand kindnesses, interchanges of civilities, and patronising influences, that the higher classes ought to practise and exert upon the lower'.[70]

What was the remedy? Mercer actually drew up a set of proposals upon which a new constitutional system might be based. He called for an executive to be elected for a period of eight or ten years and not be re-eligible. The candidate required real estate to the value of 20,000 dollars and needed to have reached the age of forty. The single legislative chamber was to be elected every four years; candidates had to be at least thirty years of age and to have real estate worth 10,000 dollars. Electors meanwhile had to be citizens and had to own either fifty acres of land or a town lot with a house worth at least a hundred dollars. In a final flourish Mercer threw out the principle of trial by jury on the grounds that jurymen were too ignorant.[71]

The entire system was intended to infuse a new vigour into government and in particular into the Federal government. Just as radical Democrats insisted on a limited government and wanted a

[70][Charles F. Mercer], *The Weakness and Inefficiency of the Government of the United States of North America by a Late American Statesman* (London, 1863), 57, 304-7, 328, 65.

[71][Mercer], *Weakness and Inefficiency, 347-50.*

populistic system to secure it, so this arch-conservative, adopting a neo-Federalist stance, desired a strong government removed from direct popular influence. Mercer's hope was a Democrat's fear: an active government would afford scope to the inequalities within society. In that he sought a return to an older age, characterised by paternalism and deference, Mercer's outlook was quintessentially that of a reactionary. But whatever abusive epithets he loaded upon Jefferson, Jackson and the democratic tradition, he had only respect and praise for Henry Clay and the Whig party.[72]

Although it is impossible to determine how widespread such views were within the Whig party, it is nonetheless clear that they were more common than most historians have acknowledged. The party contained within it men whose views were remarkably reactionary. Colton apologised to his transatlantic readers for American democracy; Mercer resurrected Federalist arguments and devised a High-Federalist constitution. Both looked to the Whig party for salvation. Yet even these luminaries were progressive by comparison with the three editors of the *Independent,* a Whig newspaper set up at the end of 1841 in Washington D.C. The chief editor of the *Independent* was Jonathan H. Pleasants (also the editor of the influential *Richmond Whig*) and the newspaper was intended to complement the rather sedate *National Intelligencer.* Nowhere were more reactionary views expressed than in this paper's columns; nowhere did the Whig party receive more whole-hearted support.

'Democracy', according to the Prospectus of the *Independent,* 'is a mob'. 'Nor', the editors added, 'can it be anything else.' They boasted that they were themselves 'republicans'. Yet even this was a concession. In an article entitled 'Rights here and in England', the editors affirmed that they preferred English liberty, on the grounds that it was less speculative and all-embracing. The American constitution had sanctioned too many bad actions or deeds. 'Its supposed securities' had 'almost entirely failed' with the result that Americans were left with 'a School-boy government'. Democracy, the constitution – the *Independent* repudiated both. The Declaration of Independence met the same fate. Here were 'wild principles' which afforded 'authority for every species of disorganization'; 'agrarianism' was 'their direct consequence'. Pleasants and his colleagues thus denounced the entire course which American goverment had taken since the separation from England.[73]

[72]*Ibid.,* 83-4.
[73]*Independent,* prospectus in e.g. *Richmond Shield,* 13 Nov. 1841; *Independent,* 17, 27 May 1841.

The *Independent's* social theory was equally contentious. The editors did not trouble to deny the existence of a class of rich men, nor of a class of poor. Who were the rich? The paper gave a frank answer:

> The most intelligently active, the most orderly, the most attentive to their occupation, the most capable, the best behaved, the most painstaking, the most moral are, as a class, the richest, and make up the great body of the wealthy.

And who were the poor?

> Usually, the idle, the wasteful, the foolish, the ill-behaved; men neglectful of their own good, who love vice or sloth, who discharge in a very indifferent manner, or not at all, their duty to themselves, their families, their neighbors, and society.

The *Independent* was prompted to these observations when reviewing Andrew Jackson's Presidential performance. His had been the satanic influence that had tried to array the poor against the rich. For Jackson had laboured 'continually' to 'kindle up' a 'gross, grovelling and envious enmity of the Poor against the Rich'.[74]

But, according to the editors, the Whig party was there to defend them. In the present crisis Whig sympathies were 'most of all with that denounced class of successful citizens, rich without a crime and powerful without oppressing anybody'. The rich were 'the surest rampart against the Tyranny over the people themselves' which demagogues were trying to establish. The duty of the Whig party was to defend the rich and therefore, the paper implied, with a Hamiltonian flourish, promote the good of society as a whole.[75]

The Independent was as committed to the Whig party as, for example, Theophilus Fisk was to the Democrats. At one time or another the newspaper singled out those conservative Whigs whose course it approved. These included Henry Clay (who was eulogised), Senators Archer of Virginia and Berrien of Georgia, together with Congressmen Arnold, Poindexter and Saltonstall (of Tennessee, Mississippi and Massachusetts respectively). Similarly it applauded the conservative Whig *Louisville Journal* as well as the *Richmond Whig*. The paper's editors were dedicated to the Whig cause and the Whig programme. The banking system, they asserted, was 'among the highest inventions and noblest results of modern civilization'.[76]

However enthusiastic their partisanship, Pleasants and his col-

[74]*Ibid.*, 29 April 1841.
[75]*Ibid.*, 14 Dec. 1841.
[76]*Ibid,* 4, 22 Feb., 8, 22 March, 22 April, 3, 21 June, 20 May 1841.

leagues on the *Independent*, along with men like Charles Mercer and Calvin Colton, occupied an ideological position that was at one extreme of the Whig party. But their presence within the party is not difficult to account for. When they examined the democratic system in America, Whigs in the mainstream of their party did not share the utter dismay of their more reactionary colleagues; still less, however, did they share the enthusiasm of the Democrat. Democracy was not yet a matter of consensual agreement in politics and typical Whig utterances do not suggest that it was. Hence the anti-democrat naturally joined the Whig ranks.

The philosophy of the most conservative of the Whigs lays bare the logic of the Whig response to democracy. Essentially democracy was still perceived in the Jacksonian era as the atomistic and egalitarian creed that it had been in 1776. Conservatives feared not the idea of ultimate popular control over government which democracy now conveys but instead the idea that it then conveyed of a political equality rooted in a society of independent co-equal citizens. It was the levelling tendency in American democracy, clearly visible in Jacksonian Democratic theory, from which the conservatives drew back in fear. Thus the failure of the Whig party to enthuse over democratic institutions owed nothing to chance and even less to bad tactics. In embracing democracy, most of them felt that they would be embracing the social theory, with all its implications and assumptions, upon which democracy rested. 'Government by the people', according to one historian, was by the Jacksonian era, 'largely a matter of consensus and wont'.[77] It may well be doubted whether anyone who accepts this formulation will perceive the ideological cleavage that separated Democrat from Whig or understand the fury with which their battles were so often fought.

The Dialogue

Historians belonging to the so-called 'consensus' school of American history have frequently rested no small part of their case upon an analysis of the Jacksonian era. Underlying the struggle between Jacksonian Democrat and Whig, they claim, there is visible that consensus, that agreement upon fundamentals which has characterised so much of the American past. In essence consensus historians have found the decisive agreement to have existed over democracy and capitalism.

There can, of course, be little doubt that a discernible area of

[77] Meyers, *Jacksonian Persuasion*, 13.

agreement must necessarily surround the protagonists in any political conflict, even one which ends in revolution, carnage or civil war. In a relatively stable political system, such as that in which the Democratic and Whig parties operated, the agreement is inevitably greater. And the consensus that enclosed the Jacksonian era is easily identified. Thus both parties wished to preserve the American republic; neither wished to introduce a monarchy or a titled aristocracy. Similarly both parties believed in the institution of private property; neither one was socialistic and neither was feudal. Here was a not inconsiderable 'consensus'.

But the discovery of this agreement, fundamental as it undoubtedly was, is unlikely either to stimulate interest or to promote understanding. And, in analysing the consensus, it is impossible to go beyond these truisms without making important qualifications and, in particular, without specifying which sections of the two parties are under consideration.

As far as the two groups occupying the extreme positions in the political spectrum are concerned – conservative Whigs and radical Democrats – the area of agreement extended only a little further. Both groups believed in rule by law, in the ultimate beneficence of the Federal constitution (the *Independent* was an exception) and in equality before the law. But they differed sharply as to how these laws were to be passed, how the constitution was to be interpreted, where ultimate sovereignty lay, and whether that equality had been adequately guarded. Similarly both parties believed that men were not absolutely equal in talent, ability or merit and both believed that a precise equality of wealth could not be established. But here the extremes clashed bitterly, reaching dramatically different conclusions about the degree of equality which should prevail. At this level the area of agreement was highly uncertain.

It may well be questioned whether an emphasis upon consensus and agreement now furthers or hinders the analysis. Very little more can be adduced in favour of the 'consensus' theory that is not open to this objection. Thus both parties believed in 'liberty' and in a 'fair' reward for labour just as both presumably sought the good society and the good government. But agreement upon these fundamentals does not preclude disagreement within them. Such disagreement existed on a grand scale in the Jacksonian era.

In the dialogue between Democrat and Whig the basic nature of American government and society was at issue. Had liberty been attained in the United States? Did equality of opportunity truly exist?

Should the nation be a republic or a democracy? The answers given by conservative Whigs to these questions were the opposite of those offered by radical Democrats. The parties clashed over the role of government, the division of power, the legitimacy of certain basic occupational pursuits, and the degree of justice in society. Conservative Whigs desired an organic society of interdependent units, differentiated so as to permit a wide range of occupational pursuits and giving fair and therefore unequal rewards to unequal talents. They sought a republic administered by an élite and based upon a public will that was guided by the most worthy among the electorate. Radical Democrats, on the other hand, fought for an overwhelmingly agrarian society, essentially undifferentiated, and permitting much narrower economic inequalities. Their desired government was a populistic democracy, spontaneously transmitting popular impulses into government and manned by a group that was virtually indistinguishable from the electorate as a whole. Where conservative Whigs wanted a political system based on and reflecting social inequalities, radical Democrats wanted a polity that was still more egalitarian than the society of near equals from which it sprang. Ultimately, the clash was over the nature of man and of his relationship, through government and society, to other men.

The two sets of partisans were themselves dimly aware of this deep rooted difference. But because it was so fundamental and because it governed so many of their perceptions of the world in which they lived, it was difficult for either group to recognise the authenticity and the legitimacy of the world view of the other. Historians have generally dismissed as rhetorical excesses the charges which each party brought against the other. In so doing they have denied themselves a valuable insight into the politics of the era. For the charges themselves throw light upon accusers and accused alike.

Among the allegations and counter allegations that were tossed around the political arena none have received less respect from historians than the derisory labels of 'agrarians' and 'aristocrats' which Whigs and Democrats respectively sought to fasten upon each other. The idea of an aristocracy, scholars presumably reason, or of an agrarian equalisation of property, is patently absurd. Perhaps the use of such terms has even tended to discourage analysis of the parties' ideologies. (Why study the utterances of men so indifferent to truth and accuracy?) Yet questions remain unanswered. Why were these particular labels selected? Why were they so commonly employed? The philosophy of conservative Whigs, juxtaposed with that of radical Democrats, exculpates partisans from the charges of

128

hypocrisy, insincerity or gross fatuity which have been levelled against them.

If these terms are worthy of examination it is necessary to define them closely. When Democrats employed the term 'aristocracy' it was meant in a special sense. They did not, of course, intend to convey the idea of rule by the best which the Greek derivation suggests. Nor did they intend to suggest a hereditary or titled class of nobility such as those which existed in Europe. Instead they had abstracted what they took to be the essential, all-sufficient feature of an aristocracy, that quality which gave it its distinctive, unalterable nature. To the extent that a political system contained this quintessential feature within it, they argued, so it was to that extent an aristocracy. What was this feature? Committed to the idea of a natural equality among men, faced with a direct challenge to that ideal in the social system of Europe, and aware that the titles of the European aristocracy and the privileges which they secured came from government, Democrats argued that governmental aid to a favoured class was aristocracy. On this reasoning it was absurd to imagine that aristocracy was merely a system of titles and hereditary honours. It was not and John Taylor of Caroline, the greatest theorist of the Democratic party, wrote his famous *Inquiry* in order to demonstrate that it was not. 'An opinion that aristocracy can only exist in the form of a hereditary order or a hierarchy', Taylor declared, 'is equivalent to an opinion, that the science of geometry can only be illustrated by a square or a triangle.' Indeed Taylor readily acknowledged that America was in no danger of succumbing to a European-style aristocracy. 'Nobility and hierarchy', he conceded, 'cannot acquire in the United States the article of wealth, necessary to constitute a separate order or interest.' They could 'only be used as feints to cover the real attack'. For aristocracy was, Taylor reminded his readers, 'a Proteus, capable of assuming various forms'. Consequently 'some test' was needed 'to make the forms appear in the hideousness common to the features of the family'. Taylor specified what the test should be: it was 'an accumulation of wealth by law without industry'. 'Title without wealth is the shadow', he warned, 'an accumulation of wealth by law is the substance.' This was the essence of aristocracy. 'A transfer of property by law', he concluded, 'is aristocracy, and aristocracy is a transfer of property by law.'[78]

This was the sense in which the Democrats employed the term. According to *The Globe,* an aristocracy was 'any body of men raised above their fellows by the possession of privileges which others do not

[78]Taylor, *Inquiry,* 86, 255, 352.

enjoy or by a legal exemption from burdens which others are compelled to bear'. Most Democrats believed, of course, that privilege was the source of the increasingly severe economic inequalities which vitiated the natural equality among men. Hence it was understandable that they should employ a term which they found not only justifiable and accurate but which, by its connotations, was polemical and controversial. And when they heard the Whig demands for an active government, the Whig defence of the network of gross privileges that comprised the banking system, and the hostility of many Whigs to democracy itself, the equation of Whiggery with aristocracy was complete. However incongruous the term may now appear, the bulk of the Whig party was indeed, according to Democratic preconceptions, an aristocracy.[79]

Yet when the Whigs heard such a charge, they could scarcely even take it seriously. In a society which offered unprecedented opportunities to all, in which rich and poor were closer than in any other, where liberty had been established and equality attained, and where economic growth had occurred at an astonishing rate, the idea of an aristocracy, whether commercial or landed, supposedly hostile to the people yet in fact able to command the support of approximately half of an exceptionally wide electorate, was an absurdity. A speech by Daniel Webster before the United States Senate captures this disbelief:

> They call it aristocracy. They beseech the poor to make war upon the rich, while, in truth, they know not who are either rich or poor. They complain of oppression, speculation, and the pernicious influence of accumulated wealth. They cry out loudly against all banks and corporations, and all the means by which small capitalists become united, in order to produce important and beneficial results. They would choke up the fountains of industry, and dry up all its streams. In a country of unbounded liberty, they clamor against oppression. In a country of perfect equality, they would move heaven and earth against privilege and monopoly. In a country where property is more equally divided than anywhere else, they rend the air with the shouting of agrarian doctrines. In a country where the wages of labor are high beyond all parallel, and where lands are cheap, and the means of living low, they would teach the laborer that he is but an oppressed slave.

Webster then questioned the sincerity of these men:

> Sir, what can such men want? What do they mean? They can

[79] *Globe*, 20 Sept. 1839. See also *The Crisis Met* (n.p., n.d.), 2.

> want nothing, sir, but to enjoy the fruits of other men's labor.
> They can mean nothing, but disturbance and disorder, the
> diffusion of corrupt principles, and the destruction of the moral
> sentiments and moral habits of society.

Between Webster's outlook and that of the Democrats who talked of 'aristocracy', there was no real point of contact.[80]

The Whigs nevertheless countered the charge with their own favourite term of abuse: 'agrarian'. Thomas Govan has provided a succinct definition of the term. 'Agrarianism', he points out, signified 'the forced equalization of the ownership of cultivated land.'[81] The Whigs employed the term in this sense except that they applied it not merely to land but to all property. It is of course true that no Democrat, indeed no American of the entire era, ever called for such an equality. But the Whigs were making a projection for the future based upon their experience of the present and past. The egalitarian thrust of Democratic theory, the attack upon wealth and talent in government, the suspicion of wealth and capital in society, comprising in all a demand for a greater measure of equality, and for a society and a government that were based upon the similarities among men – all this made the charge understandable. Democrats did rail against the existing inequality of property, the National Reformers did advance an avowedly 'agrarian' scheme of land distribution, and the congressional Democratic party did sanction such measures as preemption, which could be constructed as an indirect attack upon property rights. Set against this, Democratic references to the sanctity of private property and Democratic disclaimers against an equal division counted for little. It was natural for men who were in any case uncomfortable with the growth of democracy to wonder where the egalitarian path would lead. Brownson's articles of 1840, effectively advocating an equalisation of property after death, marked, it seemed, the next and penultimate stage. Whigs noted that he held a Federal office and they shared his opinion that the programme represented a culmination of Democratic theory. This was the view of the *National Intelligencer*, the leading Whig newspaper in the nation:

> There is nothing in it [the article], to be sure, for which the public
> might not have been fully prepared, by former revelations of the
> LOCOFOCO [i.e. Democratic] creed: and it contains no

---

[80]*Cong. Gl.*, 25 i App., 634.

[81]Thomas P. Govan, 'Agrarian and Agrarianism: A Study in the Use and Abuse of Words', *J.S.H.*, XXX (Feb. 1964), 35-47. Govan applies this definition to the Jeffersonian era; it is equally applicable to the Jacksonian period.

proposition which is not clearly deducible from premises which have all along been the admitted elements of the creed.[82]

The Democrats were attempting to introduce an excessive and unnatural degree of equality into the nation. The Whigs were convinced that it could not be done, and that it would result only in increasingly wild and tyrannical measures and the destruction of liberty. But to alert the electorate a dramatic appeal was needed. The charge of 'agrarian' was thus as necessary as it was justified.

In accounting for the heat generated by the confrontation of Democrat and Whig, it is perhaps more relevant to consider the ideological distance between the two poles of the political spectrum rather than the proximity of the two parties around the centre.[83] For the presence of an extreme wing within a party tends naturally to discredit that party as a whole in the eyes of its opponents. Thus the recriminations, the abuse and the declarations of hostility that flew across the political divide should perhaps been seen as a reflection of the lack of consensus between radical Democrats and conservative Whigs. Here was a disagreement of great proportions. Here were two groups who believed, in essence, that the emerging democratic order contradicted the nature of the commercial society that was accompanying it. Radical Democrats espoused democracy and feared the burgeoning capitalist system; conservative Whigs embraced the commercial economy and lamented the growth of democracy. The chasm between them grew out of contradictory views of man, and of man's relationship with his fellow men. The rhetoric of the era, and especially the terminology of 'agrarian' and 'aristocrat', disclose this chasm. The confrontation of 'agrarian' with 'aristocrat' was the clash of egalitarian with élitist. Utimately it was a clash of democracy with capitalism.

---

[82]*Nat. Int.*, 11 Aug. 1840.

[83] Historians arguing for consensus have often fallen into this trap without realising or acknowledging it. Thus Lee Benson ignores the conservative wing of the New York Whig party even though it was quite prominent and highly vocal – Lee Benson, *The Concept of Jacksonian Democracy* (Princeton, 1961), *passim.*

4

THE LIBERAL CAPITALIST CONSENSUS

Conservative Democrats

In May 1844 the Democratic party assembled in Baltimore for the purpose of choosing its candidate for the forthcoming Presidential election. An uninformed observer could have been forgiven for wondering how the different factions and groups had ever been united within the same political organisation, so bitterly opposed did they appear to be. The greatest intensity of feeling was probably displayed by the Van Burenites who had until recently been confident of success. By the time of the convention they feared they were to become the victims of a conspiracy. 'The very atmosphere', reported John L. O'Sullivan, the Van Burenite editor of the *Democratic Review*, 'is burthened with the putrid odor of the corruption so rotten and rife in men's hearts'.[1]

The gloomy forebodings of the Van Buren men were to be amply justified by the course of events at the convention. The ex-President's staunchest supporters were enraged at the process by which their man was set aside. Benjamin F. Butler, leader of New York's Van Burenite delegation, on one occasion 'became white with excitement' and 'actually jumped up three or four times from the floor two or three feet high'. Some of the Ohio men, also strongly in favour of Van Buren, were prepared to split the party rather than nominate another candidate. The threat of a bolt by the anti-Van Buren groups did not deter one Ohioan. 'Let them do it and be damned', he exploded. When it became clear that their favourite could not succeed, some of the Ohioans almost left the convention in disgust, before any nomination had been secured. So great, however, was their hostility to Van Buren's leading challenger, Lewis Cass, that they were prevailed upon to stay. The same delegate, writing to Senator William Allen, also a staunch Van Burenite, explained what was the 'true and brave position of the Ohio delegation':

> twenty in number, stripped for the fight – determined at least that if Van Buren could not be saved, then that the Jackson and Van Buren policies and its [sic] gallant defenders should not be offered up on the altar of venality, corruption, and proscription;

[1] O'Sullivan to Van Buren, 27 May 1844, in Charles G. Sellers, Jr., *James K. Polk, Continentalist* (Princeton, 1966), 88.

133

and that if Lewis Cass and his friends were determined that the guillotine should do its work, then that the *damned, rotten, corrupt, venal* Cass cliques from one end of the Union to the other should be guillotined.

Accordingly the Ohio men deliberately began '*a real western fight –* rough and tumble'. Van Buren was not saved but Cass was punished and James K. Polk, hitherto a Van Burenite himself, won the nomination. Butler 'wept like a child' over the defeat; O'Sullivan reported that he and his friends were 'weeping with one eye while we smile with the other at the overthrow of the intriguers and traitors'. It was an extraordinary scene and the emotions which were aroused were to have a profound effect upon the history of the Democratic party.[2]

Van Buren at Baltimore was the accredited hard money candidate. It was no coincidence that Ohio, with the most radical Democratic party, was also the staunchest of the Van Buren states. Lewis Cass, on the other hand, was the leading conservative candidate. The *Plebeian,* a Van Burenite newspaper in New York city, contemptuously referred to Cass as a man with 'too little soul' and 'too much love of monarchical institutions and European courts . . . to be a Democrat'. Nor was Cass the only conservative Democrat to generate such hostility within his own party. Men who inclined to the radical wing of the Democracy displayed a constant fear and resentment of their more conservative colleagues. This intra-party division was particularly deep in New York where by the mid-forties the radicals were known as 'Barnburners' and the conservatives as 'Hunkers'. The antagonism was, however, of long standing. So temperate and unexcitable a politician as Silas Wright had in 1837 (in a letter to Van Buren) warned that too many Democrats were 'immersed' in 'speculation'; this, he assumed, explained their votes in favour of banks and other corporations. Wright was firm if also philosophical:

> Sometimes we have been compelled to sink below the surface to permit this rotten matter to float off, and were it two years earlier I should fear a defeat might be necessary at this time; but as the presidential election of 1836 is past I have, as yet, no fear . . . for I shall not consider a reduction of our strength in the Legislature an injury if that should be a consequence, which I doubt.

[2]Francis W. Pickens to Calhoun, 28 May 1844, in Sellers, *Polk, Continentalist,* 88; H.C. Whitman to Allen, 27, 29 May 1844, in Edgar A. Holt, 'Party Politics in Ohio', *O.S.A.H.Q.,* XXXVIII (Jan. 1929), 89, 91; O'Sullivan to Van Buren, 29 May 1844, in Sellers, *Polk, Continentalist,* 98. Sellers' biography of Polk is indispensable to an understanding of Democratic factionalism – see *Polk, Continentalist,* Chapter II for the events of the Baltimore convention.

In some counties in the state that year the party actually had rival organisations with rival tickets, one radical and one conservative. Preston King, another Van Burenite, reacted in what was perhaps the characteristic radical manner. He was not sorry to see the split, since 'by casting all traitors from their camp, the pure democracy will alone achieve true victory'. King wrote in private but the intra-party struggle he described was often waged in public. The result was that the two wings came to resent each other almost as much as they disliked the Whigs. It was a schism which created intense hatreds and which ended lifelong friendships.[3]

Nor was the radical-conservative split limited to New York state. In New Hampshire in the early 1840s the *Patriot* heaped abuse upon Isaac Hill, the state's leading conservative Democrat. Hill was 'the great champion of corporate monopolies', a 'jackal of corporations and prince of stock mongers and the money power'. He was also 'a hyena'. Far away in Wisconsin, meanwhile, similar antagonisms were ripening. During the Constitutional Convention of 1846 Edward Ryan, a militantly anti-bank Democrat, voiced his fear of the soft money men within his own party:

> I fear the softs. They cannot be killed. The hundred heads of the hydra might be lopped off, but the "softs" have no heads. They spring up on every hand; they sway and govern the legislatures. Look at the new states – democratic, "hard" as are the body of the people; see how the "softs" have carried all their measures and involved the people. Let it not be so in Wisconsin.

In terms of his own political creed Ryan was right to fear the influence of the softs. For in virtually every state there was, during the post-Panic years, a radical-conservative division within the Democracy. But the split did not begin in the Jacksonian era; rather it was as old as the Democratic party itself. Its origins must be sought in the 1790s.[4]

[3]*Plebeian* in *Madisonian,* 7 April 1843; Wright to Van Buren, 13 May 1837, in James R. Sharp, *The Jacksonians versus the Banks* (N.Y., 1970), 299; King to Azariah Flagg, 22 Nov. 1837, in Ernest P. Muller, 'Preston King: A Political Biography' (Ph.D. thesis, Columbia, 1957), 179. See also *Albany Atlas,* 9 Feb. 1847, in Patricia E. McGee, 'Issues and Factions: New York State Politics from the Panic of 1837 to the Election of 1848' (Ph.D. thesis, St. John's University, 1969), 174, 176; Wright to Flagg, 21 July 1847, in Sister Theresa Fournier, 'The Political Career of Azariah Cutting Flagg, 1823-1847' (Ph.D. thesis, Middle Tennessee State University, 1975), 154; Dix to Van Buren, 7 June, 1836, in Martin Lichterman, 'John Adams Dix, 1798-1879' (Ph.D. thesis, Columbia, 1952), 90. On the radicalism of the Ohio Democracy see *Dem. Exp.,* 24 Jan. 1846.

[4]*N.H.P.,* 24 March, 16 June 1842; Milo M. Quaife (ed.), *The Convention of 1846* (Madison, Wisc 1919), 85.

It is now generally recognised that the party which formed in the 1790s around Thomas Jefferson was united in little more than its desire to oust the allegedly anti-republican Federalists. It sought to replace them with men who were unequivocally republican and unreservedly committed to the principles of majority rule. But within the Republican party of the 1790s and 1800s there were serious divisions. There was a radical (Old Republican) wing, represented by men like John Randolph, John Taylor of Caroline and Nathaniel Macon, and a moderate wing, led by James Madison and others. As Richard E. Ellis has pointed out, the two groups were often bitterly divided. The radicals were the heirs of the Antifederalists, deeply suspicious of government (and especially of the Federal government) and hostile to banks and corporations. For them Jefferson's election was merely the first stage in what would be a process of constitutional restoration. Federalists were to be purged, the commercial system inspired by Hamilton was to be uprooted and the power of revolutionary egalitarianism was to be consolidated by a thorough democratisation of the judiciary, the last refuge of unrepentant Federalism. But for the moderates Jefferson's election was enough. Other issues could be compromised. Many of the moderate Republicans soon began to fear the radicals as much as, or more than, the Federalists. By 1805 the radical-moderate schism was the major division in politics. Although the radicals achieved certain isolated successes, it was the moderate wing which triumphed.[5]

It was a significant victory. As Ellis notes, 'American economic growth between 1800 and 1828 generally took place in the way moderate Republicans envisaged it would'. Tariffs, internal improvements and banks (both state and national) were the engines of growth which the moderates had either introduced or defended. This in turn had an effect upon political ideology the importance of which can hardly be exaggerated:

> The moderate Jeffersonians, during the years of their ascendancy created a new political and economic synthesis from the old dichotomies of the Revolution. For in the years immediately following independence most people generally believed that business enterprise and democracy were incompatible; what the moderate Jeffersonians did was to democratize business.[6]

But the new synthesis was not preserved. It was undermined, upon the

---

[5]Richard E. Ellis, *The Jeffersonian Crisis: Courts and Politics in the Young Republic* (N.Y., 1971), 19-32, 271-83.

[6]*Ibid.*, 283. It is significant that the moderate Republicans chartered far more banks than had the Federalists.

one hand, by the advance of democracy, intellectually inseparable from the levelling egalitarianism which had existed only on the radical wing of the Jeffersonian coalition and, on the other hand, by the emergence of a newly commercialised society, whose growing pains were most severely felt in the Panics of 1819 and then of 1837. The moderate Jeffersonian synthesis was thus pulled from opposite directions; the resulting ideological rupture received its institutional expression in the second party system.

The struggles of the 1790s and 1800s bear more than a casual resemblance to those of the Jacksonian era. There is a clear continuity between the radicals of the 1790s and the anti-bank Democrats of the 1820s. Similarly those of a neo-Federalist persuasion were, in the later period, found in the Whig party where they helped form its conservative wing. But the continuity between the first and second party systems is blurred by the course of the moderate Republicans. The heirs of Madison were found in both parties. But those who were in the Democratic party experienced great discomfort. In the post-Panic years especially, they were an unhappy, incongruous and often bewildered minority.[7]

As the Jacksonian hard money policy took another step forward with the introduction of the Independent Treasury, conservative Democratic resentment reached a new peak. Throughout Andrew Jackson's second term there had been a steady procession of Democrats leaving the party to join the Whig opposition. Most of the permanent defections were caused by the banking controversy but many opponents of the hard money policy were still in 1837 to be found within the party. The radical-conservative division was deepened by the Panic of that year and a sign of its new depth came on 16 August 1837, with the appearance in Washington of a new conservative Democratic newspaper, aptly entitled the *Madisonian*.[8]

The anti-bank crusade of the 1830s and 1840s was seen by those Democrats who were involved in it as a reaffirmation of the Jeffersonian creed. Jefferson and his party had indeed on various occasions denounced banking institutions in quite unmeasured terms even though their actions had often fallen short of their rhetoric. The anti-bank Democrats of the 1830s clothed themselves in the Jefferson mantle and invoked the doctrine of progress to justify and legitimise their greater militancy. But to those within the party who did not share

---

[7]*Ibid.*, 283-4

[8]The Conservative Democrats have not been adequately studied. See, however, Rush Welter, *The Mind of America, 1820-1860* (N.Y., 1975) 425-9 and *passim.*

the suspicion of, or hostility towards, banks the voice of the past spoke in quite different tones. 'Through its whole history', the *Madisonian* argued with considerable force, the Democratic party had 'avoided the extremes of federalism on the one hand, and radicalism on the other.' But the doctrines now endorsed by Van Buren were 'revolutionary and levelling'. They were designed to set the rich against the poor, the farmer against the merchant, the labourer against the employer. Hence 'their inevitable tendency' was 'to unhinge society; to break down our institutions; to demoralize and degrade the Government' and even 'to produce what led to the revolution in France'. It was thus 'the duty of every good member of society' to 'resist this mad crusade of wickedness and folly'.[9]

As the war with the banks gathered momentum, so the *Madisonian* became increasingly shrill in its predictions of impending ruin. Its editor, Thomas Allen, warned in July 1838 that 'one of the most terrible conflicts that ever this country witnessed is rapidly approaching'. It would be 'a war of the poor against the rich'. At the beginning of 1840 the newspaper reviewed President Van Buren's Message to Congress, correctly observing that it was 'the most radical . . . that has ever been sent to Congress from the American Executive'. In July of that year, after the appearance of the first 'Laboring Classes' article, it warned that Brownson's doctrines would be next on the agenda. By this time the *Madisonian* was openly supporting Harrison, the Whig Presidential candidate.[10]

This was not a chance association. Conservative Democrats tended to share the underlying social philosophy of the Whigs rather than that of the Democrats. Thus the *Madisonian* declared that all classes were 'mutually and reciprocally *dependent*', while William C. Rives, the Virginia Senator who unofficially led the conservative Democrats, felt that 'all pursuits and all classes' were 'blended in one common interest'. Hence the politics of conflict described by the Democratic radicals was as inaccurate as it was dangerous. Conservative Democrats also shared the Whigs' basic satisfaction with the economic growth and commercial expansion which had been achieved in the recent past. Nathaniel Tallmadge, conservative Democratic Senator from New York, in a letter to Rives stated his conviction that the Van Burenites were seeking to 'prostrate our whole credit system which has done so much for the prosperity of our country'. At a meeting of conservative Democrats in New York in

[9]*Madisonian*, 16 Aug., 17 Oct. 1837. See also 12 Sept. 1837.

[10]*Ibid.*, 28 July 1838, 1 Jan. 1840

January 1838, the delegates, having warned against 'all radical and destructive doctrines and sentiment', then accused Van Buren of deserting the principles of Jefferson and Madison. The administration, they felt, had declared war upon the credit system, a system that was 'the peculiar offspring of liberty . . . essentially democratic, equal and universal'. The delegates partly attributed New York's rapid economic growth and social improvement to the operations of her banking institutions. In Maine a group of conservatives offered the electorate the opportunity to emulate the achievement. 'Through the intervention of banks and a well regulated system of credit', they urged, 'you may do in ten years to come, what New York has done the ten years past.' 'Surely nothing has done more for this nation – nothing is doing more', argued the *Madisonian*, 'than commerce and credit.'[11]

The conservative Democrats approved of the credit system for reasons that were similar, if not identical, to those advanced by the Whigs. Both groups were convinced that it facilitated the upward mobility for which American society was justly renowned. The system enabled 'every man who bears a tolerable character, coupled with industry' to have an opportunity 'of bettering his condition'. Thus it had been 'the great lever of our advancement as individuals, and as a nation in wealth and prosperity'. Because of the abolition of primo-geniture and entails, the *Madisonian* argued, and because of the unique fluidity of American society 'one generation, in this country' was 'enough to bring those now at the bottom of the wheel of fortune to the top'. Hence the Van Burenite assault upon the banks and the credit system, by blocking the avenues of enterprise, was in fact undermining a system which 'has made us at once the wonder and glory of the civilized world'.[12]

Thus when the conservative Democrats objected to the Independent Treasury, correctly interpreting it as a vote of no confidence in the banks, they were not merely defending the right of certain isolated financial institutions to hold and employ the government's revenues. Nor were they simply defending the banking system in general. Instead they were voicing their approval of the process of commercialisation, with all its ramifications, which the nation was undergoing, of the existing social structure, and of the present prospects for advancement. They

[11] *Ibid.,* 2 Sept. 1837; Tallmadge to Rives, 31 May 1837, in Sharp, *Jacksonians versus Banks,* 12; *Proceedings of the Great Democratic Republican Meeting in the State of New York, Jan. 2, 1838* (Washington, D.C., 1838), 12; 'Meeting of Maine Conservatives', in *Madisonian,* 1 Aug. 1838.

[12] *Pros. of Dem. Rep. Meeting,* 12-3; *Madisonian,* 27 March 1841, 16 Aug. 1837.

were expounding a social philosophy that was squarely within the Madisonian, moderate Republican tradition.

Yet because the political universe had significantly altered between the Jeffersonian and Jacksonian eras the latter day Madisonians had to attempt a new synthesis. For many conservative Democrats were closely associated with, and sympathetic to, the political egalitarianism which Jacksonian Democracy had stimulated.[13] Some were as fully committed to the new populistic democracy as their more radical colleagues. Thus with the victory of 1840 the *Madisonian* expressed its gratification in terms which were as populistic as any which an orthodox Democrat might have employed:

> The people were its authors – they are its real governors. Those who are elected to perform the details of office, are not masters but servants. . . . Mankind have thoroughly tried, and reject, all governments but that which is most untried *viz*: that which is most perfectly Democratic. To that sort of government philosophy and humanity tend. There is progress. The Democratic principle moves forward, not backward. Benevolence, morality, and Christianity aid it and encourage it.

There was nevertheless a sharp contrast between this enthusiastic response to political democracy and the guarded wariness with which the conservatives reacted to even the mildest hint of social protest. The conservatives were progressive political democrats but in their 'devotion to the *existing* institutions of the country' and their 'unconquerable resistance to schemes of wild *innovation* and *destruction*', they had effectively furthered the process by which the agrarian traditions of American democracy were transformed in order to accommodate the needs of a burgeoning capitalist society. As the conservatives embraced democracy they almost imperceptibly abandoned the traditional agrarian conception of the classless, undifferentiated and unhierarchical society. The society with which they had now come to terms, however much it emphasised upward mobility, however much it insisted upon the harmony of the classes and however much it sought to protect the interests of all, was nevertheless unmistakably class based. The conservatives had exchanged classlessness for class mobility; essentially they had begun to dilute equality of conditions into equality of opportunity. They had attempted a marriage between democracy and capitalism.[14]

[13] Some Democrats were considerably more conservative in their political outlook. These individuals were thus even closer to the Whigs than those who subscribed to the more orthodox Democratic view of politics and government while rejecting its social philosophy. See Welter, *Mind of America*, 425-9.

[14] *Madisonian*, 13 Nov. 1840; William C. Rives in *Cong. Gl.*, 25 ii App., 610.

The significance of the conservative Democratic ideology lay in its predictive character rather than its representative nature. For if they had anticipated, in the broadest sense, the future development of American social and political thought, this success did not provide them with an easy passage through the post-Panic years. Caught between the advocates of 'agrarianism' and the upholders of 'aristocracy', the conservative Democrats experienced great difficulty in maintaining their position. The purists within the group endeavoured to maintain a strict neutrality, delivering alternate warnings about the wickedness of the two major parties. Thus the *Ulster Sentinel* appealed to moderate opinion to discredit Whigs and orthodox Democrats alike. While the Whigs sought to establish an oligarchy, the newspaper claimed, the Democrats in reality favoured a mobocracy. The interests of the majority of the people clearly lay elsewhere.[15]

Yet with the polarisation of politics that took place during the years of Van Buren's Presidency, the conservatives were ultimately forced to make their choice between the two parties. Their fortunes can be followed at both state and national level. When the twenty-fifth Congress convened in 1837 there were probably four Democratic Senators who could be termed conservative and approximately fourteen Representatives. Together they represented the states of Virginia, Georgia, South Carolina, New York, Massachusetts, Maine, Indiana and Illinois – a varied selection geographically. The conservatives' strength was probably greatest in Virginia, where in the state's House of Delegates they managed for a time to hold the balance of power, running their own candidates wherever possible. But even here they had difficulty in remaining united, some favouring the Democrats, others the Whigs and others preferring independence. In New York, perhaps their second strongest state, the conservatives were by 1838 united with the Whigs, Senator Tallmadge winning re-election with a combination of Whig and conservative Democrat votes. Elsewhere conservatives were often unable to win the endorsement of the regular Democratic organisation with the result that they were forced into retirement. But it was the course of the *Madisonian* in Washington, closely linked with the Virginia conservatives, and widely regarded as the mouthpiece of William Rives, which was most crucial for the fate of the conservatives.[16]

Initially the *Madisonian* claimed to be a regular Democratic

---

[15] *Ulster Sentinel* in *Madisonian*, 3 Oct. 1837.

[16] *Whig Almanac and Politician's Register for 1838* (N.Y., 1838); Raymond C. Dingledine, Jr., 'The Political Career of William Cabell Rives' (Ph.D. thesis, University of Virginia, 1947), 329-34.

newspaper, loyal to the new administration and differing with it on the single question of the Independent Treasury. At this time its editor, Thomas Allen, regularly flayed the Whigs; he hoped that the Independent Treasury, after being defeated in the House, would not be reintroduced. But when it became apparent that these hopes were illusory, Allen gradually began to dissociate the newspaper from the Democratic party and to move it tentatively towards the Whigs. By May 1838 Henry Clay was praised as 'thoroughly Madisonian' in his principles. It is a mark of the significance that was universally attached to the Independent Treasury, with its implicit radicalism, that Allen now disliked it far more than the alternative of a national bank, against which Rives and the conservatives had been battling for almost five years. Yet, in asking the conservatives to consider offering support to the Whigs, the *Madisonian* was careful to distinguish the more liberal Whigs from their conservative, neo-Federalist colleagues. Although there was 'not a whit' of difference 'between a Conservative Democrat and a Democratic Whig' yet a complete union was unthinkable since 'the Conservatives hold the ultra Whigs in as utter abhorrence and detestation, as they do the *loco focos'*. Thus there could be 'no more affinity between the Conservatives and ultra Whiggism than between Conservatism and loco focoism'. Both were 'alike obnoxious and intolerant'. In mid-1838 Allen was still insisting upon a separate organisation in order that the conservatives should hold the balance between the two parties. He both praised the Whigs for conceding to the conservatives those rights which the Van Burenites had denied them whilst at the same time warning against the influence of the reactionary elements within the party. Consequently the nomination of Harrison, less closely identified with the old National Republican party than Clay, enabled the conservatives to unite to defeat Van Buren and, they hoped, radicalism. Although one or two conservatives had returned to the Democratic party by 1840 yet, as one historian has suggested, 'the Rives conservatives existed in name only and were in reality merely an appendage of the Whig party'.[17]

Reinforced by their alliance with the conservative Democrats, the Whigs achieved the first and their greatest Presidential victory in the famous 'Log Cabin' campaign of 1840. But the death, within a month of taking office, of General Harrison, placed John Tyler of Virginia in the White House. Within a matter of weeks the chain of events was

---

[17]*Madisonian,* 12 Sept., 17 Oct. 1837, 5, 29, 26 May, 28 July, 4 Aug., 13, 15 Dec. 1838; Sharp, *Jacksonians versus Banks,* 238.

under way which was to result in an open breach between the President and the Congressional Whigs. Tyler was finally expelled from the party and, after a brief and unsuccessful attempt to form a viable independent third force in politics, he was permitted to rejoin the Democrats (whom he had left during the nullification crisis). Somewhat optimistically, perhaps, Tyler attempted to secure the Democratic nomination for President; he and his supporters attached themselves firmly to the conservative wing of the party.[18]

Although Tyler had not, of course, been in the Democratic party in the late 1830s, he nevertheless shared many of the views and opinions of the conservative Democrats. Hence when the rupture with the Whigs came, it was fitting that he should employ, as the official mouthpiece of his administration, the *Madisonian*. It was fitting also that he should find in William Rives, still a United States Senator, one of his staunchest Congressional supporters.

Tyler's Inaugural Address announced that the new President looked forward to a speedy termination of the war which, he charged, Van Buren had waged against the banks. But the Whigs ought perhaps to have remembered that Tyler had believed a national bank to be unconstitutional for a quarter of a century. The President ultimately vetoed the two bank bills passed by Congress in the summer of 1841. In December of that year, in his first Annual Message, Tyler stated his conviction that the suspension of specie payments which was accompanying the recession, was inexcusable. He thus staked out his position; it was emphatically not that of an orthodox Whig.[19]

Instead Tyler's view of banking placed him midway between the orthodox of both parties. Similarly the *Madisonian* on the one hand lauded the President for the firmness with which he vetoed the bank bills, knowing as he did that 'certain stock-jobbers and overgrown capitalists who prey like sharks upon the poor' would be antagonised. But on the other hand, the editor acknowledged that banks had done the nation much service. Whatever mischief they had caused was 'more owing to their management, or rather mismanagement, than anything necessarily inherent in the nature of these institutions'. The editor filled many of his columns with attacks upon the 'Ultras' of both parties and repeatedly urged moderate opinion to support the President's middle course.[20]

[18] See below, pp. 170-4.

[19] James D. Richardson (ed.), *A Compilation of the Messages and Papers of the Presidents, 1789-1897*, 10 vols. (Washington D.C., 1897), IV, 39, 83.

[20] *Madisonian*, 16 Nov. 1841, 29 May 1843. See also 21 Sept., 19 Dec. 1842, 16 Jan. 1844.

Tyler found some support in Congress. Henry A. Wise of Virginia, also opposed to the 'dangerous extremes of both parties', looked to Tyler to establish 'Constitutional Republicanism in the place of Agrarianism on the one hand and of Federalism on the other'. Another supporter was Caleb Cushing of Massachusetts who had in the thirties warned of the evil influences at work within each party. But the effort to build a third party was a pronounced failure. Tyler at the end of 1842 could claim only two supporters in the Senate and a mere six in the House. It was indeed, as his critics derisively observed, a mere 'corporal's guard'.[21]

In the states the administration pursued the same goal. With the Federal patronage available Tyler was able to launch several strategically located newspapers and to take over others. In addition he recruited a considerable number of individuals, of varying stature and fame, to fill Federal offices. But as the hopes of a third party faded the administration began to drift towards the Democracy. Carefully, it dissociated itself from the hard money wing.[22]

The Tylerite third party of the 1840s was thus as numerically feeble as the conservative Democrat third party of the 1830s. The two groups were ideologically similar yet neither managed to mobilise the full strength of the conservative Democrats. Probably a majority of Democratic partisans whose views resembled those of the conservative defectors remained loyal, despite the mounting strength of the radicals. They preferred to fight within the party rather than join the Whigs. Still less, it is safe to assume, did they wish to form a third party.

Consequently the Democracy was, in the late thirties and early forties, convulsed by intra-party disputes. They were especially severe in some of those states where the party enjoyed a virtually unassailable superiority over the Whigs. This was certainly the case in New Hampshire, perhaps the strongest Democratic state in the Union. Here Isaac Hill, an original Jacksonian of 1828, was set aside by his more radical colleagues in the early 1840s. The vicious infighting which then broke out led to the establishment of a newspaper claiming to speak for the entire party but in fact the organ of the conservatives, entitled *Hill's New Hampshire Patriot*. It then existed

[21] Letter from Henry Wise, 5 Nov. 1841, in *Madisonian*, 14 Dec. 1841; *Cong. Gl.*, 25 ii App., 573-4; Sylvan H. Kesilman, 'John Tyler and the Presidency: Old School Republicanism, Partisan Realignment, and Support for his Administration' (Ph.D. thesis, Ohio State University, 1973), 66, 75-6; *Whig Almanac and United States Register for 1843* (N.Y., 1843), 17.

[22] See below, pp. 170-4.

side by side with the *New Hampsire Patriot*, spokesman for the dominant radical wing. In true conservative fashion *Hill's Patriot* combined the populism of its rival with denunciations of its rival's radicalism, insisting that enterprise should be stimulated and that radicalism was 'a direct departure from democracy'. Significantly, while the radicals backed Van Buren, Hill was sympathetic to Tyler, eventually receiving a Federal appointment. Far away in Missouri, meanwhile, an equally fierce struggle was taking place between the followers of Thomas Hart Benton, virtually the embodiment of the hard money policy (and an ardent Van Burenite), and the conservative soft money faction which was centred on St. Louis. The *Missouri Reporter*, the leading defender of the softs, stated its desire for a 'reform' of the banking system rather than its annihilation and voiced its approval of 'well-guarded banks of issue'. The *Madisonian* not unnaturally sided with the *Reporter* and gave the softs much aid and encouragement.[23]

Thus the conservative-radical schism transcended state boundaries. In New Hampshire, *Hill's Patriot* declared its distaste for the views of the *Bay State Democrat*, organ of the radical wing of the Massachusetts Democracy, for the opinions of Ohio's radical Democrats and for the ideas of the New York Barnburners – all prominent Van Buren groups. On the other hand it praised the more conservative *Albany Argus* as well as conservative leaders like Richard M. Johnson of Kentucky and Governor David Porter of Pennsylvania. In Massachusetts Tyler looked not to the faction led by George Bancroft and Marcus Morton and represented by the *Bay State Democrat* but instead to men like Robert Rantoul, who had been midway between the two wings of the party and to David Henshaw, who was clearly identified with the conservatives. Rantoul's middle position is apparent from some remarks made in the course of an Oration which he delivered at Worcester in 1837. Rantoul denounced the Whigs as aristocrats and the Workingmen as anarchists. While openly criticising what he believed to be excesses of radical zeal, he nevertheless remained firmly within the party.[24] Similarly Daniel S.

[23] *Hill's Pat.*, 2 Feb., 13 May 1843; *Madisonian*, 24 Feb. 1842; *Missouri Reporter* in *Madisonian*, 4 Feb. 1843. See also *Madisonian*, 17 Dec. 1842.

[24] *Hill's Pat.*, 13 May, 9 Nov. 1843, 8 Feb. 1844; Robert Rantoul, 'Oration at Worcester', in Luther Hamilton (ed.), *Memoirs, Speeches and Writings of Robert Rantoul, Jr.* (Barton, 1854), 563. On Rantoul see Robert D. Bulkley, Jr., 'Robert Rantoul, Jr., 1805-1852: Politics and Reform in Ante-Bellum Massachusetts' (Ph.D. thesis, Princeton, 1971) – an unusually rich and thorough survey; Arthur B. Darling, *Political changes in Massachusetts* (New Haven, Conn., 1968), 284-5. Note the contrast between Rantoul's view of the Workingmen and their relations with Marcus Morton – see above, p. 93.

Dickinson, the New York Hunker and a future United States Senator, managed to combine assaults upon radicalism with loyalty to the Democratic party. On the one hand Dickinson objected to the prevailing spirit of reform as 'wild, heedless and Robespierrian', a spirit which, 'under the imposing and specious garb of *natural rights*' sought 'to ride in havoc over our happy land spreading in its desolating course seeds of wickedness, disease and death'. On the other hand he identified the opponents of tariff reduction as the representatives of 'overgorged capital' and viewed the entire tariff controversy as a stage in 'the same great struggle between the few and the many which has marked the footsteps of man from the earliest periods of his history'. Dickinson could thus alternately echo the convictions of the committed of both parties. Finally in James Buchanan, already a leading Democratic Senator, the conservative Democratic persuasion had a still more august spokesman. Buchanan, who made a half-hearted attempt at the Presidential nomination in 1844, remained squarely within the party; he managed also, by dissociating himself from Pennsylvania factions, to avoid the stigma which fell upon conservatives of the Dickinson stamp. In essence he straddled the conservative-radical division, agreeing with the radicals, for example, that 'money is equivalent to a title of nobility in our larger commercial cities' while at the same time disavowing hostility to banking in principle and dissociating himself from the militant hards. Buchanan's social perceptions were consonant with his opposition to the hard money creed:

> From the very nature of our institutions, the wheel of fortune is constantly revolving and producing such mutations in property, that the wealthy man of today may become the poor laborer of tomorrow. . . . A large fortune rarely lasts beyond the third generation, even if it endures so long.

Perhaps Buchanan's stance can best be termed 'semi-conservative'.[25]

Thus it can only be a convenient simplification to talk of a radical/conservative dichotomy within the Democratic party. Because of the differences within these two groups and because of those individuals who were somewhere between the two camps, it would be perhaps more accurate to envisage a spectrum of Democratic opinion. By the late 1830s a discerning observer could have placed most politicians somewhere along this spectrum, although in response to changing

---

[25] John R. Dickinson (ed.). *Speeches, Correspondence, etc., of the Late Daniel S. Dickinson of New York*, 2 vols. (N.Y., 1867), I, 79, II, 386; *Cong. Gl.*, 26 i App., 132, 735; *Globe*, 22 Feb. 1840; Sharp, *Jacksonians versus Banks*, 12.

circumstances (both political and economic) and changing perceptions, some were compelled to alter their position.

It was a spectrum which encompassed a wide range of social thought and theory ranging from the anti-capitalist protest of the radicals to the entrepreneurial commercialism of the conservatives. The critical positions are readily identifiable. Those radicals for whom class divisions had already reached an intolerable depth were essentially in the Eastern cities; they were not in a position of power within the party.[26] The Van Burenites, who typically feared for the intensification of existing social inequalities, were powerful in every section of the Union and, until 1844 at least, probably dominant in the nation as a whole. Occupying the ground between the urban radicals and Van Buren himself were journals like the *Democratic Review* and the *Western Review*, newspapers like the *Evening Post* as well as prominent statesmen like William Allen of Ohio. This section of opinion was in 1844 almost solidly behind Van Buren. Although a small group of conservatives (including especially Thomas Ritchie of Virginia) also backed Van Buren, the conservative vote was largely divided between Richard M. Johnson of Kentucky, Lewis Cass of Michigan and John C. Calhoun[27] of South Carolina. Depending whether fear of radicalism or dislike of Whiggery was uppermost in their minds, conservative Democrats either left, remained in, or rejoined the party. Thus, outnumbered and disunited, the conservative Democrats were unable, until the introduction of the Texas issue, to block Van Buren's nomination or even significantly influence party policy.

The ascendancy of the radicals was, of course, partially attributable to the effects of the economic recession. Consequently, as the nation began to recover, the radical impulse grew weaker and a conservative entrepreneurial reaction ensued. By the end of 1847 President Polk, adopted in 1844 as the Texas candidate who was most acceptable to the Van Burenites, could state that the 'toiling millions' were 'receiving higher wages and more steady and permanent employment than in any other country or at any previous period of our history'. The slight movement along the spectrum of Democratic opinion represented by Polk's nomination, coupled with the larger shift resulting from the return of good times, had done much to diminish the force of Democratic radicalism. The crisis, it was felt, had passed.[28]

[26] It is possible, however, that regular Democrats were influenced by their ideas.

[27] For Calhoun's ambiguous position see below, Chapter 6. (Thomas Ritchie was, of course, to desert Van Buren in May 1844 over the Texas question).

[28] *Messages of Presidents*, IV, 554.

Liberal Whigs

'The principles of the new school of Whigs', wrote the *New York Express* in 1845, 'naturally tend to the lowest and basest appeals to the human heart'. Inside the party, the editor feared, lay 'a crop of demagogues'. Although these individuals should not strictly be termed Whigs (since 'nothing is more odious to a true Whig than the despicable character of a demagogue'), they had somehow insinuated themselves into a position of power within the party. Not surprisingly the *Express* instead considered its own views to be the true Whig doctrines. By the mid-forties it was openly suggesting a separation from the members of 'the new school'.[29]

The *Express* adhered rigidly to the principles of conservative Whiggery. For this reason alone it almost inevitably came into collision with those within the party who were of a more liberal persuasion. To the conservatives the liberal presence was anathema. The stability of the nation, they felt, was now being threatened not only by their avowed enemies, the Democrats, but also by unprincipled traitors within their own ranks. Essentially the conservatives feared the deference which the liberals displayed, apparently unashamedly, towards the masses. 'The Whigs are at this day', Horace Binney lamented, 'more democratic in their devices and principles than the Democrats in the days of Jefferson.' To conservative Whigs like Binney this was a deplorable prospect.[30]

If Binney had stated that some Whigs were now more democratic than some Jeffersonians, his claim would have been well founded. For there was indeed a liberal/conservative division within the Whig party and the liberals could plausibly cast themselves as defenders of some of the articles of the Jeffersonian faith. This division was neither as widespread nor as deep as the corresponding split in the Democratic party but it was nonetheless of considerable significance, especially in New York, the largest and most powerful state in the Union. The liberal Whig persuasion in certain respects resembled the ideology of the conservative Democrats and the resemblance is perhaps a measure of the maturity and sophistication of the second party system. Clustered around the centre of the political spectrum there lay a consensus of opinion; essentially it was an agreement upon the 'fundamentals' of liberal capitalism.

[29] *New York Express* in *Cincinnati Daily Enquirer,* 10 Sept. 1845.
[30] Charles C. Binney, *Life of Horace Binney* (Phil., 1903), 451.

It was, perhaps, inevitable that any party which sought to recruit support among the democratic masses should have begun to address them in the language of democracy. As realistic politicians the Whigs were often compelled to modify or even to abandon the élitism towards which many of them seemed to incline. But it would be a mistake to dismiss liberal Whiggery as a cynical attempt to advance Hamiltonian views by employing Jeffersonian terminology. For the heirs of what can loosely be termed the moderate Republican tradition experienced no greater discomfort when they associated with the neo-Federalist conservatives in the Whig party than when they enlisted with the radicals in the Democracy. Their presence in each party contributed in no small measure to the establishment of a viable two-party system – in a sense the first the nation had seen.

The liberals did not, however, entirely reformulate Whig ideology. Rather they placed additional emphasis upon some of its constituent parts to the neglect of others. Thus when Joseph D. Hoag of Iowa, seeking to convince the state's constitution makers of the merits of manufacturing, insisted that 'the operatives often made more than the owners' and that 'common hands who were stronger and careful, would in a comparatively short time, be able to buy small farms or otherwise go into business for themselves', he was voicing an opinion from which no conservative Whig could have seriously dissented. Similarly, when James Dunlop of Pennsylvania ridiculed Charles J. Ingersoll's radical report on banking, his arguments might in essence have been approved by the most reactionary of Whigs. According to Dunlop, Ingersoll's fear of an aristocracy was absurd since the banks were owned by 'widows and orphans, frail old women and toddling children'. 'Junius' likewise argued that corporations (provided they were not too large) promoted 'a wider and more democratic division of powers' while William Henry Harrison, a Whig propagandist reported, was 'opposed to all measures which shall tend to build up distinctions of WEALTH among the people'.[31]

These statements set the more liberal Whigs apart from their conservative colleagues in the party not because they were controversial but because they betokened a greater confidence in the electorate to which they were addressed. Similarly the liberals shared the standard Whig optimism concerning the future of a commercial and industrial society. 'Never was there a measure of public policy',

---

[31] *Iowa C.C.*, 147; *Pa. C.C.*, I, 378; *The 'Junius' Tracts* (N.Y., 1844), 99; [Jacob B. Moore], *The Contrast* (n.p., n.d), 6. It is perhaps necessary to add that Dunlop was an Antimason. In Pennsylvania the Antimasons united with the Whigs against the Democrats. They in effect represented liberal Whiggery.

Thurlow Weed declared in 1844, 'which exerted a happier influence upon the wealth and prosperity of a nation than the Whig Tariff of 1842.' Along with both Democrats and Whigs, Weed identified that tariff with protection and then associated protection with manufacturing and an increasingly differentiated economy. Thus, however liberal they might be, the liberal Whigs remained Whigs.[32]

Even so, as they reached out for the votes which would ensure the triumph of their policies, they were driven to make concessions. The Whigs believed, of course, in the value and beneficence of a banking system. But, faced with the battery of Democratic attacks upon banking and the Democratic success in mobilising popular opinion against the banks, the liberals were often cautious in their defence. 'Junius' again set an example which others followed:

> The Whigs are accused of being the bank party. If this means that they want a *sound* banking system, always paying specie on demand; that they want *few* banks, and the least amount of bank capital that will answer the necessities of the country, then the charge is true. They have made *few* banks and with few exceptions, *good* ones.

The manner in which 'Junius' qualified his approval of banks displayed a clear awareness of the disastrous consequences for any party that was too closely associated with them. If all Whigs were conscious of this, the liberals were yet more willing to act upon the realisation in their dialogue with the electorate. But many liberals went somewhat further. In New Harmony, Indiana, the *Disseminator* sought to turn the fear of banking against the Democrats themselves. In common with other Westerners, its editor (no doubt reflecting the experience of the West with wildcats) argued that a national bank was needed to restrain, regulate, and provide a numerical check upon, the state banks. The choice was between a national bank and a limited number of state banks, on the one hand and, on the other hand, 'a host of State banks and shaving shops, responsible and irresponsible, unknown out of their own neighbourhoods, and consequently subjecting us to loss from their depreciated paper'. The *Disseminator* avowed itself in favour of the principles of Jefferson – and those of Harrison. In nearby Vincennes the *Gazette* went still further when it actually employed the egalitarian rhetoric of the Democrats against the Independent Treasury, cornerstone of the Democratic anti-bank policy. 'Shall we', it asked, 'bow our necks to the landed and monied aristocracy, which is now attempted to be forced upon us through the instrumentality of the sub-treasury?' The *Gazette* did not, of course,

[32]*A.E.J.*, 13 May 1844.

offer any hint of true social protest, instead enjoining its readers not to display any prejudice against, for example, banks or merchants. But its willingness to employ the language of social conflict sharply differentiated its editor from the large number of Whigs to whom such language represented a dangerous incitement of the masses. For this terminology was, to the conservative Whigs, if not demagoguery, then at least an unwise appeal to the passions, one which could only serve to undermine confidence in the fabric of society. Similarly suspect were the declarations of the Whigs of Westfield county, New York, who, in deriding the Barnburners' famous 'Stop and Tax' law, termed it a policy that 'unnecessarily' taxed the people 'for the benefit of the Banks, Brokers and Stock-Jobbers'. The Westfield county convention declared its determination to sustain the Whig party until 'the cause of LIBERTY, PROTECTION, AND EQUAL RIGHTS shall be triumphant throughout our beloved land'. It was a newer and more populistic Whiggery.[33]

But despite their emphasis upon upward mobility, their reluctance to offer an unqualified defence of banking, and their utilisation of the language of social conflict, it was the liberals' view of political democracy which most clearly distinguished them from conservative Whigs. In the Wisconsin Constitutional Convention of 1846 Moses S. Gibson declared himself in favour of an elective judiciary, an innovation which horrified conservative Whigs. Because Gibson believed that 'the people were capable of self-government' he could reason that 'the nearer the officeholder was brought to the people' (who were 'the source of all political power') 'the better'. James Dunlop in the Pennsylvania convention likewise boasted an almost boundless confidence in the people. While the conservative Whigs were appalled at the radicalism of the Ingersoll report on banking and fearful of the consequences if it should be widely publicised, Dunlop was instead confident that the reaction of the masses would be akin to that of the statesmen. 'The people', he insisted, 'are just made of the same materials as ourselves.' They were 'quite as competent judges of truth and error as ourselves'. When Dunlop claimed to have 'entire confidence in them', he backed the claim by asking that the report be distributed as widely as possible. It was a 'perfectly harmless report' – comparable to the stories of the Arabian nights – and its only effect could be to reduce Democratic strength. In true liberal fashion

[33] *Junius' Tracts*, 31; *The (New Harmony, Indiana) Disseminator*, 23 April 1840; *Vincennes States Gazette*, 25 July 1840; 'Convention of the Whigs of Westfield Co., N.Y.', in *A.E.J.*, 27 Dec. 1844.

Dunlop invoked the name of Jefferson, 'the great apostle of liberty', in a plea that error be tolerated.[34]

Like the conservative Democrats the more liberal Whigs insisted that the party of Jackson and Van Buren had departed far from the sacred Jeffersonian path. The *Boston Atlas* in 1840 claimed that the Jeffersonian heritage had been transmitted instead to the Whigs, while 'Junius' castigated the Democrats as 'Federalists of the worst stamp, uniting in their creed the most obnoxious principles of that obsolete school, such as admiration of the veto and other high Federal and monarchical powers, with the most radical and revolutionary doctrines'. The combination made up 'the seed and type of absolute government'. Other Whigs gleefully seized upon the names of former Federalists who were active in the Democratic party in order to discredit their pretensions to democracy.[35]

Despite these rhetorical successes, however, some of the more liberal Whigs encountered certain difficulties in reconciling their liberalism and their Whiggery. Nowhere were these problems more clearly confronted than in the state of New York where the triumvirate of Thurlow Weed, Horace Greeley and William H. Seward was engaged in a running battle with the conservatives in the party. The career of each is pertinent to a discussion of liberal Whiggery.

The political career of Thurlow Weed was an exceptionally long one. Born in 1787 he had by the age of twenty acquired an interest in politics that was maintained until his death in 1882. In the earlier part of his career Weed was actively involved in the Anti-Masonic movement which swept the 'burned over' district of western New York in the late 1820s. In 1830 he founded, and began an involvement of thirty years' duration with, the *Albany Evening Journal*, a newspaper which rapidly became the most authoritative voice of New York Whiggery. With the demise of the Whig party Weed became an equally prominent member of the Republican party. Never much concerned with office himself, he was content to play a role which was less familiar in his own times than it has since become – that of party boss. He played the role with consummate skill.[36]

As a Whig and Republican, Weed's first impulses were those of a conservative. But in his role as a party manager he was constantly

[34] Quaife (ed.), *Convention of 1846*, 588; *Pa. C.C.*, I, 376-7.

[35] *Boston Atlas*, 4 Aug. 1840; *'Junius' Tracts*, 31; 'Junius', *The Crisis of the Country* (Phil., 1840), 12.

[36] Harriet A. Weed (ed.), *Autobiography of Thurlow Weed* (Boston, 1884), I, 360 and *passim.*

aware of the need for concession and compromise. In a revealing passage in his *Autobiography* he recalled the views he had held on that most awkward of topics for a conservative, a national bank. Weed confessed that he believed a national bank to be 'necessary'. Yet he also recognised that it was an electoral liability. In the *Evening Journal* of 24 June 1842, he insisted that the party could not 'go down to the People, at a Presidential election, in favor of a United States Bank'. Weed then delivered a threat. 'The moment the Whig Party determines to refer the Bank issue to the Ballot Boxes', he warned, 'we will cheerfully surrender our place and our paper.'[37]

The same recognition of the need for compromise and concession governed Weed's attitude to the state banks. He was conscious that public opinion, as well as the demands of justice, required that banks which were financially unsound or which contravened the laws of the state, should be penalised. This, he argued, was necessary to protect the system itself. Hence Weed was being consistent when he attacked those banks which had been created by the Albany Regency and which he considered unsound or politically corrupt. He was even able to accuse the Democrats of being 'the bank party'. And when conservatives like James Watson Webb of the *Courier and Enquirer* protested against this course of action, Weed replied by denouncing Webb as the tool of the Wall Street aristocracy. Not unnaturally, these charges were disturbing to the more conservative elements within the party. Philip Hone, writing in his diary, praised Weed as a 'firm supporter of the Whig cause'. But he added that he was 'somewhat of a radical, however'.[38]

Yet Hone's judgment was unsound. In no sense was Weed a radical. In 1840 he informed the *Evening Journal's* readers of the significance of the party battle in which they were engaged. It was 'vain', he wrote, 'to attempt to blend the lines which now separate parties' for the Whigs represented the conservative principle and the Democrats the destructive. According to Weed, Silas Wright was 'a leveller'; the Independent Treasury was 'destructive' in 'its intent, its means, and its end'. In the light of these pronouncements it is difficult to disagree with Glyndon G. Van Deusen's conclusion that Weed possessed a 'natural conservatism'. It was, in Van Deusen's words, because of his assumption that 'economic achievement was . . . good

[37] *Ibid.*, 371; *A.E.J.*, 24 June 1842; Glyndon G. Van Deusen, *Thurlow Weed; Wizard of the Lobby* (Boston, 1947), 89.

[38] *A.E.J.*, 31 March, 28 May 1838; Van Deusen, *Weed*, 150; Allan Nevins (ed.), *The Diary of Philip Hone, 1828-1851* (N.Y., 1936), 659.

achievement' that he was unable 'to view the activities of businessmen in a critical spirit'.[39]

The same fundamental conservatism, shrewdly tempered with a dose of realism, determined Weed's ideas on government and the suffrage. In his *Autobiography* he recalled that he had opposed the adoption of the Constitution that was drawn up in the New York convention of 1821. That convention, he recollected, 'had developed under the leadership of Mr. Van Buren, strong radical tendencies' with the result that, while many of its provisions were acceptable, he had taken 'strong ground' against it. For he had 'dreaded the effect of extending and cheapening suffrage.' Nevertheless, a quarter of a century later, when pressure was building up for a new convention and further reforms, Weed took a more liberal attitude. He frankly admitted that his opinions had altered:

> Time has shown us there is more of patriotism in the Cottage than in the Palace. Republican institutions derive truer support from humble cabins than from stately Mansions. Wealth is too often sordid and grasping. Public virtue resides more with the Middle and the Labouring classes. The Young Men, and the Poor Men, cast impulsive and disinterested votes. We go, therefore, for 'the largest liberty' in relation to Suffrage. Let us have UNIVERSAL SUFFRAGE in practice as well as in theory. The great system of self-Government will not have been perfected, until all its Subjects are citizens.

The people, he proclaimed, desired 'more freedom – more equality'. They should therefore be given a new constitution.[40]

There is some doubt, however, whether Weed was here being entirely sincere. It is true that the optimism which he displayed regarding public opinion was not a casualty of electoral defeat. When it became clear that the Presidential election of 1844 had been lost, Weed acknowledged that Texas must now be annexed and the tariff lowered. If the two measures proved ruinous, then, he was confident, 'the people will rise up in their majesty and hurl their oppressors from power'. Yet in his *Autobiography* he wrote that in 1821 he 'feared then, *as I have ever since feared* [My italics] that universal suffrage would occasion universal political demoralization, and ultimately overthrow our government'. On the assumption that Weed could not have been mistaken as to the opinions he had held on so

---

[39]*A.E.J.*, 6 Aug. 1840, 19 Sept., 27 Dec. 1844; Van Deusen, *Weed,* 24, 226. See also *A.E.J.,* 25 May 1842.

[40]*Autobiography of Weed,* 89; *A.E.J.,* 10 Nov., 1845; 1 June 1846. See also 25 June 1842, 11 Jan. 1844, 6 April 1846.

important a matter it is clear that in 1846 or in 1880 he had at least distorted the truth. Perhaps his views on universal suffrage were analogous to his attitude towards a national bank: he would not defend what could not be successfuly defended. Weed was always conscious that the spirit of the age was essentially liberal. In opposing the nativist demand for a reform of the naturalisation laws, he argued that it would only achieve results opposite to those which were intended. For 'ALL popular movements in relation to suffrage teach but one lesson'. Thus in advocating universal suffrage, Weed was perhaps merely accepting the inevitable. Certainly he was attempting to ensure that its arrival would be on the most favourable terms for the Whig party.[41]

Whatever the process of reasoning behind it, the attitude was clearly that of the pragmatist. But to be prepared to concede Weed required a certain confidence in that electorate to whom his case would be put. He opposed radicalism perhaps as ardently as the reactionaries in his party yet had sufficient faith in democracy to allow the people to pass judgment upon it. Thus it would be quite erroneous to conclude that politicians of the Weed stripe, however 'pragmatic' they might be, had no ideological commitment. A staunch defender of Whig economic policies, and an advocate of concession and compromise on issues relating to political democracy, Weed was a prominent representative of liberal Whiggery. Yet he devised no coherent philosophy; his solution to the problem of the liberal Whigs was to pretend that it did not exist.

If Thurlow Weed's career reflected the need for the conservative to compromise and to concede what could not be defended, the life of Horace Greeley shows the difficulties encountered by the conservative who tried to grapple with what he admitted to be enormous and deep-seated social evils. Greeley had, like Weed, been a member of the Anti-Masonic party. Unlike Weed, however, he had settled in New York city. After editing the *Jeffersonian,* the *New Yorker* and the *Log Cabin* (the foremost Whig campaign newspaper of 1840), Greeley in 1841 launched the New York *Tribune,* destined to be one of the most influential political newspapers of the century. The fact that Greeley lived and worked in the largest city in the nation is of more than biographical significance. It provides a key to his social thought.[42]

---

[41]*A.E.J.,* 16 Nov. 1844; *Autobiography of Weed,* 90; *A.E.J.,* 18 Nov. 1844. Other Whigs were probably guilty of some dissimulation including, of course, Calvin Colton.

[42]On Greeley see Glyndon G. Van Deusen, *Horace Greeley, Nineteenth Century Crusader* (Phil., 1953); Horace Greeley, *Recollections of a Busy Life* (N.Y., 1868); Jeter A. Iseley, *Horace Greeley and the Republican Party, 1853-1861* (Princeton, 1947).

Despite certain radical leanings Greeley was in many respects an orthodox Whig. In a short pamphlet entitled 'Why I Am a Whig', he argued that although order and liberty were both indispensable to a nation, and both open to abuse, yet 'the tendency, the temptation', to err 'in a Democracy like ours' was 'almost wholly on the side of the latter'. Elsewhere Greeley drew attention to one of 'the great distinguishing principles and aims of the Whig party'. This was 'the assertion and maintenance of the supremacy of Law over Will or Force or Numbers'. Because Americans were living in an 'age of incessant Agrarian upheaval and Radical convulsion' there was a need for 'something which holds fast, something which opposes a steady resistance to the fierce spirit of Change and Disruption'. This need would be met by the Whig party; the Whigs were emphatically 'the champions of Liberty based on Order'.[43]

This letter-perfect conservatism was matched by a comparable dedication to the success of standard Whig policies. Greeley was wont to argue that credit was a benevolent agent of prosperity, virtue and republicanism and that banking originated with, and was inseparable from, freedom itself. Similarly he spared no effort to convince his readers that the Whig policy of protection was essential to the nation's welfare, earning in the process a reputation as one of the foremost tariff theorists in the country. He likewise advocated internal improvements, claiming that the two together 'worked from opposite directions to one common end – namely the diminution of expense in the transportation from producer to consumer'. Tariffs brought production itself nearer; internal improvements facilitated transportation. Finally, Greeley was, until the mid-forties at least, squarely behind the Whig land policy, dismissing the Democratic measures of graduation and pre-emption as evidence of 'the unhallowed spirit of plunder'. Consequently few men were more devoted to the Whig cause than Horace Greeley. In 1844 he campaigned for Henry Clay with such fervour that he was for six months covered with boils, sometimes as many as fifty or sixty at once.[44]

Yet there was another side to Greeley's thought. According to Glyndon G. Van Deusen, his biographer, Greeley was greatly disturbed by the effects upon the nation of the Panic of 1837. His eyes were opened for the first time, Van Deusen suggests, to the evils

[43] Horace Greeley, *Why I Am A Whig* (n.p., n.d.), 2-3; Van Deusen, *Greeley,* 73; *The Whig Almanac and Politicians' Register for 1846* (N.Y., 1846), 63-4.

[44] *Jeffersonian,* 12 May, 15 Sept. 1838; Greeley, *Why I Am A Whig,* 11; *Tribune,* 23 June 1841; Arthur M. Schlesinger, Jr., *The Age of Jackson* (Boston, 1946), 440. See also *Jeffersonian,* 28 Oct. 1838; *Tribune,* 3 July, 28 Aug. 1841; *Whig Almanac for 1846,* 24.

within urban society. Whatever the explanation there is no doubt that by the late 1830s Greeley was willing, as conservative Whigs were not, to draw attention to the need for fundamental reforms. The social radicalism consequent upon this was in a sense superimposed upon the Whiggery to which he was still committed. The result was not so much a synthesis as an amalgam of opinions, and one which belonged to Greeley alone.[45]

Thus by the 1830s he was convinced that there were not only 'individuals' but whole 'classes in the most favored countries' whose condition was 'as bad now as it ever can have been'. Among America's female employees he singled out those seamstresses who were employed at pitifully low wages in the nation's towns and cities. The plight of many male workers, especially those supporting families, was equally desperate. Greeley repeatedly drew the attention of his readers to the poverty and destitution that were widespread within their city in the hope of arousing their concern and mobilising their support. But he also warned that the remedy to which they might naturally incline, moral reform, was inadequate. Greeley broke with the conservative Whigs and, in a wider sense, with conservative tradition, when he insisted that social evils could not be eradicated by a crusade that merely sought to inculcate the values of the protestant ethic. It was, he argued, 'a very common and pernicious error' that 'the evils which afflict the Poor are such as might be entirely removed by economy, temperance and industry'. It was an error which had a paralysing effect upon reform movements since it effectively confused the cause of suffering with its consequences. The poor might be immoral; moral reform was nevertheless insufficient. For a life of incessant toil was 'the unvarying condition' of thousands in New York city alone and 'penury and privation' was 'its reward'. Humanitarian reformers tended to view the suffering of the poor as an unfortunate but perhaps necessary consequence of an otherwise beneficent social order. Greeley, on the other hand, was convinced that for millions the social mechanism which rewarded effort and stimulated virtue had broken down. Thus he was able to recognise that 'many a good artisan lives miserably as a poor drudge because he can find no employment in the vocation for which he has fitted himself and in which he alone excels'. A moral reform movement, however well-intentioned, could not combat evils of this magnitude.[46]

[45] Van Deusen, *Greeley*, 31.

[46] *New Yorker*, 17, 24 July 1841. See also *Tribune*, 13, 29 July 1841, 30 Nov. 1843, 28 Jan. 1845. Greeley also argued that the currency schemes favoured by Whigs and Democrats, whether for hard money or a national bank, were also quite inadequate as remedies – *Tribune*, 22 July 1841.

What then was the solution? In the Jacksonian era there was, of course, a position within the political spectrum for the individual who held these opinions. The weight of tradition and the force of contemporary political controversy tended naturally to propel him, with considerable momentum, towards the radical wing of the Democratic party. But Horace Greeley was unable to take up such a position and for reasons which transcend personal considerations. Greeley's opinions cut across the political spectrum; he could not be accommodated in any single position.

Probably the major obstacle preventing Greeley from joining the Democratic party was simply his Whiggery. This was not merely a question of membership of an institution. Although it was rare for prominent Whigs to become Democrats, the example of Alexander Everett of Massachusetts suggests that it was by no means impossible. Essentially Greeley's problem was that his Whig beliefs had provided him with insights and opinions which he could not and would not surrender. The underlying social philosophy which had prompted him to enlist with the Whigs might have significantly altered but the commitment to policy and the intellectual insights which he had derived from it had acquired an independent vitality. The result was a fascinating combination of ideas and an idiosyncratic career as a partisan.

One example of Greeley's insight came when, in the columns of the *New Yorker,* he took the radical Democratic editors of the *Evening Post,* William Cullen Bryant and William Leggett, to task for their adherence to orthodox Democratic principles. The *Post,* faithful to its *laissez-faire* philosophy, opposed a proposal to regulate steamboats. Noting that steamboat explosions were a commonplace, and that they often resulted in loss of life, Greeley in reply argued that regulations were clearly in the public interest. The freedom to be blown up in a steamboat was not, he declared, a freedom which the American people needed. The duty of government was here, as elsewhere, clear: 'it must act in its high capacity as conservator and guardian of the public interest'. It is easy to understand, and sympathise with, Greeley's attachment to active government on so clear-cut an issue.[47]

If his views on the role of government tended to repel him from the Democracy, his sympathy for the employer and his appreciation of the growth rates which the economy was achieving almost inevitably had the same effect. Again Greeley had a tilt with the *Evening Post*;

[47]*New Yorker,* 12 May 1838.

again he gave as good as he received. This time the *Post*, in support of a group of strikers, had hailed their conflict as that of wealth against poverty. Greeley conceded that strikes might be justified and even that they might be justified in a majority of instances. But, he asked, 'where is the criterion?' Wages could not be an exact equivalent of what the worker earned or deserved but instead only 'a guess at it'. It was impossible to be more precise, if only because there was no consensus on how to measure the value of labour. Thus Greeley had sensed the difficulties inherent in applying the labour theory of value to American society as it now was; he had identified one of the problems which had led Brownson to denounce the entire wage system.[48]

But Greeley was not prepared to endorse the radical solutions that Brownson had advocated. Repeatedly he proclaimed to his readers that he despised the politics of conflict pursued by the radical Democrats. 'We abhor', he declared, 'most unequivocally the schemes of the pretended reformers who preach distrust, hatred, discord and destruction.' 'In short', he concluded, 'we abhor Loco-Focoism.'[49]

For Greeley retained a strong sympathy with the employer. Often genuinely unable to pay higher wages and often compelled to dismiss his employees, the capitalist too was the victim of circumstances. In many situations, Greeley believed, higher wages would merely lead to bankruptcy with consequent unemployment. The evils thus inhered in the system.[50]

Greeley had other reasons for condemning Democratic policy. The agrarian society of autonomous individuals had no appeal to one whose perceptions were so thoroughly urban and commercial. On one occasion Greeley chided the *Democratic Review* for promoting 'a savage and jealous individual independence, regardless of social and general well-being'. He complained that 'on no single point' was 'the spirit of the *Review* constructive, creative, hopeful of the future'. In his view the existence of the city, the growth of manufacturing, the spread of business – all must be accepted, even welcomed. The problem, however, was to eliminate the evils of the system. It was a problem on a grand scale.[51]

[48] *Tribune,* 18 May 1843.

[49] *Ibid.,* 22 June 1841. See also 4 April 1844, 5 Sept. 1845; *Log Cabin,* 5 Sept. 1840. For Greeley's objections to Brownson's reform programme see *Tribune,* 7 May 1841.

[50] *Ibid.,* 10 Nov. 1843.

[51] *Ibid.,* 2 Sept. 1842.

Any individual who subscribed to what was in many respects a radical critique of society and yet remained fearful of social unrest was, not unnaturally, awkwardly placed. In Greeley's case ideology and politics were out of alignment. He was convinced that the Democratic solution, involving, as he believed, a blatant appeal to self-interest, and entailing a retrogressive, pernicious and utterly unrealistic social philosophy, was as dangerous as the evils which it sought to remove. Poignantly, Greeley asked his readers whether some other social system could not be devised. If not, the outlook for a society divided into capitalists and labourers was indeed bleak:

> Must there be a constant struggle on one side to get more and on the other to give less? – giving to that basest of characters, the mere grog-shop politician, a chance to step in between them, declare the employer a tyrant and oppressor of the poor, set the latter against the former, and extend the consequence and power of his worthless self by professing to be the champion of the Working Men, and so carrying them off to the support of projects and policy hostile to the welfare of both employer and employed.

Greeley was ready with his answer. It was the Fourierite programme, rechristened by its leading American spokesman, Albert Brisbane, as 'Associationism'. Horace Greeley became in the early 1840s one of its most enthusiastic champions.[52]

The Fourierite blueprint for the reconstruction of society called for the establishment of a number of communities, each of 1,620 persons, entitled 'phalansteries'. Its attraction for Greeley was that while it proposed what would ultimately be an extraordinarily radical change in society it nevertheless eschewed all compulsion and promised to avoid any real social turmoil. In an address given before an Association meeting Greeley informed his listeners that, as far as reform was concerned, he was, by inclination and temperament, a pessimist. The good that reformers sought was not always achieved; the evil that they caused in pursuing their goals could rarely be avoided. But Association, he explained, removed this difficulty:

> I think this broad and comprehensive objection is fully obviated by the system of Association. This system requires no immediate sacrifice as a condition precedent of ultimate benefit. While it may well satisfy the most thorough Radical, it need not alarm the most timid Conservative. While it will ensure independence and comfort to the Poor, it increases rather than diminishes the wealth and enjoyments of the Rich. And this is the feature of the

[52]*Ibid.*, 18 May 1843.

system which has won for it *my* sympathies, and enlisted in its behalf my earnest and hopeful exertions.

Hence Association provided an escape from Greeley's ideological impasse. Radical reform on a voluntary basis – this was its promise.[53]

How then is Greeley's outlook to be summarised? Because he believed in active government (and even in government spending to relieve unemployment),[54] and because he drew attention to urban poverty and deprivation, some historians have concluded that his thought comes close to anticipating that of the New Dealers.[55] But this is highly misleading. Governments of the Jacksonian era proposed little or no governmental intervention which involved coercion of the rich and powerful in order to benefit the poor and weak. Greeley sympathised with both groups and, because of the nature of Democratic radicalism (which he felt able, on theoretical grounds, to repudiate), he was never called upon to decide which, in the final analysis, would command his loyalty, if their interests conflicted. Thus, if he had lived a century later it is at least doubtful whether, if forced to determine his priorities, he would have voted for Franklin D. Roosevelt.

This doubt itself is attributable not merely to the eccentricities of Greeley but also to the ideological currents of the age in which he lived. In certain essentials, Greeley's thought was quite different from that of other partisans. But the unresolved dualism that was its unique feature – the tension between his Whiggery and his radicalism – this was permitted to exist precisely because of the opinions and beliefs of his colleagues. And these beliefs suffused the age.

Horace Greeley was, in the Jacksonian era at least, primarily a journalist; Thurlow Weed was essentially the party boss. The third member of the triumvirate, William Henry Seward, was the statesman. Like the other two Seward was from Western New York. Like them he had risen to prominence in the Anti-Masonic movement. Unlike them he had consistently involved himself directly in politics. His career at

---

[53] *Ibid.*, 20 April 1842.

[54] Greeley also called for reading rooms, lectures, libraries and lyceums for the city's labourers. Later in the 1840s he reversed his previous opinions and became an enthusiastic campaigner for free land and homesteads – see Van Deusen, *Greeley*, 111-12.

[55] Lee Benson, *The Concept of Jacksonian Democracy* (Princeton, 1961), 109; Dexter Perkins, 'William H. Seward', *N.Y.H.*, XV, (April 1934), 160-74. This view obviously contradicts that of Arthur M. Schlesinger, Jr. who argued that the Democrats were the forerunners of the New Dealers. Reviewing the controversy, one historian has recently suggested that the Benson view is, on the whole, more persuasive. See Bernard Sternscher, *Consensus, Conflict and American Historians* (Bloomington, Ind., 1975), 203.

161

state level culminated in 1838 with his election to the Governorship, a position which he held for four years. Subsequently Seward became a United States Senator and was, until the election of Abraham Lincoln at least, probably the Republican party's most popular leader. Under Lincoln he served as Secretary of State.[56]

Although Seward was close to both Greeley and (especially) Weed, his social and political philosophy differed significantly from theirs. Less of a conservative than Weed, less of a radical (and of a conservative) than Greeley, his outlook was quintessentially liberal. It was Seward more than anyone who clearly articulated the creed of liberal Whiggery.

As a liberal, Seward was also a democrat. In 1839 in his first Annual Message to the Legislature the new Governor avowed that he was 'conscientiously holding the principle of universal suffrage, and indulging in no apprehension of evil from its practical operation'. Indeed universal suffrage, he later declared, was 'the perfection of political justice, because it is political equality'. Seward's faith in American democracy was a generous one; he believed that the example which the nation offered to other countries was 'more precious than any other knowledge not derived by immediate illumination from the source of all Light'. Like a Democrat Seward was confident that a self-governing people could create a society that was more just and equitable than any which the world had yet seen. This view of progress contrasted sharply with the gloomy forebodings of the conservative Whigs.[57]

Yet ironically, a faith in progress and in social improvement could also, in the Jacksonian era, conflict with a faith in democracy. Because he did not share the other beliefs which comprised the Democratic worldview, Seward was compelled to voice his criticism of what he believed to be excesses of democratic zeal. He took exception to the claim (which Democrats like George Bancroft came close to making) that the voice of the people was the voice of God on earth. To the extent that it merely demanded a system of majority rule, the dictum was, of course, unexceptionable. But in its literal sense it was 'as absurd as the doctrine of the divine right of Kings' and 'as dangerous as it is impious'. Warning of the dangers to which this absurd notion exposed a community, Seward in effect demonstrated why he was a Whig and not a Democrat:

[56] The best biography of Seward is Glyndon G. Van Deusen, *William Henry Seward* (N.Y., 1967).

[57] George E. Baker (ed.). *The Works of William H. Seward,* 5 vols. (Boston, 1884), II, 197, III, 17-8.

162

> Men in their collective capacity, in masses, and in communities, as well as in their individual action, may, and often do, err in judgment. All that moral and intellectual cultivation, which is requisite to enable them to distinguish truth from error, and reason from prejudice, in the exercise of private judgment, is no less necessary in their congregated action. There is even greater danger of error in masses, because there is greater scope for passion and prejudice, and there is also a diminished sense of responsibility. There can, therefore, be no security against error in communities, other than what protects individuals against it, habits of virtue and cultivated intellects.

The progress which Seward envisaged would not be promoted by resting society squarely upon the self-interest of its members, as the Democrats supposed. Rather it would be generated by measures which would improve their physical and spiritual existence. Such measures would operate collectively upon society as a whole; hence governmental action was needed. Thus Democratic eulogies of the people threatened to impede their improvement as individuals while Democratic insistence upon *laissez-faire* threatened to stunt the moral and material growth of society.[58]

Because he denied that a society which permitted the free exercise of self-interest would automatically be self-improving, Seward had to find another base for the political superstructure. Liberty alone (which allowed the pursuit of self-interest) was inadequate. It had to be supplemented by another principle. This was no less than 'Order'. Here was 'the first instinct of the Whig party' – 'public order'. In Seward's view order and liberty were not in conflict; rather, each was necessary to the other. The French revolutionaries, he told a Mass Meeting of Whigs in 1844, had sought to base a republic on the principles of liberty and equality. Their experiment had failed simply because they overlooked the vital 'element of order'. Even in the United States there had recently been 'frequent popular disorders – outrages in which the inalienable rights of citizens have been violated, the majesty of the laws defied, and the violators of the public peace shielded by popular opinion'. If liberty, equality and self-government were to be maintained the State must intervene, with the express purpose of preserving order.[59]

Seward did not, however, conclude from this that order would be preserved solely by repression or by various policing activities. Rather

[58]*Ibid.*, III, 139-40. See also III, 136, for the argument that excessive confidence in the people discourages, for example, educational reform. See also III, 237, 245.,
[59]*Ibid.*, III, 261-2, 141.

he looked to those actions of government which would simultaneously promote social improvement. Here was a second reason for him to repudiate the Democratic *laissez-faire* philosophy.

Although Seward was earnestly committed to progress, he felt no despondency or alarm when he examined society as it now was. Americans could, he felt, congratulate themselves on the fact that 'an aristocratic order, or influence', such as that which guided British society, was 'unknown'. Similarly wealth was distributed more evenly in the United States than elsewhere. It only 'rarely' happened in America that fortunes large enough 'to be productive of public injury' were amassed. Conversely, 'the universality of the motive to obtain a competence' and 'the facility of acquiring it' together prevented the emergence of rigid class barriers. Indeed Seward believed that 'the rich in this country – if any may justly be called so where such effective restraints are imposed upon accumulation – are more liberal and public spirited; and the poor – if such there are where actual destitution is unknown – are more honest than the relative classes in other countries'. Thus the distance between rich and poor in both economic and social terms was, in the United States, a small one. It was one of the nation's greatest triumphs.[60]

Here Seward's social philosophy accorded with that of a majority of his Whig colleagues. He was also in agreement with his party in defending the banking system. Surely, he asked, 'no harsh or injurious spirit' would be 'indulged towards institutions which, deriving their powers from public grants, have performed their trusts with general fidelity, and whose stability is intimately connected with the public interest and the general welfare'? Society was not radically defective; banks need not be assaulted.[61]

But Seward was loathe to spend time defending banks. He preferred to assert the need for a still more equal society. According to orthodox Whig theory, governmental intervention had played an enormously significant role in shaping the distinctively egalitarian society in which Americans now lived. Most Whigs added that this was (approximately) the greatest degree of equality that any advanced and prosperous society could sustain. Seward, however, pushed the argument a little further. More equality was desirable; the same Whig policies could produce it.

This then was the duty of the Whig party. In 1844 Seward co-wrote an Address of the Whig Members of the Legislature. The

[60] *Ibid.,* III, 135-7.
[61] *Ibid.,* II, 300.

party's aim, it was avowed, was to establish a greater degree of equality. But, the document continued, the Whig party 'levels upward, not downward'. It would achieve its goal by 'education and benignant legislation, not by subverting established laws or institutions'. Whereas the Democrats envisaged a politics of conflict, intending to secure or to recapture for the 'producer' those fruits of his labour which were sought by the 'aristocrats', the liberal Whigs clung to their vision of an organic, harmonious society and trusted in the effects of enlightened legislation. Specifically Whigs of the Seward stripe looked to internal improvements and to education.[62]

In one of his messages to the legislature Governor Seward explained the attraction of an internal improvements programme. It would, he argued, promote equality by fostering cultural, material and intellectual advancement:

> Whilst it invades no rights, and promotes the convenience of all, it visits with peculiar beneficence citizens of humble circumstances and assiduous industry, indirectly augmenting capital, diminishing the necessity for its use, and reducing the cost of subsistence and exchange, and at the same time bringing leisure and facilities for intellectual enjoyment, and permitting all, instead of the few, to go abroad on errands of inquiry, interest, duty, and affection.

Hence internal improvements would help 'remove inequalities of local advantage'; they would 'produce harmony and mutual affection'.[63]

But an even more powerful weapon than internal improvements was education. In a Fourth of July discourse delivered on Staten Island in 1839 Seward called for an 'equality of social condition'. Since 'the beginning of time', he declared, 'aristocracy has existed' and 'society has been divided into classes – the rich and the poor – the strong and the dependant – the learned and the unlearned'. To this inequality 'the ignorance, the crime, and sufferings of the people' were in no small measure attributable. Such an aristocracy existed even in the United States where it 'prevents the diffusion of wealth and prosperity'. Seward exhorted his fellow Americans to put an end to this inequality:

> We should be degenerate descendants of our heroic fore-fathers did we not assail this aristocracy, remove the barriers between the rich and the poor, break the control of the few over the many,

[62] *Ibid.*, III, 394.
[63] *Ibid.*, II, 312.

extend the largest liberty to the greatest number, and strengthen
in every way the democratic principles of our constitution.

Seward was here speaking at a Sunday School celebration. He told
the educators that 'the work in which you are engaged' would deal the
aristocracy severe blows. For since 'knowledge' was power and thus
'the secret of aristocracy', it followed that 'Sunday schools and
common schools' were 'the great levelling institutions of the age'. Five
years later Seward delivered substantially the same message to a
Mass Meeting of Whigs. 'Universal education', he declared, 'is the
great agrarian agent – the leveller we must use to prevent wealth and
power from building up aristocratic institutions, and dividing society
into unequal classes.' It was precisely the 'agrarian agent' which a
Whig could employ. For 'education tends to produce equality, not by
levelling all to the condition of the base, but by elevating all to the
association of the wise and good.' Its effects would thus be wholly
analogous to those of a wisely planned internal improvements
policy.[64]

The effects of the two in conjunction would be decisive. The under-
privileged would benefit as society progressed towards equality.
Simultaneously, public order would be guaranteed since an intelligent
and prosperous nation could not conceivably be an unruly one. Here
then was the best protection both for individuals and for society as a
whole. 'The most complete security' for the constitution was 'to be
effected by the highest attainable equality in the social condition of
our citizens.' Since 'power will always unite with the few or the many,
according to the extension or limitation of knowledge', it followed that
'the highest attainable equality is to be accomplished by education
and internal improvement as they distribute among the whole
community the advantages of knowledge and wealth.' An active
government, intervening in society to diffuse knowledge, to promote
equality and therefore to guarantee both order and liberty – this was
Seward's vision.[65]

How realistic were these hopes? Whether the increasingly
commercialised market economy was, as Seward claimed, an agent of
equality or, as the Democrats retorted, a cause of ever-increasing
inequality is still uncertain. Research into the distribution of wealth in
ante-bellum America tentatively suggests that some fast-growing
regions, including particularly towns and cities, were characterised by
greater, not less inequality. While it would be difficult to deny

[64] *Ibid.,* III, 209-10, 263. See also III, 148.
[65] *Ibid.,* III, 213.

Seward's main point that a newly constructed road or canal would increase the wealth of a particular area, it would also be necessary to consider any detrimental effect upon that, or any other, community. Even after this calculation had been made, the total effect upon the entire economy, including any changes in commodity prices, in the availability of goods, in the redeployment of labour, in migration (and emigration) and in the rate of return upon capital would have to be taken into account. Such data will probably never be available. Yet since the debate over capitalism and equality still persists, it might be fair to conclude that Seward's view was at least plausible.[66]

Similarly Seward's seemingly extravagant claims for the egalitarian power of education should at least be treated with respect. Throughout the Western world liberals have, for over a century, concentrated much of their reformist energy upon schools, often with the hope of creating a more egalitarian society in the process. Indeed the reform programme of the 1960s, promoted by John F. Kennedy and Lyndon B. Johnson, concentrated so heavily upon education for precisely this reason. The attraction was, as late as 1966, what it had been in 1837 – equality without dispossession. Again it was to be a levelling upwards. Only recently has this approach fallen into some disrepute.[67]

The major weakness in Seward's reform programme lies elsewhere. Whether he was right or wrong he failed to explain in detail the mechanism by which internal improvements and education would produce the desired results. The Democrats repeatedly argued that an active government inevitably furthered the interests of the dominant groups in society. Surprisingly perhaps, Seward failed to confront the question.

In spite of this, Seward's outlook is unmistakably modern. Hopeful for the future, committed to the principles of self-government, and confident that a capitalist economy would produce a society of free and reasonably equal citizens, he had constructed an image of America which is still easily recognisable. The view of democracy, with its perception of order and liberty as opposite sides of the same coin and the vision of a differentiated society characterised by dynamic growth and interdependent occupational groups linked through the market mechanism effectively anticipated the self-image of industrial, democratic America. Nevertheless his assumption that equality could be produced without in any way antagonising the more

[66] Some of the advocates of the new monetarism claim that an essentially unregulated market economy produces the highest substantial degree of equality.

[67] See Christopher Jencks, *Inequality* (London, 1975).

powerful interests in society sets his liberalism apart from that of, for example, the New Deal. And this difference is surely enough to negate the whole comparison. His was essentially the ideology of liberal Whiggery. It differed from that of the Democratic party – of 1836 or of 1936.

Yet whatever its limitations, Seward's liberalism was sufficient to create antagonisms within his own party. Even in New York he and his fellow liberals encountered serious opposition from the conservative Whigs. By 1842 the Governor had decided to retire from politics. He would not seek re-election, partly because of the hostility displayed by sections of the Whig party. In a private letter Seward gave his reasons for not seeking renomination:

> My principles are too liberal, too philanthropic. . . for my party. . . Those principles. . . .do not receive fair consideration and candid judgment. There are some who know them to be right, and believe them sincere. These would sustain me. Others whose prejudices are aroused against them, or whose interests are in danger, would combine against me. I must, therefore, divide my party in a convention.[68]

Some historians have seized on the pronouncements of liberal Whigs like Seward, Weed and Greeley and taken them as representative of the party as a whole. From this they have concluded that the two major parties were fraternal twins: the Whigs were no less democratic than the Democrats. It is a misleading judgment. The liberals were themselves fully aware of their differences with their conservative colleagues and not for one moment did they believe that the parties were ideologically indistinguishable. After the party's defeats of 1841 Seward, again in a private letter, drew attention to the party's failings. Because it 'sympathised not with the masses', he wrote, it 'was always held at bay'. This was a theme to which he frequently returned. Similarly Horace Greeley (whose radical opinions should never be regarded as typical of, or even connected with, the party) felt the need publicly to explain why 'in other respects Liberal and Progressive' he should yet 'sympathize and act with, the American Whig party, rather than its great antagonist'. 'Hitherto', Greeley had written, some years earlier, in a private letter to Weed, 'all the advocates of social reform of any kind, all the advocates of a higher destiny for labor, all the combatants against injustice and false social principles, in short, all the social discontent of the country' had been 'regularly repelled from

---

[68] Seward to Christopher Morgan in Frederick W. Seward (ed.), *William H. Seward: An Autobiography* (N.Y., 1891), 547.

the Whig party and attracted to its opposite'. Greeley feared that the Whigs were in danger of being 'considered the enemies of improvement and the bulwarks of an outgrown aristocracy in the country'.[69]

Thus both Seward and Greeley were aware that their opinions and principles were controversial even within their own party. The conservatives were still more aware of it. By 1838 Philip Hone was lamenting the absence from the state assembly ticket of any 'leading Federalist or National Republican' name. Similarly Daniel D. Barnard, a conservative Whig congressman, felt that the liberals threatened 'the structure of civil society'. According to Barnard, Thurlow Weed was no more than a 'demagogue'. James Watson Webb of the *Courier and Enquirer* likewise warned that 'a portion of the Whig Press' was 'as radical as that of the worst portion of the Loco Foco' so that 'from them nothing can be expected'. According to Webb, the views set forth in Greeley's *Tribune,* the primary offender, were 'utterly hostile to that wholesome *conservatism* which, more than other feature, is the peculiar mark and glory of the Whigs'. In 1846 when the party nominated John Young, a prominent liberal, for Governor, Webb in disgust left the state convention.[70]

What were the relative strengths of the two wings of the party? In New York state the liberals were perhaps dominant,[71] although the conservatives made up an important minority. But elsewhere the balance was probably different. The *New York Express*, vociferous in its attacks upon the liberals, on one occasion suggested that by expelling them the party could improve its electoral performance. Its principles and membership would then, the article continued, be more closely in line with those of the Whig party in other states:

> Now there is no reason why the Whig party in this State should
> not always be in power, as it is in Massachusetts, Vermont, or

[69] e.g. Lee Benson, *Concept, passim;* Seward to Weed, 12 April 1835, in John J. Reed, 'The Emergence of the Whig Party in the North; Massachusetts, New York, Pennsylvania and Ohio' (Ph.D. thesis, University of Pennsylvania, 1953), 299-300; Greeley, *Why I Am A Whig,* 1; Greeley to Weed, 27 Jan. 1841, in Thurlow W. Barnes, *Memoir of Thurlow Weed* (Boston, 1884), 93. Benson, it should be noted, found significant differences between the parties on ethnocultural questions. (See below, Chapter 5, for a critique of this view).

[70] Herbert Kriedman, 'New York's Philip Hone, Businessman – Politician-Patron of Arts and Letters' (Ph.D. thesis, New York University, 1965), 228-9; Sharon H. Penney, 'Daniel Dewey Barnard: Patrician in Politics'(Ph.D. thesis, State University of New York at Albany, 1972), 117; *Courier and Enquirer,* 19 March, 28 April 1845. See also 19 May, 5 Aug. 1845, 16 April, 1844. On Webb see James L. Crouthamel, *James Watson Webb, a Biography* (Middletown, Conn., 1969), 104.

[71] It must be repeated, however, that Greeley's radicalism was in no way representative of New York Whiggery.

Rhode Island, or generally, as in Connecticut, but except that it is demoralised by such [liberal] principles. . . . We have more Whig interests in property at stake than any Whig State in New England, or in the Union – *but this New York is the only one of the Free States where in the Loco-Foco party there is nearly, if not quite as large an amount of property as there is in the Whig party* – and the cause of this is that such principles as the Albany Evening Journal and its slavishly following echoes in different parts of the State promulgate and defend, keep back from us men of property in the Loco-Foco ranks and divert from us men of property in the Whig ranks.

Even when allowance is made for partisan exaggeration, this statement cannot be entirely discounted. Among the Eastern states New York's Whigs may have been atypical.[72]

Yet although the liberal-conservative division was nowhere as deep as it was in New York, some generalisations can be made. Thus where urban and mercantile interests predominated, conservative Whiggery tended to flourish. In New York state, the conservatives, known as 'Silver Grays', were centred on Buffalo, Albany, Binghampton and, especially, New York City. 'Urban location', according to one historian, 'was the key factor in fostering Silver Gray support'. In 1839 the conservatives generally backed Henry Clay for the party's Presidential nomination. New York City delegates to the convention, according to Philip Hone, were 'out and out Clay men'. Clay was identified with the conservative wing of the party; the liberals, from central and western New York, looked instead to Winfield Scott or William Henry Harrison. In New England liberal Whiggery was less prominent and the conservatives were far more successful than in New York. New England Whigs perhaps resembled a Philip Hone rather than a William Seward.[73]

Although further research is needed to demonstrate the proposition more conclusively, it seems likely that the pattern was similar elsewhere in the nation. Henry Clay was the accredited conservative leader (although his support was broad enough to encompass men from all sections of the party). The *Madisonian* conceded that Clay was strong with the mercantile interests in the cities. In New Jersey, the Whigs from the Eastern area of the state were, in the late 1830s, Clay supporters; in the West Harrison was favoured. In Pennsylvania

[72]*New York Express,* 25 Aug. 1845, in *Cincinnati Daily Enquirer,* 10 Sept. 1845. For a similar statement by Daniel D. Bernard see Penney, 'Barnard', 129.

[73]Lee H. Warner, 'The Silver Grays: New York State's Conservative Whigs, 1846-1856' (Ph.D. thesis, University of Wisconsin, 1971), 145-157, 171; Kriedman, 'Hone', 256. See also *Autobiography of Weed,* 481; *Memoir of Weed,* 89.

170

the Anti-Masonic party (which was allied with the Whigs against the Democrats) was powerful in the Western sections of the state. It effectively replaced liberal Whiggery. Many of the Anti-Masons in 1839 wanted to support Harrison; some even left the state convention when Clay was nominated. The Whigs proper 'came principally from the Philadelphia area'. In Delaware there was also a split between 'reform Whigs' and 'old Whigs', while in Maryland the Baltimore contingent were 'real staunch Clay Whigs'. Similarly there was a cleavage in North Carolina between what one historian has called the 'Federal Whigs', who were strongly in favour of a national bank, and the 'Republican Whigs', who were more liberal on the question. Another scholar has hinted that a similar division even existed in the Florida territory. Although it did not attain the depth of the comparable schism within the Democracy, the liberal-conservative division within the Whig party was a prominent feature on the political landscape.[74]

John Tyler and the Alliance of the Centre

If agreement upon 'fundamentals' was not characteristic of the politics of the Jacksonian era, it could nevertheless be argued that the moderates in each party were not separated by any basic ideological disagreements. The consensus upon democracy and capitalism which some historians believe to have underlain the entire era in fact united conservative Democrats with liberal Whigs. But this unity remained ideological rather than organisational. The defenders of 'liberal capitalism' were divided between the two parties and a relative weakness was the inevitable result. The bitter strife and seemingly gross partisanship which characterises Jacksonian politics as well as the maturity and relative stability of the two party system are attributable in no small measure to the disunity of the moderates.[75]

[74] *Madisonian,* 2 July 1842; Walter R. Fallow, 'The Rise of the Whig Party in New Jersey' (Ph.D. thesis, Princeton, 1966), 307-10; *Proceedings of the Democratic Whig State Convention held in Chambersburg, Pa, 13-14 June 1839* (Chambersburg, 1839), 12-26; *Proceedings of the Whigs of Chester County, Pennsylvania Favorable to a Distinct Organization of the Whig Party* (n.p., n.d.), 6, 21; Charles M. Snyder, *The Jacksonian Heritage, Pennsyslvania Politics 1833-1848* (Harrisburg, Pa., 1958), 45; Richard A. Wire, 'John M. Clayton and the Search for Order: A Study in Whig Politics and Diplomacy' (Ph.D. thesis, University of Maryland, 1971), 136 (Wire gives no details of the split within the party), Sister Mary St. Patrick McConville, *Political Nativism in the State of Maryland* (Washington, D.C., 1928), 12; J.G. de Roulhac Hamilton, 'Party Politics in North Carolina', *J.S.H.P.,* vol. XV (Durham, N.C., 1916), 68; *Tallahassee Florida Sentinel,* 13 Aug. 1841.

[75] Much of what has been written on the Jacksonian era in support of the consensus overview is well applicable to the agreement between conservative Democrats and liberal Whigs.

In the early 1840s, however, a serious attempt was made to unite the moderates under one political banner. When John Tyler succeeded to the Presidency his refusal to approve a bill to incorporate a new national bank marked the beginning of an attempt to attract moderate opinion within both parties. Tyler hoped to launch a new party, an alliance of the centre against the two extremes. According to the *Madisonian*, 'every Whig is not an ultra-Bank man; nor every Democrat a Bentonian humbugger', and it was 'to the *moderate* men that the country looks for salvation'. Backed by the power and influence of the Presidency, the projected third party not unnaturally alarmed both Whigs and Democrats alike. Thus Samuel J. Tilden was one Democrat who feared that Tyler might draw some Jacksonians into his orbit while Millard Fillmore by January 1842 was in despair in case the Whig party should 'break up from its very foundations'. According to Fillmore the party had 'no common principle – no common head'. But these fears proved groundless and Tyler's third party never even came close to becoming a major political force.[76]

The story of Tyler's break with the Whig party has often been recounted. Although some of the details remain unclear, the basic facts have been established. There is no doubt that Tyler at the outset promised to approve a national bank of limited powers. But he regarded this as the maximum possible concession and as a proof of his desire to co-operate with the Congressional party. The Congressional Whigs, however, passed a bill for a more traditional bank, hoping to force Tyler into signing it, but assuming that, in the event of a veto, they could then obtain the more limited institution to which he had already assented. Tyler, not unnaturally enraged at what he took to be an attempt at coercion, then retreated into his original opposition to virtually any national bank and vetoed not only the first but both bills. This apparent breach of faith sealed his fate with the Congressional Whigs and he was eventually expelled from the party.[77]

Some historians have criticised the actions of Tyler and of Henry Clay during the crisis of 1841-2. But the cause of the breach lay in the divergence of opinion between Tyler, a states-rights Whig, and the

---

[76] *Madisonian*, 25 Feb. 1842; Tilden to Nelson J. Waterbury, 11 Sept. 1841, in John Bigelow (ed.), *Letters and Literary Memorials of Samuel J. Tilden*, 2 vols. (N.Y., 1908), II, 8; Fillmore to Weed, 22 Jan., 1842, in Frank H. Severance (ed.), *The Millard Fillmore Papers*, 2 vols. (Buffalo, 1907), II, 227.

[77] Good accounts of the crisis are to be found in Sydney Nathan's *Daniel Webster and Jacksonian Democracy* (Baltimore, 1973), esp. 163-95; George R. Poage, *Henry Clay and the Whig Party* (Chapel Hill, N.C., 1936); Lyon G. Tyler, *The Letters and Times of the Tylers*, 3 vols. (Richmond, Va., 1894-6), esp. vol. II.

172

overwhelming majority of the party who advocated orthodox Whig policies. The Whigs had not yet achieved the degree of unity which the Democrats could boast, and indeed full unity was not attained until the expulsion of the Tylerites had been completed. Tyler's opinions had scarcely been considered when he had been nominated. Thus the unexpected death of Harrison, the first White House incumbent to die whilst in office, made the rift probable if not inevitable.

Although agreement could have been reached, had the Whigs been prepared to compromise at the outset, it was not merely obstinacy or tactical ineptitude which prevented this. When William Rives, Tyler's spokesman in the Senate, suggested that the compromise bank bill be introduced as an 'experiment', Henry Clay made a reply which accurately portrays the mood of the Whigs:

> The Senator tells us that if *his* experiment fail, we may then make a Bank after the old model. Why, sir, what have we been struggling against for the last eight years? Experiment after experiment until our country has been brought to the very brink of ruin. And, at the moment when we have not merely seen land, but got, as all had hoped, into a safe port; when storms and tempests and experiments were at an end, and the bright sun of hope and prosperity was bursting upon our joyful vision, the Senator from Virginia comes forward and asks us, once more to put to sea with him on a distant and perilous cruise, and to try *another* experiment.

Having campaigned in a recent election against executive power, the Whigs could not perhaps have been expected to compromise with a President who held office, it seemed, only because of fortuitous circumstances. The Whigs' room for manoeuvre was limited by their own ideological commitment.[78]

Nevertheless, when the partyless President introduced his new fiscal policy, proposing to establish an 'Exchequer', some Whigs did not look unfavourably upon it. Liberal Whigs like Weed (who had, of course, for many years been seeking to rid the party of its commitment to a national bank) were willing to support the measure. But the difficulty for Tyler, as he pursued a middle course, was that virtually his every action alienated some elements within the party. Thus Weed and the liberals were prepared to concede ground on the bank issue; they were incensed at Tyler's lukewarm support for the tariff. Western Whigs, less concerned with a protective tariff, were outraged when Tyler prevented a distribution of the surplus government

[78]*Cong. Gl.,* 27 i App., 354.

revenues. Northern anti-slavery Whigs were antagonised by Tyler's desire to annex Texas; they looked with suspicion or contempt upon the states-rights doctrines which he had espoused throughout his career. Thus the Whigs were alienated by Tyler's attempts to recruit Democratic support; they were less than enraptured by his efforts to retain theirs.[79]

Conversely, the Democrats were able to object to Tyler's repeal of the Independent Treasury and to his response to the Dorr controversy.[80] They could afford to observe from afar the spectacle of a Whig President at odds with a Whig Congress. Some conservative Democrats were willing to invite Tyler to rejoin the Democratic party; a few were even prepared to consider him as a Presidential candidate. But they had no reason to desire a realignment of parties, which would surely have weakened them, at least in the short term.

The two party system thus withstood the shock of the Tyler crisis. Perhaps there was a critical point after which Tyler's support would have snowballed; the Tyler party never came close to attaining this degree of strength. Each of the major parties, presumably frightened that any division would result in the triumph of its enemy, managed to retain its unity. The moderates in each party no doubt resented their more extreme colleagues. But they were almost certainly repelled by the extremists in their opponents' ranks. Hostility and revulsion were perhaps the decisive feelings.

Although it is possible to identify the clash over democracy and commercialism as the ideological foundation of the two party system, it would be an error to assume that party loyalty was a mere reflex of ideas. The partisan who had enlisted with the Democracy or the Whig party had by the 1840s acquired an attachment to the policies for which the party stood,[81] to his colleagues within the party and even to

---

[79]*A.E.J.*, 10 June 1842. Weed and the liberals, as has already been noted, were consistent advocates of a protective tariff. Distribution was a favourite measure with Western Whigs – see Raynor M. Wellington, *The Political and Sectional Influence of the Public Lands, 1828-1842* (Cambridge, Mass., 1914), 105; George M. Stephenson *The Political History of the Public Lands from 1840 to 1862 – from Pre-Emption to Homestead* (Boston, 1917), 56, 84. The Northern Whig party was generally more militantly anti-slavery than the Democracy, see below Chapter 5. Essentially Whig economic policy was a package of measures, each designed to appeal to one or more sections of the Union, see below, Chapter 6. Tyler's attempts to pick and choose among them threatened the entire package.

[80]On the Dorr War see below, Chapter 6.

[81]Thus conservative Democrats generally adhered to Democratic *laissez-faire* principles; liberal Whigs remained governmental activists. The resulting division over policy was probably greater than any ideological divergence which underlay it.

the party itself as an institution.[82] This multi-faceted loyalty was matched by a corresponding antagonism towards the opposing party and the combined force of these pressures was enough to guarantee the survival of the second party system – at least until the emergence of the slavery controversy. The consensus over liberal capitalism in a sense linked the two parties; it was an agreement which prevailed at the centre of the spectrum of political opinion. But the ideological cleavage between Whig and Democrat cannot be encompassed within it.

[82] See below, Chapter 6 for a discussion of these other motivations.

PART THREE

THE ROLE OF IDEOLOGY

5

THE ETHNOCULTURAL DIMENSION

By the Jacksonian era American society already exhibited an extraordinary heterogeneity. In its ethnic composition this society was almost uniquely diverse; in the multiplicity of religious faiths espoused by its citizens it was no less remarkable. Historians have traditionally recognised, of course, that these different ethnic and religious groups did not always co-exist harmoniously. More recently (and more controversially), however, some historians have insisted that disagreements over what are termed 'ethnocultural' issues were often the major sources of political conflict in the United States.

Such was the contention of Lee Benson in his influential work *The Concept of Jacksonian Democracy*. Writing in 1961, Benson in effect sought to give an entirely new direction to Jacksonian historiography. While historians had for years debated the significance and meaning of the term 'Jacksonian Democracy', Benson argued that the term had 'forced' historians 'to operate within an inadequate framework of ideas' and should be discarded. Benson endorsed the consensus formulation of agreement upon 'fundamentals' and concluded that in the Jacksonian era such agreement clearly existed between the two parties. Both political parties were capitalistic, both were democratic.[1]

Benson did not, however, suggest that fundamental agreement necessarily produced harmony. Instead, he claimed, it would 'permit almost every kind of social conflict, tension and difference to find political expression'. Benson, whose work was limited to New York, and his former student Ronald P. Formisano, who analysed Michigan politics, argued that such conflicts arose primarily over ethnic and religious problems. Since 'both masses and élites agreed on the basics of political economy', political partisanship 'did not originate in class antagonism'. Instead the 'presence of sharp ethnic and religious conflict . . . cut vertically through class groups and inhibited class resentments.' Thus Jacksonian politics did not express class conflicts; they muffled them.[2]

---

[1] Lee Benson, *The Concept of Jacksonian Democracy* (Princeton, 1961), 335. For a critique of this work see Michael A. Lebowitz, 'The Significance of Claptrap in American History,' *S.L.* (Winter, 1963), 79-94.

[2] Benson, *Concept,* 27; Ronald P. Formisano, *The Birth of Mass Parties: Michigan, 1827-1871* (Princeton, 1971), 55. Another work in the same vein is Paul Kleppner, *The Cross of Culture: A Social Analysis of Midwestern Politics, 1850-1900* (N.Y., 1970). Important criticisms of the ethnocultural school include J. Morgan Kousser,

According to Benson and Formisano the parties differed in their atttudes towards ethnic and cultural homogeneity and in their ideas on group and individual responsibility. Essentially the Whig view of government was interventionist: social evils such as intemperance were the responsibility of the entire society and therefore of the government which served it. The spirit of Whiggery was thus that of an evangelical protestantism; the Whig party gave expression to the desire for cultural uniformity and homogeneity that was widespread among evangelical Protestants. Its natural enemies were thus the immigrant, the Roman Catholic (and especially the Roman Catholic immigrant) and the anti-evangelical Protestant. The crusade which it fought for moral improvement and cultural homogeneity also entailed a distinctive view of politics itself. The political party fell under suspicion.[3] As Formisano explains:

> Men who desired society unified by shared moral codes tended to assume that government and society possessed organic unity. Party organisation contradicted these assumptions and mocked the idea that government existed to promote the commonweal and by suffrance of the commonalty.

Whiggery was thus evangelical, interventionist and moralistic.[4]

The mirror image of the Whig outlook was that of the Democrats. An opposition to evangelicalism enlisted various of the Protestant sects together with the Roman Catholics, the non-believers and the immigrants in the defence of cultural and ethnic diversity. Individual responsibilty for intemperance (or slavery) implied a non-interventionist role for government while the recognition of heterogeneity removed an obstacle to the acceptance of political parties. The Democrats, in contrast to the Whigs, stressed cultural heterogeneity, ethnic diversity and 'laissez-faire'.

It is easy to acknowledge that the perspective offered by Benson and Formisano has enabled historians to explain phenomena that were otherwise unintelligible and to formulate additional hypotheses

'The "New Political History": A Methodological critique', *R.A.H.*, IV (March 1976), 1-14; Richard B. Latner and Peter D. Levine, 'Perspectives on Antebellum Pietistic Politics,' *ibid*, 15-24; Richard L. McCormick, 'Ethno-Cultural Interpretations of Nineteenth-Century Voting Behavior', *P.S.Q.* LXXXIX (June 1974), 351-77; Donald J. Ratcliffe, 'Politics in Jacksonian Ohio: Reflections on the Ethnocultural Interpretation', *O.H.* (Winter, 1979), 5-36; James E. Wright, 'The Ethnocultural Model of Voting: A Behavioral and Historical Critique', *A.B.S.*, XVI (May/June 1973), 653-74.

[3] Anti-party is not discussed in detail by Benson. However it is here treated alongside issues that were more obviously ethnocultural in nature.

[4] Formisano, *Birth of Mass Parties,* 77.

with which to examine the politics of the era. Yet, in denying Democratic hostility to capitalism and Whig reservations about democracy, the ethnocultural interpretation leaves many questions unanswered. How, for example, is party conflict to be explained in those regions (especially in the South) where there was great ethnic homogeneity, little immigration and a Whig party which showed 'unwillingness to join the movements for humanitarian reform'?[5] Roughly the same degree of party competition prevailed in these areas as in Michigan or New York. Even more significant, why (especially in the post-Panic years) did banking become the crucial subject in politics, the major area of disagreement between the parties, the foremost concern of both rhetoricians and legislators? Finally, why did the Whigs fail 'to muster against the Democrats . . . a competitive egalitarian appeal'?[6] Formisano notes this fact but the ethnocultural interpretation is powerless to account for it.[7]

Immigration

There can be little doubt that hostility to the immigrant was expressed through the Whig party rather than through the Democracy. Daniel Webster in 1844 expressed his 'deep and strong conviction' that a reform of the naturalisation laws was an urgent necessity. No less than 'the preservation of the Government' demanded it. Webster was speaking in the aftermath of Henry Clay's defeat in the Presidential election of 1844. The result, it was widely felt, had been determined by the immigrant vote. Yet Webster's hostility was not of such recent

---

[5]Herbert Ershkowitz and William G. Shade, 'Consensus or Conflict? Political Behavior in the State Legislatures during the Jacksonian Era', *J.A.H.*, LVIII (Dec. 1971), 591-621; Formisano, *Birth of Mass Parties*, 8. See also Burton W. Fulsom II, 'The Politics of Elites: Prominence and Party in Davidson County, Tennessee, 1835-1861', *J.S.H.*, XXXIX (Aug. 1973), 359-78.

[6]To explain this Formisano in effect employs a conspiracy theory, claiming that the Democratic class-conscious rhetoric and 'vocabulary' was 'borrowed from the true radicals of the day'. It functioned 'as a smokescreen for clever, opportunistic men'. Largely because he fails to make allowance for the factional splits within the Democratic party, and especially for the factional split between radicals and conservatives, Formisano does not see the similarity between his 'true radicals' – the Eastern Workingmen – and the radical Democrats. In effect he points to the behaviour of conservatives to discredit the utterances of radicals. The failure to recognise intra-party disputes is the more surprising since Floyd B. Streeter *(Political Parties in Michigan, 1837-1860* (Lansing, 1918) – a book to which Formisano frequently refers) actually analysed the parties according to their factional composition. See Formisano, *Birth of Mass Parties*, 30, 55.

[7]This chapter does not attempt a full analysis of nativism, social and moral reform movements, or pro and anti-party theory. The aim is to show how and where these movements and ideas intersected with, and influenced, party ideology.

origin for he had 'seen the pernicious influence of these foreign votes for the last thirty years'. Willie P. Mangum, Whig Senator from North Carolina, displayed an even more intense dislike of foreign 'influence' in opposing the 1838 Pre-emption Act. The act, by offering full and equal pre-emption rights to the immigrant, attracted 'the bandit of the Appenines, the mercenary Swiss, the hungry loafer of the cities of the Old World, the offal of the disgorged jails, penitentiaries and houses of correction of foreign countries'. Senator Merrick of Maryland (also a Whig) attempted to amend the bill so as to exclude non-citizens from its provisions; his support came exclusively from his own party.[8] It was thus natural that when in the 1830s and 1840s, Native American[9] parties sprang into existence in the urban centres of the nation, the Whigs were far more sympathetic than the Democrats. Henry Clay, though opposed to a complete amalgamation, admitted that 'with the Natives, we have strong sympathies and ought to cultivate amicable relations'. Alexander Porter, Whig Senator from Louisiana and himself an Irish immigrant, yet agreed with the Nativists that the naturalisation period should be extended, while one Clay supporter confessed that 'for forty years' his opinion had been that 'there should be no citizens of the United States except those born within its limits'. In New York city, a focus of Nativist influence, the bargains made between Whigs and Nativists impelled one Catholic newspaper to point out to 'a naturalized citizen' that 'if he supports the Whig party, he supports the cause of nativism, and aids it in its unholy crusade against his own rights'. 'The truth', according to Democrat James Bowlin of Missouri, was that 'these Native Americans' were 'nothing more than a wing of the Whig party'.[10]

Bowlin described nativism as a 'noxious plant' which 'flourishes in corruption'. This was the standard Democratic response. The Nativists were themselves denounced as 'the worst and most unnatural of aliens' and Democrats were prepared to 'explicitly disclaim all

[8]J.W. McIntyre (ed.), *The Writings and Speeches of Daniel Webster,* 18 vols. (Boston, 1903), XIII, 303, 321; *Cong. Gl.,* 26 i App., 48, 25 ii App., 129.

[9]These were sometimes called 'Native American' parties, sometimes 'American Republicans' and sometimes 'American' parties. Here the term 'Nativist' is employed to cover all.

[10]Clay to Clayton, 2 Dec. 1844, in Richard A. Wire, 'John M. Clayton and the Search for Order. A Study in Whig Politics and Diplomacy' (Ph.D. thesis, University of Maryland, 1971), 186; Porter to Crittenden, 2 Jan. 1841, in William H. Adams III, 'The Louisiana Whig Party' (Ph.D. thesis, Louisiana State University, 1960), 127; E Pettigreu to Clay, 1 Jan. 1845, in Calvin Colton (ed.), *The Life and Works of Henry Clay,* 10 vols. (N.Y., 1904), V, 519; *Truth Teller* in Herbert I. Loudon, 'The Nativist Movement and the American Republican Party in New York City during the Period 1843-1847' (Ph.D. thesis, University of New York, 1966), 208; *Cong. Gl.,* 29 i App., 44.

fraternity of feeling and connection with such men'. The Democratic
national platforms of 1840, 1844 and 1848 contained the following
resolution:

> That the liberal principles embodied by Jefferson in the
> Declaration of Independence, and sanctioned in the Constitution,
> which make ours the land of liberty, and the asylum of the
> oppressed of every nation, have ever been cardinal principles in
> the Democratic faith; and every attempt to abridge the present
> privilege of becoming citizens, and the owners of soil among us,
> ought to be resisted, with the same spirit which swept the alien
> and sedition laws from our book.

This does not, however, convey the outrage which some Democrats
felt towards the Nativists. Alexander Duncan of Ohio told Congress
that they were 'base demagogues', 'infamous despoilers of the elective
franchise', 'calumniators and foul detractors of the American
character and Republican principles' and 'political swindlers'. The
very name of Nativist, he added, 'sickens me'.[11]

It is significant that Duncan was one of the most radical Jacksonians
to win a seat in Congress. Extremism on ethnic questions accompanied
economic radicalism. This was no coincidence. Duncan's attitudes
towards banks and towards nativism, like those of his colleagues
within the party, and also those of his Whig opponents, were
intimately related and mutually reinforcing. The nativist controversy
is explicable only in terms of the fundamental differences in ideology –
in social and political philosophy – between Whig and Democrat.

It was perhaps inevitable that, as the tide of immigration swelled in
the 1830s and 1840s, thinking men of all persuasions should be
impelled to confront the problems which it brought and to consider the
issues which it raised. The immigrants tended to arrive in large
numbers in the nation's seaboard cities and to settle in what were
already, or what rapidly became, the poorer quarters. Often unskilled
and illiterate, they naturally sought companionship with their countrymen and found consolation from the drudgery of manual labour or the
misery of unemployment in drink or the church. The largest ethnic
group were the Irish, whose fierce patriotism and intense loyalty to the
Roman Catholic church made them a conspicuous, seemingly alien,

---

[11]*Cong. Gl.,* 29 i App., 43; Henry E. Riell, *An Appeal to the Voluntary Citizens of
the United States* (N.Y., 1840), 3; Kirk H. Porter and Donald B. Johnson, *National
Party Platforms* (Urbana, 1966), 2, 4, 11; *Cong. Gl.,* 29 i App., 44. Whig presidential
platforms contained no reference to immigration.

and unassimilable element. The Irish areas were often those with the highest crime rate; the Irish made up a large proportion of the paupers in the almshouses of Boston, Philadelphia, New York, and other Eastern cities. The presence of the Irish in particular, and of immigrants in general, was thus in direct conflict with Republican America's traditional self-image: the nation of law-abiding Protestants, comprising a society that was fluid and harmonious, unified and prosperous.[12]

This image was the one which the Nativists saw. American society, they felt, was unique in offering the poor opportunities for wealth, success and self-advancement. Lewis Levin, Nativist Representative from Philadelphia, challenged Congressmen to show him 'a nation where mankind can obtain so abundantly all the comforts of life, at so little cost of labour'. William S. Miller, one of New York city's Native Americans who won election to Congress, stated what was merely the necessary and almost inevitable corollary when he argued for the unity of interests among the different classes and occupational groups. 'Labor', he reminded the Democrats, 'cannot flourish without imparting prosperity to the capitalist; nor can you tax and oppress the capitalist without ultimately taxing the labor of the country'. Miller admitted that it was possible to 'strip the rich man' but in so doing, he warned, 'the poor man you both strip and starve'. This same highly conservative attitude was struck by his colleague Thomas A. Woodruff, who reacted strongly to the Democratic charge that the tariff made the rich richer. Woodruff was willing, as few politicians were, to deny that this was an unfortunate consequence. His indignation was unmistakable:

> In the name of heaven, is it in this free land of ours a crime to be rich? Is it a fault by the sweat of our brow to accumulate wealth? Has it come to this, that Americans are to be taunted and denounced because, from the exercise of their intellect, skill, and industry, from the employment of their capital and their strict adherence to business, they have become rich? . . . What if the system should make the "rich richer": is not the wealth still here, and is it not diffused among the community? I have yet to learn that the accumulation of wealth by honest industry and enterprise should be regarded as a national calamity

[12] This paragraph is based on Ray A. Billington, *The Protestant Crusade 1800-1860* (N.Y., 1938); Oscar Handlin, *Boston's Immigrants* (Cambridge, 1959); Leo Hershkowitz, 'New York City, 1834-1840, A Study in Local Politics' (Ph.D. thesis, University of New York. 1960); Robert F. Hueston, 'The Catholic Press and Nativism, 1840-1860' (Ph.D. thesis, Notre Dame University, Indiana, 1972); Ira M. Leonard, 'New York City Politics, 1841-1844; Nativism and Reform' (Ph.D. thesis, University of New York, 1965); Loudon, 'Nativist Movement'.

The description which New York Nativist William W. Campbell
offered of himself is applicable to the entire party. Campbell was 'no
friend of radicalism – no exciter of hostile feelings between different
classes and pursuits'.[13]

This social conservatism entailed a matching political philosophy.
The Washington *Native American* noted an article published in the
Democratic Review on the Supreme Court. Its author (Charles J.
Ingersoll), the paper reported, 'is opposed to the venerableness of the
Supreme Bench, scoffs at the reverence for old rules and orders – and
old opinions – for old wisdom and old virtue'. 'Is he aware', the editor
asked with pathos, 'that he scoffs at the dearest doctrines we
possess?'[14] Similarly Nativists embraced the highly conservative
ideal of the single, separate national character. A social equality being
a manifest absurdity, the cement of society, they felt, would be the
spirit of brotherhood, the mutual respect that obtained in the
family, extended so as to enclose the whole of society. For 'in a
Republican form of Government . . . nothing tends to produce the
greater degree of national and private happiness so much as the
unanimity of sentiments, the similarity of action on the part of the
people'. 'Unanimity', essential to the preservation of social and
political tranquillity, could 'only be obtained and preserved by the
continuance of a national and separate character.' What was this
national character? 'Americanus', writing in the *Native American*,
defined it as 'that individuality of language, habits, thought, action
and fraternal love which characterizes every nation and tribe of
people. . . . That complete bond of union, that perfect unity of purpose
which distinguish every section and division of mankind'. The
Nativist aim, according to the New York Executive Committee of the
party, was 'to become a single, great people, distinct in national
character, political interest, social and civic affinities, from all the
other nations of the earth'.[15]

The openly conservative outlook of the Nativists made them
natural allies for the Whig party. Thus their Congressmen and
newspapers were able to endorse the Whig economic programme, to
demand, for example, a protective tariff and the circulation of small
banknotes in the District of Columbia. One of their Representatives
went so far as to lament, in public, Henry Clay's defeat in 1844.[16]

[13]*Cong. Gl.*, 29 i App., 47, 1076, 1069, 620.

[14]*Nat. Am.*, 24 Feb. 1838.

[15]*Nat. Am.*, 19, 27 Aug. 1837; *Address of the General Executive Committee of the
American Republican Party of the City of New York* (N.Y., 1845), 14.

[16]*Cong. Gl.*, 29 i App., 1066-70; *Nat. Am.*, 14 Oct. 1837; *Cong. Gl.*, 29 ii App., 393.

Yet when the Nativists turned their gaze upon society as it was, and particularly as it was in the urban centres, they saw an assault upon their most cherished ideals. Here, for example, was the spectacle of paupers 'tottering by the hundreds and thousands to our poor houses'. The Nativist's intense conservatism, his genuine conviction that the social structure to which he was committed was best suited to the needs and capacities of Americans, his assumption that urban growth and the wage system were inherently good and valuable to the rich employer and the poorer wage-earner alike – all this ensured that the blame for this poverty should be placed upon the immigrant himself rather than the social system. The immigrants were 'idle' and 'vicious'; they comprised 'the ignorant, the poor, and the criminal'. Louisiana Nativists considered them 'destitute of any intellectual aspirations', being merely 'the pauper, the vagrant, and the convict', groups whose upkeep cost the American people as much as their own navy! But it was an anonymous writer, author of a pamphlet entitled *The Crisis*, who was perhaps most virulent in his denunciations of immigrants. Foreign influence, he argued, was 'an extraneous and unnatural fungus that has continued to drift in detached masses across the Atlantic from the rotten governments of Europe, the corrupt and wretched stews, pauper houses and prisons of overburdened and decrepid transatlantic monarchies'. Was America, he asked, to become 'the great slough-hole for the deposit of the world's filth'?[17]

The social conditions in the cities where immigration had been heaviest were doubtless responsible for much of the Nativist anxiety. Yet there was no concern for the immigrant himself; rather it was the calamitous consequences for the native population that were deplored. Of all the crimes of which the immigrant was convicted none was more serious than that of fostering radicalism. Nativists agonised over 'the radical influences' of which it was 'needless to speak' and which 'the foreign vote has introduced'. The fact that many labour and radical leaders were of European extraction was repeatedly emphasised. Thus the *Native American* drew attention to the 'levelling or agrarian system' which, it feared, was 'advancing with a stride that is truly alarming to every patriot'. 'This odious doctrine', the newspaper claimed, which was 'so much at war with good government', had been

---

[17] *Nat. Am.*, 14 Oct. 1837; *The Crisis! An Appeal to Our Countrymen, on the Subject of Foreign Influence in the United States* (N.Y., 1844), 6, 15, 64; *Address of the Louisiana Native American Association to the Citizens of Louisiana and the Inhabitants of the United States* (New Orleans, 1839), 4. Nativists occasionally attacked those immigrants who had amassed great wealth – see *Nat. Am.*, 14 Oct. 1837. This was not, however, a major grievance.

'first introduced into this country by foreigners'. From Europe had come radicals who sought 'to uproot society', to overthrow government, and to end the rule of law. Nativists saw indications that 'we have . . . reason to feel anxiety for the security of our country from anarchy and mob law'; the foreign origin of many radical leaders made them an obvious target for abuse.[18]

Yet it was not simply the leaders of the radical groups who were feared. These were no more than a tiny minority whose presence would presumably be little affected by a lengthening of the naturalisation period, the major Nativist demand. Rather it was the political power and influence of the immigrant masses which presented the major problem. Thus it was claimed that the Democratic party's 'disposition to array the poor man against the rich' was manifested in, and encouraged by, the existence of 'pauper foreigners'. The Nativists dreaded, in essence, the political consequences of the immigrant's presence, the scope which it offered to the demagogue and the radical (usually one and the same). 'Those who dream on in peace, fearing nothing', Campbell warned, 'will yet wake up to the reality of danger when it will be too difficult to avert it'.[19]

Nativists believed that many immigrants brought with them a spirit of blind obedience 'imbibed in their early youth' which made them easy prey for the party autocrat, who wished to mobilise them as a European monarch mobilised his subjects. They thus formed mindless masses, pawns in the hands of the corrupt, demagogic spoilsman. Alternatively, if in Europe they had effectively resisted 'the laws which govern them' then there was the equally grave danger that they would have 'that spirit of sedition and insubordination', that tendency towards 'unbridled licentiousness' which would prevent them from submitting 'to the sacred obligatons of law'. Going from Europe to America, immigrants would have passed 'from one extreme to another'. Seeking now a degree of liberty that was unreal and unattainable, they would be at the mercy of those base radicals who promised to give it them. According to the Louisiana Nativist Association, 'it would be a miracle, were they to stop precisely at the point of temperate liberty'. The Nativist's fear of radicalism, which itself sprang from his deeply conservative outlook, was a fundamental cause of his hostility to the immigrant.[20]

[18] *Cong. Gl.,* 29 i App., 621; *Nat. Am.,* 9 June, 1838, 10 Aug., 1837; *The Crisis,* 60; J.S. M'Farlane, *Address to the Public Authorities of the United States by the Louisiana Native American Association* (New Orleans, 1836), 11.

[19] *Nat. Am.,* 24 Feb., 1838; *Cong. Gl.,* 29 i App., 48.

[20] M'Farlane, *Address,* 11; *Address of Louisiana Native American Association,* 10.

The Louisiana Nativists' concern for 'temperate liberty' points towards one of the fundamental articles of the Nativist creed. Opposition to the immigrant both reinforced, and grew out of, a particular conception of liberty, a distinctive attitude towards popular government. To the Nativist democracy was a highly unstable form of government, one which was peculiarly exposed to the dangers of anarchy or tyranny. The Nativist lived in constant fear of a democracy 'growing out of exaggerated conceptions of liberty'. The editor of the *Native American* proclaimed himself and his colleagues 'the true disciples of liberty'. But, he added, 'we worship her for *her virtues*, not for *her vices*'. 'We should despise her', he continued, 'if she were to remove from us the restraints necessary for the good order of civilized life, and suffer us to sink into the indulgence of the beastly gratifications which are disgusting even in the barbarian'. Liberty in America was 'recognized, defined, and limited by the law' but if 'committed to the guardianship of those who do not appreciate her virtues', the result wuld be 'all kinds of excesses . . . anarchy and ruin'. The immigrants, it was clearly implied, were a group 'who do not appreciate her virtues'.[21]

The Nativist crusade in effect catalogued the dangers which men of a frankly conservative persuasion feared from democracy as it was perceived in the 1830s and 1840s. Many of their pronouncements can be seen as rejoinders to the populistic slogans which were being employed by the Democrats (and some of the Whigs). The *Native American* noted that radicals drew upon the doctrine of 'equal rights' which was indeed 'the virtual principle of our Government'. The editor tried to salvage something by emphasising that it was a principle 'restrained . . . by the wise and just provisions of our Constitution'. Yet he was clearly alarmed at the scope for radicalism which such a doctrine offered. 'Give it', he warned, 'the unbridled, licentious construction contended for by the agrarian or *foreign party*, and it assumes the form of a demon, that threatens all that is excellent in our civil and social systems.' Other Nativists drew attention to the 'cry raised here of natural rights'. This, they acknowledged, might be justified in a revolutionary situation, but in America it was 'little better than the ravings of insanity'. For 'individuals under an organized Government can claim no rights not embraced in their legal institutions'. When the Democrats, defending the immigrant suffrage, contended that place of birth was entirely accidental and therefore not a necessary qualification for political rights, the dismay of many Nativists was complete. For this idea seemed to set at nothing the

[21]*Nat. Am.*, 24 Feb., 9 June 1838; *Cong. Gl.*, 29 i App., 48.

prescriptive force of the past, to threaten the organic society with immediate dismemberment. If, irrespective of his birthplace or his individual merits, the immigrant could claim a political equality (for this was what the suffrage now denoted), the social fabric itself was in danger. For the Nativist naturally assumed a close relationship, virtually a mathematical ratio, between social and political inequality. If the place of birth held no political significance, it might soon become socially irrelevant. Thus inherited property would be threatened so that by this 'untenable and preposterous doctrine', the 'entire system of domestic relations would be broken up, – the legal possession of property would be destroyed, and there would be an end of civil government'. The Nativist was able to connect two such apparently unrelated issues as immigrant suffrage and the transmission of hereditary property only because of his particular attitude towards democracy. Many Nativists semed to visualise America's populistic government as an inverted pyramid, balanced on its point. The adoption of proposals as unsound as that of alien voting threatened to send the whole structure crashing to the ground.[22]

Hence, when Nativists demanded an extension of the natural-isation period, they were contending for principles which went far deeper than any purely ethnic hostility might suggest. Was it right, one Nativist wondered, that here 'where *all* depends upon the popular will', immigrants should almost immediately enjoy full political rights? By delaying the enfranchisement of the foreigner, the Nativist hoped to eliminate the spirit of radicalism from America, a spirit which was in every sense foreign and alien, dependent upon the social evils created by immigration and fed by the foreigners' ignorance of politics and constitutional republicanism. Thus he hoped to raise the tone of political life, to restore respect for the suffrage, to create social and political harmony and to check the destructive and anarchic tendencies within American democracy.[23]

It is, as David Brion Davis has pointed out, ironic that in pursuing his goals, the Nativist in fact aggravated the evils which he sought to eradicate. Thus he presumably intensified any feelings of hostility or of grievance which the immigrant may have felt and injected yet another hugely controversial subject into politics. His entire

---

[22] *Nat. Am.,* 9 June 1838; *Cong. Gl.,* 29 i App., 48; *Address of Louisiana Native American Association,* 14. Significantly, the author of *The Crisis* bitterly resented Fanny Wright's attacks on 'great Americans like Robert Morris, Fisher Ames, Alexander Hamilton and John Jay' – *The Crisis,* 60.

[23] *The Crisis,* 64. It should perhaps be emphasised that there was a genuine reforming impulse within the Nativists movement. In New York city, for example, Nativists improved local amenities and services and increased governmental efficiency.

programme was unlikely to have resulted in a more harmonious social and political order even if it had been implemented for it seems clear that the causes of social unrest and political radicalism were more deeply rooted than he allowed. In campaigning for support and in publicising his hostility, the Nativist probably vitiated rather than furthered his aims. Yet the paradox was ultimately that which faced all ultra-conservatives in Jacksonian politics. How could men who still openly admired the old Federalists, including even Hamilton, who believed that it required twenty one years to learn the letter and spirit of the American constitution, and who argued that republicanism demanded not 'mere maturity' but 'additional intimacy with the nature of American government' as well as 'additional wisdom' – how could these men secure power in a populistic democracy like that of the United States? It was a gargantuan task.[24]

Although in the 1830s and 1840s Nativism failed to make much headway as an independent political force, it was nevertheless able to exert considerable influence upon the Whig party. It was, predictably, the conservative wing of the party that was, in general, sympathetic; these conservatives employed arguments similar if not identical to those used by independent Nativists. In New England the editor of the conservative Whig *Providence Journal* began what would ultimately be almost a fifty year period of service to nativism, a record which, it has been suggested, is 'perhaps unsurpassed in the annals of American nativism'. In Hartford, Connecticut, the *Courant*, an ex-Federalist and now a conservative Whig newspaper, was similarly disposed towards the immigrant. Five years, it believed, were not enough for him to 'acquire that degree of intelligence and that interest in free institutions' necessary to earn the suffrage. From Philadelphia, the *American Quarterly Review* complained that the immigrants were poor and ignorant without the necessary knowledge of 'liberty and free institutions' while further South in Raleigh, North Carolina, the *Register* worried about the dangers to be apprehended from foreign immigrants incited by 'the base appeal of demagogues'.[25] Both the *Review* and the *Register* were Whig in sympathy. Although there were few immigrants in the South-West (except in New Orleans), Whigs here occasionally expressed in the familiar terms, their

[24] David Brion David, 'Some Themes of Counter-Subversion; An Analysis of Anti-Masonic, Anti-Catholic, and Anti-Mormon Literature', *M.V.H.R.*, XLVII (Sept. 1960), 205-24, esp. 223; M'Farlane, *Address,* 8.

[25] Patrick J. Conley, 'Rhode Island Constitutional Development, 1636-1841; Prologue to the Dorr Rebellion' (Ph.D. thesis, Notre Dame University, 1970), 233; *Hartford Courant,* 16 Nov. 1844; *A.Q.R.,* XXII (Sept. and Dec. 1837), 59; *Raleigh Register,* 22 Nov. 1844. The *Providence Journal* was still in 1841 sympathetic to the Federalists – see 20 June 1841.

hostility or lack of sympathy. The Vicksburgh *Constitutionalist* believed that ninety per cent of immigrants were 'totally unfit, in every respect, to be allowed the liberty of suffrage'. Likewise, from the older West, Senator Alexander Porter claimed that many immigrants formed 'such a mass of ignorance and passion' that they were easy prey for demagogues.[26] Further North, in Michigan the Detroit *Journal and Courier* warned that the Irish had come to overthrow 'our social system' while William Woodbridge, future United States Senator and Governor, informed the delegates at the Constitutional Convention of 1835 that to be a voter, a man needed more than 'general intelligence' and 'an abstract devotion to liberty'. Accordingly, he and three Whig colleagues entered a formal protest against the principle of non-citizen voting. Thus the arguments used by those Whigs who inclined towards nativism indicate that they shared the basic social and political outlook of the independent Nativists. It is perhaps significant that when Senator Smith of Indiana sought to defend the character of Western immigrants, he felt it necessary to assure his Whig colleagues that they were 'not the class of political foreigners who hangs around your sea ports, and the suburbs of your large cities, making politics their trade, preaching agrarian and locofoco doctrines in the daytime, and lighting locofoco matches and rioting at night – the levellers down because they cannot level up'.[27]

It was, however, in New York, that the Nativists made perhaps their greatest impact upon the Whig party. Their pressure did not result in the absorption of their creed into New York Whiggery, but it undoubtedly widened the split in an already deeply divided party. Conservative Whigs like Philip Hone, James Watson Webb, Daniel D. Barnard and Millard Fillmore together with newspapers like the *American* and the *Commercial Advertiser* endorsed nativism for the standard reasons. Yet the liberal wing of the party, headed by Seward and Weed and supported by Greeley's various presses, opposed nativism strongly. Seward in particular was fiercely hostile:

> This right hand drops off before I do one act with the Whig or any other party in opposition to any portion of my fellow citizens, on the ground of their nativity. . . . No pretence of policy, no sense of injury, shall induce me to join, aid or abet, such miserable efforts.

Yet Seward shared the Whig and Nativist desire for the single national

---

[26] *Vicksburg Constitutionalist,* in David N. Young, 'The Mississippi Whigs, 1834-1860' (Ph.D. thesis, University of Alabama, 1968), 144-5; Porter to Crittenden, 2 Jan., 1841, in Adams, 'Louisiana Whig Party', 144-5.

[27] *Detroit Journal and Courier,* 8 April 1835, in Formisano, *Birth of Mass Parties,* 90; *Mich. C.C.,* 226-8; *Cong. Gl.,* 26 i App., 68.

character. 'The Americans', he declared, 'are a homogeneous people, and must remain so; because however quickly they expand, they swell in one great and unbroken flood. All exotic elements are rapidly absorbed and completely assimilated.' The Seward wing differed with the conservatives over many issues of which nativism (considered as an example of ethnocultural preference) was not the most fundamental. With an expansive faith in democracy, a deeper commitment to universal suffrage and a fear of radicalism that was of only slight proportions, Seward was able to welcome the immigrant where the conservatives could only fear him.[28]

Thus the sympathy which many Whigs felt for nativism derived from assumptions about the nature of liberty, the causes of urban vice and poverty, and the structure of the good society. Since these assumptions were antagonistic to those of the Democrats, it was natural that the Democrats should be antagonistic to nativism. Conflicting responses to nativism grew out of, and reinforced, conflicting social and political philosophies.

If the more conservative Whigs and the Nativists were alike fearful of the dangers to which democracy exposed a nation, Democrats were convinced that the populistic institutions of America were no less than a 'glorious heritage of uncontrolled freedom'. John M. Pumroy, attacking nativism, reminded his readers that America was 'the last hope for the liberty of the world'. This belief was an integral and essential component of the Democratic ideology and it was, of course, expressed with similar enthusiasm on other issues, the most notable of which was perhaps that of territorial expansion.[29]

In establishing the claims of the immigrant to the liberty afforded by American institutions, Democrats were compelled to refute the arguments employed by the Nativists. Whereas a majority of the Whigs probably agreed with the Nativists that American republicanism was of organic growth, the culmination of an evolutionary process that had been in motion for centuries, the Democrats believed that 'our

[28] Allan Nevins (ed.), *The Diary of Philip Hone* (N.Y., 1936), 677; *Courier and Enquirer*, 28 April 1844; Sharon H. Penney, 'Daniel Dewey Barnard: Patrician in Politics' (Ph.D. thesis, State University of New York at Albany, 1972), 238; John D. Morris, 'The New York State Whigs, 1834-1842, A Study of Political Organization' (Ph. D. thesis, University of Rochester, 1970), 199; Glyndon G. Van Deusen, *Horace Greeley, Nineteenth Century Crusader* (Phil., 1953), 93; Van Deusen, *Thurlow Weed: Wizard of the Lobby* (Boston, 1947), 91-2; George E. Barker (ed.), *The Works of William H. Seward*, 5 vols. (Boston, 1884), III, 388, 111. Seward also argued that immigration increased national wealth. See *Works of Seward*, II, 198.

[29] *Dem. Exp.*, 16 Aug., 1845; John N. Pumroy, *A Defence of Our Naturalization Laws. . .* (Phil., 1845), 10.

institutions are not so complex'. A twenty one year naturalisation period was absurd for 'a government so simple as ours'. 'The principles of our government', James Brent of Louisiana pointed out, 'are few and simple'. Significantly, Brent added that he had 'great confidence in man's capacity for self-government'. It was a pertinent comment.[30]

Beneath the Democrats' faith in the people lay, of course, their still more controversial ideas about the nature of liberty in a democratic state. Many Jacksonians did not deny that the immigrants were poor or ignorant; instead they denied that this was a satisfactory reason for withholding political rights. This attitude was clearly expressed by Pumroy:

> Ignorance and poverty, particularly in a land of oppression and of an overgrown population, where labor brings but a few pence per day, are not crimes. Shall we deny a man the right of citizenship in consequence of his ignorance and poverty? There is no such doctrine taught in our Declaration of Independence.

The fact than an immigrant might be poor could be no disqualification since, in the words of Senator Anderson of Tennessee, 'the poor of every land' were 'the same'. They were 'the lovers of liberty, wherever you find them, because they have been made to taste the bitter cup of degradation'. Anderson assured his fellow Senators that there was 'nothing to fear from such men'. Nor could the immigrant's contact with despotism be adduced as an argument against his rapid enfranchise ment. The only legacy of such contact, it was insisted, was a deep hatred of all forms of tyranny. According to the *Globe*, immigrants were 'haters of despotism and friends of liberty'. Anderson told the Senate how 'the iron of resistance' had entered 'deep into [the immigrant's] heart against the titular nobleman before whom he was compelled to bow, and against that king who had ruled him with a despot's rod'. Iowa Democrat Sylvester G. Matson was even 'inclined to believe' that, because driven to America by oppression, the immigrants 'know *better* how to appreciate the inestimable blessings of liberty than we do'. For many Democrats an experience of despotism strengthened the claim for political rights.[31]

When replying to this argument, Whigs and Nativists generally maintained that it was not the love of liberty but merely the need to

---

[30] *La. C.C.*, 90; Thomas L. Nichols, *A Lecture on Immigration and the Right of Naturalization* (N.Y., 1845), 33.

[31] Pumroy, *Defence*, 8-9; *Cong. Gl.*, 26 i App., 46; *Globe*, 2 Aug. 1837; *Iowa C.C.*, 330.

escape from poverty, which brought the immigrant. Democrats were unmoved by such reasoning. For them the distinction did not, indeed could not, exist. For democracy rested upon individual self-interest and even in America it was, ultimately, the need to avoid poverty which impelled men to labour. Thus the *Globe* wanted 'no better title to nativity than striking the first axe into the forest, and ploughing the first furrow in the field'. This, the newspaper believed, was a just claim 'to the rights of citizenship'. Since it was 'human nature for men to protect and defend what belongs to them', then as Thomas L. Nichols pointed out, 'you bind men to your country and government' by 'the very act of naturalization'. Thus 'the quickest and best way of making men good citizens' was 'to confer upon them as soon as possible, the rights, and to require of them the responsibilities, of citizenship'. Hence the force of self-interest and the love of liberty from which it sprang would merge in the immigrant, as in the native born, to guarantee his patriotism and loyalty. Conversely, however, if the immigrant were denied political rights, his self-interest would turn him against the government. For, as James Bowlin reminded Congress, 'every government is arbitrary and despotic, no matter what its forms or name, to the man disfranchised from all political rights'. The highly egalitarian force of self-interest thus demanded a political equality since, in the words of Thomas Nichols, 'in a country of free institutions and equal laws, to deprive any class of men of the right of suffrage, would be making odious distinctions, engendering heart burnings and hatreds'. It was in this connection that Theophilus Fisk, discussing the immigrant question, declared that 'the Christian and the Patriot look upon all mankind as brethren – made of one blood'. On the immigration issue Democratic egalitarianism – and it was once more a levelling egalitarianism – was again reaffirmed.[32]

Consequently, the more radical and egalitarian the Jacksonian's social and political philosophy, the more likely he was to favour the rapid enfranchisement of the immigrant. Fisk was prepared to reduce the naturalisation period to a single year; many other radicals were prepared to allow alien voting. Conservative Democrats, on the other hand, looked with disfavour upon these proposals. Yet inter-party differences remained even within pro or anti-immigrant ranks. As Formisano points out, opposition (in Michigan) from Democrats to alien voting 'usually lacked the nativism . . . often expressed by Whigs'. Similarly Seward's hostility to nativism was based upon a purely assimilationist attitude to immigration which was not stressed in

[32] *Globe*, 20 Jan. 1841; Nichols, *Letter on Immigration*, 33-4; *Cong. Gl.*, 29 i App., 44; *Dem. Exp.*, 16 Aug. 1845.

the Democratic response.[33] A Democrat's stance on nativism was dictated by his commitment to the political equality of white men in the agrarian, atomised society. Thus in general, the nativist controversy suggests not a reinterpretation of the ideological clash between Democrat and Whig, but instead an additional perspective on it.[34]

Religion and Morality

If the Whig party often showed sympathy towards the Nativist movement, it is no less true that it manifested that commitment to Protestant Christianity to which historians have drawn attention. Religion was, of course, one of the major obstacles to the absorption of many immigrant groups and particularly to that of the Roman Catholic Irish. Orestes Brownson even believed that nativism arose primarily from opposition to Catholicism[35] and there is no doubt that Nativists were often alarmed at the prospect of a large and seemingly ever-increasing Catholic population. They feared the temporal power of the Pope and the Catholic clergy – events in New York did nothing to allay their fears[36] – in which they saw a direct threat to the separation of church and state. Thus James Watson Webb in the *Courier and Enquirer* declared his conviction that 'the Roman Catholic religion is at war with civil and religious freedom'. Webb was even prepared to state that 'no people, the great mass of whom recognize the power and authority of the Pope and a Priesthood [sic], are qualified for, or will sustain, Republican institutions'.[37]

But it was not simply the doctrinal tenets or the institutional structure of the Catholic church which aroused the concern of Nativists. It was also the morals and habits of the immigrants which, it was often assumed, were a product of the Catholic faith. New York's Nativists complained that 'the low filthy grogshops of our cities' were filled by immigrants and that the sanctity of the Sabbath was violated by their 'dance houses' which remained open on that day. These

---

[33] *Dem. Exp.*, 11 Oct. 1845; Formisano, *Birth of Mass Parties*, 96.

[34] Democrats rarely confronted the problem of urban growth consequent upon immigration, often assuming that the immigrants went, or should go, West.

[35] *Br. Q. R.*, II (Jan. 1845), 84.

[36] There was undoubtedly some Catholic intervention in politics and however justified and essentially nonpartisan the Catholic hierarchy might have been, it gave credence to Whig fears. See esp. Vincent P. Lannie, *Public Money and Parochial Education: Bishop Hughes, Governor Seward and the New York School Controversy* (Cleveland, 1968).

[37] *Courier and Enquirer*, 28 Sept. 1843.

194

Nativists believed that 'three fourths of. . . .[New York's] pauperism is the result of intemperance, moral depravity and sheer idleness'. They blamed the immigrant for all three.[38]

Nevertheless, concern for the preservation of religious values, and particularly for those of the Protestant religion, was not limited to those who joined the Nativist parties. Jacksonian America saw the creation or growth of a large number of essentially Protestant and evangelical societies, such as the American Bible Society, the American Tract Society, the American Sunday School Union and the American Temperance Union, designed to inculcate within the community those moral principles which evangelicals believed were being undermined or ignored. The motives of these reformers is a subject of some debate among historians but it is not necessary to adopt in full the 'social control' thesis to recognise that a strong element of social and political conservatism was present. Thus Joseph Tuckerman, a pioneer in the development of American philanthropic organisations, was prepared to admit that 'the poor suffer from low wages'. But he quickly added that it was 'not half as much as from a misapplication of the wages they receive'. He believed that three quarters of the vice and crime in Boston came from 'the free use of intoxicating liquors'. Similarly Neil Dow, the most prominent temperance reformer of the ante-bellum years, stated in 1834 that he did not 'remember a single instance of suffering in the families of sober and industrious people'. Thus, like the Nativists, Tuckerman and Dow perceived evils and ills in American society yet assumed that its fundamental economic structure and organisation were sound.[39]

Although both Tuckerman and Dow were Whig in allegiance, it is probably Theodore Frelinghuysen, Senator from New Jersey and Henry Clay's running mate in 1844, whose career best illustrates the evangelical thrust of Whiggery. Frelinghuysen was a member of most

[38] *The Crisis,* 56, 31.

[39] Joseph Tuckerman, *The Principles and Results of the Ministry at Large in Boston* (Boston, 1838), 301, 166; Dow quoted in Frank L. Byrne, *Prophet of Prohibition: Neil Dow and His Crusade* (Madison, Wisc., 1961), 22. See also Clifford S. Griffin, *Their Brother's Keepers: Moral Stewardship in the United States 1800-1865* (New Brunswick, N.J., 1960); Lois W. Banner, 'Religious Benevolence as Social Control: A Critique of an Interpretation', *J.A.H.,* LX (June, 1973), 23-41; Emil C. Vigilante, 'The Temperance Reform in New York State, 1829-1851' (Ph.D. thesis, University of New York, 1964); John J. Rumbarger, 'The Social Origins and Functions of the Temperance Movement in the Reconstruction of American Society, 1825-1917' (Ph.D. thesis, University of Pennsylvania, 1968); Michael J. Heale, 'Harbingers of Progressivism: Responses to the Urban Crisis in New York City, 1845-1860', *J.A.S.,* X (April 1976), 17-36, 'From City Fathers to Social Critics: Humanitarianism and Government in New York, 1790-1860', *J.A.H.,* LXIII (June 1976), 21-41.

of the moral reform movements of the era and is now perhaps chiefly remembered for his role in the Sunday mails controversy. Frelinghuysen opposed the introduction of a Sunday postal service because he believed that the Sabbath was essential to 'cherish' those 'moral influences' through which 'alone' a 'free people can preserve their liberties'. Indeed so important did he consider the sanctity of the Sabbath that he gave its preservation a higher priority than commercial progress and expansion. Although he doubted whether the absence of a Sunday delivery would in fact result in a reduction of profits, he explicitly denied that this was a relevant consideration. For with the Sabbath inviolate 'we shall possess a moral excellence as a people, a thousand fold more valuable than all the wealth and splendors of commercial greatness'. Frelinghuysen hoped and believed that 'we shall never graduate public worth by dollars and cents' and exhorted his fellow Americans to 'reject the miserable pelf that is amassed by labor, pursued on a violated sabbath'. Thus the case of Frelinghuysen demonstrates that some Whigs perceived a possible conflict between moral purity and commercial progress and, even more significant, that faced with a choice between the two, they would take the former.[40]

The effects which Frelinghuysen anticipated from the uncontaminated Sabbath were many and varied. He saw in its influence a counter-balancing force to that of 'selfish cupidity' and argued that without it 'the heart would become the victim of a cold and debasing selfishness, and have no greater susceptibility than the nether millstone'. Frelinghuysen endorsed the view that a moral community must be founded upon 'religious obligation' for otherwise, he warned, morality would have 'no vital principle' and would be 'a mere sounding brass to amuse the ear'. Without an effective moral code, he feared, there would be 'no salutary restraint upon the conduct of men'. Hence the sabbath would encourage 'intelligence and integrity', 'public and private virtue'. It would be 'a great moral lever in the absence of which, an augmenting flood of evil' would engulf the nation. Without the observance of the Sabbath as a day of rest, he believed, irreligion and immorality would become rife and since 'all your penalties and prisons will oppose an utterly inefficient check', laws would be trampled upon or openly ignored.[41]

Many of the fears and hopes displayed by Frelinghuysen were widespread among the more conservative Whigs. Daniel D. Barnard

[40]Theodore Frelinghuysen, *Speech . . Concerning Sabbath Mails, 8 May 1830* (Washington D.C., 1830), 6, 11. For details of Dow's 'intensely partisan' political stance see Byrne, *Prophet of Prohibition,* 34.

[41]Frelinghuysen, *Speech on Mails,* 7-8, 11-3.

believed that 'the principle of obedience would sit lightly on the people, unless it were enforced by a common sense of religious obligation', while Alonzo Potter, after delivering a warning about the dangers to be apprehended from labour unions, suggested that, in order to counter their essentially wicked influence, 'redoubled efforts' should be made 'to spread among our countrymen the influence of a pure and undefiled religion'. 'Without this', he added, 'we are inevitably lost – we may be lost soon.' Similarly, clergymen like Hubard Winslow noted that the 'reckless and revolutionary' spirit of infidelity was making some mechanics 'dangerous men to the Republic'. It was, consequently, 'highly important that special attention should be given to their intellectual and moral cultivation'. Winslow observed that 'the progress of temperance' had done much.[42] Other Whiggish reformers suggested that religion might ease class tensions; in so doing they revealed their characteristic assumption that such divisions, or at least the division between rich and poor, was natural and inevitable. Thus Tuckerman strove to instill 'a deeper sense of the relation which Christianity recognizes between the more and less favored classes of society – between the rich and poor'. Jonathan M. Wainwright, for his part, in his Address entitled *Inequality of Individual Wealth the Ordinance of Providence, and Essential to Civilization* looked to religion to 'assure' all that 'these distinctions are to terminate here'. Wainwright also developed a typically Whiggish line of thought when he argued that religion would, 'by promoting industry, sobriety, integrity, and all the habits that advance individual prosperity. . . . lessen the number of the poor'. Hence religion was 'the poor man's friend'; it 'elevates him and his family'.[43]

The demand for religion as an essentially conservative social force helps explain the connection of social reformers with the Whig party. Moral reform was envisaged as a necessary support for, and restraint upon, a self-governing people. It was in a sense a counterbalancing force to that of liberty, in that it reduced or even eliminated the dangers to which liberty was exposed. Social reformers feared that the atomistic society with which democracy was increasingly associated was in danger of repudiating all external authority; individual morality, they feared, was jeopardised by democratic individualism

---

[42] Daniel D. Bernard, *A Plea for Social and Popular Repose* (N.Y., 1845), 8; Alonzo Potter, *Political Economy; Its Objects, Uses and Principles* (N.Y., 1841), 301; Hubard Winslow, *The Means of the Perpetuity and Prosperity of Our Republic* (Boston, 1838), 27.

[43] Joseph Tuckerman, *On the Elevation of the Poor* (Boston, 1874), 92-3; Joseph Wainwright, *Inequality of Individual Wealth the Ordinance of Providence, and Essential to Civilization* (Boston, 1835), 51-2; Frelinghuysen, *Speech on Mails*, 12.

and the cult of the autonomous, self-sufficient and self-interested democrat. These fears were clearly articulated in a *Report of the American Sunday-School Union:*

> There are considerations connected with our country, that present cause for melancholy apprehension. The spirit of freedom, with all its rich benefits, is not without its dangers. Every mind in any measure acquainted with its own operations, knows that there are propensities within us which require control – that must be brought into subjection to wholesome regulations and discipline.

The *Report* then specified these dangerous tendencies and in so doing abstracted what were several of the main components of Democratic ideology. The principle of self-government, its absorption into America's national identity and self-image, its redefinition in terms of individual rather than merely collective self-rule – all were clearly recognised and critically examined:

> Now one startling danger lies in the very heart of our blessings. We are too proud of our liberties and of our country. Self-confidence is engendered and a spirit of individual independence almost *too strong for law.* We are *our own rulers* – we boast. Politically, it is true – The fear is reasonable that we shall practically refuse or deny the authority even of *our own rulers.* There is a constant tendency to break away from all restraints. "Resistance", "liberty", "independence", "the rights of man" are so familiar, and so grateful too, I grant, – that we are prone to forget, not only Him, whose unspeakable goodness has made us to differ, but to forget, also that these animating terms, and the glow of patriotism, and the love of country, if not sustained and cherished by sound principles, will become the mere watchwords for licentiousness and all misrule.

Calvin Colton, writing anonymously, and in a manner and tone far different from those he employed for the 'Junius' Tracts, showed the same concern when he argued that 'Christianity, morality and piety, in connexion with the intelligence of the common people' were 'the last hope of the American Republic', and, more significantly, that they were 'the only adequate means of bridling and holding in salutary check that rampant freedom, which is so characteristic of the American people'. Of course neither Colton nor the men in the Sunday School Union wished to repudiate liberty. Rather, by curbing its dangerous tendencies – tendencies which they believed could only result in anarchy or tyranny – they sought to support and preserve it.[44]

[44]*Eleventh Annual Report of the American Sunday-School Union* (Phil., 1835), 9; [Calvin Colton], *A Voice from America to England* (London, 1839), 60.

The fears of conservatives like Colton and of those evangelicals who supported the Sunday School Union propelled them towards the Whig party. Although not all Whigs were ardent social or moral reformers, the party's basic ideology made it an attractive home for evangelicals. Considerations which applied to economic policy were relevant in the separate though not unrelated sphere of moral reform. Just as the Whigs were eager to employ the power of government to facilitate economic growth they were able to contemplate its use to promote essentially moral causes. The assumptions underlying both types of intervention were similar, if not identical. Both proceeded from a view of society which placed the community before the individual. Thus the Ann Arbor Society for the Promotion of Temperance passed a resolution

> that we look upon our interests, our rights, all our earthly hopes and means of future happiness as identified with the well being of community, and that we regard the injuries done to intemperance as encroachments on our public and individual rights which as good citizens we consider it our duty to resist.

Similarly, moral reformers and Whigs alike assumed that society's natural aristocracy, whether of talent or virtue, should direct and lead. 'Our constituents', Frelinghuysen told the Senate, 'look up here for correct moral lessons'. It was thus of great symbolic importance that government should not itself be seen to encourage the violation of the Sabbath. 'Let the guilt rest upon individuals', he urged, 'but let the government be clear'. Neil Dow, who believed throughout his life that the clergy should rule in God's name for His greater glory, declared his conviction that 'the intelligent, the virtuous and the learned' ought to rule and reform 'the ignorant, the depraved, and vicious'. Moral reformers like Dow and Frelinghuysen clung to an organic view of society which, in the Jacksonian era, almost necessarily entailed the full acceptance of, and an emphasis upon, the inequalities between man and man. It was thus natural for Whigs of a conservative persuasion to embrace moral reform. 'So far from omitting to carry Temperance into politics', said Massachusetts Whig Richard Hildreth, 'I would have not only Temperance, but the whole of morality carried there'.[45]

Although Hildreth did not see so wide-ranging a scheme effected, the Whigs were nevertheless able to give some support to causes like temperance and thus to obtain piecemeal successes within the states.

[45] Ann Arbor Society for the Promotion of Temperance quoted in Formisano, *Birth of Mass Parties,* 78; Frelinghuysen, *Speech on Mails,* 10; Dow quoted in Byrne, *Prophet of Prohibition,* 7; Richard Hildreth, *Letter on Political Action* (Boston, 1840), 11-12.

Research on the voting behaviour of Illinois legislators has shown that Whigs were far more likely to favour temperance than Democrats and there is considerable evidence to suggest that this pattern was reproduced in Maine where the temperance cause was strongest, in Massachusetts, where the Whigs passed the notorious fifteen gallon law, and in other Northern states.[46] Yet there was no unanimity among the Whigs upon moral reform; the South remained relatively indifferent and the more liberal elements in the North were perhaps less enthusiastic than the conservatives. As a political cause, moral reform, like nativism, tended to be espoused by conservative Whigs.[47]

Democrats, on the other hand, were, in general, not merely indifferent or unenthusiastic but deliberately and consciously hostile. Frequently they voiced their approval of temperance or an unviolated Sabbath; many expressed their faith in the Christian religion and, in particular, in Protestantism. Yet they refused to sanction the introduction of specifically religious and moral causes into politics. Thus Theophilus Fisk 'highly approved of the regular observance of Sunday as a day of rest and devotion' but he wished it 'to be observed by the power of reason and moral suasion, and not by physical force, or penal enactments'. The editor of the New Orleans *Picayune* expressed his conviction that 'all attempts to screw men by fine or imprisonment into particular religious observances, produce effects directly opposite to those intended by bigoted sectarians'. Similarly many Democrats personally favoured the cause of temperance yet resisted all attempts to enforce it by law. John P. Hale of New Hampshire is a typical case. 'Few men', according to his biographer, 'worked harder than Hale in the temperance crusade', yet Hale believed temperance laws to be 'absurd and ridiculous'. This attitude was prevalent wherever the question of temperance arose. In Ohio the *Cincinnati Enquirer* deprecated 'the thrusting of the great moral enterprise of *Temperance* into the political arena'. According to the *Enquirer* this was 'a prostitution of a great object in morals and in happiness'. The question ought to be 'one of moral force – moral suasion – the means moral – and all urged without intemperate fanaticism and bitter intolerance'. In Massachusetts a group of Democrats opposing the fifteen gallon law affirmed their support for temperance but exhorted the reformers

[46] Rodney O. Davis, 'Illinois Legislators and Jacksonian Democracy' (Ph.D. thesis, University of Iowa, 1966), 310-6; Ershkowitz and Shade, 'Consensus or Conflict?' *passim;* Neil Dow, *The Reminiscences of Neil Dow: Recollections of Eighty Years* (Portland, Me., 1898), 340-3; Arthur M. Schlesinger, *The Age of Jackson* (Boston, 1945), 256.

[47] A clear exception to this generalisation is the Free Soil (and then Republican) movement, although there were other than moral considerations involved here.

to 'resort, as all moral reformers who were not persecutors and bigots, always have done, to reason and argument, the still small voice of moral suasion'. They should not 'apply the terror of the law to restrain poor man's appetites'. James Bowlin of Missouri made what was the classic Democratic response to moral reform when, lumping together temperance, abolition and nativism, he pronounced all three 'bad in their tendencies' since all three 'fanned the flames of discord and animosity'.[48]

The Democratic rejection of moral reform as a political cause was rooted in the desire for an absolute separation of religious and moral questions from politics. 'A man's religious belief', according to Thomas L. Nichols, 'and the manner in which he chooses to worship his Maker' were 'a matter which belongs not to society or government, and over which they can have no control'. For, it was argued, 'to control conscience in matters of religion, is a prerogative that belongs to God alone'. Religion was thus 'a matter resting entirely between man and his creator'. Hence, as the *Missouri Reporter* concluded, 'no man's civil and political rights should depend upon his religious faith, or his lack of religious faith'. 'Between politics and religion', the *Missourian* noted, 'there is, and ought to be, an entire separation.' 'Government', in the words of John Pumroy, 'has no concern with man, except as a member of civil society.'[49]

Democrats denied the legitimacy of state intervention in religious matters for the same reasons that they resented governmental interference with the economy. Thus the fifteen gallon law was opposed as 'a dangerous legislative premium held out to ultras. . . .to get up combinations and sects, in order to control legislation and press their particular creeds into the form of the law'. The smallest deviation from the principle of religious toleration was as dangerous a precedent as a piece of legislation designed to benefit only one economic interest. Each was a violation of the democratic principle, a denial of the voluntary ethic. 'Virtue', according to the *Missourian*, was a '*voluntary* striving after conformity to the law of righteousness and goodness'. John Pumroy explained that 'the restriction of law to

---

[48] *Dem. Exp.*, 6 Sept. 1845; Richard H. Sewell, *John P. Hale and the Politics of Abolition* (Cambridge, 1965), 25; *Cincinnati Enquirer*, 27 Sept. 1843; Benjamin F. Hallett *et al.*, *Investigation into the Fifteenth Gallon Law of Massachusetts. . .* (Boston, 1839), 21; *Cong. Gl.*, 29 i App., 45. An analysis of party support for temperance in Illinois finds that of the legislators classed as favourable 64% were Whig; of those opposed 88% were Democrat. Those classed as moderate were almost evenly divided between the two parties. See Davies, 'Illinois Legislators', 310-3.

[49] Nichols, *Lecture on Immigration*, 28; Pumroy, *Defence*, 13; *Missouri Reporter* and *Missourian* in *Dem. Exp.*, 27 Dec. 1845.

the interests of civil society' resulted from 'the principle, that there can be no *merit* or *demerit* without the liberty of choice'. It was impossible to be 'good or bad upon compulsion' since 'it is only as a free agent, in matters of religion, that men can deserve praise or blame'. Most Democrats assumed that coercion from government was in any case ineffectual or counter-productive, but even if it were not, their objections would probably have remained. 'Freedom', said Brownson, 'requires us to recognize in each individual certain rights, rights which we may no more invade to do the individual good, than to do him harm'. The Democrats recognised the justice of temperance and other moral causes but their desire to improve individual morality was less potent than their love of liberty.[50]

If the enactment of moral legislation was a denial of liberty, it similarly violated the principle of equality. Just as partial legislation benefited either those who enacted it or those whose economic interests it served, so moral legislation represented for Democrats, as indeed it did for many of the reformers themselves, an attempt to impose the supposedly superior morality of one section of the community upon another. The *New Hampshire Patriot* showed the egalitarian thrust of this viewpoint when declaring its hostility to 'the idea of a few arrogant men assuming to dictate, control, and order the disposition of everything of a public or private character'. But it was George Sidney Camp who developed this theme most fully. Camp claimed in effect that the moral faculty lay in the individual; it had no separate existence in society. Hence moral power could not legitimately be exercised by one group or individual against the will of another:

> We are not made for authority over our fellow beings. That moral nature, by virtue of which alone we could claim it, has evidently been given us for the regulation and government of ourselves alone. Moral duties are revealed to our species by nature as individuals, and discoverable by us, each for himself, solely upon the separate inspection of his own heart. There is nature's sole depository of the immutable law of right and wrong, justice and injustice, in its applicability to human actions. Its only natural sanction is vested in every man's individual conscience, whch reproaches or applauds him for his own actions merely. Thus Nature has made each, for himself alone, the executor of her laws, and she qualifies no man to prescribe and act for another. His moral attributes are not more than sufficient to accomplish him for his own responsibilities.

[50] Hallett, *Investigation,* 16; *Missourian* in *Dem. Exp.,* 27 Dec. 1845; Pumroy, *Defence,* 13; *Bo. Q.R.,* I (Oct. 1838), 488.

Here was the moral rationale for Democratic individualism. Just as Democrats claimed for the autonomous individual an equality of social and political power with his fellow citizens, so they effectively insisted on an equality of moral responsibility. Camp phrased this demand in terms which convey the levelling tendencies of Jacksonian Democracy:

> Ih the absence of Divine authority, and while we are conversant with but one order of intelligent beings, universally the same in their essential attributes, one in *genus* and one in *species,* all are morally equal, that is, equal in those respects which constitute moral accountability. . . and each has a right to determine the limits prescribed to his actions by the moral law for himself.

Camp here supplied what was the moral underpinning for Democratic egalitarianism. 'When our Saviour propounded the law of human conduct', he reminded his readers, 'he reduced mankind to a level.' For 'mankind are our equals and not our superiors, and we owe to "neighbour" neither obedience nor allegiance.'[51]

Thus Democrats saw in the attempt to legislate morality and religion an assault upon their most valued principles of liberty and equality. It was this assault rather than any moral relativism which most influenced them. Temperance and religion were good; liberty and equality were better. It is safe too, to assume that Democrats had not forgotten Federalist attacks upon Jefferson as an infidel, for there was a strong current of anticlericalism in many of their pronouncements. According to Martin Van Buren, the clergy were one of 'two classes' (the other being the judiciary) 'whose interference in politics is always and very naturally distasteful to sincere republicans'. Van Buren drew attention to 'their want of sympathy for popular rights'. While extreme conservatives looked to the church as a major support for a Republic, many radicals saw it as a formidable opponent of democracy and liberty. George Bancroft complained that the church in America 'is as faithful to the doctrine of Absolutism, as it can be in a democratic country', while Orestes Brownson similarly noted that it invited men to acquiesce in gross social inequalities. It had thus become 'false to its founder' and was now 'a constabularly force at the service of the police', the 'greatest of all obstacles to intellectual and social progress'. It is a significant comment upon the ideological configurations of the Jacksonian era that when Brownson advocated the abolition of

---

[51] *N.H.P.,* 29 Feb. 1844; George Sidney Camp, *Democracy* (N.Y., 1845), 45-7, 54.

hereditary property he also recommended the destruction of the priesthood.[52]

These were radical and doubtless unusual demands. But many Democrats would have supported the still contentious proposition that the Roman Catholic and even the non-believer could be as good a citizen as the Protestant. Thus Thomas L. Nichols acknowledged that, 'though educated... in the straitest sect of Protestantism', he had 'yet to learn that Protestants are better men, better citizens, or better Christians than Catholics'. Elsewhere Democrats voiced their opposition to attempts to restrict officeholding to those believing in 'a state of future rewards and punishments'.[53]

Thus the Democrats were able to appeal to non-evangelical Protestants, to Roman Catholics and to non-believers. It was an impressive achievement, but one that depended upon a rejection of the traditional claims for religion that republicans had made and which conservatives indeed continued to make. In denying these claims, moreover, Democrats necessarily rejected the traditional – and still current – assumptions about the role and importance of virtue in a republic. Religion and moral reform had been visualised as a means of propping up individual virtue, of restraining individual and group self-interest, and hence of deriving harmony and unity from the potential excesses of liberty and self-government. But since Jacksonian man was governed by self-interest, it followed that neither religious nor moral legislation was needed. George Camp again made explicit a line of thought that was surely common to many Democrats. Contrary to the widely accepted belief, Camp affirmed, the individual in a republic did not need to exercise self-restraint in order to ensure the welfare of the community; nor was he expected to sacrifice his interests if they came into conflict with those of other individuals or groups. Why should this be so? Camp gave three reasons. Firstly, he maintained that since individuals were equal none could dominate. There would thus be many different self-interests and it would be possible to 'harmonize and reconcile' them by 'justice alone'. This was 'the only neutral ground on which all parties can meet', the only effective code by which self-interest could be pursued. Secondly, Camp argued, in classic Democratic manner, that 'all men are sufficiently moral where neither passion nor interest perverts the decisions of conscience'. Hence justice, he implied, would be

[52] Martin Van Buren, *Inquiry into the Origin and Course of Political Parties in the United States* (N.Y., 1867), 365-6; *Bo. Q. R.*, I (Oct. 1838), 461, 463, 468, III (July 1840), 386.

[53] Nichols, *Lecture on Immigration*, 29; *Missourian* in *Dem. Exp.*, 27 Dec 1845.

maintained by the power of the majority. (He did not consider the possibility of a conflict of interest involving a majority of the community, presumably because orthodox Democratic theory assumed that this could not happen.) Third'y, the rule of justice, he believed, was the most expedient foundation for any society. It was naturally adopted, he noted, even by a community of pirates. From these three considerations it followed that self-restraint was not required. Hence 'the law of justice will form the rule of legislative conduct, no matter what may be the particular and accidental shade of the moral character of a people'. Camp concluded that 'republican government does not rely upon the state of the public morals, but upon the union of the virtuous impulses of a moral nature with the strong motives of a personal interest'. He added that 'whatever doubts may be entertained, under various possible circumstances of the sufficiency of either separately, there can be no doubt of their being all sufficient in a state of combination'. This was the Democratic theory. It was the theory of John Taylor of Caroline.[54]

Self-interest operating in an atomised society of equalised social and political power – this and not religion or even virtue, was the foundation upon which American democracy rested. Camp's assumption that in the absence of governmental intervention harmony would ensue was typically Jacksonian. But perhaps the clearest statement of the Democratic attitude to religion and virtue was made by the party's semi-official magazine, the *Democratic Review*. Tocqueville's assessment of the role of religion prompted a reviewer of his *Democracy in America* to give a Jacksonian estimate of its importance. The writer (possibly John L. O'Sullivan) set out to correct Tocqueville's assertion that religion had a direct effect in maintaining the democratic form of government. He agreed that 'religion operates directly upon the moral habits of the individual citizen', but this made its influence 'consequently subsidiary to that of the enterprise and industry which form. . . . the actual basis of good moral habits'. The certainty of a satisfactory reward for labour, he implied, which itself depended upon the absence of partial, exploitative legislation, impelled men to labour and this ensured good morals. Hence the most that religion could do was to 'concur with a good government in producing good moral habits'. Democracy and the political equality which it guaranteed rested, the reviewer continued, not upon religion but upon the equality of conditions; this was 'the single cause of the existence and stability of our democratic institutions'.

---

[54]Camp, *Democracy*, 94-104; John Taylor, *An Inquiry into the Principles and Policy of the Government of the United States* (London, 1950), *passim.*

Without this social equality, he declared, religion would be powerless to support democracy:

> If any change in the condition of the people of the United States should lead to a change in the principle of the government from *democracy* to *aristocracy* or *despotism,* the influence of religion would have no tendency to prevent this change from taking effect. The form must follow the substance, and when that changes must change with it. If an essential inequality of condition should ever take place among the people of the United States, the principle of aristocracy would immediately prevail in the government.

Hence 'religion has no tendency to maintain the democratic form of the government, or to prevent its change to a different one'. Interestingly, the writer suggested that under another, and therefore inferior, form of government, its influence could be greater. In these circumstances it might 'resist the moral plague, which would then tend to flow in upon society to furnish new motives for good conduct, in lieu of the *worldly prosperity* which might then not so uniformly follow it' [My italics]. Religion was thus a less potent social force than self-interest. The *Review* implied that as the world progressed, so religion, as a social and political force, became increasingly irrelevant. Of course, this writer, in common with the vast majority of Democrats, no doubt revered the moral code of Christianity and respected the truth of religion as a metaphysical entity. But the suggestion was that equality and self-interest were more important social forces. The *Review* did not state that democracy could survive in a nation that had abandoned religion, but it was strongly implied. Here was the ideological base upon which the baffling and contradictory Democratic alliance between freethinkers, Protestants and Roman Catholics was built.[55]

Party: The Theory

It is one of the ironies of American political history that although the second party system was in many senses the most fully developed and evenly balanced that the nation has ever seen, yet acceptance of party itself as a legitimate and permanently established institution was by no means complete. Hostility to parties was, of course, older than the Republic itself and although it inevitably diminished as party and party strife became increasingly familiar to Americans it nevertheless remained as a force – and ironically, too, as a force that perhaps helped to intensify party competition – in Jacksonian politics. Limited

[55]*Dem. Rev.,* I (July 1838), 350-2.

almost entirely to the anti-Democratic ranks, anti-party sentiment served to reinforce conservative opposition to, and resentment of, the party of Jackson, Van Buren and Polk. This hostility had some roots in the cultural values of evangelical Protestantism; hence it has been treated (by Formisano, for example) as an ingredient of ethnocultural politics.

That the relationship between anti-party and ethnicity was a close one is suggested by the hostility of Nativists to the political party. The anonymous author of the pamphlet entitled *The Crisis* was convinced that 'among the causes which have brought into action and stimulated foreign influence, and which will hereafter continue its evils is *party spirit*'. While the author's boast that the Nativists 'love country more than party' did not suggest a preference that was in any sense controversial, it nevertheless denoted a conflict of interests which many Americans simply did not perceive. Similarly the Louisiana Native American Association complained of 'the malign influence of party spirit'. It was a major grievance of Nativists everywhere that the existence of a mass of ignorant foreign-born voters stimulated party organisation and encouraged an unnecessary degree of party conflict. The Nativists, when they formed their own party, were in effect constructing an anti-party party.[56]

Their hostility towards party was shared by many fierce Whig partisans. As Lynn Marshall has pointed out, the highly partisan opposition to Jackson which developed in the early 1830s was slow in acquiring organisational structure precisely because of the reluctance of men like Daniel Webster to accept party discipline or to employ party techniques. Contemporaries of both parties recognised that the Whigs were unable to match the Democrats in organisation and unity. Whigs indeed were prone to deplore the depth of partisan feeling. When William Henry Harrison, after one of the most intensely partisan election campaigns in American history, delivered his Inaugural, he warned that the violence of party spirit 'must be greatly mitigated, if not entirely extinguished, or consequences will ensue which are appalling to be thought of'. According to Joseph Story party was 'the curse of our country, and will probably be the destruction of our Liberties', while Alonzo Potter in the *New York Review* complained that 'allegiance to party is getting to be rewarded, we had almost said, honored, before allegiance to country'. To Washington Hunt 'the most deplorable and appalling evil of the time' was 'that the unclean spirit of party has been permitted to invade the tribunals of justice'. Harrison and Story, Potter and Hunt desired a greater degree

[56] *The Crisis*, 9, 46; *Address of Louisiana Native American Association*, 16.

of political unity; this desire was widespread within the Whig party. As late as 1844 John P. Kennedy found the 'glory of Mr. Madison's administration' in the fact that 'it made peace between the parties'. In 1841, in the aftermath of Harrison's victory, Daniel Ullmann expressed his belief that parties 'often need to be resolved into their original elements' and added that 'such an era has now arrived'.[57]

As Formisano has noted, one of the major sources of anti-party sentiment was the desire for social harmony and unity. Many Whigs assumed that this was the natural state of American society, provided it received proper direction from government. Social and politial conflict was thus attributable to the deliberate and premeditated actions of party politicians. According to the *American Magazine* parties were 'inimical to the peace and harmony of society' and therefore 'fatal to rational liberty'. William Cost Johnson of Maryland complained to Congress that 'the strong fanaticism of party' meant that 'no public man, who was not an ultra on one side or another, could receive the confidence of any large portion of the people'. Most Whigs acknowledged that some political discord would necessarily exist in a republic but they feared that it was in the interests of party and party politicians to augment and intensify it. Hence they were suspicious and resentful of organisations whose strength was obtained only at the expense of unity, agreement and consensus.[58]

To this extent anti-party was clearly another product – along with nativism and moral reform – of the desire for social homogeneity and unity that typified evangelical Protestantism. Yet, even here the social conservatism of Whig anti-party theorists was prominent. Underlying the idea of gratuitous strife was the assumption that American society was just and equitable. Deep political divisions, it was implied, need not exist because the social structure did not give rise to the grievances necessary to sustain them. To the anti-party Whig, party conflict might conceivably represent disagreement but not true social conflict. In attacking party, however, they had before them the image of the Democratic party. Hence the identification of party with social strife is an understandable one.

[57]Lynn Marshall, 'The Strange Stillbirth of the Whig Party', *A.H.R.*, LXXII (Jan. 1967), 445-68; Harrison's Inaugural in *Madisonian*, 4 March 1841; Story quoted in William W. Story, *The Life and Letters of Joseph Story*, 2 vols. (London, 1851), II, 481; *N.Y.R.*, II (Jan. 1838), 48; *Cong. Gl.*, 29 i App., 64; [John P. Kennedy], *A Defence of the Whigs* (N.Y., 1844), 22; Daniel Ullmann, *An Address. . . before the Tippecanoe and other Harrison Associations of the City of New York, Feb. 22 1841* (N.Y., 1841), 38-40.

[58]*A.M.* quoted (and endorsed) in Nat. Am., 20 June 1840; *Cong. Gl.*, 25 ii App., 581-2.

Many Whigs held that the party, by means of its institutional apparatus and permanently functioning machinery, enabled a small minority to exercise a tyrannical control over the electorate. By the demagogic arts of flattery and deceit party leaders – and here anti-party men were clearly referring to Democratic leaders – were able to mobilise the masses and even to induce them to act in opposition to their own best interests. James Watson Webb in the *Courier and Enquirer* charged the Democrats with plotting a deliberate conspiracy against the public welfare:

> The men who work the wires of the party machinery – that portion of them who do most in directing the movement of the masses who go against us – are unquestionably doing all they can to injure the interests of those masses, and a great many of them we believe are conscious of it themselves. They are generally, however, too cunning to let either their convictions or their dishonesty appear to the public. They deceive in the dark – they look one way and now another, and while they are wily in their proofs of regard for the people, are at heart their very worst enemies – and *know it.*

Although this was a conspiracy theory, it is not necessary to assume that it stemmed from the psychic instability of paranoia. Rather it reflected the confidence of the partisan, with strongly held convictions, that his principles were just and true. To Webb Whig policy was self-evidently correct; the Democratic opposition was, therefore, sinister and insincere.[59]

This line of thought was common to many Whigs. Parties, according to the *American Magazine,* were 'the madness or folly of many for the benefit of a few'. If party spirit were violent it followed that 'the contest will be for personal and selfish purposes'. According to William Henry Harrison the spirit of party was 'hostile' to 'the people's best interests'; it was a spirit 'contracted in its views – selfish in its objects', looking to 'the aggrandizement of a few, even to the destruction of the interest of the whole'. Parties were thus 'destructive of public virtue'. The party was an agency which, by demanding unconditional loyalty, undermined the sound judgment of the statesman and threatened the public spiritedness of the good citizen. Here was a major complaint against parties, although one which had been heard ever since factions or parties had existed. For the spirit of party 'engenders the bitterest feelings, palsies the social virtues, warps the judgment, stifles the civilities of life and freezes up the warm gushes of philanthropy'. Equally, the tyranny of party enabled 'a few ambitious

[59] *Courier and Enquirer,* 27 Sept. 1842.

and corrupt, or misguided leaders' to control the masses who were 'in effect disfranchised'. Individual freedom of conscience was thus violated. It was, then, little wonder that party should be opposed by those who were most aggressively committed to Protestantism. Criticism of the party was often couched in the same terms as criticism of the Pope. Daniel Ullmann, at the beginning of a long anti-party tract, made the connection explicit when he declared that 'the unrestricted exercise of the right of private judgment is the essence of protestantism in religious matters and of democracy in matters political'. Private judgment was threatened by party and Pope alike.[60]

Many Whigs who did not oppose party in itself nevertheless perceived a conflict between individual freedom and party loyalty. Whigs generally lagged behind Democrats in the perfection of organisational techniques and sometimes this was acknowledged by their spokesmen. In Iowa the *Bloomington Herald* observed that the Democrats were able to maintain the greater degree of unity but pointed out that this was obtained only by sacrificing freedom of opinion:

> That this harmony among the dominant party is the source of their power we cannot doubt – nor are we ignorant of the fact that difference of opinion has been the stumbling-block in the way of the Whigs. That party is not formed of the right material to be drilled and marshalled by aspiring leaders. . . . With the Whigs the individual is never sufficiently merged into the partisan to make an efficient, ready tool; and we glory in a defeat which grows out of such independence – men's views are different, their modes of reasoning various, and any constant unanimity must grow out of the overbearing dictation of the few, or the subserviency of the mass.[61]

It is, of course, true that in any political party individual freedom of opinion must necessarily, to a greater or lesser degree, be diminished. For several reasons Democrats were less likely to confront the problem, but for these Whigs it bulked large if only because party brought few, if any, compensations. In addition, it was electorally more advantageous for anti-party men to emphasise this feature of the party system than to voice their other objections.

For their opposition was ultimately that of the social and political conservative to the dangerous tendencies of American democratic

---

[60]*A.M.* in *Nat. Am.*, 20 June 1840; *Madisonian*, 4 March 1841; *The Crisis*, 12; Ullmann, *Address*, 31-2, 9.

[61]*Bloomington Herald* in *Iowa C.C.*, 395.

politics. Not only could they see no social conflict upon which a party system might be based, they also felt that parties endangered the traditional methods of leadership in a republic. The political theory upon which anti-party arguments tended to be based was that of republicanism as opposed to democracy. Party placed in office the opportunistic politician, not the disinterested statesman that republican theory had postulated. Whigs of a conservative persuasion were dismayed that the military chieftain Jackson had been succeeded by Van Buren, the archetypal party politician. One of the eighteen reasons 'why Van Buren ought not to be re-elected' in 1840 was that 'he is the instrument of a party and not the President of the Union'. During the Presidential campaign of 1844 the *Whig Text Book* compared the stature of the two major candidates. Clay was a statesman 'whom every nation on earth would be proud to call her own', whereas Polk was 'a partizan of the lowest order'. According to traditional republican theory, to which conservative Whigs still clung, the statesman was expected to exercise his talents and superior abilities in the interests of the entire community. He should not merely represent their interests and voice their opinions. Party pressure, however, impeded the independent action of the statesman. It is significant that when Horace Mann of Massachusetts made this complaint he specifically objected to the politician's too-close representation of his constituency, rather than merely his loyalty to party:

> Now I would ask any sober and reflecting man, whether he would not prefer to have his own and his country's interests represented on the floor of Congress by [honest] individuals. . . . though widely differing from him on a particular point, rather than to have them represented by a base party chameleon, who always reflects the political complexion of the district he resides in; – or outdoing the chameleon himself, changes to the complexion of the district he means to go to.

Similarly William Cost Johnson of Maryland lamented the absence of true statesmen from the political stage and attributed it to the spirit of party. It was this, he complained,

> which makes both of the two strong parties in this country cordially dislike, and bitterly persecute, every high-minded man who will not be as rancorous as themselves; that makes a gentleman, who boldly throws himself upon his pride of feeling, and stands upon his Americanism, and deigns to think and act for himself, at once placed between the cross-fire of both parties, and denounced by each. The very man who most deserves the confidence of the people, is the last, too often, to gain it; whilst a time serving politician, who is sometimes on one side, sometimes

on the other, the loudest wherever he is to be found, is called a patriot, and the most to be caressed by each, and the first to be honored and promoted.

Johnson in effect contrasted the republican statesman, whom the anti-party men revered, with the newer party politician whose rise had accompanied the growth of democracy.[62]

Anti-party was thus rooted in a set of values that were not only cultural, but also political and socio-economic. Men who objected to party tended to be conservative both socially and politically; like Johnson they usually belonged to the conservative wing of the Whig party. Although it was theoretically possible to have complete faith in the people's capacity for self-government and yet to be critical of party very few anti-party theorists maintained this position. Instead they were men anxious for the fate of popular government in America, republicans rather than democrats. After accusing Democratic party workers of treachery or deceit, James Watson Webb declared his conviction that the party 'would look exceedingly small the next time it goes to the polls' – 'if the people could understand and coolly and dispassionately act upon the great questions before them'.[63]

Webb represented, of course, the conservative wing of the New York Whig party. The liberal wing, led by Seward and Weed, had repudiated the neo-Federalist outlook of the conservatives, their fear of democracy, their mistrust of the people, their dread of radicalism. Hence it largely ignored, if it did not entirely dismiss, the anti-party theories with which that outlook was associated. And in fact a majority of Whig partisans generally suppressed whatever reservations they may have had about parties and party conflict; a few even joined the Democrats in their attempts to refute anti-party theory. For where the parties tended ideologically to converge, there was a common set of ideas and assumptions about party. It was no doubt easy for men who were in the thick of party conflict to see the struggles in which they were engaged as a continuation of what could already be described as the American tradition of political partisanship. At any rate, Whigs in this situation devoted little time to anti-party theorising.

Instead they would perhaps have endorsed the view that party was the inevitable result of disagreement over principles and policy. It was 'vain', the *New York Review* believed, 'to expect uniformity of

[62]*Madisonian,* 23 Jan. 1840; *The Whig Text Book, or Democracy Unmasked* (n.p., n.d.), 29-31; Mary Mann, *The Life and Works of Horace Mann,* 5 vols. (Boston, 1891), IV, 352-3; *Cong. Gl.,* 25 ii App., 582.

[63]*Courier and Enquirer,* 27 Sept. 1842.

opinion'. If only because men reasoned differently, saw different facts, had different interests, and were influenced by different passions, parties were unavoidable. The *Review* was Whig in its politics; for the Democrats Jabez D. Hammond similarly argued that 'among a free people' disagreements naturally produced parties. Few Democrats would have disputed this proposition. Both Hammond and the writer in the *New York Review*, however, went further than a mere acknowledgment of the inevitability of party. According to the writer in the *Review*, party conflict operated as a check upon government. An opposition party's function included that of safeguarding the rights of a threatened minority; similarly it scrutinised the political activities of every officeholder in order to expose his corruption or incompetence. Thus a separation of parties in effect reinforced the separation of powers. The *Madisonian* in its Whig days likewise recognised this feature of party competition when noting that 'a long lease of power to one party tempts corruption'. Hence, the newspaper concluded, 'two great parties there must always be in every country, to watch, and keep each other in check'. The adverse effect on anti-party sentiment of the Whig successes of the late 1830s and 1840 is clear from the *Madisonian's* confidence that 'when the faults of Government become flagrant' then 'the other party succeeds to reform abuses'. For this had happened 'lately with us'. The *Madisonian* was, of course, first Democratic, then Whig, finally Democratic again. The same pro-party posture was taken by more orthodox Democrats. According to Martin Van Buren party competition was 'inseparable from a free government' not least because 'the disposition to abuse power, so deeply planted in the human heart, can by no other means be more effectually checked'. Thus the argument that parties helped to check and balance the government was itself bipartisan.[64]

Whigs and Democrats alike found other virtues in party. The *New York Review* and the *Democratic Review* while as far apart ideologically as they were close geographically, both argued for party as an educative force. Political discussion, public knowledge of, and interest in, political events, concern for individual rights and liberties – all, the journals agreed, were encouraged by the party dialogue. Other partisans posited a dialectical basis for the two party system. Theophilus Fisk for the Democrats suggested that of Reform *versus*

[64]*N.Y.R.*, VIII (April 1841), 396, 400-1; Jabez D. Hammond, *A Political History of the State of New York (including the Life of Silas Wright)* 3 vols. (N.Y., 1852), III, 670; *Madisonian*, 19 March 1841; John C. Fitzpatrick (ed.), 'The Autobiography of Martin Van Buren', *American Historical Association, Annual Report for the Year 1918*, II, 125.

Conservatism, while Horace Greeley for the Whigs saw Liberty *versus* Order. There was a clear similarity between them.[65]

Yet it is significant that the virtues of party could only be perceived by those who were not blinded by their fear of the people or suspicion of democracy. Where this fear still existed, anti-party was its natural companion. Men like Greeley and Weed, organs like the *Madisonian* and (on this occasion) the *New York Review* neither lamented the decline of the republican polity nor feared for the stability of the social edifice. In proportion as these anxieties were removed, the fear of party diminished.

Nevertheless, relatively few Whigs engaged in theorising about party; they maintained instead a practical and energetic silence. Democrats were bolder and far less equivocal. For them party was an undoubted, a positive good. 'Party', Alexander Duncan told Congress, 'is the salt of the nation.' According to Democratic Senator William Roane of Virginia, 'the only way in which we can go efficiently for our country' was 'through the medium of party'. Democrats were highly suspicious of men who disclaimed any allegiance to party. When James Buchanan, during a debate on the currency question, claimed to be acting above party considerations, his colleague Robert Strange of North Carolina immediately rebuked him. Strange was reported as being 'sorry to hear the Senator adopt the cant so frequently used by the Opposition – that he was above party consideration. No public man commended himself to his confidence by saying that he was above party consideration.' Strange's was the typical Democratic response. The traditional opprobrium with which the party politician had been regarded – and was still widely regarded – no longer influenced Jacksonians. Jabez D. Hammond praised Silas Wright's dedication to party as proof of his selflessness. Wright, he pointed out, 'was not selfish: to him his party was everything – himself nothing'. This was an accurate description so far as Wright was concerned. In 1846, aware that he would probably fail to win re-election as Governor of New York, Wright consoled himself with the thought that 'if I fall, I shall have the sound democracy of the state to fall with me'. 'Separate from them', he added, 'I am nothing and can be nothing.' This was a statement which could hardly have been made by a Whig; it would probably have met with contempt from Henry Clay or Daniel Webster.[66]

---

[65]*N. Y. R.*, VIII (April 1841), 402; *Dem. Rev.*, IX (Oct. 1841), 345; *Dem. Exp.*, 20 Sept. 1845; Horace Greeley, *Why I Am A Whig* (n.p.,n.d.), 1–3.

[66]*Cong. Gl.*, 26 i App., 52, 219, 25 iii App., 191; Hammond, *Political History*, III, 53; Wright to John R. Russell, 10 March 1846, quoted in Ransom H. Gillet, *The Life*

This complete acceptance of party by Democrats permitted its use in ways which Whigs could not bring themselves to accept. When discussing the duties of a politician, Jackson himself employed a military metaphor which gives credence to Whig fears that party threatened independence and liberty. Writing to Blair in 1840, Jackson reminded his old friend that 'the Democratic members are expected to sit like brave men who hold the safety and perpetuity of our republican system in their hand and who are relied on to die at their post before they will deliver up the ship to the enemy'. Such a remark would have confirmed many Whig suspicions about party. Similarly, although both parties practised rotation in office (and rotated offices so as to benefit their own supporters), it was the New York Democrat William L. Marcy who coined the famous phrase 'to the victor belong the spoils'. No Whig seems to have endorsed this maxim. To Hammond it was 'an evidence of frankness'. To Theophilus Fisk it was 'a sentiment which we endorse at all times and under all circumstances'.[67]

How were Democrats able to adopt so remarkable an attitude to party? Some historians, such as Richard Hofstadter and Michael Wallace, have argued that the Jacksonian acceptance of party, and particularly of the opposition party, was achieved in large part at the expense of ideology and principle. Whereas partisans of the Federalist-Republican era, they argue, had been generally opposed to party, men of the Jacksonian era were able to accept its existence because the ideological gap between the parties was much narrower. Party battles, in effect, were admissible because victory or defeat signified less. Thus the party system, and acceptance of party itself, was a product of ideological consensus and agreement.[68]

As an explanation for the growth of party organisation and pro-party thought this is highly unsatisfactory. The Democrats, pioneers in both, were able to embrace party without any sacrifice of ideological purity. It is not necessary, it is perhaps not even possible,

and Times of Silas Wright, 2 vols. (Albany, 1874), II, 1731-2. Clearly the Calhoun Democrats, who were of course strongly opposed to party, present an exception to this rule. Yet the rule is perhaps proved by this exception since the Calhounites were also opposed to the rule of the numerical majority. See below, Chapter 7.

[67] John S. Bassett (ed.), The Correspondence of Andrew Jackson, 7 vols. (Washington D.C., 1926-35), VI, 67; Ivor D. Spencer, The Victor and the Spoils: A Life of William L. Marcy (Providence, 1959), 59-60; Hammond, Political History, II, 429; Dem. Exp., 2 Aug. 1845.

[68] Richard Hofstadter, The Idea of a Party System: The Rise of a Legitimate Opposition in the United States, 1780-1840 (Berkeley, 1969), esp. 246-8; Michael L. Wallace, 'Ideologies of Party in the Ante-Bellum Republic' (Ph.D. thesis, Columbia University, 1973), esp. 389-451.

to determine whether ideological acceptance of party was responsible for its organisational development or whether the relationship was reversed. Yet it is clear that Democratic social and political philosophy was consonant with a pro-party stance. Indeed it is tempting to suggest that the more radical a Democrat was, the more easily he accepted the idea of party conflict and competition. Paradoxically, the more opposed he was to the Whig party, the more readily he might acknowledge its existence, and even its permanent existence. Party in this sense worked to solidify rather than diminish ideological conflict.

There were in fact many considerations which helped make Democrats more favourable to party than Whigs. Democratic ideology tended to rob anti-party arguments of much of their force or to permit Democrats to suspend consideration of problems that were urgent to the Whigs. Thus, believing in limited government, Democrats were not compelled to face the possibility that parties inevitably employed their political power so as to further the economic interests of their supporters. This perhaps removed one traditional obstacle to the development of party. Similarly, with their more vivid and less qualified fear of power, Democrats could tolerate an opposition party which, if its opposition were effective, might check those in power and thus further restrict the activities of government. Party was an additional means of checking and balancing power; Democrats were usually more favourable than Whigs to checks and balances. More important, the Democrats, with their greater faith in the people, envisaged party as a channel of communication along which popular opinion passed before reaching government. They thus applauded party for the very reason that conservative Whigs condemned it. And since, according to Democratic theory, the representative's task was merely to voice the opinions and defend the interests of his constituents, it followed that a tyranny of opinion – at least over the majority – was impossible. Thus the Democrats easily dismissed many of the charges which anti-party theorists brought.[69]

These factors are nevertheless of only minor importance in accounting for the Democratic enthusiasm towards party. Essentially, Democrats were able to plunge into party organisation, and to ignore,

[69] Assuming party loyalty as a necessary fact, George Sidney Camp argued that it permitted only the moderately great statesman to be elected. Reversing the traditional formulation, however, he approved of this on the grounds that it reduced the scope for individual ambition and necessitated concern for the public welfare – Camp, *Democracy*, 139-41. As Regina Morantz has pointed out, 'party, as the instrument of majority rule, was a levelling influence which guaranteed the supremacy of the collective wisdom of the common mind' – Regina A.M. Moratz,' "Democracy" and "Republic" in American Ideology, 1787-1840' (Ph.D. thesis, Columbia University, 1971), 206-7.

or overlook, traditional and contemporary arguments against party because they perceived a socio-economic and even a socio-psychological basis for the two party system. This itself was a perception which fitted compactly into the structure of their beliefs. In effect, Democrats argued that an opposition to their principles and policies was inherent in human nature; it could not but arise in a free society. With the recognition of a permanent opposition, the major obstacle to an unqualified endorsement of party was removed.

If Martin Van Buren can be regarded as the epitome of the new breed of party politician, then his celebrated *Inquiry into the Origin and Course of Political Parties in the United States* can be regarded as the standard Democratic exposition of the pro-party philosophy. In what was basically a history of the major political parties Van Buren noted that the 'political seed' of Federalism – incorporated banks, tariffs, and other examples of partial legislation – had 'never been eradicated'. He added that 'it seems not susceptible of eradication'. Here was the entirely plausible basis upon which party conflict rested. Support for, or opposition to, the Hamiltonian economic policy would create a permanent political division in the United States. The contending parties would be the Democrats and an Opposition, whose name might alter, whose character and policy might occasionally be slightly changed, but whose underlying principles would remain constant. Hence the Democrats had to rally their supporters to oppose their Federalist adversaries.[70]

Van Buren was not content merely to take note of the permanent existence of Federalism; in addition he sought to account for it. He found its roots in inequality, whether consisting of privilege, of wealth, or simply of the desire for superiority. The danger from wealth in particular was ever-present:

> To be allied to power, permanently, if possible, in its character and splendid in its appendages, is one of the strongest passions which wealth inspires. The grandeur of the Crown and of the landed aristocracy afford a fair vent to that in England. Here, where it is deprived of that indulgence, it maintains a constant struggle for the establishment of a moneyed oligarchy, the most selfish and monopolizing of all depositories of political power.

Van Buren thus recognised that human nature might create the same evils in the United States, a republic, as in England, a monarchy. It was an idea consonant with the Democratic emphasis upon self-interest and Democratic fears of 'aristocracy'.[71]

[70] Van Buren, *Inquiry*, 267.
[71] *Ibid.*, 166.

217

Van Buren added that only 'the democratic spirit of the country' (by which he really meant the Democratic party), prevented the successful realisation of the aims of the wealthy. Moreover, as the wealthy, or those who aspired to great wealth, acquired control over the government, and obtained, by the use of its powers, special privileges, so their natural tendency to consider themselves superior to the rest of the community would be strengthened. The enjoyment of such privileges, Van Buren warned, 'is certain sooner or later to produce distrust of the less favored body of the people, and distrust grows apace to the proportions of prejudice and dislike'. By this means the aristocracy of Federalism was formed. It was united by special interests, and could be checked only by the people's active supervision of the affairs of government. Party was the instrument they were to use.[72]

Significantly, Van Buren was careful to point out that the feelings of superiority engendered by wealth and privilege were (with few exceptions) 'not the fruit of infirm purposes or characters'. To stress this point he admitted that this change of feelings operated on three out of every four Democrats who obtained privileges. Hence for Van Buren, the opposition, although an incipient aristocracy, although anti-democratic and thus virtually treasonous in its views, was an impersonal element. Criticism and perhaps even persuasion were useless; dedication to the Democratic party was the only means of combating it. Federalists might thus, as Van Buren repeatedly acknowledged, be men of great personal merit, they might sincerely believe in the principles they espoused and they might possess a genuine if misguided love of country. They would always exist; the Democracy had to be ready to do battle with them.[73]

This line of thought was not limited to Van Buren. Frank Blair was convinced that the 'undying' principles of democracy and federalism were 'at the bottom of all our contests'.[74] In the Pennsylvania Constitutional Convention Thomas Earle traced the history of political parties and found their origin not in the Federalist era, nor even in the era of the English Civil War, but in the classical age. Parties had 'existed in ancient Greece and Rome', and were in fact 'the same which have existed in all other countries'. One of these parties

[72]*Ibid.*, 224.

[73]*Ibid.*, 225. Hence Van Buren's scrupulous fairness to, and even praise for, the Federalists in no way implied an even partial acceptance of their principles or programme – see pp. 29, 71, 167-8 and *passim*. Similarly the fact that Democrats did not try to eliminate their opponents is not evidence of any real ideological consensus, as Wallace implies – Wallace, 'Ideologies of Party', 157.

[74]*Globe*, 3 Aug. 1838. See also 16 Nov. 1842.

'was termed the democracy and the other the aristocracy' and these were the parties which would 'perpetually exist, so long as truth and error continue to have a separate existence'. Democratic spokesmen frequently identified the struggle between the parties as that of producers against non-producers, or of those desiring a strong central government against those who favoured an inactive, economical government, or of those with faith in the people against those who feared and mistrusted them. John G. Floyd, however, who fittingly represented New York, pushed the Democratic theory of party to its logical conclusion when he argued that party conflict was a war of rich against poor. Not surprisingly he acknowledged that his speech might be thought to possess a spirit of 'radicalism' or of 'Jacobinism'. But, undeterred, he stated his conviction that in the United States,

> every great political contest has been, and every great political contest upon principle will be, a war between the rich and the poor – on the part of the rich, a war of aggression, on the part of the poor, a war of defence. The arrogance of wealth is almost universal – the possessor of riches most naturally slides into the belief that the property which gives him advantages in the procurement of the luxuries of life over his poor neighbour, should confer additional personal importance and superior political rights.

Here was the social war, a war between rich and poor, which was the ultimate horror to anti-party and conservative theorists, actually incorporated into political theory and thus legitimised. Floyd here stood the traditional anti-party philosophy upon its head.[75]

The Democratic pro-party outlook thus accorded easily with the Democratic social and political theory. Experience of active government in the United States (and, no doubt, especially of its progress during the partyless era of 'good feelings') had induced Jacksonians to reject the traditional no-party republican ideal, which had been upheld by John Taylor of Caroline as well as (though inconsistently) by Jefferson, and to recognise that the danger from self-interest, from government and from 'aristocracy' was as great in republican America as in feudal Europe. Democratic theory was thus anchored once again in the motive of self-interest. The political party was the instrument by which the self-interest of the majority could neutralise that of the privileged élite. Accepting an opposition as inevitable, the Democrats viewed their own party as the representative of the forces of liberty and equality and hence as the custodian of American democracy.

---

[79] *Pa. C.C.*, I, 116; *Cong. Gl.*, 26 i App., 590.

Ethnoculture and Politics

It was because they laid most stress upon the motive of self-interest, because they were anxious to preserve equality as they understood it, and because they were enthusiastic champions of popular government that the radical Democrats were the most articulate defenders of party. For the same reason they were apt to be unequivocally opposed to the introduction of moral and religious issues into politics and highly sympathetic to the immigrant. Conversely it was the conservative Whigs who, mindful of the inequalities that necessarily must exist in any civilized community, fearful of the social conflict which democracy threatened to provoke and suspicious of Democratic demands for liberty and self-government, were most inclined to resent the immigrant, to condemn the political party and to seek legislation for religious and moral reform. A politician's stance upon ethnocultural issues was thus likely to be consistent with his response to issues that were socio-economic or more narrowly political in nature.[76]

The dichotomy that is implied by Formisano and Benson between socio-economic and ethnocultural questions[77] must therefore be replaced by an emphasis upon world vision and ideology in their broadest sense.[78] Without this dichotomy it becomes possible to

[76] I am here dealing with tendencies rather than with iron laws. Thus some politicians cannot be so readily placed on the spectrum of opinion which I have constructed. I believe, however, that a statistical analysis would confirm the reliability of the model.

[77] Formisano occasionally offers a hint that ethnoculture was linked to socio-economic and poltical issues, noting, for example, how 'class and cultural attitudes blended' in the thinking of two Michigan Whigs, that 'intemperance caused a blurring of social distinctions', that Presbyterians (who were rich and not very liberal) were separated from the Irish by 'class and culture' and that parties probably 'gave the death blow to the deference politics of the aristocratic state republics of the early national period'. But his suggestions are not followed up. Probably because of his immersion in the contemporary social sciences Formisano transfers the ideological patterns of the post-1945 era into the Age of Jackson. (Is it significant that conflict between ethnic or religious groups no longer suggests any real disagreement over democracy or political economy?) Any historical investigation which assumes that the 'laws' of contemporary social science are universal is likely to discover a homogeneous past – Formisano, *Birth of Mass Parties,* 88, 117, 161, 182.

[78] The ethnocultural issues which Formisano emphasises – temperance and alien voting – were considerably more important at state than at national level. Those strongly committed to temperance (e.g. Dow in Maine) or hostile to the immigrants (the Nativists) were both more active and more successful in state politics than in Federal elections, where the topics rarely arose. The state was the obvious theatre of operations for these men and the influence of ethnocultural issues was presumably greater there. Similarly, if anti-party was a major, *independent* ingredient of Whiggery then it is at least arguable that it should have resulted in reduced Whig strength at Federal elections (where problems of organisation were greatest). Thus if ethnocultural factors were paramount then the Whigs and their supporters might well have concentrated their efforts on state elections. In fact the reverse happened and party support fell away during state campaigns – see Formisano, *Birth of Mass Parties,* 24.

recognise, and account for, the presence of ethnocultural conflict without assuming (as Benson and Formisano do) that it is concealed behind the mere window-dressing of rhetoric and social and political theory. There will now be no reason to believe that the ethnocultural issues played any more than the secondary role in party conflict that their relatively infrequent intrusions into both rhetoric and legislative chamber would suggest. Ethnocultural preferences were undoubtedly present among the contending partisans; their importance should not be exaggerated.[79]

Thus the ethnocultural interpretation is perhaps inadequate on two accounts. Firstly it would seem to overestimate the importance of purely ethnocultural issues. Secondly it apparently fails to recognise their intimate relationship to the other issues of the era. Ironically too, the presence of the ethnocultural issues – immigrant voting, political partisanship, religion and morality in politics – is most apparent in the conflicting attitudes of the two extreme groups, the radical Democrats and the conservative Whigs. For it is here that the validity and justice of the term 'Jacksonian Democracy' which Benson and Formisano are keen to discard, are most evident. Despite the belated recognition of ethnoculture, the concept can be retained.

The confinement of the evangelical, anti-party outlook to the conservative section of the Whig party is the explanation for its relative lack of importance. Whigs in the mainstream of their party might sympathise with the outlook but it required innovatory proposals for subjecting the judiciary to the evils of party, for enfranchising aliens or for dispensing with the Protestant Bible in American schools to make them rally to the cause. Even here they supported the *status quo,* and in the absence of any local groundswelling of opinion (as

---

[79] Although it is not the purpose of this work to analyse electoral voting (upon which much of the ethnocultural case rests), several considerations may be relevant. As far as Formisano's work is concerned – for a devastating critique of Benson's presentation of quantitative data see Lebowitz, 'The Significance of Claptrap' – it is noteworthy that many of his statistics cover the years 1848-1852 when, by his own admission, 'the familiar issues of Democratic-Whig strife' were 'ritual themes'. Especially serious here is the inclusion of the Free Soil vote of 1848 (which presumably included some of the support that the radical Democrats had enjoyed, since Martin Van Buren was the Free Soil candidate for President) as illustrative of anti-Democratic strength. Generalisations about the Jacksonian era based on this must be highly suspect. The treatment of parties as monoliths is also misleading in this connection. It is certainly true, as Formisano points out, that some rich men voted Democratic but it is also true that some non-evangelicals, e.g. Episcopalians, voted Whig. The Episcopalians were usually rich; the Democratic rich may well have been non-evangelical or alien. To decide how voters whose economic interest pulled them one way but whose ethnocultural loyalties pulled them another resolved their problems is clearly a major difficulty and one which has yet to be overcome – Formisano, *Birth of Mass Parties,* 81-2, *passim.* See also the works cited in note 2, especially McCormick.

occurred in the early 1850s in Maine over temperance) these essentially defensive successes were all that was achieved. The lack of success is perhaps less than surprising. Anti-party could not stand before the need to resist Democratic policy and principle, the weight of an already powerful tradition bore down upon all attempts to mix religion with politics, and opposition to the immigrant was more likely to intensify strife than to diminish it. In each case the demands of the conservatives for the ethnocultural programme could, with some justification, be sacrificed in the interests of a conservatism more widely defined. By 1837 the *status quo* included parties, the rapid enfranchisement of immigrants and a long established and agreed separation of religion and politics. The attempts that were made to alter these conditions, and the deep-seated values and preferences of partisans combined to create an ethnocultural dimension to the ideologies of Democrat and Whig. Though its existence must be recognised, its importance need not be exaggerated. Nor should it be pointed to as proof positive of the truth and validity of consensus history.

A Note on Race

A sad postscript to the politics of ethnicity concerns the fate of the racial minorities in the United States. For although the 'middle period' of American history saw what was in a sense the decisive stage in the process by which the nation accommodated itself to the fact of continued ethnic diversity, it was also an era in which the white man's oppression of blacks and Indians intensified. As democracy accepted and even welcomed the immigrant, it rejected and spurned the red and the black man.

This paradox culminated in Democratic theory. Acknowledging and even demanding the equal rights of the immigrant, Democrats generally refused to recognise those of the Indian and the black. Historians have noted that this ideological pattern was widespread: those favourable to the immigrant were usually deeply racist and hostile to blacks and Indians; conversely the racial minorities received much sympathy from nativists.[80] This was a paradox which would have profound effects upon the course of American history.

Perceiving the suffrage as the superstructure which rested upon equality in both society and politics, and finding the support for this equality in the natural similarities among men, Democratic theory

---

[80] See for example Chilton Williamson, *American Suffrage: From Property to Democracy, 1760-1860* (Princeton, 1960), 261-7.

was unable to accommodate a class of secondary or inferior voters. In the Michigan Constitutional Convention of 1835-6 Democratic leader John Norvell, although not opposed to Indians voting, nevertheless felt compelled to oppose a motion enfranchising only those of the race who paid taxes. Norvell was hostile to this resolution 'because it contained a barbarous phrase, which drew a line of distinction between different classes of the inhabitants of the state entitled to vote'. The implication was that such a distinction was undemocratic; Norvell preferred to forbid the Indians to vote rather than allow the suffrage to be contaminated by contact with the force of inequality. Even more significantly, at the same convention Norvell avowed that he would oppose the enfranchisement of blacks 'until we [can] consent to treat them as equal with us in all respects'. There can be no clearer or more succinct statement of what political equality denoted for the Democrats.[81]

Before the Democrat could enfranchise the black man he thus needed to acknowledge a complete equality between the races. There were enormous barriers to such an admission. For if the blacks were indeed equal and if they did merit equal rights then the existence of slavery could no more be justified (on abstract grounds) than an attempt to enslave the white population. Slavery would thus become an absolute, intolerable evil. Its implicit recognition at the time of the Revolution and the acceptance that was implied as a condition of Southern entry into the Union would throw the nation itself into disrepute. The matrix of ideas and concepts composed of Democratic notions of 'the Union', of 'mission', of 'manifest destiny' and of 'Providence' would become a mockery. Not surprisingly, Democrats, from North and South alike, asserted the superiority of the white race.

With a few exceptions the Whigs were equally firm believers in white superiority. Yet they were also less concerned to maintain a society or polity of equals. Placing far more stress upon the differences and inequalities between man and man, Whigs could find a place for blacks or Indians in the hierarchy they envisaged– even if it were the bottom place. Similarly their collective view of morality (which was closely related to the hierarchical view of society) impelled many Whigs to feel a responsibility for the Indian, the slave and the free black.

Consequently, most of the truly racist utterances of the Jacksonian era came from Democrats. Blacks were 'ignorant, degraded, vicious', a race of 'human brutes', 'quite incapable of improvement' and unable

[81]*Mich. C.C.*, 247, 157.

to pass 'the point at which intellectual aspirations overcome animal propensities'. Indians were 'without any tendency to improvement', utterly 'destitute of any intellectual propulsion' and 'repulsive [in] nature'. The Democratic commitment to racism was almost as intense as the Democratic commitment to democracy.[82]

Nevertheless, however much Democratic spokesmen might point to the wretched condition of the blacks, Democratic racism did not rest upon empirical data. Convincing as this might have proved – and no doubt did prove to some – it was insufficient. For in championing the immigrant Democrats had dismissed all such evidence. The squalor in which the Irish, for example, lived, the fact that they had never experienced liberty but instead had been tyrannised for centuries, the spectacle of poverty and ignorance which they presented – all such considerations had been swept aside in the interests of political equality in its most fundamental sense. Since all men were equal, the immigrant's claim to equal rights could not be rejected by reference to his condition. But similarly, the condition of the blacks was, of itself, insufficient to justify his continued enslavement or disfranchisement. The concept of black inferiority receded further into the Democratic consciousness and it hardened into dogma.[83]

Thus the intellectual route by which greater respect and concern for the black man could have been acquired was not merely visible to the Democrat, it was glaringly apparent. And the more willingly he embraced the immigrant, the more apparent did the route appear and the more rapidly he was compelled to block it with the giant boulder of racism. By 1860 the ideal of racial equality was as far off as ever, blacks were not merely unequal; they were hardly human at all. The progress of democracy and the growth of egalitarian sentiment had, instead of carrying the Negro and the Indian with them, virtually left them behind. Here was the great paradox – and the great tragedy – of the ante-bellum era.

[82] *Cincinnati Enquirer,* 14 Feb. 1845; *Dem. Rev.,* XXVIII (June 1851), 503, XXV (Dec. 1849), 512, XXVIII (May 1851), 432, 429.

[83] See Duncan J. MacLeod, *Slavery, Race and the American Revolution* (Cambridge, 1974).

SECTIONS, PARTIES AND IDEOLOGY

The politician of the Jacksonian era, whether Whig or Democrat, was committed to a set of beliefs and ideas which together made up a coherent world-view. This ideology not unnaturally influenced his behaviour, whether in the legislative chamber, at the hustings or in the executive office. It frequently helped determine his activities within the party organisation. It could affect his conduct as a representative of his constituents. It could function as a springboard from which he might hope to advance his own career. For the committed partisan, behaviour was almost necessarily governed, in part, by ideology.

Yet there were other pressures to which a statesman was exposed. If membership of a political party offered an opportunity for an intending politician to direct the affairs of government in accordance with certain stated principles, it also put additional demands upon him. For parties were not simply vehicles for ideology; they also had a partially independent existence. The partisan necessarily owed some measure of loyalty to the party as an institution. Similarly, as a representative of a constituency, whether it be a ward, a town, a district or an entire state, the politician was obliged to consider the wishes of those who elected him. In some instances these wishes might run counter to the course suggested by his own principles. Thus party and electorate were apt to create forces which might challenge the pressure exerted by ideology. It is necessary to measure the strength of these competing pressures in order to determine the effect of ideology upon behaviour.

Ideology and Behaviour

In their official party pronouncements, the two major parties were, of course, compelled to make frequent reference to the increasingly democratic form of government that was emerging in the Jacksonian era. Party rhetoric suggests that though neither party was monolithic in structure or uniform in opinion Democrats and Whigs yet entertained significantly different views of this most fundamental development. It is necessary, therefore, to determine whether, in the practical application of principle, this most crucial difference was retained.

A comparison of the ideology of the two major parties leads inevitably to the conclusion that the Democratic party was considerably more enthusiastic towards the advancing democratic ethos than were its Whig opponents. For their part, the Whigs were seriously divided between conservative elements, to whom democracy was anathema, and a liberal wing, which could boast a confidence in popular rule which occasionally even rivalled that of the Democrats. Thus if behaviour were consonant with ideology, the Democratic party might be expected to have spearheaded the drive towards, for example, universal (white) male suffrage in the states, while the Whigs might be expected to have furnished whatever serious opposition was mustered. Yet there is no reason to assume that the more liberal Whigs would have lagged far behind the Democrats.

According to the historian of the suffrage, this is approximately what happened. After surveying various movements (within many states) aiming at a liberalisation of the suffrage, he concludes that 'more Whigs than Democrats had reservations about a democratic suffrage'. Although 'generally speaking most Whigs would go along with Democrats on the road to suffrage reform', yet 'the initiative. . . remained. . . with the Democrats'.[1] In Congress the suffrage question rarely arose. In 1842, however, there was, in the House of Representatives, an attempt to amend the charter of the town of Alexandria in the District of Columbia (over which Congress exercised, of course, direct control). The amendment sought to liberalise the suffrage by enfranchising all white males over twenty one who had resided for at least one year in the town. It received the support of 92 per cent of the Democrats in the House but only 26 per cent of the Whigs. The vote suggests a wide divergence between the parties on the suffrage issue.[2]

But opinion on the suffrage is only one measure of a party's commitment to democracy. The ideological division which separated the parties was a more fundamental one. It concerned in effect the extent to which power or sovereignty lay with the people. This, far more than the suffrage, was the question on which opinions were virtually irreconcilable and it is this issue which, better than any other, discloses the gulf between the two parties.

The vexed question of sovereignty might have remained of only theoretical importance but for a curious sequence of events which took place in the tiny state of Rhode Island during the early 1840s. The citizens of Rhode Island had lived since 1663 under a colonial charter whose terms now both disfranchised over half the adult male population and gave to less than one third of the electorate a majority

[1] Chilton Williamson, *American Suffrage from Property to Democracy, 1760-1860* (Princeton, 1960), 261, 263.

[2] *H.J.*, 27 ii 901-2.

of the seats in the lower house. After several years of unsuccessful attempts at reform the proponents of constitutional revision dramatically invoked the original rights of the people to rule and in effect set aside the ancient constitution entirely. They drew up a new constitution and submitted it not to those enfranchised under the provisions of the Charter, but to the entire people. It was triumphantly approved and ratified and the leader of the reform movement, Thomas W. Dorr, became Governor of Rhode Island.[3]

There were now two governments in Rhode Island. The Charter government, condemning the Dorrites as revolutionaries, sought to suppress the new regime by force. A series of confrontations took place and for a time it seemed that wholesale violence might ensue. But Dorr's supporters shrank from a show of strength and the Charter government re-established itself. Dorr himself fled from the state in order to recruit support. He was eventually captured, tried and sentenced to life imprisonment.

As the two sides faced each other in the streets of Providence, so the two rival political parties, Democrats and Whigs, came into sharp conflict over the merits of Dorr's course of action. Although the situation was an explosive one, Democrats with few exceptions rallied to Dorr. From the United States Senate Levi Woodbury, Secretary of the Treasury under Jackson and Van Buren, wrote a confidential letter to the newly proclaimed Governor. Although counselling caution, Woodbury stated his belief that if his cause were unjust then 'the whole fabric of our American liberties rests on sand and stubble'. Dorr received similar declarations of sympathy from two other leading Democratic Senators, Thomas Hart Benton of Missouri and Silas Wright of New York. Representative Edmund Burke of New Hampshire, who was 'with the people of Rhode Island heart and soul', was confident that the entire New England Democracy shared his opinions. William Allen of Ohio, speaking in the Senate, went so far as to pronounce the Charter government, as it had existed from the Revolution to 1842, 'a sheer, a downright, a blasphemous usurpation'. But support came from even higher quarters. Andrew Jackson himself, in a letter to Frank Blair, argued that since 'the people' were 'the sovereign power', they had 'a right to alter and amend their system of Government when a majority wills it, as a majority have a right to rule'. Martin Van Buren, the unofficial leader of the

[3] On the Dorr war see Patrick T. Conley, 'Rhode Island Constitutional Development, 1636-1841: Prologue to the Dorr Rebellion' (Ph.D. thesis, Notre Dame, 1970); Peter J. Coleman, *The Transformation of Rhode Island 1790-1860* (Providence, 1963); Marvin E. Gettleman, *The Dorr Rebellion, A Study in American Radicalism* (N.Y., 1973); Arthur M. Mowry, *The Dorr War* (Providence, 1901).

Democratic party, wrote a public letter to a gathering of Dorr supporters in which he offered them his 'most hearty sympathy. . . in their efforts to secure for the people of Rhode Island the enjoyment of the rights and privileges to which they are entitled'. Frank Blair in the *Globe* meanwhile warned the Charter authorities that if they sought to put down the Dorr government by force, the attempt would be met with force.[4]

With an impressive degree of unanimity, Democrats throughout the nation expressed sympathy with Dorr and his followers. In addition to the *Globe* newspapers like the *Augusta (Maine) Age*, the *New Hampshire Patriot*, the *Boston Post*, the *Detroit Free Press*, and the *Democratic Statesman* (of Nashville) voiced their approval. Amos Kendall, although 'pacific. . . in principle and inclination', assured the readers of his *Expositor* that he would 'unquestionably enrol. . . among the traitors' if he were a citizen of Rhode Island. Similarly at Democratic State Conventions in New Hampshire and Vermont and at Tammany Hall resolutions favouring the Dorr faction were passed. Other prominent Democrats who identified themselves with Dorr included Senator Richard M. Young of Illinois, Governor Marcus Morton of Massachusetts and William Cullen Bryant, Samuel J. Tilden, Ely Moore, and Churchill C. Cambreleng of New York. Except for the supporters of John C. Calhoun, few Democrats came out against the suffrage party.[5]

If the Dorr episode be considered as a test of Democratic sincerity it is clear that the overwhelming majority of Democrats passed the test. Their often expressed faith in popular government and their repeatedly professed belief that sovereignty lay at all times with the people clearly governed their response to the Rhode Island crisis. But the most convincing translation of Democratic theory into practice came when Dorr was being pursued by the Charter government. The authorities called upon the Governors of neighbouring states to assist them by apprehending and returning the fugitive. But Chauncey Cleveland, the Democratic Governor of Connecticut, frankly refused to co-operate. In a letter addressed to the Charter Governor of Rhode

[4] John B. Rae, 'Democrats and the Dorr Rebellion', *N.E.Q.*, IX (Sept. 1936), 476-83; *Cong. Gl.*, 27 ii 506; Jackson quoted in Gettleman, *Dorr Rebellion*, i; Van Buren in *N.Y.T.*, 14 Sept. 1842; *Globe*, 13 May 1842.

[5] Louis C. Hatch, *Maine: A History*, 4 vols. (N.Y., 1919), II, 312-13; *N.H.P.*, 12, 19 May 1842; *Boston Atlas*, 10 May 1842; *Courier and Enquirer*, 24 June 1842; *Democratic Statesman*, 19 April 1845; *Kendall's Expositor*, II (14 April 1842), 113-4; Gettleman, *Dorr Rebellion*, 269-70, 170; *Globe*, 29 April 1842; *Letter of Richard M. Young, Declining his nomination as a candidate for Governor* (n.p., n.d.), 15-17; *Providence Daily Journal*, 21 Jan. 1843.

Island he justified his course of action by suggesting that Dorr himself might be the legal Governor – an idea which naturally enraged the recipient of the letter. In New Hampshire meanwhile, Governor Henry Hubbard, also a Democrat, explained that he too was unable to comply with the request. In so doing he declared his support for 'Governor Dorr':

> If the views of those who oppose the course *Be right,* then, in my judgment, our revolution which was to secure to free men, just and equal rights, – to give to man an independent and sovereign charter, and to implant in his soul the inherent principle of personal and political liberty – *has proved a solemn mockery.*

The Democratic Governors of the neighbouring states were thus in complete sympathy with Dorr and his cause. Some years later, President Polk added his voice to the chorus of approval by pointedly conferring much patronage upon the Dorrite Democrats.[6]

But if Dorr became a Democratic hero, he remained a Whig villain. For party opinion was polarised on the question to a striking degree. In an official statement the Whigs of Maine gave what was the standard Whig reaction to the Dorr controversy. 'A revolution by force of arms', they argued, 'can be justified only by its necessity, as the last resort of the people in their efforts to throw off oppressive and intolerable government'. It could not be justified in Rhode Island since 'no such necessity exists in the free States of this Union'. Daniel Webster, in effect arguing on behalf of the Charter Government (in the case of Luther v. Borden) explained that in the absence of this necessity sovereignty must be exercised 'through the prescribed forms of law'. Otherwise 'anarchy' and 'a tumultuous, tempestuous, violent, stormy liberty' would ensue. The discrepancy between Whig and Democratic opinion on sovereignty was clearly displayed at this trial. For Webster claimed that a constitution, far from being the instrument by which majority rule could be secured, was intended to protect government against 'the sudden impulses of mere majorities'. Similarly, the *Boston Atlas* complained that the Dorrites had advanced 'wild and licentious notions of popular sovereignty' which, 'if carried out, would subvert every existing State Government in the Union', while according to the *National Intelligencer* 'the proceedings in Rhode Island' had been 'from the beginning, only an unlawful action of men, disappointed in ambitious aspirations, seeking to attain, by an overturn of the State Government, political elevation,

---

[6]Cleveland quoted in *Providence Daily Journal,* 2 Sept. 1842; *N.H. Senate Journal* (1842), 16; Gettleman, *Dorr Rebellion,* 166.

which they have not been able to achieve by fair competition with their fellow citizens'.[7]

The most conservative Whigs sought to defend the narrow suffrage which the Charter had created. James F. Simmons, a Whig Senator from Rhode Island, actually defended the property qualification on the floor of the Senate. 'It creates', he claimed, 'a feeling of cherished regard to home and to country, unknown to the mere itinerant adventurer.' But it was the sovereignty issue rather than the suffrage question which united the Whigs in defence of the Charter. Some were terrified at the spectre of rebellion and anarchy which now loomed before them. The solidly conservative *Hartford Courant*, the leading voice of Connecticut Whiggery, called for repression:

> It is high time that the pernicious sentiments promulgated in this country respecting government, personal security, and the rights of persons and property, by foreign and domestic levellers and agrarians – the Fanny Wrights, Robert Dale Owens, O.A. Brownsons, and their fellow laborers against the social systems of our country – should be put down; and nothing will do this as effectually as the strong arm of the law.

Other Whigs emphasised the gravity of Dorr's offence. Cuthbert Powell of Virginia was one of many who believed the uprising treasonous, while in New York City George Templeton Strong urged the authorities to hang Dorr in order to deter other agitators from embarking upon similar courses of action. To those on the conservative wing of the party the entire movement constituted a threat to the very foundation of society.[8]

Although some Whigs were aware that repression might confer martyrdom upon Dorr and his followers, all nevertheless went out of their way to pronounce an unqualified condemnation of his activities and of the theory of government upon which he had acted. According to Henry Clay the entire episode represented a 'wanton defiance of established authority'. No Whig seriously questioned this judgement. It was echoed by the *Whig Review,* and by an impressive number of party newspapers including the *Kennebec Journal,* the *Portland Advertiser,* the *Providence Journal,* the *Independent,* the *Natchez*

[7] Gettleman, *Dorr Rebellion,* 269, 191; *Boston Atlas,* 12 April 1842; *Nat. Int.,* 9 May 1842.

[8] Simmons in *Nat. Int,* 24 May 1842; *Hartford Courant,* 2 July 1842; *Letter of Mr. Cuthbert Powell, to the People of the Fourteenth Congressional District of Virginia* (n.p., n.d.), 11; Allan Nevins and Milton H. Thomas (eds.), *The Diary of George Templeton Strong,* 4 vols. (N.Y., 1952), I, 180.

Daily Courier and the *Detroit Daily Advertiser.* Even more significantly, the Whig Governor of Vermont expressed his detestation of Dorr's action and of all that it implied. In contrast to the Democratic Governors of the neighbouring states, Whig incumbents were eager to aid the Charter government.[9] Governor John Davis of Masachusetts promised to apprehend Dorr if the opportunity arose. In New York the Governor's chair was occupied by William Henry Seward, among the most prominent of New York's liberal Whigs. Seward gave the clearest expression of his views on the affair some two years later. 'An attempt has been made', he informed an audience at Yates county, 'to subvert the republican government of Rhode Island and to erect another in its place.' Seward believed that the attempt constituted 'treason' and he heaped abuse upon the Democrats for encouraging it. Seward, like his colleague Thurlow Weed, recognised the justice of the claim for a wider suffrage but he was no less opposed to the strategy employed, and the philosophy underlying it, than the reactionaries within his party. Hence he too in 1842 was willing to assist the Charter governor.[10]

Thus the Dorr war, as it came to be known, was fought not only in Rhode Island but within the nation as a whole. Democrats with few exceptions were whole-heartedly committed to Dorr; Whigs with even fewer (if any) exceptions opposed and denounced him. This division can be suggested quantitatively. In Congress in 1845 a series of resolutions was introduced from New Hampshire's state legislature concerning the Dorr controversy. They effectively endorsed Dorr's entire case, asserting that he had been legally elected Chief Magistrate and had been wrongfully imprisoned. The House then voted on the question of suspending its rules to allow the resolutions to be presented. In a vote which suggests the extent to which party opinion was polarised on the issue, Democrats by 107 to 7 favoured the suspension while the Whigs by 67 votes to 6 opposed it. Each party thus achieved over 90 per cent unity on the question.[11]

Thus the entire episode demonstrated the existence of a fundamental divergence of opinion on the vexed and troublesome issue of sovereignty and offers a dramatic illustration of the importance in

[9]Gettleman, *Dorr Rebellion,* 165; *Whig Rev.,* II (Nov. 1845), 448; Hatch, *Maine,* II, 312-3; *Portland Advertiser,* 27 May 1842; *Providence Journal,* 20 June 1842; *Independent,* 24 May 1842; *Natchez Daily Courier,* 3 Oct. 1844; *Detroit Daily Advertiser* in *Courier and Enquirer,* 24 June 1842; Governor Paine of Vermont in *Providence Daily Journal,* 28 Oct. 1842.

[10]Gettleman, *Dorr Rebellion,* 239-40; Seward in *A.E.J.,* 29 Oct. 1844; *A.E.J.,* 1 June 1842.

[11]*H.J.,* 28 ii 182-3.

practical, behavioural terms, of the differences between Whig and Democratic political theory. It was a difference that was perhaps masked by the wider (though still far from complete) agreement which existed on the question of suffrage.

Although conflicting attitudes towards suffrage and sovereignty were a significant manifestation of the ideological division between Democrat and Whig, it was of course the economic and financial questions of the era which dominated Jacksonian politics. Paramount among these was the banking question, the issue which, in the post-Panic years, aroused the greatest controversy and the highest intensity of partisan emotion. If behaviour were consistent with ideology on this most important of subjects the Democrats might be expected to have displayed considerable hostility towards the banks; there is no reason to believe, however, that the party would have acted with anything approaching unanimity. Instead a combination of (conservative) Democrats in alliance with an almost wholly united Whig party might be expected to have defended the banks.

At national level, however, the Democrats, true to their official pronouncements, concentrated upon the Independent Treasury. Since it became the test of Democratic orthodoxy, the party quickly united on the issue. The Whigs, after the departure of the Calhounites, were virtually unanimous in their opposition. Tables I and II[12] show the degree of party unity on the question in both House and Senate between 1837 and 1846. It is clear that by the time the Independent Treasury finally passed in June of 1840 the two parties, with only trivial exceptions, stood united in both House and Senate, the Democrats in favour and the Whigs against. This high degree of partisan cohesiveness was maintained when the Whigs in 1841 repealed the act and when the Democrats sought to reintroduce it in the House in 1844 (unsuccessfully) and in both House and Senate in 1846 (successfully).

Whig banking policy involved, in place of the Independent Treasury, a national bank. (Some Whigs, however, gave only a qualified approval to this plank in the party's platform; others opposed it outright.) In 1837 resolutions were passed concerning the expediency of a national bank; the Whigs voted overwhelmingly in favour of a new bank. In 1841 (by which time the party's strength was far greater and sectionally more even), they succeeded in passing two bank bills only to have their hopes thwarted by the vetoes of President Tyler.

---

[12] See below, Appendix, for the Tables referred to in this chapter.

Finally, the House in 1844 again voted upon resolutions concerning a bank. The votes of each party in both House and Senate are given in Tables III and IV. They indicate that both parties achieved great cohesiveness on the bank question. With few exceptions the Democrats were against a national bank, the Whigs in favour. Thus in the post-Panic years the Democratic policy of an Independent Treasury combated the Whig policy of a national bank. As far as Congressional voting was concerned, each party on the banking question sought to legislate in accordance with the principles and policies to which it was committed.

With the abandonment of the pet bank system, however, and its replacement with the Independent Treasury scheme, the chief battle ground in the war with the banks shifted from Washington to the twenty-six state capitals. Yet here too behaviour matched principle. For in virtually every state the Democratic party in the years following the Panic began a systematic campaign against the banks, with goals that ranged from reform to outright annihilation. The Whigs, with equal consistency played the part of defenders of the banks. They were joined in most cases by those soft money Democrats who refused to endorse the antibank policies pursued by their colleagues. Although the Democrats met with varying degrees of success, the pattern of partisan behaviour, closely in line with party pronouncement, was broadly similar in every section of the Union.

Jacksonian Democracy thus came to a culmination in the struggle within the states against the banks. In virtually every state the Democratic party concentrated its reforming energies on the banking question. Where they did not demand the annihilation of the banks partisans called for reductions in bank capital, and checks upon paper money. They sought larger ratios of specie to paper, the elimination of small bills, unlimited (or at any rate fuller) liability for bank directors and stockholders and stricter penalties against those banks which suspended specie payments. In some states they insisted that all bank charters were in principle repealable; elsewhere they worked to exclude the paper money issued by other states' banks. The Whigs for their part rallied to the defence of the banking interest, often opposing attempts to effect a reduction in bank capital and defending those banks which had been forced to suspend specie payments. They demanded the retention of limited liability and looked with favour upon small notes. In every state of the Union they answered Democratic denunciations of the banks by pointing to their role in fostering economic growth and diversification. Thus the controversy dominated politics in all but a few of the twenty-six states. Banking was the major issue in the post-Panic years both at Washington and in the state capitals.

The war that was conducted against the banks within the states has been surveyed by many historians. As a result there is now a considerable amount of quantitative data which demonstrates the extent to which the parties were able to act in accordance with their professed principles. Thus in New York the years of radical Democratic dominance in the legislature (1834, 1835 and 1837) witnessed a halt in the increase of credit facilities in the state, whereas in the years of conservative Democrat and Whig control (1836, 1838 and 1839) expansion took place at an accelerated pace. In neighbouring New Jersey a key legislative vote (in 1838) saw 72 per cent of Democratic legislators placing themselves on record condemning bank suspensions and 82 per cent of Whigs acquiescing in them. Further West in Ohio Democratic radicals experienced a decade of frustration and ultimate failure in their attempts to reform the banks. They pinned their hopes on the constitutional convention of 1850. When the convention assembled the Democrats voted 43 to 9 in favour of a provision to destroy the existing banks. Each measure failed, however, in the face of unanimous opposition from the Whigs. In the same year a constitutional convention assembled in Indiana. Here 43 Democrats (approximately half the party's contingent) voted to prohibit banking in the state. The Whigs were divided, some favouring a general free banking law and others preferring to perpetuate the state bank. The prohibition was defeated. In Iowa, on the other hand, a new constitution was drawn up in 1846 in which banking was officially prohibited. In the crucial vote all the Democrats were pitted against all the Whigs.[13]

Events followed a similar pattern South of the Mason-Dixon line. In Virginia anti-bank Democrats voted against relief for banks, against the circulation of small notes, in favour of coercing the banks into resumption and in favour of increased liability for bank stockholders. A large majority of Whigs (typically 90 per cent) adopted the opposite stance and defended the credit system. In Missouri a survey of voting in the state legislature indicates the degree of partisan voting on the banking question. Between 1836 and 1840 69 per cent of Democrats on average voted against the incorporation of financial institutions.

[13] Ernest P. Muller, 'Preston King: A Political Biography' (Ph.D. thesis, Columbia, 1957), 158; Peter D. Levine, 'Party in the Legislature: New Jersey, 1829-44' (Ph.D. thesis, Rutgers, 1971), 194; James R. Sharp, *The Jacksonians versus the Banks* (N.Y., 1970), 156-7; William G. Shade, *Banks or No Banks: The Money Issue in Western Politics, 1832-1865* (Detroit, 1972), 129; Erling A. Erickson, 'Banks and Politics before the Civil War: the Case of Iowa, 1836-1865' (Ph.D. thesis, University of Iowa, 1967), 141.

But an overwhelming majority of Whigs (89 per cent) were favourable to these measures. From 1836 to 1844 84 per cent of Democrats were generally opposed to attempts to expand the currency while 85 per cent of the Whigs supported them. Finally 43 per cent of Democrats were favourable to a liberalisation of banking operations (to give the banks greater freedom); 80 per cent of the Whigs registered their approval. The parties adopted similar stances in Tennessee. Under the Governorship of James K. Polk a series of efforts was made to reform the state's banking system. Thus a Senate vote saw seven Democrats and two Whigs in favour of an immediate forced resumption of specie payments. The measure was opposed by eight Whigs and six Democrats. In the House a bill designed to force resumption and to impose additional regulations was defeated by a single vote. Twenty-nine Whigs and two Democrats opposed the proposal; thirty-one Democrats and one Whig supported it. Finally, a Senate bill demanding rapid resumption, making charters repealable and prohibiting all notes under one dollar failed in a tie vote with six Democrats deserting their party and joining a united Whig opposition. Governor Polk himself favoured these measures – as befitted a Van Burenite Democrat.[14]

Thus the evidence suggests that the two parties waged the bank war in accordance with their stated principles and beliefs. This was also the conclusion reached by Herbert Ershkowitz and William G. Shade in their investigation of legislative voting in the states. Examining the voting patterns in the legislatures of six geographically dispersed states, Ershkowitz and Shade demonstrated quite clearly that in the aftermath of the Panic a majority of Democrats generally stood in direct opposition to a large majority of Whigs when the subjects of banking and the currency arose. Almost invariably the Whigs were more favourable to the banking interest and to small notes than the Democrats. In virtually every instance too, party antagonism deepened in the post-Panic years.[15]

At this point it is possible to revert to Congressional voting. Although Congress had no control over banks within the states, it was, of course, responsible for those within the District of Columbia.

[14] Sharp, *Jacksonians versus Banks,* 239-46; Paul W. Brewer, 'The Rise of the Second Party System: Missouri, 1815-1845' (Ph.D. thesis, Washington University, St. Louis, 1974), 403-416; Charles G. Sellers, Jr., *James K. Polk, Jacksonian* (Princeton, 1957), 387-94.

[15] Herbert Ershkowitz and William G. Shade, 'Consensus or Conflict? Political Behavior in the State Legislatures during the Jacksonian Era', *J.A.H.,* LVIII (Dec. 1971), 591-611.

Tables V and VI[16] show Democratic and Whig voting on matters connected with the rechartering of the District banks in the House and Senate respectively. Similarly Tables VII and VIII record party voting on motions calling for restrictions on small notes. Finally, Table IX documents party voting on proposals for increased liability for bank directors and stockholders. The voting indicates that, with a striking degree of unity, Democrats attacked and Whigs defended the banking interest in the District.

Thus at national level and in state politics the two major parties successfully translated their partisan declarations into legislative voting. Party rhetoric implied an alignment of hard money Democrats against a coalition of Whigs and softs. There is little reason to suppose that this rhetoric was belied by behaviour or that either party was unable to vote according to the principles with which it was identified.

Sections

In his role as a representative, the politician was, of course, expected to consult, if not necessarily to obey, the wishes of his constituents. Since these wishes were not always satisfied merely by the triumph of the party to which he belonged additional pressures were brought to bear upon the political system. The most important of these were sectional; in representing a particular section of the nation (or indeed of a state), the partisan was often compelled to modify or adapt, ignore or even jettison, the principles which his party affiliation implied. The result was that sectional forces were never an insignificant factor in Jacksonian politics.

The United States in the Jacksonian era was already a nation of striking geographical diversity. Most noticeably there were, of course, the Southern states set apart, to some extent at least, by the institution of slavery with all that it implied for the economy, social system and cultural life of the section. But scarely less startling was the contrast between some of the Eastern states, where urban growth, diversification and industrial development were preparing to take major strides, and the states of the newer West, where conditions of an unspoilt frontier wilderness still obtained. Politicans and their constituents were, of course, well aware of these differences between the various sections; historians have been no less aware of them.

As far as the differences between East and West are concerned, the historiographical controversy centres upon the role of the frontier in Jacksonian politics. Frederick Jackson Turner, who drew attention

---

[16] See below, Appendix.

to the importance of the frontier in the overall development of American democracy, insisted on the primary role of the West in creating the Jacksonian Democratic upsurge of the second quarter of the nineteenth century. Arthur M. Schlesinger Jr., on the other hand, in his seminal *Age of Jackson* took issue with the Turnerian interpretation and replaced it with the view that the East, and specifically the cities of the North East seaboard, were the breeding ground of Jacksonian Democracy. Since Schlesinger placed great emphasis upon anti-bank sentiment as a measure of commitment to Jacksonian ideals the controversy can be reviewed by comparing the experience of both East and West with their respective institutions and contrasting the political developments which ensued.[17]

The economy of the West was, of course, less mature and less stable than that of the East. Thus while the North Eastern and South Eastern states were able to benefit from a banking system that was already by the time of the Panic well integrated into the economy of the regions, the banks which had sprung up in the West frequently proved unable to withstand the shocks of the recession. Because they were of more recent origin, and because their numbers had multiplied so quickly during the flush times of the early thirties, the banks of the West proved highly vulnerable when the economic climate changed. Many failed outright; others became the targets of Democratic agrarian radicalism.[18]

Prior to the Panic of 1837 both parties had been responsible for a serious overextension of credit facilities in the West. Consequently the reaction which followed was the more severe. In many of the Western states serious attempts were made to prohibit banking entirely; in Louisiana and Arkansas the prohibition was effected. Indeed by the early 1840s the Democratic party in most of the Western states was a hard money party. Whereas in the East the official policy was one of reform, in the West destruction became the stated goal. Moreover the war with the banks endured longer and attained a greater ferocity in the West than in the East. Thus there can be little doubt that, insofar as hostility to banking provides a measure of the strength of Democratic principles, the ideas of Jacksonian Democracy were most successfully practised in the West.

Yet it remains true that in the West the banks were of more recent origin and, therefore, of less importance to the economy. Hence their

---

[17]Frederick J. Turner, *The United States, 1830-1850* (N.Y., 1935); Arthur M. Schlesinger, Jr., *The Age of Jackson* (Boston, 1946), 209.

[18]Sharp, *Jacksonians versus Banks, passim;* Shade, *Banks or No Banks, passim.*

destruction was here a more feasible goal than in the East. The Democrats who led the anti-bank crusade in the Western states were determined to prevent the emergence of a new and alien economic order. As they themselves recognised, that order was already becoming a reality in some Eastern states. The abolition of banks and the elimination of paper money was thus a far more drastic proposal in, for example, New York City than on the farms of southern Illinois. Arthur M. Schlesinger Jr. identified Jacksonian Democracy as 'a problem of classes' and there is no doubt that the radical, class-conscious and embittered Democrat, unable to accept the class structure as it *now* existed, was generally Eastern and urban. The Eastern city was the focus of Democratic fears; the Western farm was the focus of Democratic hopes. While actual class conflict was most intense in the East, the anti-bank movement, which it undoubtedly encouraged, triumphed in the West.[19]

This East-West tension also made itself felt within the Whig party. The most conservative of Whigs, like the most radical of Democrats, tended to be found in the Eastern cities; their often vehemently anti-democratic utterances were echoed only faintly in the West. The currents of liberal Whiggery, although much in evidence in the Eastern states, usually emanated from the western areas of those states. They were generally directed against the conservatism of the mercantile and industrial interests on the seaboard and in the larger towns and cities. Thus in the West Whig opposition to democracy was muted just as Democratic opposition to banking was amplified. In both East and West the two parties acted in accordance with the principles which they propounded. Frederick Jackson Turner argued long ago that the effect of the frontier was to facilitate the advance of democracy and to retard the development of class conflict. Because East and West were at different stages of economic and social development, there was a significant sectional tension within each of the major parties.

But however important the differences between East and West they were, of course, to be rendered almost insignificant by the growing hostility between North and South. With the re-emergence of the slavery controversy in the 1840s and 1850s politics became increasingly sectional in orientation. The two major parties of the Jacksonian era proved unable to withstand these sectional pressures and each finally disintegrated. Some historians have concluded from this that the second party system itself was 'artificial' in that it sought to exclude from politics those sectional conflicts which formed the

[19]Schlesinger, *Age of Jackson,* 263.

238

fundamental political divisions within the nation. Alternatively, it has been suggested that the sectional antagonism between North and South resulted in the capture by militant Southerners of the Democratic party. It is claimed that because the South controlled the Democratic party, and because the Democratic party (usually) controlled the Federal government, the South was 'in the saddle' throughout the Jacksonian era. It is thus necessary to measure the importance of this sectional antagonism in order to determine its effect upon the behaviour of Whig and Democrat.[20]

Although the Missouri Compromise had promised a permanent settlement of the slavery controversy, the question was continuously agitated throughout the Jacksonian era. In response to what it considered an oppressively high protective tariff and to the growth of anti-slavery sentiment in the North, the state of South Carolina had in 1832 formally nullified the Federal tariff law.[21] Other Southern states did not follow South Carolina's lead but Andrew Jackson's hostile reaction to the state's 'treason' drove many Southern states rights enthusiasts out of the Democratic party and into the ranks of the nascent Whig opposition. Their unofficial leader was South Carolina's foremost statesman, 'the great nullifier', John C. Calhoun. The influence upon the party struggle of the sectional controversy between North and South cannot be understood without an examination of the ideas of Calhoun and the pro-slavery faction.

By the time of the nullification crisis Calhoun had constructed a distinctive ideology.[22] It rested, of course, on the assertion that slavery, rather than a necessary evil to be endured, was instead a postive good to be cherished. Calhoun claimed that blacks, when freed, fell into a condition of degradation; as slaves they received protection and were generally well cared for by their masters. Still more important were the advantages which slavery secured for the white race. Abel P. Upshur, another pro-slavery ideologue, claimed that the feeling of racial superiority fostered self-respect and an appreciation of the benefits of liberty that could not otherwise be

[20]Richard P. McCormick, *The Second American Party System* (Chapel Hill, 1966), 353; Richard H. Brown, 'The Missouri Crisis, Slavery and the Politics of Jacksonianism', *S.A.Q.*, LXV (Winter 1966), 55-72.

[21]On the nullification crisis see especially William W. Freehling, *Prelude to Civil War: The Nullification Controversy in South Carolina* (N.Y., 1966).

[22]There is no entirely adequate study of Calhoun's thought. Richard N. Current's *John C. Calhoun* (N.Y., 1963) is generally perceptive but ignores or under-estimates Calhoun's hostility to the alleged aggressions of Northern capital and to capitalism itself. Current takes issue with Schlesinger's view (p. 161) but Schlesinger has the better of the argument. See Schlesinger, *Age of Jackson*, 244-7.

promoted. For Upshur slavery was 'a great positive good, to be carefully protected and preserved'; for Calhoun it was 'the most safe and stable basis for free institutions in the world'.[23]

One of the most important arguments deployed in defence of slavery – and it was one which was immensely significant in determining the political allies of the pro-slavery forces – concerned its effect upon social inequalities. Upshur argued that where slavery prevailed there was 'a remarkable independence, freedom and equality among all classes of the whites'. Because the most menial jobs were performed by the blacks, one of the grossest forms of inequality was removed – as far as the white race was concerned. Upshur explained that slavery was ideally suited to republican institutions because it paradoxically produced the highest attainable degree of equality in society:

> There is no form of regular government which can preserve an equality of wealth among individuals, even for a day; and it would be absurd to say that domestic slavery can produce any such result. But it approaches that result much more nearly than any other civil institution, and it prevents, in a very great degree, if not entirely, that gross inequality among the different *classes* of society from which alone liberty has anything to fear.

The result was that Southerners were 'equal in our rank' and 'equal in our fortune'. Thus 'the spirit of levelling sees nothing to envy'; 'the spirit of agrarianism sees nothing to attack'.[24]

But the pro-slavery forces were not content merely to defend slavery. In addition, and to reinforce their defence, they denounced the alternative free labour system practised in the North. According to Calhoun, Northern society was divided into different and opposing classes. One was a class of exploiters, the other a class of the exploited. Indeed the history of the world furnished no example of 'a wealthy and civilized society in which one portion of the community did not, in point of fact, live off the labor of the other'. It was inevitable since 'there is and always has been in an advanced stage of wealth and civilization, a conflict between labor and capital'. In the South, however, 'the condition of society. . . exempts us from the disorders and dangers resulting from this conflict'. But in the North the time would soon come when 'the war upon capital must commence'. 'Liberty', Upshur concluded ominously, 'cannot survive this contest'.[25]

---

[23]Richard K. Cralle (ed.), *The Works of John C. Calhoun,* 6 vols. (Columbia, S.C., 1851-5), V, 337-8; Abel P. Upshur, 'Domestic Slavery', *S. L. M.,* V (Oct. 1839), 677-87 – esp. 678, 687; *Cong. Gl.,* 25 ii App., 62.

[24]Upshur, 'Domestic Slavery', 679, 685.

[25]Cralle, *Works of Calhoun,* II, 631-2; Upshur, 'Domestic Slavery', 685.

Calhoun's solution was the famous concurrent majority system. Under a government which gave power to a mere numerical majority, he argued, taxpayers were exploited by those who stood to benefit from an increase in government revenues (whether the numerical majority itself or those who administered the government). The consequent redistribution of wealth would inevitably widen the gap between rich and poor as well as encouraging the rise of demagogues and spoilsmen (who sought to wield the immense powers of government). If instead, however, all legislation had to be approved by a majority of those within each significant interest group, exploitation would cease. Oppressive majorities could not be formed, the interest of every group would impel it to compromise, wise and patriotic men would be chosen as representatives and, because the wealthy and intelligent would now have an identity of interest with the poor and ignorant, social harmony would be the inevitable result. Each interest group would be represented within the nation by one or more states; within each state a suitably devised constitution (like that of South Carolina) would similarly protect the various groups. Thus the theory of the concurrent majority, upon which Calhoun built his defence of nullification, offered an opportunity for Northern society to escape its otherwise unavoidable doom.[26]

The price to be paid was, of course, permanent acquiescence in the slave system as it existed within the Southern states. Calhoun invited Northerners to protect the South not merely for its own sake but in order to preserve Northern Democratic institutions. The South, he explained, was the harmonising, conservative influence:

> In this tendency of conflict in the North between labor and capital, which is constantly on the increase, the South has been and will ever be found on the Conservative side; against the aggression of one or the other side, which ever may tend to disturb the equilibrium of our political system.

By preserving Southern society, with its slave labour base, Northerners, according to Calhoun, could guarantee the stability of their own section and, therefore, of the entire nation.[27]

Because Calhoun's outlook was overtly sectional, both he and his followers had difficulty in attaching themselves to either of the major parties. There were to be sure good reasons for them to consider joining the Whig party. In their belief that slavery permitted the maximum degree of equality that any society could sustain they

[26]Cralle, *Works of Calhoun*, I, 13-22, 25, 45-6, 48-51 and *passim*.
[27]*Cong. Gl.*, 25 ii App., 62.

repeatedly emphasised the dangers of an excess of egalitarian zeal. According to Calhoun inequality of condition was 'A necessary consequence of liberty'. Indeed it was 'this inequality of condition between the front and rear ranks in the march of progress' which gave 'to progress its greatest impulse'. Representative Francis Pickens, one of Calhoun's most committed followers, believed that 'the history of mankind proclaims that there is "an elect and chosen few" '. Pickens then asked the House to imagine a society in which a hundred men began with an equal amount of wealth at their disposal. Within five years, he claimed, forty would own property while sixty would have none. Thus there was a danger that oppressive governments or demagogic politicians might seek to appropriate large fortunes in the name of a levelling egalitarianism. According to Upshur 'the great danger which liberty has to fear in the United States' was 'to be found in that agrarian spirit which strikes at all that is above it, and spares nothing that is good or great in the institutions of society'. These were the sentiments of a conservative Whig.[28]

The pro-slavery theorists shared other opinions with the conservative Whigs. According to Calhoun liberty was 'a reward to be earned, not a blessing to be gratuitously imposed on all alike'. Here was a view which contrasted sharply with the Democratic insistence upon liberty as a function of self-interest. Upshur likewise believed that liberty was understood and appreciated by very few. Similarly, in their opposition to majoritarian democracy and their disdain for party machinery, party discipline, the spoils system and indeed virtually the entire theoretical justification for party, the pro-slavery ideologues were following closely in the Federalist tradition. The conservative wing of the Whig party might thus have been their natural resting place.[28]

Yet there were also good reasons for the pro-slavery forces to enlist with the Democratic party. To defenders of states rights the Whigs with their greater attachment to centralised Federal power were clearly less attractive than the Democrats. Thus Calhoun was strongly opposed to internal improvements when directed by the Federal government and to the proposed distribution of the government's surplus revenues – both policies with which the Whig party was closely identified. Similarly the pro-slavery men were apologists for the agrarian society of the South. Upshur employed a standard Democratic argument when he claimed that agriculture fostered virtue, patriotism, frugality and a 'quiet uniformity' while simultaneously

[28] Cralle, *Works of Calhoun,* 56-7; *Cong. Gl,* 24 i App., 290; Upshur, 'Domestic Slavery', 684.

[29] Cralle, *Works of Calhoun,* I, 55; Upshur, 'Domestic Slavery', 678.

discouraging ostentation, corruption and the love of luxury. Like the Democrats Upshur viewed the large cities of the North East with apprehension; his outlook, like theirs, was agrarian and essentially pre-capitalist.[30]

Yet there was perhaps an even more compelling reason for the Calhounites to rejoin the Democratic party. Their fear of the levelling forces within American society was balanced by a corresponding hostility towards those policies which, they feared, would create unacceptably severe inequalities. When at the time of the nullification crisis Calhoun criticised the tariff for 'its tendency. . . to make the poor poorer, and the rich richer', he was not merely referring to the inequality between the two sections. At present, he acknowledged, the tariff 'operates sectionally'. But when the South was exhausted, he warned, it would 'oppress the wage-earner'. Similarly, in a speech before the Senate, Calhoun argued that the nation's banking system also had detrimental effects not merely upon liberty but upon the distribution of wealth in society:

> I have great fears that it will be found hostile to liberty and the advance of civilization – fatally hostile to liberty in our country, where the system exists in its worst and most dangerous form. Of all institutions affecting the great question of the distribution of wealth – a question least explored and the most important of any in the whole range of political economy – the banking institution has, if not the greatest, one of the greatest, and, I fear, most pernicious influences.

Other Calhounites voiced this orthodox Democratic objection to the banks. Robert Barnwell Rhett, one of Calhoun's South Carolina followers, claimed that 'of all the devices for giving capital the ascendancy over labor, the banking system as generally existing is the most subtle and complete'. Thus like the Democrats, and in complete contrast to the Whigs, Calhoun and his associates denounced banks and tariffs as the instruments of an artifical and fraudulent inequality.[31]

As a result, and because the sectional, pro-slavery philosophy cut across the ideologies of Whig and Democrat, Calhoun and his followers were unable to become orthodox members of either party. After the nullification crisis, leading South Carolinians and other pro-slavery militants defected from the Jackson party in order to resist the extension of executive power. In so doing, however, they (like the orthodox Whigs) also opposed the advancing democratic ethos,

[30] Upshur, 'Domestic Slavery', 678-80.
[31] Cralle, *Works of Calhoun*, VI, 25-6, II 333-4; *Cong. Gl.*, 25 ii App., 506.

scorning Van Buren, now heir apparent to the White House, as the archetypal party spoilsman. Upshur was to remain within the Whig party, serving as John Tyler's Secretary of State, until his unfortunate death (the result of a steamboat accident) in 1843. Calhoun himself in the early 1830s had hoped to recruit the support of Northern capitalists for the defence of slavery. He proposed an agreement by which they would refrain from interfering with slavery and the slaveholders would prevent a social revolution in the North. Unrealistically perhaps, Calhoun expected events to compel the Northern capitalists to accept his analysis of Northern society, his prognosis and even the comparison between Northern labourers and Southern slaves. In 1836, speaking in the Senate, he delivered a grave warning to them:

> The sober and considerate portion of citizens of the non-slaveholding States, who have a deep stake in the existing institutions of the country, would have little forecast not to see that the assaults which are now directed against the institutions of the Southern States may very easily be directed against those which uphold their own property and security. A very slight modification of the arguments used against the institutions which sustain the property and security of the South would make them equally effectual against the institutions of the North, including banking in which so vast an amount of its property and capital is invested.

Unfortunately for Calhoun the warning went largely unheeded.[32]

Calhoun had advocated as early as 1834 a divorce of bank and state. Hence when the Van Buren administration introduced the Independent Treasury Calhoun rejoined the Democratic party. He and his little band gave enthusiastic support to the hard money policy and even firmer support to the doctrines of free trade to which the party increasingly inclined. Perhaps because of the orthodoxy of his views on all the great financial questions of the era, Calhoun began once again to covet the Presidency. Convinced of his own sincerity and of the consistency of his opinions (at least since the nullification crisis), he soon hoped to secure the Democratic nomination in 1844. Again his judgement was lacking. He now expected to convince men of standing within the Democratic party that they must adopt a man

---

[32] Cralle, *Works of Calhoun*, V, 207. If Calhoun had had a better grasp of the process by which ideology is created, or if he had been less confident of the power of his own logic, he would have realised that Northerners were deeply committed to the idea of a free, upwardly mobile society. A rebellion of factory operatives in the North would not have convinced the factory owners that the factory system was exploitative any more than a slave rebellion would have altered Calhoun's view of slavery.

who not merely defended slavery as a positive good but who regarded majoritarian democracy as a sham. Since most prominent Democrats had spent virtually their entire careers expressing their faith in the majoritarian principle, they not unnaturally refused to nominate him. Confident that his critique of majoritarian democracy was irrefutable, Calhoun had presumably expected to re-educate the entire party. But the Rhode Island controversy exposed the gulf between the two views. Upshur called the uprising 'the very madness of democracy, and a fine example of the workings of the majority principle', while Calhoun went so far as to write a public letter condemning the theory of sovereignty upon which the Dorrites had based their case and of which virtually the entire party had expressed approval. Although it won solid support in some areas of the South, the Calhoun candidacy never came near to success. When he realised that his hopes would not be fulfilled Calhoun withdrew from the contest, joined the Tyler administration as Upshur's successor and, still seeking a guarantee for the South and her peculiar institution, devoted all his energies to the acquisition of Texas.[33]

With the political opinions of a conservative Whig, the commitment to policy of a radical Democrat and a view of equality which condemned him to share the fears of both, Calhoun was essentially without a party to support him. Whilst he differed with the Whigs over virtually all significant issues of policy, his disagreement with the Democrats was an equally fundamental one. At the core was his view of majority power. While the Democrats followed John Taylor of Caroline in the belief that it was generally impossible for the majority to live off the proceeds of the labour of the minority, Calhoun argued that it was not merely possible but virtually inevitable. On this premise he constructed a set of beliefs that could not well be accommodated within the second party system.

How widely was this pro-slavery, anti-democratic ideology accepted? When he rejoined the Democratic party Calhoun took with him only a dozen Congressmen, all of whom represented Southern states. In 1844, however, the Calhoun candidacy attracted a number of dissidents within the party although many of them shared his views only in part (if at all). In the North some extreme urban radicals, including former Locofocos like Fitzwilliam Byrdsall, supported Calhoun in preference to Van Buren. Presumably they were attracted to the South Carolinian's analysis of class conflict within the North, to

[33] Upshur quoted in Sylvan H. Kesilman, 'John Tyler and the Presidency; Old School Republicanism. Partisan Realignment, and support for his Administration' (Ph.D. thesis, Ohio State University, 1973), 161.

his anti-bank and free trade sentiments and to his general orthodoxy on financial questions. In complete contradiction, however, some conservative Democrats in the New England states, including men like David Henshaw of Massachusetts, rallied to Calhoun, partly because he was clearly identified with opposition to the dominant Van Buren wing and partly because he was, on his own admission, a conservative as well as being a Democrat. But Calhoun was in truth neither a conservative nor a radical Democrat. Thus Theophilus Fisk, as ardent a radical as any in the party and one who proclaimed that the famous dictum 'to the victor belong the spoils' had his approval 'at all times and under all circumstances' was an enthusiastic Calhounite, even though Calhoun thought the proposition monstrous. Similarly, the conservative Democrats in the North who followed Calhoun could not have met the pro-slavery tests of orthodoxy if the Southerners had sought to impose one. The Northern Calhounites, although forming only a small minority within the party, were themselves hopelessly divided.[34]

In the South, however, Calhoun's strength was considerably more solid. It is difficult to determine whether all who backed his candidacy entirely shared his beliefs. But there was within the Southern Democratic party and even, as a legacy of the nullification crisis, within the ranks of the Whigs, a core of Southerners who, in accordance with the pro-slavery viewpoint, saw politics primarily in sectional, states-rights terms. Yet their importance should not be exaggerated. For in the South as in the North, the political debate was dominated by the banking controversy. The Calhounite Democrats were a complicating factor but essentially the controversy produced similar political alignments, similar points of debate and similar voting patterns both North and South of the Mason-Dixon line.

As far as the banking question was concerned, the differences between North and South were slight in comparison with those between East and West. Conditions in the South East and South West resembled those in the North East and North West respectively. In the South Atlantic states, as in New England and the Middle Atlantic states, banks were generally under sound and conservative management. Because they were well integrated into the regional economy they were less deeply affected by either the boom of the early 1830s or the subsequent recession. As a result Democratic

---

[34] See 'The Correspondence of Calhoun', *Annual Report of the American Historical Association for the Year 1899* (Washington, D.C., 1900), *passim;* Schlesinger, *Age of Jackson,* 406-10, 434; Richard R. Westcott, 'A History of Maine Politics 1840-1856; The Formation of the Republican Party' (Ph.D. thesis, University of Maine, 1966), 31-2; *Dem. Exp.,* 2 Aug, 1845.

attacks were similarly restrained. In the South West, by contrast, the Panic struck with devastating effect. Of all sections the South West had participated most freely in the credit expansion of the early thirties; it consequently experienced the greatest distress in the early forties. Thus the South Western Democrats were in the vanguard of the struggle against the banks.[35]

There were thus significant sectional differences within the two parties when the subjects of banking and the currency arose. Yet the important differences were between East and West rather than North and South. Even these, however, did not serve to diminish the hostility between the two parties. Because Whig and Democrat differed so strikingly in their perceptions of government, of society and ultimately of man himself, the banking controversy attained a degree of intensity which has rarely, if ever, been surpassed in the history of American party politics. As far as the banking question was concerned the differences between Whig and Democrat easily overrode those between North and South. They were prominent on the written page, at the hustings – and in the legislative chamber.

For this reason it can only be a distortion to read back the sectionalism of the Civil War era into the 1830s and early 1840s. In many of the Southern states only an insignificant or negligible minority of politicians displayed a greater concern for sectional than party conflict. Most Southerners, like most Northerners, were oriented towards the party of which they were members; unlike Calhoun and his followers they perceived no threat from the Free States. This can be shown most clearly in a state by state analysis.[36]

The border states of the South were least imbued with pro-slavery particularism. The Whig party in Delaware, Maryland, Missouri and Kentucky was little more than a rechristened National Republican party. It lacked a states rights wing. Similarly there were few, if any, prominent Calhounites within the Democratic party in these states. Instead politicians like Henry Clay for the Whigs and Thomas Hart Benton for the Democrats sought a middle position on the slavery

[35] Sharp, *Jacksonians versus Banks* is invaluable on the sectional differences within the Democracy concerning the banking controversy.

[36] The analysis of Southern sectionalism given here closely follows that of Charles G. Sellers, Jr. in his article 'Who Were the Southern Whigs?', *A. H. R.,* LIX (Jan. 1954), 335-46. It is also based upon a wide variety of primary and secondary sources – see bibliography. In particular newspapers proved a valuable source. Only the most important citations will be listed. For an alternative view see William J. Cooper, *The South and the Politics of Slavery, 1828-1850* (Baton Rouge, 1978). Cooper does, however, concede the supremacy of financial issues in the post-Panic era.

question. Benton for example deprecated pro-slavery agitation as much as he disliked political anti-slavery while Clay throughout his career attached far more importance to party than to section. In the border states slavery was, of course, less firmly entrenched than in the deep South; this was reflected in the politics of the region.

There were, however, other states in which the exponents of nullification and states rights doctrines were in a position of relative impotence. Perhaps because of the importance of New Orleans as a major commercial centre Louisiana's Whig party (almost alone among the states of the deep South) had always been little more than the old National Republican party with which Henry Clay was so clearly identified. Nor did the Louisiana Democracy contain any significant number of Calhounites. Similarly, in North Carolina the second party system had firm roots and was not threatened by Southern pro-slavery militancy. Even in the 1830s the North Carolina Whigs were faithful to the leadership of Henry Clay and committed to the Bank of the United States. Neither of the parties in North Carolina was much affected by the nullification crisis of the early thirties nor by the Tyler crisis of the early forties. Indeed in the nullification era each party had sought to stigmatise the other by identifying its supporters with the discredited South Carolina 'traitors'. Thus the Whig party, far from expressing the particulist conservatism of the states rights enthusiasts, was imbued with an aggressive and forward-looking commercialism comparable to that displayed in the most prosperous Northern states. North Carolinians were seriously divided along party lines; they did not feel the need to coalesce in defence of their section.[37]

A similar situation began to take shape in Tennessee in the late 1830s. Until this time Tennessee Whigs had embraced a states rights commercialism which approved of state banks but looked askance at a national bank. Yet by the time the Van Buren presidency was under way, many Whigs, especially in the commercial centres of Nashville and Memphis, were moving closer towards Henry Clay and the path of orthodoxy. At the same time the Democrats received an important, if small, accession of strength when the followers of Calhoun left the Whig party. Thus in Tennessee, party rather than section determined the course of political controversy.[38]

Of the remaining South Western states Arkansas, by population one of the smallest states in the Union and therefore of little strategic

[37] See Message of Governor Edward B. Dudley in *N.C.S. & H.J.* (1839), 276-85.
[38] See Sellers, *Polk, Jacksonian, passim.*

importance, was not a Calhounite stronghold. But in Alabama and Mississippi Southern sectionalism presented a challenge to the second party system. In Mississippi Jefferson Davies, future President of the Confederacy, was one of a small but dedicated band of Calhounites. Following their leader back into the Democracy these states rights enthusiasts helped to give the party an almost permanent ascendancy over the Whigs. The Democrats were equally powerful in Alabama. Here the Calhounites, led by Dixon H. Lewis, drew their strength from the southern half of the state where slave density was greatest. Elsewhere the Democrats were powerful in those northern areas characterised subsistence farming and lack of access to transportation facilities. In the case of Alabama (and there is little reason to doubt that the conclusions are applicable to Mississippi) there have been two significant attempts to evaluate the relative strength of the Van Buren and Calhounite elements. In 1844, prior to the state's nominating convention, the *Democratic Gazette* sought to assess the popularity of the two foremost candidates – Van Buren and Calhoun. The Van Buren delegates, it argued, represented two thirds of the total Democratic strength within the state. They were out-and-out Van Buren men. Since the Calhoun areas in the south contained some pockets of Van Buren support the newpaper concluded that the majority for Van Buren was probably in excess of two thirds. The *Gazette* was undoubtedly a partisan source. Yet one historian who has specifically considered this question with reference to Alabama has basically endorsed the judgment. 'Until late in the final decade of the ante-bellum period', he concludes, 'the men who had followed Dixon Lewis out of the Whig party in the summer of 1838. . . made few converts to their extreme strict constructionist outlook within the Democracy, and thus remained a small minority whose numbers were, however, relatively stable.' The conclusion that 'the followers of Calhoun were a vexatious but small minority', can be applied to all except one or two of the Southern states.[39]

The states where Calhoun was strongest were probably Georgia, Virginia and, of course, South Carolina. In Virginia the eastern lowlands and tidewater were the strongholds of pro-slavery particularism. Calhoun's support was impressive on the tidewater; men like R.M.T. Hunter, a Speaker of the House and an ardent Calhounite, represented eastern Virginia. Similarly states rights Whigs of the John Tyler stamp hailed from the coastal regions of the state. Yet the states rights devotees were a minority within each party.

[39] *Democratic Gazette*, 10 Jan., 1844; Jonathan M. Thornton, III, *Politics and Power in a Slave Society: Alabama 1806-1860* (Baton Rouge, 1978).

The National Republican wing dominated the Whig party and the Van Burenite Democrats, marshalled by Thomas Ritchie, Van Buren's ally of an entire generation, and by George Dromgoole, were too strong for the Calhoun men. Thus despite the influence of the states rights elements, the subjects and the course of political debate in Virginia closely resembled those in other states.

The politics of Georgia were even more complex than those of Virginia. Of all the Southern states Georgia was the one in which the South Carolina nullifiers found most support. In response to the nullfication crisis Georgia's politicians divided into two camps; the Unionists, who backed Jackson against the nullifiers, and the States Rights party whose members, whilst not overtly suppporting the principle of nullification, were nevertheless highly alarmed at Jackson's handling of the affair and particularly at his apparent departure from the path of states rights orthodoxy. Yet the Unionists were themselves unionists of the Andrew Jackson stamp rather than of the Daniel Webster persuasion. Hence both parties could claim to be the champions of states rights. As the banking controversy deepened, however, both at Washington and in Georgia, the Unionist and States Rights parties were gradually transformed into the Democratic and Whig parties respectively. It was a slow and painful process in the course of which many prominent statesmen changed sides (particularly in response to the Independent Treasury). The transformation was only completed in 1842 when the Whig-States Rights party, by nominating Henry Clay for President, finally fell into line. By this time Calhoun's support within the Georgia Democracy had been strengthened by the defection (over the banking controversy) of states rights advocates like Walter Colquitt, a future United States Senator. In 1843 Calhoun won the official nomination of the Georgia state Democratic party for President only to have it withdrawn after the party sustained a heavy defeat in the subsequent elections. Georgia's Whigs were at this time busily dissociating themselves from extreme Southern states rights principles. Thus the re-emergence of the banking issue in the late 1830s had begun a process of reorientation in politics. The divisions that were a legacy of the nullification crisis had given way to a realignment that was based upon the financial issues of the era and upon the ideological conflict that underlay them. Sectional feeling independent of the banking controversy and of party ideology never disappeared in Georgia but as in Virginia it assumed an importance that was probably secondary.

A different situation obtained in South Carolina, surely the most atypical state in the Union. The second party system here had shallow roots, largely as a result of the nullification crisis, which had pitted nullifiers against unionists rather than Democrats against Whigs (or National Republicans). Calhoun dominated South Carolina as no other statesman dominated any state. Hence when he returned to the Democratic column in 1837 he was able to bring almost the entire strength of South Carolina with him. The small South Carolina Whig party was also imbued with the states rights philosophy to the extent that it pledged only conditional support for Harrison in 1840. Because Calhoun dominated South Carolina politics and because he always sought to retain the support of the entire state (in order the better to resist the encroachments of the Federal government) political strife between Democrat and Whig never attained a consistently high level of intensity.

But despite its undoubted success in South Carolina, Southern sectionalism was unable in the post-Panic years to break the bonds of the party system. Because the differences between Whig and Democrat were deemed to be of such significance, party rather than section was the rallying point for all but a small minority of Southerners. The Calhounites themselves recognised this truth. Thus James A. Seddon, a future Confederate leader and Cabinet minister, in February of 1844 wrote to Calhoun to try to persuade him not to divide the party by contesting the Presidential election as an Independent. Whoever the nominee might be, and whatever section he might represent, Seddon implied, party loyalty was felt to be of paramount importance:

> a great majority of your friends in this state thought much was to be gained in a contest between Mr. Clay and any Democratic candidate by the election of the latter, and much reluctance was felt to pressing any third candidate, even yourself, to the extent of destroying the ascendancy of the Democratic party and ensuring the triumph of the Whigs.

The party system was thus able to withstand the efforts of the Calhounites (and of the Northern anti-slavery militants) to divide the nation along sectional lines.[40]

Although the supremacy of party was apparent when statesmen responded to the twin issues of banking and the currency, there were, of course, other financial subjects upon which the parties differed. Prominent among these was the land question. Democrats in general favoured a liberal land policy, offering generous pre-emption rights to settlers and desiring to reduce and graduate the price of those lands which were not readily disposable at the standard rates. The Whigs, seeking instead to preserve the enormous acreage for future generations

[40]*Correspondence of Calhoun,* 924. See also pp. 902-3.

and to set some limit on the pace at which it was settled, espoused a more conservative policy. They officially opposed pre-emption and graduation and desired to distribute the revenues obtained from the sale of lands to all the states of the Union in order to encourage state spending on internal improvements and education. The Democrats, in turn, opposed the distribution policy.

Democratic policy, aimed at a rapid and easy settlement of the lands, had an obvious Western orientation. Whig policy, geared towards a slower settlement and recognising the needs of the original thirteen states (many of which were losing population as a result of Western migration), had an equally clear appeal to the East. Because of this some Democrats in the East and some Whigs in the West effectively dissociated themselves from their official party policy. Thus Iowa Whigs proclaimed their support for pre-emption; Virginia Democrats disliked graduation.[41] Consequently, voting on the land question was often a compromise between sectional and party pressures. Eastern Democrats and Western whigs often defected and voted with their opponents.

As far as distribution was concerned, however, the parties maintained an impressive degree of unity. Table X records party voting on the distribution policy between 1841, when the Whigs passed the measure, and 1844, when the Democrats repealed it. The voting indicates that the Democrats were unanimously opposed to distribution; all but a small minority of Whigs supported it.[42]

On the actual disposal of the lands, however, sectional tensions impaired the unity of both parties. As Tables XI and XII suggest, the Democrats in both House and Senate were far more favourable to a liberal land policy than the Whigs. Yet Eastern Democrats and Western Whigs were frequently unable to maintain ranks. Among these defectors there was a slight tendency for Northerners to favour pre-emption and graduation more than Southerners. The average support (in the Senate) from each section is recorded in Table XIII. The evidence therefore suggests that as far as land policy was concerned, party membership was probably the major determinant of voting behaviour. A majority of both Whig and Democratic legislators were able to vote according to the stated principles of their party. Each party nevertheless modified its stance in the section in which its official policy had least appeal. Thus the determinants of voting

[41] Louis Pelzer, 'The History and Principles of the Whigs of the Territory of Iowa', *I.J.H.P.*, V (Jan. 1907), 46-90. For the views of Virginia's Democrats see the roll calls used in Table XI (Appendix).

[42] See below, Appendix.

behaviour on the land question, it would appear, were, in ascending order of importance, loyalty to North or South, identification with East or West, commitment to Whig or Democratic doctrine.

More important than the land question (at least after 1842 when the Compromise Tariff expired) was the controversy over protection. Democrats officially opposed a high tariff, viewing it as an instance of an active government invading the equal rights of the people in order to confer financial benefit upon a privileged minority. The Whigs, on the other hand, concerned to promote national self-sufficiency, and desiring to create a diversified economy, sought to build up American manufactures behind a tariff wall. Their victory in 1840 allowed them to enact the Tariff of 1842 to whose repeal the Democrats immediately pledged themselves. After an unsuccessful attempt during the years of the twenty-eighth Congress the Democrats in 1846 passed the Walker Tariff which effected a clear reduction in tariff rates.

The official Democratic policy was to permit a tariff for revenue only. Within the confines of the revenue principle, however, they were prepared to discriminate for incidental protection. The Whigs continued officially to favour protection unequivocally. Table XIV records Congressional voting on the tariff question between 1842 and 1846.

Sectional pressures were of considerable importance on the tariff issue. Within the Democratic party Pennsylvania was known to favour high discriminatory rates, whether incidental or not (largely to protect Pennsylvania iron). In New York and New Jersey protectionist sentiment was also rife within the Democracy and in Massachusetts and Vermont the party, although able to elect few Congressmen, also supported high duties. In the House nine Democrats from New York, ten from Pennsylvania and one from Massachusetts supported the Tariff of 1842; in the Senate both of Pennsylvania's Democrats and one Democrat from each of the states of Maine and New York backed the measure. Without these defections the bill could not have passed.

In the aftermath of the Tariff of 1842 Democrats from these states sometimes officially opposed any reduction in tariff rates. In New York Hunkers like Samuel Beardsley defended the 1842 act stoutly and the Democratic Legislative Address of 1844 came out against any material alteration in its terms. In Pennsylvania the *American Volunteer,* a Democratic newspaper, in 1843 proudly reminded its readers that all Pennsylvania's Representatives and Senators had voted for the 1842 act, which, it claimed, was now 'the settled policy of the state'. The tariff bill of 1844 saw eight Democrats from

Pennsylvania, ten from New York, four from New Jersey and a total of six from the states of Connecticut, Massachusetts, Kentucky and Vermont voting with the Whigs. Two years later twelve Democrats from Pennsylvania together with four from New York, two from New Jersey and one from Maryland voted against the Walker Tariff. The Democrats from much of the North East, it seemed, could not be relied upon to support tariff reduction.[43]

Conversely the Whigs in these states were enthusiastic advocates of protection. They here lost no opportunity to pin the free trade label on the Democrats. In the North West the party was less enthusiastic but still willing to endorse the protective principle. But the Southern Whigs had some difficulty in holding their ranks. In Kentucky, Clay's home state, and in Louisiana, where the sugar interest required protection, the party was not embarassed by its national stance. Similarly, in Delaware the tariff was generally a popular measure. Yet elsewhere the Whigs were unable to give consistent support to their Northern colleagues. In the 'Log Cabin' campaign of 1840 Addresses by the Georgia and Virginia Whigs claimed that Harrison favoured the Compromise tariff while Van Buren was the protection candidate. Similarly George Badger of North Carolina in that year denied that Harrison favoured protection. Consequently, the Tariff of 1842 was opposed in the House by thirty-one Southern Whigs, of whom only three were Tylerites. (Only six Northern Whigs opposed the measure.) In the Senate all the nine dissenting Whigs represented Southern states. Many Southern Whigs were as yet out of line with the rest of the party.[44]

Gradually, however, they moved towards the path of orthodoxy. John M. Berrien of Georgia in 1844 spoke for many when he explained that 'the march' of the 'manufacturing spirit' was 'still onward and southward'. For Georgia, he claimed, was 'awakening to the conviction that a portion of her productive labor may be better employed'. She was 'becoming more and more convinced of the advantage of a division of labor'. In Virginia the influential *Richmond Whig* was also proclaiming the need for diversification in the South while in North Carolina Senator William Graham, who, in common with almost every other Congressman from his state, had voted against the Tariff of 1842, was now publicly endorsing it. The *Raleigh*

---

[43] Muller, 'Preston King', 269; *American Volunteer,* 28 Sept. 1843.

[44] *Address of J. C. Alford, William C. Dawson et al. to their Constituents, May 27, 1840* (n.p., n.d.), 17; *Address of the Whig Convention for the Nomination of Electors, To the People of Virginia* (n.p., n.d.), 11-2; George E. Badger, *Speech delivered at the Great Whig Meeting in the County of Granville, 3 March 1840* (Raleigh, 1840), 9.

254

Register, an important Whig newspaper, in 1846 was to complain that the Walker Tariff would make duties too low. In Tennessee, meanwhile, the Whigs had in the Gubernatorial compaign of 1843 (and as a result of Democratic pressure) nailed the protective flag to their mast. They had, moreover, carried the election– against no less a figure than James K. Polk.[45]

Thus by the time of the election of 1844 an increasing number of Southern Whigs overtly favoured protection. In some Southern states (Missouri, Arkansas, Alabama and Mississippi) it was widely claimed that Clay favoured incidental protection only or that he generally followed a middle course on the issue. These, however, were states in which the Whigs were relatively weak. In South Carolina, also a strong Democratic state, the party probably did not move towards protection. But elsewhere pro-tariff sentiment had increased. The Georgia Whig-States Rights party had originally favoured even lower duties than the Democrats and the *La Grange Herald,* a Whig newspaper, had in 1843 proclaimed that 'the Whig party of Georgia are as much opposed to a [high protective] tariff as it is possible for any individual to be'. They desired 'a Tariff that will supply revenue enough for the Government and no more'. But the following year the party was defending the Tariff of 1842 as a revenue measure while in 1846 Georgia's Whigs in Congress actually opposed the Walker Tariff. In Georgia, as elsewhere in the South, pro-tariff sentiment within the Whig party was on the increase.[46]

It is then undeniable that, as far as the tariff was concerned, the parties were considerably affected by sectional tensions. Yet this did not alter the fact that the Democrats were identified with free trade, the Whigs with protection. Thus it was recognised virtually throughout the nation in 1844 that a victory for Polk would be the signal for tariff reduction and that if Clay were elected, protection rather than revenue would determine the rates of duties on imports. The sectional pressures were contained within the party system. By 1846 the men who had engineered the Compromise Tariff of 1833 might have congratulated

---

[45] John M. Berrien, *Speech on the Tariff* (Washington, 1844), 16; Robert H. Tomlinson, 'The Origins and Editorial Policies of the *Richmond Whig and Public Advertiser,* 1824-1865' (Ph.D. thesis, Michigan State University, 1971), 105-16; J.G. de Roulhac Hamilton, *Party Politics in North Carolina 1835-1860* (Durham, N.C., 1916), 85; Robert N. Elliott, *The Raleigh Register, 1799-1863* (Chapel Hill, 1955), 83; Sellers, *Polk, Jacksonian,* 489.

[46] *The Mill Boy,* n.d.; Gene Wells Boyet, 'The Whigs of Arkansas, 1836-1856' (Ph.D. thesis, Louisiana State University, 1972), 209; *Harry of the West,* 24 April, 1844; David N. Young, 'The Mississipi Whigs, 1834-1860'(Ph.D. thesis, University of Alabama, 1968), 114-5; *La Grange Herald,* 28 Sept. 1843.

themselves upon the final results. After a ten year interlude the tariff had once more emerged as a major subject. But the party system had done much to reduce its disruptive effects and the Act of 1846 proved to be the last major tariff controversy before the Civil War era.

Another of the issues on which party and section jostled for supremacy was that of internal improvements. Officially the Democrats were opposed to Federal improvements except where the projects were truly national in scope. All others, they argued, were attempts to tax the people for the benefit of a privileged minority. Henry Clay's American System, on the other hand, had originally called for the creation of a large network of transportation projects, planned and built by the Federal government and serving to bind the nation together. Roads, canals and railroads, it was held, would, by diminishing transportation costs, provide a spur to economic growth from which the entire nation would benefit. Yet partly as a concession to Southern states rights sentiment Clay had gone some way to surrendering the internal improvements policy. Distribution, he hoped, would permit the states to finance their own projects. Because of this, and because there were not, in the post-Panic years, sufficient funds to embark upon new schemes, internal improvements was not, at least until the mid-forties, an issue of the first magnitude.

Sectional pressures, were, nevertheless, of some importance in determining a politician's response to internal improvements. The Whigs in the North East favoured the projects (although few were now planned that would directly benefit the section). In the West they favoured them still more whole-heartedly; the Cumberland Road project was one of several designed to improve the section's transportation facilities. But in the South some dissent was expressed. In the campaign of 1840 Virginia's Whigs, although denying that internal improvements was an issue, nevertheless tried to link Van Buren with them and, therefore, to cast odium upon him. Harrison, it was asserted, could be no worse. Georgia's Whigs were similarly unenthusiastic, endorsing only those projects which were truly national and voicing a clear preference for distribution. In Alabama the party at first opposed all federal intervention in this sphere and then approved only those projects which the states alone could not undertake.[47]

These sectional pressures affected the Democrats. In the South East and New England the party remained firmly committed to its

[47]*Address of Whig Convention. . . to the people of Virginia,* 11-12; *Address of Alford, Dawson et al,* 17; Carlton L. Jackson, 'A History of the Whig Party in Alabama, 1828-1860' (Ph.D. thesis, University of Georgia, 1962), 16-17.

official policy. But Westerners, arguing that hitherto the East had derived great financial advantage from federal expenditure on rivers, canals and harbours, demanded, and with increasing stridency after 1844, a share for their section. This demand was voiced most strongly in the states of the North West but Democrats from, for example, Arkansas and Tennessee made the same appeal. This pressure culminated in the passage through Congress in 1846 of a Rivers and Harbours Bill, specifically designed to benefit the West. President Polk, however, vetoed the bill, basing his action on orthodox Democratic theory.[48]

Historians who have investigated Congressional voting on the subject of internal improvements have found that sectional loyalties cut across commitment to party. According to Thomas B. Alexander the Cumberland Road project during the twenty-fifth Congress was supported by North Westerners, whether Whig or Democrat. North Easterners, he found, were divided 'somewhat along party lines' while in the South 'the little support given came from Whigs'. Thus while 'a party tendency affected attitudes on the Cumberland Road extensions', it was nevertheless 'generally subordinated to local sectional interest'. Similarly, in the twenty-sixth Congress, voting on the Cumberland Road and on measures connected with rivers and harbours improvements suggests, Alexander argues, that 'consistent [party] attitudes were present but somewhat distorted by local-interest pressures'. Internal improvements projects, he concludes, continued to be 'issues on which a degree of sectional influence warped party lines'.[49]

In another survey of Congressional voting Joel Silbey has endorsed this judgement. Silbey found that during the twenty-seventh Congress 'both parties split apart' when the questions of the Cumberland Road and river and coastal defence projects were debated. When Congressmen voted 'party loyalty' was 'replaced by a heightened localism.' This pattern continued so that throughout the forties 'sectional and local considerations played important roles'.[50]

This did not, however, obliterate loyalty to party and party ideology. Employing scalogram analysis, Silbey demonstrated that

[48] Donald E. Fehrenbacher, *Chicago Giant, A Biography of 'Long John' Wentworth* (Madison, Wisconsin, 1957), 26, 45; Melinda Meek. 'The Life of Archibald Yell', *Ark. H.Q.,* XXVI (1967), 11-23, 162-84, 226-43, 353-78, 167, 363.

[49] Thomas B. Alexander, *Sectional Stress and Party Strength* (Nashville, 1967), 26, 31.

[50] Joel H. Silbey, *The Shrine of Party* (Pittsburgh, 1967), 56, 63.

Whigs from every section of the Union were far more likely to favour internal improvements than Democrats. Although sectional differences were of great importance, party loyalty markedly influenced the voting of Representatives and Senators alike.[51]

Within the states similar voting patterns have been discerned. Again the parties splintered as a result of local pressures. But as the recession began to be felt and the financial condition of the states to deteriorate the Democrats became somewhat less sympathetic to internal improvements. In the West, where many states had overreached themselves, a reaction set in. Thus in Indiana the Democrats in 1840 demanded that the projects cease; they agreed that they had been bipartisan in origin but now hinted that a constitutional prohibition might be necessary. In Illinois the Democrats by 1839 were also swinging against internal improvements and they now lagged behind the Whigs in bestowing legislative support on them. In the South Whig reservations about federal improvements did not apply to those sponsored by the states. Whigs in Virginia, North Carolina and Georgia, for example, were often enthusiastic in their advocacy of an entire network of projects. [52]

Nevertheless local pressures continued to be of great importance in many states. In their survey of legislative voting Ershkowitz and Shade found an increasing divergence between the parties after 1837. Yet these differences virtually disappeared when the parties voted to give corporate charters for the projects.[53]

In some states, however, ideological commitment may well have been a more cohesive force within the two parties. In New York both the Whigs and the Hunkers favoured internal improvements strongly, and after his victory in the Gubernatorial race of 1838 William Seward launched an extensive programme of canal and road building. The Barnburners, however, were outraged at this prodigality. They enacted the famous Stop and Tax Law of 1842, which required the approval of the electorate for any increase in the state debt. The same year a serious intra-party struggle broke out within the Democracy with Hunker Governor William Bouck in favour of continuing the canal programme and the Barnburners seeking instead to terminate it. The canal issue in New York, like the banking question throughout the

[51] Silbey, *Shrine of Party*, Chapters IV, V, Appendix II.

[52] *South Western (Ind.) Sentinel*, 6 March 1840; Theodore C. Pease, *The Frontier State 1818-1848* (Springfield, 1918), 239; *The Essays of Camillus* (Norfolk, 1841), 61-2; Message of Governor Dudley in *N.C.S. & H.J.* (1839); *Address of Alford, Dawson et al.*, 17, 28.

[53] Ershkowitz and Shade, 'Consensus or Conflict?', *passim*

nation, pitted Whigs and conservative Democrats against radical Democrats. On the two issues the principles of each group were the same.[54]

Similarly in New Hampshire internal improvements proved an issue of great proportion and one on which party rather than local considerations predominated. In New Hampshire railroads were the burning issue. Conservative Democrat Isaac Hill, in alliance with the Whigs, sought to create a network of railroad lines within the state. He desired to incorporate the companies, to allow them the right of eminent domain and to give the companies limited liability. The radicals fought each proposal. The *New Hampshire Patriot* in 1842 argued that it would be better to 'drive capital from New Hampshire' by refusing to charter the companies than 'to endure the greater evils resulting from the unnecessary sacrifice of individual rights'. As a result the radicals checked the progress of the railroads, refused them the rights of eminent domain and forced them to pay all claims for land damages. The radical programme had, according to one historian, 'sent capital into Maine and Massachusetts'.[55]

In New Hampshire the railroad controversy was of greater importance than the banking struggle (although the alignments created and the principles involved were identical). Yet in most states, and at Washington, internal improvements was a relatively minor issue in the post-Panic years. Party was generally a significant determinant of voting behaviour and the geographical differences on the question were local rather than sectional (apart perhaps from the fairly widespread Southern objection to federal improvements). Politicians were responding to the demands of their constituents both in the state legislatures and at Washington. It is thus misleading and inaccurate to claim that internal improvements simply divided North from South. Voting on the issue was complex but because internal improvements was not, for the most part, a decisive area of policy, temporary defections were tolerated. Because Whig and Democrat were so clearly differentiated on the major issues of the day, the often inconsistent voting on internal improvements projects did not pose a serious threat to the two party system.

On the various issues of economic policy which separated Whig and

[54]On the New York canal issue see especially Patricia M. McGee, 'Issues and Factions: New York State Politics from the Panic of 1837 to the Election of 1848' (Ph.D. thesis, St. John's University, 1969), 75-99 and *passim.*

[55]*N.H.P.,* 9 June 1842; Donald B. Cole, *Jacksonian Democracy in New Hampshire* (Cambridge, Mass., 1970), 214.

Democrat – banking and the currency, distribution, graduation and pre-emption, the tariff and internal improvements – the parties continued throughout the post-Panic years to act largely in accordance with their stated principles. Those who defected on one issue typically returned to their party on others. When the voting on all these subjects is taken together, the parties are found to have been highly cohesive. In the words of Thomas B. Alexander, Congressional voting provides 'evidence of a continuing and consistent view among the representatives concerning federal government roles in economic matters'. For on the financial and economic issues of the day the two parties 'were clearly in opposition'.[56]

Thus there can be little doubt that, although there were significant sectional differences within the parties upon most of the issues of the era, party had a considerably larger influence than section upon legislative voting. On some issues the important geographical differences were local, on others they were between East and West, or North and South. Yet on no issue of financial policy did sectional loyalties induce any large number of statesmen, whether Northerners or Southerners, Easterners or Westerners, Whigs or Democrats, seriously to consider leaving their party permanently. After analysing leglislative voting in the years from 1841 to 1845, Joel Silbey concluded that 'the men in Congress responded generally to the political institutions most meaningful to them, the national parties'. Sectional considerations, he suggests, were 'among those influences which they considered to be less important'. For in the mid-forties each party still had considerable support in every section of the Union. Only the prospect of extending the nation's frontiers Westward to Texas and to Oregon (with all that this entailed) constituted any real threat to the two major parties. And at the end of 1846 even this threat appeared to be receding.[57]

Because loyalty to party was felt to be indispensable to the implementation of desired policies, and because the policies to which men were committed sprang quite logically from their basic perceptions about government and society, statesmen were divided along party rather than sectional lines. Commitment to party and thus to party ideology was probably the major determinant of their voting behaviour, both at Washington and in the state legislatures. The fundamental developments of the era, the advance of democracy and the growth of a commercial, capitalist economy were national in scope. For this

---

[56] Alexander, *Sectional Stress,* 31.

[57] Silbey, *Shrine of Party,* 65-6. The Wilmot Proviso, introduced in 1846, made little impact initially.

reason alone the significance of sections could not rival the importance of party.

Party: The Institution

By associating with men of a similar persuasion, politicians of the Jacksonian era were, of course, better able to combat those with whom they were in disagreement. By forming political parties they could campaign the more easily for those among their colleagues who best embodied the principles for which they were striving or for those who could best present those principles to a mass electorate. As a means of transforming principles into legislation, rhetoric into reality, party was already, by the time of the Panic, virtually indispensable.

Yet the two major parties of the Jacksonian era were also in some sense 'electoral machines'. Whether operating in a locality, a state or in the nation as a whole both parties almost invariably attempted to enlist the support of a majority of the electorate. Neither the Democratic nor the Whig party desired merely to influence popular opinion or to pressurise established institutions in the hope of effecting some meaningful, if limited, reform. Instead both were parties whose avowed goal was to govern; in pursuing this goal and in seeking majority support they necessarily functioned as electoral machines.

There is little doubt that, in its role as an electoral machine, a party was much influenced by the constitutional and legal environment in which it operated. Thus those historians, chief among whom is Richard P. McCormick, who have emphasised the institutional and mechanical aspects of the second party system have rightly drawn attention to what they believe to be its distinctive features. They have noted, for example, the significance of certain changes in electoral procedures including the emergence of single member constituencies and the popular election of presidential electors. They have underlined the importance of the new breed of party manager, of the large array of activists which each party could call upon, and of the convention plan of party organisation. In describing the second party system they have observed that it was the first (and as yet the last) to produce balanced parties in every section and in virtually every state of the Union. Finally, in focusing upon the campaign style which emerged during the era of the second party system, they have concluded, quite justifiably, that it 'can properly be regarded as a significant form of American cultural expression'.[58]

[58] McCormick, *Second American Party System*, 15 and *passim*.

The problem with this essentially institutional interpretation arises, however, when its adherents seek to estimate the relative importance of ideology, on the one hand, and machinery and environment on the other. According to McCormick, 'between 1824 and 1840 the "presidential question", rather than doctrinal disputes was the axis around which politics revolved'. Moreover, the second party system, he argues, was, by the 1840s, 'artificial' in that the parties 'seemingly existed in defiance of the real sectional antagonisms that were present at the time'. Thus, in discussing the Whig and Democratic parties both during their formation and at their heyday, McCormick emphasises their institutional characteristics at the expense of the principles and ideals which they purported to represent. For this reason it is a questionable emphasis.[59]

According to McCormick the parties were formed above all for the purpose of contesting the presidency. McCormick claims that it was the regional identification of the candidates which did most to determine the sequence of party formation. Thus as Van Buren replaced Jackson at the head of the Democratic party and as a presidential candidate so, McCormick claims, an opposition and eventually a vigorous two party system began to emerge in the previously undivided Southern and Western states. In 1836 Whig strength grew in many of these states, foreshadowing the great triumph of 1840. It was an important stage in the formation of the two party system.[60]

Yet McCormick overlooks many of the forces which helped create the Whig party in the West and South. For Van Buren's succession to the White House had ideological implications which could not be ignored. Identified with the anti-bank policy that Jackson had initiated, Van Buren aroused the hostility of conservative business elements in, for example, Tennessee. Similarly, and because of his reputation as the archetypal party politician, Van Buren's candidacy shocked many conservatives who were distrustful of political parties. The Baltimore Convention of 1835 which nominated Van Buren had the effect of awakening many conservatives to the fact that 'the type of party they had railed against so arduously was not solely based on Jackson's popularity and had a life of its own'. They now realised that it was in all probability 'a permanent political fixture'. According to the *National Intelligencer* this convention marked 'AN ERA in the politics of the country'. It is not unreasonable to suppose that this

[59] *Ibid.* 353.
[60] *Ibid.* 15 and *passim.*

realisation contributed to the emergence of the two party system in those states where it was not already in existence.[61]

Thus Van Buren's succession helped define the nature of Jacksonian Democracy. Within months of the Panic it was clear that the anti-bank crusade, with all that it implied, was about to enter its most critical phase. The political party had been institutionalised, the forces of agrarian democracy seemed to be growing in strength. Because Van Buren lacked the popularity which Jackson had enjoyed, and perhaps because his regional identification made him an easier target, opposition to the Democracy intensified and began to form deeper roots in many areas of the nation. The worsening economic climate, the increasing clarity with which Democratic policies were announced and Democratic ideology restated, the apparent perpetuation of party government – all this in addition to personal and regional considerations furthered the formation of the second party system in the middle and late 1830s. To pluck out from these the factors which best relate to the institutional and non-ideological nature of a political party, and to assign them priority over all others is an arbitrary and unsatisfactory exercise.

But whatever the process by which the party system was formed there had emerged by the time of the Panic two rival organisations, affirming their commitment to two different philosophies and intent on pursuing two conflicting courses of legislative action. Thus even if the parties had been formed initially to contest the presidency they were now something more than electoral machines. Perhaps, when confronted with the evidence of voting in the national and state legislatures, the advocate of an institutional interpretation might reply that such voting patterns were a mere reflex of party as an institution, that they owed their existence to party machinery and that they had no independent vitality. He might thus attempt to subsume ideology under institutions.

This, however, would be a grave error. So far from depending for their existence upon the institutions of party, the ideological convictions of Whig and Democrat actually outlived them. It is now recognised that although the slavery question dominated national politics throughout most of the 1850s, yet at state level the banking and currency question was often 'of primary importance'. According to one historian, the Panic of 1857 'reveals the tenacity with which people held on to the images and ideas forged in the crisis of the late

---

[61] Sellers, *Polk, Jacksonian,* 251; Edward L. Mayo, 'The National Intelligencer and Jacksonian Democracy' (Ph.D. thesis, Claremont, 1969), 123-4.

thirties'. The Republican party, composed of both Whigs and Democrats, had to tread warily on financial questions like the tariff in order not to offend either group. Thus the Jacksonian issues survived into the 1850s. Their importance was undoubtedly diminished, but partisanship between former Whigs and Democrats endured even when party machinery had lost its grip.[62]

Even more significantly, the process by which the second party system was set aside owed much to the persistence of the ideological patterns which it had orginally supported. Thus the Free Soil party of 1848, forerunner of the Republican party, attracted a large number of Van Buren Democrats. Conservative Democrats remained aloof; urban radicals tended to mistrust any anti-slavery movement, affirming that it was Northern labourers rather than Southern blacks who formed the most severely oppressed class. But the Van Buren Democrats were, in general, bitterly opposed to the extension of slavery into the territories. At the National Democratic Convention of 1848 two delegations from New York arrived, each claiming to represent the state. The division was, of course, into (conservative) Hunkers and (radical) Barnburners and although the Convention devised a compromise whereby each delegation could deliver half the votes of the state, the split proved to be too deep. Reviewing the history of the last ten years, the Barnburners explained that the compromise was unacceptable:

> If the Convention recognise as the representatives of the Demo-cracy of New York men among whom may be found those who opposed the Independent Treasury; who were hostile to the debt paying policy of our state in 1842; who lobbied against the tariff of 1846; who fought with desperation against calling a Con-vention to revise our State Constitution; who denounced the result of the labors of that Convention; who treacherously defeated Silas Wright, the regular candidate for Governor in 1846; who attempted, at the Syracuse Convention in September last, to subvert the organisation and annul the usages of the party; who, living in a State which owes its greatness to the dignity and influence with which its liberal institutions have clothed the arm of free labor, unblushingly advocate the extension of slavery into territory now free, and upon that ground claim to be entitled to seats in this Convention as representatives of the New York Democracy – we have no hesitation in saying that if we should consent to divide with them our seats and our

---

[62] Shade, *Banks or No Banks*, 11, 16; Eric Foner, *Free Soil, Free Labor, Free Men* (N.Y., 1970), *passim.* See also Bruce Collins, 'The Ideology of the Ante-Bellum Northern Democrats', *J.A.S.*, XI (April 1977), 103-121.

votes, we should betray the principles and forfeit the confidence
of the pure and fearless party whose commission we bear. We
therefore respectfully decline to take our seats upon the terms
proposed by the Convention.[63]

It was no coincidence that the radical Democrats should oppose the
extension of slavery or that the conservatives should more readily
acquiesce in it. For the ideals and principles which had spurred the
radicals to take action against the banks now impelled them to resist
slavery. An official Address of the Democratic Members of the
Legislature of the State of New York delivered in 1848 and written by
Samuel J. Tilden, Martin Van Buren and others expounded the social
philosophy of the Barnburners. It began in orthodox Jacksonian
manner. 'From the first institution of government to the present time',
it proclaimed, 'there has been a struggle going on between capital and
labor for a fair distribution of the profits resulting from their joint
capacities.' At first capital had enjoyed the advantage. But in recent
times the 'tendency is stronger toward that just equality which all wise
and good men desire to see established'. The primary objection to
slavery (as to banking) was that it threatened this process. For in a
slave society 'the wealthier capitalists who own slaves disdain manual
labor', with the result that the rest of the white population were seen as
'having fallen below their natural condition in society'. Hence if slavery
were allowed into the new territories, the emigration of free whites
would be slowed, slave states would be established and the prospects
for free labour permanently dimmed. Thus the radicals were, as ever,
cautious in their view of the future. Concerned to preserve a society of
autonomous equals, they had in the thirties and early forties found the
major threat in the attempts of capitalists, both North and South, to
spread banking and manufacturing throughout the nation. In the late
forties and fifties their suspicions fell instead upon those Southern
capitalists, the slaveholders, who sought to spread slavery throughout
the West and therefore, it seemed, to ensure its dominance in the
nation as a whole. Frank Blair Jr. in 1858 gave an archetypal
Jacksonian interpretation of the sectional struggle:

> There is no question of North and South. It is a question between
> those who contend for caste and privilege, and those who neither
> have nor desire to have privileges beyond their fellows. It is the
> old question that has always, in all free countries, subsisted – the
> question of the wealthy and crafty few endeavouring to steal from

[63] John Bigelow (ed.), *The Writings and Speeches of Samuel J. Tilden,* 2 vols. (N.Y.,
1885), I, 244-5.

the masses of the people all the political power of the Government.[64]

Thus, throughout the North the radicals furnished a disproportionate number of those Democrats who joined the Whigs to form the Republican party. It was not an easy coalition. In 1848 the pious Benjamin Butler, a lifelong Van Burenite, in a letter to Van Buren expressed his fear that the Free Soil Democrats might be absorbed into the Whig ranks. He even suggested the establishment of a Northern Free Soil Democratic party which would 'teach the South a lesson' and 'thus render a great and lasting service to the country and the world'. The plan did not, of course, come to fruition but within the Free Soil and Republican parties the former Democrats remained highly suspicious of their Whig colleagues. As late as the Civil War these differences still occasionally surfaced. Despite the feelings of solidarity engendered by over a decade of sectional strife and by three years of warfare against a common enemy, Gideon Welles, a former radical Democrat, privately expressed his contempt for the former Whigs:

> The Whig element is venal and corrupt, to a great extent. I speak of the leaders of that party. They seem to have very little political principle, they have no belief in public virtue or popular intelligence; they have no self-reliance, no confidence in the strength of a righteous cause, and little regard for constitutional restraints and limitations.

Significant differences between the two groups persisted. Thus the Democrats within the Republican party were more likely to display the racism with which their party had been identified. It set them apart from many of their Whig colleagues.[65]

The Whigs for their part often remained divided into liberal and conservative camps. In the North, the conservatives were often slow to join the Republican party. Like their colleagues in the South many flirted with Know-Nothingism or joined the Democratic party in order the better to oppose the anti-slavery movement. The liberal Whigs in the North, by contrast, were quick to join the Free-Soil crusade. More concerned with the plight of the blacks than the former Democrats, more sympathetic to the immigrant than the conservative Whigs, the liberals more than any other group shaped the Republican party as it

---

[64] *Writings and Speeches of Tilden,* II, 569-71; Blair quoted in Schlesinger, *Age of Jackson,* 506.

[65] Butler quoted in McGee, 'Issues and Factions', 183; Howard K. Beale (ed.), *The Diary of Gideon Welles,* 3 vols. (N.Y., 1960), II, 122; Foner, *Free Soil, Free Labor, Free Men,* 267.

emerged in the decade before the Civil War. It was fitting that William Seward should be the party's single most popular leader. In 1858 Abraham Lincoln described the situation in his own state of Illinois. 'Much of the plain old Democracy is with us', he claimed, 'while nearly all the old exclusive silk stocking Whiggery is against us.' The generalisation was probably applicable to the entire North. The ideological divisions which had existed both between and within the Whig and Democratic parties in the Jacksonian era had their origins deep in the American past. They were still a significant factor in politics when their institutional support, the second party system itself, had virtually collapsed.[66]

It is not therefore possible to subsume ideology under institutions – any more than it is possible to reverse the formulation. To determine their relative importance is an extraordinarily difficult if not impossible task. An attempt has been made, however, by Peter D. Levine, one of Richard P. McCormick's students. Analysing almost every roll call in the New Jersey legislature betwen 1829 and 1844 Levine found evidence of orthodox partisan responses on the banking and tariff questions, with each party displaying an impressive degree of unity (particularly in the years after 1837). Yet because even greater unity was apparent when the legislators were voting on party questions like election laws and disputes, gerrymandering schemes, the allocation of printing contracts and resolutions on national issues, Levine endorses the McCormick thesis unreservedly. The evidence, he claims, 'casts doubt on interpretations that depict strong ideological or class differentiation between Democrats and Whigs'. Instead, he concludes, the parties 'operated as institutions with their own vested interests, acting not merely as mediums through which the public's demands could be transmitted but as real influences on behalf of their own special interests'. Institutions rather than ideological commitment were the driving force in politics.[67]

Yet the question cannot be resolved quantitatively. It is not enough to make a comparison of percentage points scored. Whigs and Democrats often disagreed among themselves on the crucial issues of the day; bi-factional disputes were of fundamental importance. It should come as no surprise to find that both sets of partisans united to advance the interests of the party. This action in itself merely demonstrates their continued loyalty to party without in any way

[66]Lincoln quoted in Schlesinger, *Age of Jackson,* 481; Foner, *Free Soil, Free Labour, Free Men, passim.*

[67]Peter D. Levine, *The Behavior of State Legislative Parties in the Jacksonian Era: New Jersey, 1829-1844* (Rutherford, N.J., 1977).

accounting for it. Parties were the vehicles for ideology; they were the organisations in which the ideologies of competing factions struggled for dominance. To promote the success of the party conciliation and concession were often required. The parties did possess an institutional existence of their own, just as they functioned too as electoral machines. This does not alter or even qualify the fact that they were also the vehicles in which the stated principles of Whig and Democrat were conveyed back and forth from the legislature and the executive office to the electorate.

Thus it seems clear that when dealing with the major issues of the era both Whigs and Democrats were normally able to translate ideas and statements of intent into legislative or executive action. Sectional loyalties on the banking question, for example, affected policy without significantly narrowing the gap between the two parties; on other subjects (land, the tariff and internal improvements) sectional considerations compelled each party to encroach to some extent upon the policy area of the other. Yet defections from the party remained the exception rather than the rule and the parties were probably affected by factional disputes more than by sectional tensions – at least when acting upon the great financial and economic questions of the era. To preserve the strength of the party as an institution and to preserve the harmony between the different sections of the Union a degree of conciliation and concession was required. Despite this, official party ideology provides a reliable guide to behaviour in the politics of the post-Panic era.[68]

[68] It has been argued that the self-interest of the politician was the principal driving force behind Jacksonian politcs – see Edward Pessen, *Jacksonian America: Society, Personality and Politics* rev. edn. (Homewood, Ill., 1978), For a critique see John Ashworth, ' "Agrarians" and "Aristocrats": Party Political Ideology in the United States, 1837-1846' (D.Phil. dissertation, University of Oxford, 1978), 361-8.

CONCLUSION

Although a century and a half has elapsed since Andrew Jackson's election to the White House, the era which bears his name remains deceptively familiar and "modern". Historians have abstracted from the age those developments which, they feel, portended most for twentieth century America. Not all scholars have applauded these developments; some indeed have been highly critical of them. Yet a determinism, a conviction that the significant changes were somehow inevitable, has pervaded much of Jacksonian historiography.

The result is that superficial similarities between the Jacksonian era and the modern age have been emphasised even though they have frequently masked fundamental differences. How many historians have, for example, assumed that the Democratic commitment to laissez-faire and classical economics is unchallengeable proof that the party was "capitalist" in orientation? This assumption alone compels the scholar to overlook much of the ideological content of Jacksonian politics.

Even more importantly, however, the deterministic approach has impelled many historians to ignore or to explain away the obvious differences between present and past. The historical process is visualised as a single stream which carries a set of deferential, aristocratic eighteenth century colonies into a capitalistic, democratic nation-state. This stream is the ultimate, inescapable force in American history. It nourishes the rising entrepreneur and the enthusiastic democrat; it engulfs the nostalgic yeoman and the unrepentant reactionary. There can thus be no serious conflict in the Jacksonian era since the capitalist and the democrat must win, the yeoman and the patrician must lose. The fact that political groups proclaim themselves to be in a state of real and even desperate conflict may be attributed to psychological instability, tactical ineptitude or mere opportunism. Thus Jacksonian democratic ideas require little study; they are in line with the predetermined pattern of progress. Agrarian ideals must perish and are therefore unimportant. Fears over democracy or capitalism are unreal since the triumph of both is assured.

This determinism results, of course, in a distorted view of the Jacksonian era. Individuals emerge as unprincipled, foolish or wicked; no attempt is made to achieve an empathic understanding of their thoughts and actions. Above all, their attempts to make sense of, and thus to control, the world in which they lived, are slighted.

The individual's involvement in this struggle to comprehend and control necessarily possesses a tragic quality. For it requires a breadth of vision and a detachment of which the committed partisan is almost inevitably incapable. Whether conservative, reactionary or even radical, the partisan is to some degree the prisoner of the age in which he lives. But before this can be appreciated the integrity of that age must be recognised.

Any attempt to portray the ideological patterns which governed men's thought must pay close attention to the concept of democracy. In Jacksonian America democracy was still visualised as an essentially egalitarian and populistic system of government. More importantly, it still implied a society composed of autonomous equals, most of whom would remain permanently engaged in agriculture. These co-equal social units would demand that government remain inactive and their own self-interest, by propelling them towards honest labour, would preserve their moral health and thus the health of society. This was the democratic creed.

It was a creed which was irreconcilable with the perceptions of those who were most favourable to the fundamental economic changes of the age. The commercial or capitalist ethic stressed inequality, interdependence and an active role for government in the creation of an expanding and diversified economy. Hence in the ideological universe of Jacksonian America democracy and capitalism were in conflict. Unless this fundamental truth is recognised the politics of the age will remain ultimately incomprehensible.

The Democratic concept of equality requires special emphasis. For the levelling thrust of Jacksonian Democracy has never been recognised. Yet it had implications not only for political and socio-economic policy but also for the ethnocultural issues of the era. Democrats typically assumed that one (white) man was approximately equivalent, in social and political terms, to another. With equal conviction, the Whigs proclaimed that he was not.

Hence the parties presented to the electorate two coherent ideologies and two internally consistent sets of policies. There were important divisions within each party yet paradoxically those who were able to accept and reconcile the major social and political changes of the age — the liberal Whigs and the conservative Democrats — experienced great discomfort within the second party system. Even if they were able to remain within one party, they were simultaneously attracted to some of its beliefs and repelled by others.

Also of considerable importance in Jacksonian politics were the conflicts which divided East from West and North from South. It was perhaps only because they were conscious of the ideological gulf between the two parties that men with different sectional loyalties were able to join in a common cause. The debate over democracy and capitalism ultimately transcended sectional differences.

Thus although sectional loyalities sometimes cut across party alignments (and although party functioned as an institution as well as a vehicle for ideology), Democrats and Whigs were able to translate real ideological differences into meaningful disagreements over policy. In the post-Panic years most partisans, it may be suggested, were convinced that a battle was being fought on the outcome of which the nation's basic social and political character depended.

In their attempts to influence the future development of the nation, both Democrats and Whigs scored some notable successes. Democratic reverence for a populistic system of government surely made a major contribution to the political culture of the United States while Whig enthusiasm for commercial growth and social mobility effectively anticipated the conservative ethic of the later nineteenth and twentieth centuries. There can thus be little doubt that many of the decisive and distinctive features of the American creed were either introduced or significantly reshaped during the Jacksonian era.

Yet although the men of the 1830s and 1840s left a mark upon the nation, it was not, perhaps, the mark they would have chosen. For even the traditions which stem from the Jacksonian era often bear a perverse or paradoxical relationship to the goals of those who helped establish them. It has often been remarked that the limited government and states-rights philosophy which Democrats expounded has since become the property of the Right. Similarly the interventionist traditions of Federalism and Whiggery have been taken over by the Left. In each case subsequent generations have concluded, whether rightly or wrongly, that the policies of Democrat and Whig were largely misconceived.

It is also fair to note that even where the politicians of Jacksonian America were able to perceive real problems they were unable to make much impression upon them. Thus although Democrats delivered a poignant warning of the dangers to be feared from industrialisation and urbanisation, their faith in the natural laws disarmed them far more effectively than any opponent could have hoped to do. Equally, the Whigs' disdain for many of the new practices of government resulted not in proposals for reform but merely in apocalyptic warnings about the future. These were inaccurate precisely because reactionaries were cut off by their own principles and commitments from the realities of American politics. In the case of both radicals and reactionaries principles were sincerely held; yet they obscured as much as they illuminated.

The politicans of the Jacksonian era who were disenchanted with American government or society were thus not merely unable to effect the changes they sought; they were unable even to devise the policies which might have brought the desired changes. Radical Democrats and conservative Whigs wished to alter the course which the nation was taking. The moderates in each party resisted these efforts and celebrated the emerging capitalist economy and democratic order. Yet they too were unable to control or even to comprehend the world in which they lived. Within two decades of the election of James K. Polk the nation would be plunged into Civil War; it would be a war which the ideologies of Whig and Democrat had been powerless to prevent or even to foresee.

These failures were not the result of folly, still less of wickedness. For the task of predicting the significant developments of even the near future is an astonishingly difficult one. The men who enlisted with the Democratic and Whig parties made a serious attempt to understand their society and political system. They brought logic and intelligence to the task; they acted for the most part in good faith. Sadly, it was not enough.

APPENDIX

Table I

Voting on the Independent Treasury : House of Representatives

Year (Congress)	Democrats			Whigs		
	In favour	Against	% In favour	In favour	Against	% In favour
1837 (25)	106	19	85	1	101	1
1838 (25)	96	10	91	2	96	2
1838 (25)	111	15	88	0	110	0
1840 (26)	123	3	98	0	102	0
1840 (26)	124	3	98	0	104	0
1841 (27)	86	1	99	1	133	1
1844 (28)	110	0	100	0	58	0
1844 (28)	123	0	100	0	68	0
1846 (29)	121	1	99	1	64	2
Average	—	—	95	—	—	1

Source: *H.J.*, 25 i 195-7, ii 679-80, 1157-9; 26 i 1171-2, 1175-7; 27 i 344-5; 28 i 157-8, ii 116-7; 29 i 621-2

Table II

Voting on the Independent Treasury : Senate

Year (Congress)	Democrats			Whigs		
	In favour	Against	% In favour	In favour	Against	% In favour
1837 (25)	24	7	77	0	16	0
1837 (25)	26	6	81	0	15	0
1838 (25)	27	9	75	0	16	0
1840 (26)	24	4	86	0	14	0
1841 (26)	27	2	93	0	23	0
1841 (27)	18	0	100	0	29	0
1846 (29)	28	0	100	0	25	0
Average	—	—	86	—	—	0

Source: *S.J.*, 25 i 51, 55, ii 320; 26 i 131, ii 195-6; 27 i 37; 29 i 467

Table III

Voting on national bank : House of Representatives

Year (Congress)	Democrats			Whigs		
	In favour	Against	% In favour	In favour	Against	% In favour
1837 (25)	4	116	3	85	6	93
1837 (25)	2	114	2	89	9	91
1841 (27)	0	91	0	128	7	95
1841 (27)	0	89	0	125	5	96
1841 (27)	0	75	0	103	5	95
1844 (28)	0	108	0	68	1	99
Average	—	—	1	—	—	95

Source: *H.J.,* 25 i 92-3, 147-9; 27 i 324-6, 409-10, 511-2; 28 i 1128-9

Table IV

Voting on national bank : Senate

Year (Congress)	Democrats			Whigs		
	In favour	Against	% In favour	In favour	Against	% In favour
1837 (25)	1	28	3	14	1	93
1837 (25)	2	29	6	14	1	93
1841 (27)	0	22	0	25	2	93
1841 (27)	0	21	0	25	3	89
1841 (27)	0	21	0	27	1	96
Average	—	—	2	—	—	93

Source: *S.J.,* 25 i 44, 45; 27 i 124, 193, 234-5

Table V

Voting to recharter banks in the District of Columbia : House of Representatives

Year (Congress)	Democrats			Whigs		
	In favour	Against	% In favour	In favour	Against	% In favour
1838 (25)	64	33	66	66	12	85
1840 (26)	25	87	22	89	0	100
1841 (27)	2	58	3	105	0	100
1843 (27)	0	69	0	98	8	92
1844 (28)	29	70	29	65	0	100
1847 (29)	16	77	17	62	0	100
Average	—	—	26	—	—	96

Source: *H.J.*, 25 ii 993-4; 26 i 1187-8; 27 i 381-2, iii 510-11; 28 i 910-11; 29 ii 359-60

Table VI

Voting to recharter banks in the District of Columbia : Senate

Year (Congress)	Democrats			Whigs		
	In favour	Against	% In favour	In favour	Against	% In favour
1838 (25)	28	2	93	9	0	100
1841 (27)	5	15	25	24	0	100
1842 (27)	0	15	0	21	0	100
1842 (27)	0	18	0	25	0	100
1842 (27)	0	18	0	21	0	100
1843 (27)	1	16	6	25	1	96
1844 (28)	4	14	22	18	1	95
Average	—	—	28	—	—	99

Source: *S.J.*, 25 ii 408; 27 i 140, ii 207, 212-4, iii 253-4; 28 i 276-7

Table VII

Voting to restrict the circulation of small notes : House of Representatives

Year (Congress)	Democrats			Whigs		
	In favour	Against	% In favour	In favour	Against	% In favour
1838 (25)	86	3	97	1	78	1
1838 (25)	66	0	100	11	54	17
1840 (26)	109	2	98	1	92	1
1840[a] (26)	96	1	99	0	75	0
1840[b] (26)	83	10	89	0	88	0
1840[c] (26)	60	29	67	0	77	0
Average	—	—	92	—	—	3

[a]This amendment called for a restriction on all notes under $10.
[b]This amendment called for a restriction on all notes under $20.
[c]This amendment called for a restriction on all notes under $50.

Source: *H.J.*, 25 ii 1265-6, 1278-9; 26 i 1188-9, 1202, 1190-1, 1195-6

Table VIII

Voting to restrict the circulation of small notes : Senate

Year (Congress)	Democrats			Whigs		
	In favour	Against	% In favour	In favour	Against	% In favour
1837 (25)	30	0	100	7	1	88
1838 (25)	27	2	93	0	11	0
1838 (25)	23	7	77	1	9	10
1841 (27)	22	0	100	3	25	11
1841 (27)	21	0	100	1	27	4
1841 (27)	13	0	100	6	20	23
Average	—	—	94	—	—	16

Source: *S.J.*, 25 ii 79, 373, 407-8; 27 i 117, 123, 57-8

Table IX

Voting on proposals to increase banks' liability : House and Senate

Year (Congress)	Democrats			Whigs		
	In favour	Against	% In favour	In favour	Against	% In favour
1840 (26)	90	14	87	2	76	3
1840 (26)	20	5	80	0	11	0
1841 (26)	18	3	86	0	16	0
1841 (27)	21	0	100	0	24	0
1841 (27)	20	0	100	0	28	0
1841 (27)	11	2	85	0	25	0
1843 (27)	15	1	94	0	25	0
1844 (28)	16	4	80	1	22	4
1844 (28)	20	1	95	1	18	5
Average	—	—	89	—	—	2

Source: *H.J.*, 26 i 1198-9; *S.J.*, 26 i 497, ii 208; 27 i 104, 229-30, 57, iii 245; 28 i 269-70, 270-1

Table X

Voting on the distribution policy : House and Senate

Year (Congress)	Democrats			Whigs		
	In favour	Against	% In favour	In favour	Against	% In favour
1841 (27)	0	91	0	119	14	89
1841 (27)	0	92	0	116	16	88
1844 (28)	0	113	0	63	0	100
1841 (27)	0	22	0	28	1	97
1844 (28)	0	18	0	22	1	96
Average	—	—	0	—	—	92

Source: *H.J.*, 27 i 220-1, 222-3 (these motions included pre-emption); 28 i 577-8; *S.J.*, 27 i 216; 28 i 170-1

Table XI

Voting on the pre-emption and graduation policies : House of Representatives

Year (Congress)	Democrats			Whigs		
	In favour	Against	% In favour	In favour	Against	% In favour
Pre-emption						
1838 (25)	76	13	85	31	41	43
1840 (26)	93	13	88	28	51	35
1846 (29)	84	11	88	11	35	24
Graduation						
1838 (25)	73	25	74	25	77	25
1839 (25)	76	18	81	22	81	21
1845 (28)	86	36	70	5	67	7
1846 (29)	92	24	79	0	61	0
Average	—	—	81	—	—	23

Source: *H.J.*, 25 ii 1101; 26 i 1031-2; 29 i 744; 25 iii 357-8, 364-5; 28 ii 329-30; 29 i 1093-4

Table XII

Voting on the pre-emption and graduation policies : Senate

Year (Congress)	Democrats			Whigs		
	In favour	Against	% In favour	In favour	Against	% In favour
Pre-emption						
1838 (25)	28	5	85	2	13	13
Graduation						
1838 (25)	25	8	76	2	8	20
1839 (25)	24	9	73	3	13	19
1840 (26)	24	2	92	4	6	40
1841 (27)	17	2	89	1	25	4
1846 (29)	23	1	96	2	18	10
Average	—	—	84	—	—	14

Source: *S.J.*, 25 ii 191; 25 ii 356, iii 134; 26 i 337; 27 i 156; 29 i 396-7

Table XIII

Average sectional support for pre-emption and graduation: Senate

	NE	SE	NW	SW
Democrats	68%	57%	97%	100%
Whigs	3%	4%	50%	29%

Source: Roll calls used for Table XII

Table XIV

Voting on the tariff: House and Senate

Year (Congress)	Democrats			Whigs		
	In favour	Against	% In favour	In favour	Against	% In favour
House						
1842 (27)	20	66	23	84	37	69
1844 (28)	28	98	22	77	1	99
1846 (29)	19	113	14	70	1	99
Senate						
1842 (27)	4	14	22	20	9	69
1846 (29)	3	27	10	24	0	100
Average	—	—	19	—	—	85

Source: *H.J.*, 27 ii 1385-7; 28 i 895-6; 29 i 1029-30; *S.J.*, 27 ii 629; 29 i 453

BIBLIOGRAPHY

Primary Sources

Government Documents, Official and Semi-Official
Newspapers
Periodicals
Collections of Writings, Speeches, Letters and Addresses
Addresses, Speeches, Orations, Convention Proceedings etc
Contemporary Books, Treatises etc.
Memoirs, Diaries, Autobiographies

Secondary Sources

280

Primary Sources

Government Documents, Official and Semi-Official

Bebout, John *et al.* (eds.), *Proceedings of the New Jersey State Constitutional Convention of 1844* (Trenton, 1942)

Briggs, George N., *Address of His Excellency... to the Two Branches of the Legislature of Massachusetts* (Boston, 1846)

Congressional Globe

Davis, John, *Inaugural Address of His Excellency... to the Two Branches of the Legislature of Massachusetts* (Boston, 1841)

_____ *Address of His Excellency... to the Two Branches of the Legislature of Massachusetts* (Boston, 1842).

Dodd, Dorothy (ed.), *Florida Becomes a State* (Tallahassee, 1945).

Dorr, Harold M. (ed.), *The Michigan Constitutional Conventions of 1835-1836* (Ann Arbor, 1940).

Everett, Edward, *Address of His Excellency... to the Two Branches of the Legislature of Massachusetts* (Boston, 1838).

_____ *Address...* (Boston, 1839).

Fuller, George N. (ed.), *Messages of the Governors of Michigan,* 4 vols. (Lansing, 1925-7).

Hill, Isaac, *Message of... Governor of New Hampshire, to Both Houses of the Legislature* (Concord, 1837).

Journal of the Alabama House of Representatives

Journal of the New Hampshire Senate

Journals of the North Carolina Senate and House of Commons

Journal of the South Carolina Senate and House of Representatives

Journal of the United States House of Representatives

Journal of the United States Senate

Kent, Edward, *Address of Governor Kent to Both Branches of the Legislature of the State of Maine, January 1838* (Augusta, 1838).

Address... January 1841 (Augusta, 1841)

North Carolina Public Documents, 1838-1840

Proceedings and Debates of the Convention of Louisiana (New Orleans, 1845) (Robert J. Ker, reporter).

Proceedings of the Convention of Pennsylvania to Propose Amendments to the Constitution, 14 vols. (Harrisburg, 1837-9).

Quaife, Milo M., (ed.) 'The Convention of 1846', *Publications of the State Historical Society of Wisconsin, Collections* XXVII (Madison, Wisc., 1919).

Richardson, James D., *A Compilation of the Messages and Papers of the Presidents,* 9 vols. (Washington, D.C., 1896-7).

Shambaugh, Benjamin F. (ed.), *Fragments of the Debates of the Iowa Constitutional Conventions of 1844 and 1846 along with Press Comment and Other Materials* (Iowa City, 1900).
South Carolina: Reports and Resolutions 1837.

Newspapers (Those used extensively are marked *)

Washington, D. C.

Common Sense, The Working-
man's Advocate
Democratic Expositor & United
*States Journal**
*Independent**

*Kendall's Expositor**
*Madisonian**
*National Intelligencer**
Native American
*Washington Globe**

Maine

Eastern Argus
Kennebec Journal

Portland Advertiser

New Hampshire

Hill's New Hampshire Patriot
New Hampshire Patriot and State
*Gazette**

New Hampshire Statesman

Vermont

North Star

Vermont Statesman

Massachusetts

Boston Atlas

Boston Weekly Reformer

Rhode Island

Providence Daily Journal
Providence Daily Transcript &
Chronicle

Connecticut

Hartford Courant

New York

*Albany Evening Journal**
Jeffersonian (Albany)
*New York Courier and Enquirer**
New York Express

*New York Tribune**
*Working Man's Advocate**
Young Hickory Banner

Pennsylvania

American Volunteer
Native American

Spirit of the Times and Daily
   Keystone (Philadelphia)

Ohio

Cincinnati Advertiser*
Cincinnati Enquirer*

Ohio State Journal*

Indiana

Dearboro County Democrat
Disseminator
Fort Wayne Sentinel
Franklin Democrat
Northern Indianan

People's Gazette
Richmond Palladium
South Western Sentinel
Torchlight
Vincennes Gazette

Illinois

Chicago Democrat
Illinois State Register and People's
   Advocate
North Western Gazette and Galena
   Advertiser

Michigan

Democratic Expounder
Detroit Daily Advertiser
Detroit Daily Constitutional

The Loco Foco
Michigan Times

Wisconsin

Wisconsin Whig

Maryland

Democrat and Carroll County Republican

Virginia

Commercial Chronicle*
The Crisis
The Old Dominion*
Portsmouth Chronicle

Richmond Enquirer
Richmond Shield
State Rights Republican

North Carolina

Raleigh Register

Raleigh Star

South Carolina

Carolina Gazette
Charleston Courier

Charleston Mercury

Georgia

Columbus Enquirer
Federal Union
Georgia Messenger (Macon)
La Grange Herald

Savannah Georgian
Savannah Republican
Southern Recorder

Florida

Florida Sentinel

Star of Florida

Missouri

The Mill Boy
Missourian

Missouri Reporter
St. Louis New Era

Kentucky

The Campaign

Frankfort Democrat

Tennessee

Democratic Statesman

Spirit of '76

Arkansas

Napoleon Standard and Commercial Advertiser

Alabama

Democratic Gazette
Franklin Democrat

Jacksonville Republican
Wetumpka Argus

Louisiana

Commercial Bulletin
The Great Western
Hebdomadal Enquirer
Jeffersonian Republican

Morning Intelligencer
New Orleans Bee
New Orleans Democrat
Natchitoches Constitutional
　　Adviser

Mississippi

Mississippian*
Natchez Daily Courier

Natchez Free Trader

Periodicals

The American Laborer
American Monthly Magazine
American Quarterly Review
The American Review: A Whig Journal of Politics, Literature, Art
    and Science
Atlantic Monthly
Boston Quarterly Review
Brownson's Quarterly Review
National Magazine and Republican Review
New Yorker
New York Review and Quarterly Church Journal
Niles Register
Southern Literary Messenger
United States Magazine and Democratic Review
Western Review
Whig Almanac

Collections of Writings, Speeches, Letters and Addresses

Bancroft, George, *The Life and Letters of George Bancroft* by M.A.
    De Wolfe Howe (N.Y., 1908).
Biddle, Nicholas, *The Correspondence of Nicholas Biddle... 1807-
    1844* (ed. Reginald C. McGrane, Boston, 1966).
Brown, Aaron V., *Speeches, Congressional and Political, and Other
    Writings of Ex. Governor Aaron V. Brown, of Tennessee* (Nashville,
    1854).
Brown, Bedford, 'Selections from the Correspondence of Bedford
    Brown', (ed. William K. Boyd), *Trinity College Historical
    papers,* Series VI (1906), 66-92.
Brownson, Orestes A., *The Works of Orestes A. Brownson,* 20 vols.
    (ed. Henry F. Brownson, Detroit, 1882-7).
Calhoun, John C., 'The Correspondence of John C. Calhoun',
    Annual Report of the American Historical Association for 1899
    (ed. J. Franklin Jameson, Washington, D.C., 1900).
            The Works of John C. Calhoun, 6 vols. (ed. Richard K.
    Cralle, Columbia, S.C., 1851-5).
'Camillus', *The Essays of Camillus, Addressed to the Hon. Joel
    Holleman* (Norfolk, 1841).
Choate, Rufus, *The Life and Writings of Rufus Choate* (ed. Samuel
    G. Brown, Boston, 1862).
Clay, Henry, *The Life and Works of Henry Clay,* 10 vols. (ed. Calvin
    Colton, N.Y., 1904).

Cobb, Howell, 'The Howell Cobb Papers', (ed. R.P. Brooks) *Ga. H. Q.*, V (March, 1921), 50-61, (June, 1921), 29-52, (Sept., 1921), 35-55, (Dec., 1921), 43-64.

Corwin, Thomas, *The Life and Speeches of Thomas Corwin – Orator, Lawyer and Statesman* (ed. Josiah Morrow, Cincinnati, 1896).

Crittenden, John J., *The Life of John J. Crittenden with Selections from his Correspondence and Speeches* by Mrs. Chapman Coleman (Phil., 1873).

Dickinson, Daniel S., *Speeches, Correspondence, etc. of the Late Daniel S. Dickinson of New York*, 2 vols. (ed. John R. Dickinson, N.Y., 1867).

Everett, Edward, *Orations and Speeches on Various Occasions*, 4 vols. (Boston, 1850).

Fairfield, John, *The Letters of John Fairfield* (ed. Arthur G. Staples, Lewiston, Me., 1922).

Fillmore, Millard, 'The Millard Fillmore Papers' (ed. Frank H. Severance), 2 vols., *Publications of the Buffalo Historical Society*, X (1907).

Follett, Oran, 'Selections from the Follett Papers' (ed. L. Belle Hamlin), *H. P. S. O.* Quarterly Publications, V (April-June, 1910), 34-76; IX (July-Sept., 1914), 70-100; X (Jan.-March, 1915), 2-33; XI (Jan.-March, 1916), 2-35; XII (April-June, 1918), 40-78.

Greene, William, 'Selections from the William Greene Papers' (ed. L. Belle Hamlin), *H. P. S. O.* Quarterly Publications, XIII (Jan.-March, 1918), 3-38; XIV (Jan.-March, 1919), 3-26.

Hunter, Robert M.T., 'The Correspondence of Robert M.T. Hunter' (ed. Charles H. Ambler) *Annual Report of the American Historical Association for 1916*, II (Washington, D.C., 1918).

Jackson, Andrew, *The Correspondence of Andrew Jackson*, 7 vols. (ed. John S. Bassett, Washington, D.C., 1926-35).

_____ 'The Jackson-Dawson Correspondence' (ed. John L. Whealen), *H. P. S. O.*, XVI (Jan., 1958), 3-30.

Jefferson, Thomas, *The Writings of Thomas Jefferson*, 20 vols. (ed. A.A. Lipscomb and A.E. Bergh, Washington, D.C., 1903).

Johnson, Andrew, *The Papers of Andrew Johnson* (eds. Leroy P. Graf and Ralph W. Haskins, Knoxville, Tenn., 1967-).

'Junius', [Calvin Colton] *The Junius Tracts* (N.Y., 1844).

Kennedy, John P., *The Collective Works of John P. Kennedy*, 10 vols. (ed. Henry T. Tuckerman, N.Y., 1871-2).

Lincoln, Abraham, *The Collected Works of Abraham Lincoln*, 9 vols. (ed. Roy P. Basler, New Brunswick, 1953-5).

Legare, Hugh S., *The Writings of Hugh Swinton Legare*, 2 vols. (ed. Mary S. Legare, Charleston, 1845-6).

Leggett, William, *A Collection of the Political Writings of William Leggett* (ed. Theodore Sedgwick, Jr., N.Y., 1840).

Mangum, Willie P., *The Papers of Willie Person Mangum*, 5 vols. (ed. Henry T. Shanks, Raleigh, 1950-6).

Mann, Horace, *The Life and Works of Horace Mann*, 5 vols. (ed. Mary Mann, Boston, 1891).

Pillow, Gideon J., 'Letters of Gideon J. Pillow to James K. Polk, 1844' (ed. Jesse S. Reeves), *A.H.R.*, XI (July, 1906), 832-42.

Polk, James K., 'Letters of James K. Polk to Cave Johnson, 1833-1848', *T.H.M.*, I (Sept., 1915), 209-56.

Porter, Kirk H. & Johnson, Donald D. (eds.), *National Party Platforms* (Urbana, 1966).

Quaife, Milo M. (ed.), 'The Struggle over Ratification, 1846-1847', *Publication of the State Historical Society of Wisconsin, Collections,* XXVIII (Madison, Wisc., 1920).

Rae, John B. (ed.), 'Democrats and the Dorr Rebellion', *N.E.Q.,* IX (Sept., 1936), 476-83.

Ritchie, Thomas, 'Unpublished Letters of Thomas Ritchie', *John P. Branch Historical Papers of Randolph-Macon College,* III (June, 1911), 199-254.

Seward, William H., *The Works of William H. Seward,* 5 vols. (ed. George E. Baker, Boston, 1884).

Story, Joseph, *The Life and Letters of Joseph Story,* 2 vols. (ed. William W. Story, London, 1851).

Sutherland, [Thomas J.] *Political Letters, Addressed to Dr. Nelson* (N.Y., 1840).

Tilden, Samuel J., *Letters and Literary Memorials of Samuel J. Tilden,* 2 vols.(ed. John Bigelow, N.Y., 1908).

—————— *The Writings and Speeches of Samuel J. Tilden,* 2 vols. (ed. John Bigelow, N.Y., 1885).

Toombs, Robert, Stephens, Alexander and Cobb, Howell, 'The Correspondence of Robert Toombs, Alexander H. H. Stephens, and Howell Cobb', (ed. Ulrich B. Phillips), *Annual Report of the American Historical Association for the Year 1911* (Washington, D.C., 1913).

Tyler, John and Julia G., *The Letters and Times of the Tylers* (ed. Lyon G. Tyler, Richmond, Va., 1894-6).

Walsh, Michael, *Sketches of the Speeches and Writings of Mike Walsh* (N.Y., 1843).

Webster, Daniel, *The Letters of Daniel Webster* (ed. C.H. Van Tyne, N.Y., 1902).

—————— *The Writings and Speeches of Daniel Webster,* 18 vols. (ed. J.W. McIntyre, Boston, 1903).

Winthrop, Robert C., *Addresses and Speeches on Various Occasions* (Boston, 1852).

Wright, Frances and Owen, Robert Dale, *Tracts on Republican Government and National Education* (London, 1840).

Addresses, Speeches, Orations, Convention Proceedings, etc.

Adams, John Quincy, *Address to Constituents, at Braintree, Sept. 17, 1842* (Boston, 1842).

Address to the Citizens of Louisiana on the Subject of the Recent Election in New Orleans (New Orleans, 1844).

Address of the Democratic Association of the District of Columbia to the People of the United States (n.p., n.d.).

Address of the Democratic Central Committee of Correspondence to the People of Pennsylvania (Harrisburg, 1838).

Address of the Democratic Hickory Club for the City and County of Philadelphia, recommending Mr. Van Buren as the Presidential Candidate for 1844. Also the Letter of Mr. Van Buren to the State Convention of Indiana (n.p., n.d.).

Address of the Democratic Members of Congress from the State of Tennessee, to their Constituents (Washington, D.C., 1841).

Address of the Democratic Members of the Legislature to the People of Virginia (n.p., n.d.).

Address to the Democratic Republican Electors of the State of New York (Washington, D.C., 1840).

Address of the Democratic Republican Young Men's Central Committee of the City of New York to the Republican Young Men of the State (N.Y., 1840).

Address of the General Executive Committee of the American Republican party of the City of New York, to the People of the United States (N.Y., 1845).

Address of the Louisiana Native American Association to the citizens of Louisiana and the Inhabitants of the United States (New Orleans, 1839).

Address to the Republican People of Tennessee, by the Central Corresponding Committee of the State, no. 2 (Nashville, 1840).

Address to the True Democrats of Jefferson County (Ohio) (n.p., n.d.)

Address to Working Men, on the Low Price of Wages, by a Mechanic (n.p., n.d.).

Address to the Workingmen of the United States (n.p., n.d.)

Address of the Whig Members of the Senate and House of Representatives of Massachusetts, To their Constituents, Occasioned by the Inaugural Address of His Excellency Marcus Morton (Boston, 1843).

Advance Guard of Democracy (Nashville, 1840).

Alford, Julius C., *et al., Address of J. C. Alford, William C. Dawson, Richard W. Habersham, Thos. Butler King, E.A. Nesbit, and Lott Warren, Representatives from the State of Georgia, in the Twenty-Sixth Congress of the United States, to their Constituents, May 27, 1840* (n.p., n.d.)

[Allen, George] *An Appeal to the People of Massachusetts on the Texas Question* by 'a Massachusetts Freeman' (Boston, 1844).

Allen, William, *Speech of the Honorable William Allen, delivered at the Great Democratic Festival, held at Lancaster, Ohio, 18 Aug. 1837* (Lancaster, Ohio, 1837).

Anderson, Alexander, *Letter of Alexander Anderson, of Tennessee, in reply to the Committee of Invitation...* (n.p., n.d.)

The Andover Husking; A Political Tale, Suited to the Circumstances of the Present Times, and Dedicated to the Whigs of Massachusetts (Boston, 1842).

Answer of the Whig Members of the Legislature of Massachusetts... to the Address of His Excellency Marcus Morton, delivered... Jan. 22, 1840 (Boston, 1840).

'Anti-Junius', 'Who and What is John Tyler?', *Political Tracts for the Times,* no. 2 (N.Y., 1843).

Appeal to Arms! (n.p., n.d.)

Badger, George E., *Speech Delivered at the Great Whig Meeting in the County of Granville, 3 March, 1840* (Raleigh, 1840).

Bancroft, George, *Oration Delivered Before the Democracy of Springfield and Neighboring Towns, July 4, 1836* (Springfield, 1836).

——— *The Principles of Democracy: An Address at Hartford. . . Feb. 18, 1840* (Hartford, 1840).

Barber, Edward D., *Oration at Montpelier, 4 July, 1839* (n.p., 1839).

Barnard, Daniel D., *A Discourse delivered before the Senate of Union College* (Albany, 1843).

——— *Man and the State, Social and Political* (New Haven, 1846)

——— *A Plea for Social and Popular Repose* (N.Y., 1845)

Baylies, Francis, *Speech of the Hon. Francis Baylies before the Whigs of Taunton, 13 Sept. 1837* (Taunton, 1837).

Berrien, John J., *Speech on the Tariff, delivered in the United States Senate 9 April, 1844* (Washington, 1844).

Biddle, Nicholas., *Eulogium on Thomas Jefferson* (Phil., 1827).

Bolles, John A., *Oration delivered July 4, 1839, at Medfield Massachusetts, at a Temperance Celebration* (Boston, 1839)

Boyd, Lynn, *To the Citizens of the First Congressional District in the*

State of Kentucky (n.p., n.d.).

Brownlow, William G., *A Political Register* (Jonesborough, Tenn., 1844).

Burke, Edmund, *Address delivered before the Democratic Republican Citizens of Lempster, N.H., 8 Jan. 1839* (Newport, N.H., 1839).

Butler, Benjamin F., *Representative Democracy in the United States: An Address delivered before the Senate of Union College* (Albany, 1841).

Can I Conscientiously Vote for Henry Clay? by 'a Professed Christian' (n.p., n.d.).

Cheves, Langdon, *Letter of the Hon. Langdon Cheves to the Editors of the 'Charleston Mercury', Sept. 11, 1844* (n.p., n.d.).

Chinn, Thomas W., *Letter of Thomas W. Chinn to Hon. Thomas Gibbs Morgan* (Washington, D.C., n.d.).

Clayton, John M., *Speech of Mr. Clayton of Delaware delivered at the Whig Mass Meeting held in Wilmington, 15 June* (Washington, D.C., 1844).

[Collins, George C.], *Fifty Reasons Why the Honorable Henry Clay Should be Elected President of the United States,* by an Irish Adopted Citizen (Baltimore, 1844).

Colquitt, Walter, *Speech of Mr. Colquitt of Georgia. . . on the Independent Treasury Bill, delivered in the House of Representatives, June 20, 1840* (Washington, D.C., 1840).

The Crisis! An Appeal to our Countrymen, on the subject of Foreign Influence in the United States (N.Y., 1844).

The Crisis Met, A Reply to 'Junius' (n.p., n.d.).

Curtis, George T., *The Rights of Conscience and of Property; or the True Issue of the Convent Question* (Boston, 1842).

[Cushing, Caleb] *An Outline of the Life and Public Services, Civil and Military, of William H. Harrison, of Ohio* (Newark, 1844)

Dana, Edward P., *A Voice from Bunker-Hill, and the Fathers of the Revolutionary War, in favor of the Hero of North Bend* (Bunker-Hill, 1840).

Darusmont, Frances Wright, *What is the Matter? A Political Address as delivered in Masonic Hall, Oct. 28, 1838* (N.Y., 1838).

[Davis, Charles Augustus] *Peter Scriber on Protection* (Washington, D.C., 1844).

A Defence of the President, Against the Attacks of Mr. Botts and the Clay Party (n.p., n.d.).

Dorsey, John L., *The Spirit of Modern Democracy Explained* (St. Louis, 1840).

[Dorsey, John L.,] *Observations on the Political Character and Services of President Tyler and His Cabinet* by a Native of Maryland (Washington, D.C., 1841).

Eleventh Annual Report of the American Sunday-School Union (Phil., 1835).

Everett, Alexander, *Oration delivered at Holliston, Mass. on the Fourth of July, 1839* (Boston, 1839).

Facts Involved in the Rhode Island Controversy with Some Views upon the Rights of Both Parties (Boston, 1842).

Fine, John, *Letter of the Hon. John Fine, to his Constituents, August 1840* (n.p., n.d.).

Fisk, Theophilus, *The Nation's Bulwark: An Oration on the Freedom of The Press* (New Haven, n.d.).

_____ *Capital Against Labor: An Address delivered . . . before the Mechanics of Boston* (Boston, 1835).

_____ *A Vindication of the Rights of Man: An Oration delivered in Portsmouth, Virginia* (Portsmouth, 1838).

_____ *Our Country; Its Dangers and Destiny: An Address delivered before the Cadets of the Norwich University* (Washington, D.C., 1845).

Fletcher, Richard, *Speech of Richard Fletcher to his Constituents, delivered in Faneuil Hall, Nov. 6. 1837* (Boston, 1837).

Frelinghuysen Theodore, *Speech of Mr. Frelinghuysen on his Resolution concerning Sabbath Mails, May 8, 1830* (Washington, D.C., 1830).

Garland, Hugh A., *The Principles of Democracy Identical with the Moral Improvement of Mankind: An Oration. . . in Celebration of the Second Declaration of Independence, or the Passage of the Independent Treasury Bill* (N.Y., n.d.).

[Garland, Hugh A.] *The Second War of Revolution, or the Great Principles Involved in the Present Controversy between Parties* (Washington, D.C., 1839).

Garland, James, *Letter of James Garland to his Constituents* (n.p., n.d.).

Greeley, Horace, *Why I Am A Whig* (n.p., n.d.).

Green, Willis, *The Sub-Treasury: A Tract for the Times* (Washington, D.C., 1844).

[Greene, Charles G.,] *The Identity of the Old Hartford Convention Federalists with the Modern Whig Harrison Party* (n.p., n.d.).

Groves, William T., *The Whigs of Washtenshaw Co.* (n.p., 1941).

Hallett, Benjamin F. *Oration delivered July 4, 1836, at Palmer, Massachusetts* (Boston, 1836).

_____ *Oration delivered July 4, 1838, at the Plymouth Co. Democratic Celebration* (Boston, 1838).

_____ *Oration before the Democratic Citizens of Oxford, July 5, 1841* (Boston, 1841).

_____ *Speech on Bunker Hill, July 4, 1844* (n.p., n.d.).

Hallett, Benjamin F. *et al., Investigation into the Fifteen Gallon Law of Massachusetts before a Joint Committee of the Legislature* (Boston, 1839).

Hard Cider and Log Cabin Almanac for 1841 (Baltimore, n.d.).

Hare, Robert, *Suggestions respecting the Reform of the Banking System* (Phil., 1837).

Harrison, William H., *Speech at the Dayton Convention, Sept. 10, 1840* (n.p., n.d.).

Hazard, Thomas R., *Facts for the Laboring Man* by a Laboring Man (Newport, R.I., 1840).

Henderson, John, *Letter of John Henderson, to the Legislature of the State of Mississippi, Dec. 28, 1840* (n.p., n.d.).

Hildreth, Richard, *Letter to his Excellency Marcus Morton on Banking and the Currency* (Boston, 1840).

———— *Letter on Political Action* (Boston, 1840).

[Hildreth, Richard], *The Contrast: or William Henry Harrison Versus Martin Van Buren* (Boston, 1840).

Hopkins, George W., *Letter of George W. Hopkins of Russell, to Col. James H. Piper of Wythe* (Washington, D.C., 1840).

Jagger, William, *To the People of Suffolk, of All Parties* (N.Y., 1838).

John, The Traitor: or, The Force of Accident. A Plain Story by One Who Has Whistled at the Plough (N.Y., 1843).

'Junius', [Calvin Colton] *The Crisis of the Country* (Phil., 1840).

———— *Sequel to the Crisis of the Country* (Phil., 1840).

———— *American Jacobinism* (N.Y., 1840).

———— *One Presidential Term* (N.Y., 1840).

'Junius, Jr.', *The Vision of Judgement: or, A Present of the Whigs of '76 and '37* (N.Y., 1838).

Kendall, Amos, *Address to the People of the United States* (n.p., n.d.).

[Kennedy, John P.] *Defence of the Whigs* by a Member of the Twenty-Seventh Congress (N.Y., 1844).

Kenney, Lucy, *A History of the Present Cabinet, Benton in Ambush for the next Presidency, Kendall coming in third best* (Washington, D.C., 1840).

———— *Address to the People of the United States* (n.p., n.d.).

[Kenney, Lucy] *A Pamphlet, Showing how Easily the Wand of a Magician may be Broken* (n.p., n.d.).

King, William R., Clay, C.C., Lewis, Dixon H., Hubbard, David, and Chapman, Reuben, *To the Democratic Republican Party of Alabama* (n.p., n.d.).

Letter on the Subject of the Vice Presidency, in favor of the Claims of Jas. K. Polk (Washington, D.C., 1844).

Levin, Lewis C., *Lecture on Irish Repeal. . .* (Phil., 1844).

[Mayo, Robert], *A Word in Season; or Review of the Political Life* and *Opinions of Martin Van Buren* (Washington, D.C., 1840).

M'Farlane, J.S., *Address to the Public Authorities of the United States* by the Louisiana Native American Association (New Orleans, 1836).

McRoberts, Samuel, *To the Members of the General Assembly of Illinois* (n.p., n.d.).

Miller, John G., *The Great Convention; Description of the Convention of the People of Ohio, held at Columbus, 21-22 Feb. 1840* (Columbus, n.d.).

Miner, Charles, *An Address delivered at the Democratic Whig Festival at Wilkes-Barre, Penn., Dec 4. 1840* (Wilkes-Barre, 1841).

Montgomery's Tippecanoe Almanac for the Year 1841 (Phil., n.d.).

Moore, Ely, *Trades' Unions: Address to the Members of the General Trades' Unions of New York* (N.Y., 1833).

_____ *Address on Civil Government: Delivered before the New York Typographical Society, Feb. 25, 1847* (N.Y., 1847).

[Moore, Jacob B.], *The Contrast: Or, Plain Reasons Why William Henry Harrison Should and Will Have the Support of the Democracy for President of the United States, in preference to Martin Van Buren* by a Workingman (Boston, 1840).

Nichols, Thomas L., *Lecture on Immmigration and the Right of Naturalization* (N.Y., 1845).

The Northern Man with Southern Principles, or the Southern Man with American Principles (Washington, D.C., 1840).

Parsons, Theophilus, *The Duties of Educated Men in a Republic* (Boston, 1835).

Peabody, Andrew P., *Reverence and Family Discipline* (Portsmouth, 1841).

Pictures of the Times: Or, A Contrast between the Effects of the True Democratic System, as Displayed under Jefferson, Madison and Jackson in former Times, and the Effects of the Aristocratic Sub-Treasury system as Displayed in Martin Van Buren's time (Phil., 1840).

The Presidential Question (n.p., n.d.).

Polk, James K., *Address of James K. Polk to the People of Tennessee, April 3, 1839* (Columbia, Tenn., 1839).

_____ *Answer of Ex-Governor Polk to Two Series of Interrogations Propounded to him and Governor Jones* (n.p., n.d.).

Powell, Cuthbert, *Letter of Mr. Cuthbert Powell, to the People of the Fourteenth Congressional District of Virginia* (n.p., n.d.).

Proceedings and Address of the Democratic State Convention of the State of Ohio (Columbus, Ohio, 1844).

Proceedings of a Convention of Democratic Young Men, Delegates from the Citizens of Pennsylvania, in favor of the Re-election of

Joseph Ritner, and opposed to Mr. Van Buren and the Sub-Treasury (Reading, 1838).
Proceedings of the Democratic Legislative Convention, held in Boston, March, 1840 (n.p., n.d.).
Proceedings of the Democratic Whig National Convention . . . for The Purpose of Nominating candidates for President and Vice President of the United States (Harrisburg, 1839).
Proceedings of the Democratic Whig State Convention held in Chambersburg, 13-14 June, 1839 (Chambersburg, 1839).
Proceedings of the Great Democratic Republican Meeting in the State of New York, Jan. 2, 1838 (Washington, D.C., 1838).
Proceedings of a Great Whig Meeting of Citizens of Boston . . . Oct. 10, 1838 (Boston, 1838).
Proceedings of the Republican Convention of Virginia, March 18, 1839 (n.p., n.d.).
Proceedings of the Sabbath Convention, held in the City of Rochester, July 20 and 21, 1842 (Rochester, 1842).
Proceedings of a State Convention of the Whig Young Men of Connecticut, Feb. 1840 (Hartford, 1840).
Proceedings of the Whigs of Chester Co., Favorable to a Distinct Organization of the Whig Party (n.p., n.d.).
The Prospect Before Us. or Locofoco Impositions Exposed (Washington, D.C., 1844).
Pugh, Jordan A., *Political Conservatism* (Oxford, 1841).
Pumroy, John M., *Defence of our Naturalization Laws, with a Friendly Warning to members of the Native American Party* (Phil., 1845).
Rantoul, Robert, Jr., *Oration delivered before the Democratic Citizens of the County of Worcester, July 4, 1837* (Worcester, 1837).
────── *Oration delivered before the Democrats and Anti-masons Plymouth 4 July, 1836* (Boston, 1836).
Rencher, Abraham, *Circular Address of Abraham Rencher, of North Carolina, To His Constituents* (n.p., n.d.).
Reply to the Letter of the Hon. Langdon Cheves by a Southerner (n.p., n.d.).
Riell, Henry E., *An Appeal to the Voluntary Citizens of the United States from all Nations on the Exercise of their Elective Franchise at the Approaching Presidential Election* (N.Y., 1840).
Rives, William C., *Letter from the Hon. William C. Rives, of Virginia, Feb. 15, 1840* (n.p., n.d.).
The South in Danger: Address of the Democratic Association of Washington, D.C., (n.p., n.d.).
Southern States Rights, Free Trade and Anti-Abolition Tract, no. 1 (Charleston, 1844).

Stanly, Edward, *Letter From Mr. Stanley, of N. C. . to Mr. Botts of Virginia* (n.p., n.d.).

Story, Joseph, *Discourse delivered before the Society of the Alumni of Harvard University, Aug. 23, 1842* (Boston, 1842).

Tarbell, John P., *Oration delivered before the Democratic Citizens of the North Part of Middlesex County, at Groton, July Fourth, 1839* (Lowell, 1839).

To the People of Michigan (n.p., n.d.).

The True Whig Sentiment of Massachusetts (n.p., n.d.).

John Tyler: His History, Character and Position (N.Y., 1843).

Ullman, Daniel, *Address before the Tippecanoe and other Harrison Associations of the City of New York* (N.Y., 1841).

Van Rensselaer, John S., *Address before the Whig and Conservative Citizens of Schenectady County, Dec. 30, 1839* (Schenectady, 1840).

Wainwright, Jonathan M., *Inequality of Individual Wealth the Ordinance of Providence, and Essential to Civilization* (Boston, 1835).

[Watson, William R.] *The Whig Party; Its Objects – Its Principles – Its Candidates – Its Duties – and Its Prospects* by 'Hamilton' (Providence, R.I., 1844).

Wayland, Francis, *The Affairs of Rhode Island* (Providence, R.I., 1842).

Whig Congressional Committee, *To the Whigs and Conservatives of the United States* (Washington, D.C., 1840).

The Whig Text Book, or Democracy Unmasked (n.p., n.d.).

Whipple, John, *Substance of a Speech delivered at the Whig Meeting held at the Town House, Providence, R.I., Aug. 28, 1837* (Providence, R.I., 1837).

Wickliffe, R. Jr., *Speech delivered in the National Convention of the Whig Young Men of the United States, Assembled at Baltimore, May 4 and 5, 1840* (Lexington, Ky., 1841).

Williams, P. Jr. et al., *To the People of Virginia* (n.p., n.d.).

Wilmot, Robert, *True Democracy Contrasted with False Democracy, or, Gen'l. Harrison's Cause Vindicated* (Cincinnati, 1840).

Winslow, Hubard, *The Means of the Perpetuity and Prosperity of Our Republic* (Boston, 1838).

Wright, Silas, *Speech of the Hon. Silas Wright at a Mass Meeting of the Democracy of Brooklyn, Sept. 29, 1840* (N.Y., 1840).

Young, Richard M., *Letter of Richard M. Young, Declining his Nomination as a Candidate for Governor* (n.p., n.d.).

Young, Samuel, *Oration delivered at the Democratic Republican Celebration of the Sixty-Fourth Anniversary of the Independence of the United States,* (N.Y., 1840).

295

Contemporary Books, Treatises, etc.

Adams, John Quincy, *Parties in the United States* (N.Y., 1841)
Aiken, John, *Labor and Wages, At Home and Abroad* (Lowell, 1849).
Appleton, Nathan, *Labor, Its Relations in Europe and the United States Compared* (Boston, 1844).
Beecher, Lyman, *A Plea for the West* (Cincinnati, 1835).
_____ *A Plea for Colleges* (Cincinnati, 1836).
Byrdsall, Fitzwilliam, *The History of the Loco-Foco or Equal Rights Party* (N.Y., 1842).
Camp, George Sidney, *Democracy* (N.Y., 1845)
Colton, Calvin, *A Manual for Emigrants to America* (London, 1832).
[Colton, Calvin] *A Voice from America to England* by 'An American Gentleman' (London, 1839).
Dwight, Theodore D., *The Character of Thomas Jefferson, as Exhibited in His Own Writings* (Boston, 1839).
Gibbs, George, *Memoirs of the Administrations of Washington and John Adams, edited from the Papers of Oliver Wolcott,* 2 vols. (N.Y., 1846).
Gouge, William M., *A Short History of Paper Money and Banking in the United States* (Phil., 1833).
Grimke, Frederick, *Considerations Upon the Nature and Tendency of Free Institutions* (Cincinnati, 1848).
Hammond, Jabez D., *A Political History of the State of New York (including the Life of Silas Wright),* 3 vols. (N.Y., 1852).
Lieber, Francis, *Essays on Property and Labour* (N.Y., 1841).
_____ *Manual of Political Ethics,* 2 vols. (Boston, 1838-9).
Mercer, Charles F,. *The Weakness and Inefficiency of the Government of the United States of North America* by a Late American Statesman (London, 1863).
Mines, Flavel S., *The Church the Pillar and Ground of the Truth* (N.Y., 1838).
Ormsby, R. McKinley, *A History of the Whig Party* (Boston, 1859).
Potter, Alonzo, *Political Economy: Its Objects, Uses and Principles* (N.Y., 1841).
[Richter, M.A.] *On Self-Government* (Boston, 1847).
Sedgwick, Theodore, Jr., *Public and Private Economy* (N.Y. 1836).
Taylor, John, *An Inquiry into the Principles and Policy of the Government of the United States* (London, 1950).
_____ *Tyranny Unmasked* (Washington, D.C., 1822).
Tucker, George, *The Theory of Money and Banks Investigated* (Boston, 1839).

Tuckerman, Joseph, *The Principles and Results of the Ministry at Large in Boston* (Boston, 1838).
———— *On the Elevation of the Poor* (Boston, 1874).
Van Buren, Martin, *An Inquiry into the Origins and Course of Political Parties in the United States* (N.Y., 1867).
[Warner, Henry W.] *An Inquiry into the Moral and Religious Character of the American Government* (N.Y., 1838).
Wayland, Francis, *The Elements of Political Economy* (N.Y., 1837).

Memoirs, Diaries, Autobiographies

Adams, John Quincy, *The Memoirs of John Quincy Adams,* 12 vols. (ed. Charles F. Adams, Phil., 1874-7).
Benton, Thomas Hart, *Thirty Years' View,* 2 vols. (N.Y., 1854-6).
Dow, Neil, *The Reminiscences of Neal Dow: Recollections of Eighty Years* (Portland, Me., 1898).
Ewing, Thomas, 'The Diary of Thomas Ewing, August and September 1842', *A.H.R.,* XVIII (Oct., 1912), 97-112.
Greeley, Horace, *Recollections of a Busy Life* (N.Y., 1868).
Hayes, John L., *A Reminiscence of the Free-Soil Movement in New Hampshire, 1845* (Camb., Mass., 1885).
Hone, Philip, *The Diary of Philip Hone, 1829-1851* (ed. Allan Nevins, N.Y., 1936).
Kendall, Amos, *The Autobiography of Amos Kendall* (Boston, 1872).
Polk, James K. *The Diary of James K. Polk During His Presidency, 1845-1849* (Chicago, 1910).
Strong, George T., *The Diary of George Templeton Strong,* 4 vols. (eds. Allan Nevins and Milton H. Thomas, N.Y., 1952).
Van Buren, Martin, 'The Autobiography of Martin Van Buren', *Annual Report of the American Historical Association for the Year 1918,* II (ed. John C. Fitzpatrick, Washington, D.C., 1920).
Weed, Thurlow, *Autobiography of Thurlow Weed* (ed. Harriet A. Weed, Boston, 1883).
———— *Memoir of Thurlow Weed* (ed. Thurlow W. Barnes, Boston, 1884).
Welles, Gideon, *The Diary of Gideon Welles,* 3 vols. (ed. Howard K. Beale, N.Y. 1960)

Secondary Sources

Adams, William H. III, 'The Louisiana Whig Party' (Ph.D. dissertation, Louisiana State University, 1960).

Alexander, Thomas B., *Sectional Stress and Party Strength: A Study of Roll-Call Voting in the United States House of Representatives, 1836-1860* (Nashville, 1967).
_____ 'The Presidential Campaign of 1840 in Tennessee', *T.H.Q.,* I (March 1942), 21-43.
Alexander, Thomas B. *et al.,* 'Who were the Alabama Whigs?' *A.R.,* XVI (Jan. 1963), 5-19.
Allison, Hildreth M., 'Honourable Levi Woodbury: Presidential Timber', *H.N.H.,* XXIII (Autumn 1968), 3-18.
Ames, William E., 'A History of the *National Intelligencer,* 1800-1869' (Ph.D. thesis, University of Minnesota, 1962).
Bailyn, Bernard, *The Ideological Origins of the American Revolution* (Cambridge, Mass., 1967).
Banner, James M., 'The Problem of South Carolina', in *The Hofstadter Aegis: A Memorial* (N.Y., 1974), 60-93.
Banner, Lois W., 'Religious Benevolence and Social Control: A Critique of an Interpretation', *J.A.H.,* LX (June 1973), 23-41.
Barkan, Elliot R., 'The Emergence of a Whig Persuasion: Conservatism, Democratism and the New York State Whigs', *N.Y.H.,* LII (Oct, 1971), 367-95.
Bartlett, Marguarite, *The Chief Phases of Pennsylvania Politics in the Jacksonian Period* (Allentown, Pa., 1919).
Bassett, John S., *The Life of Andrew Jackson* (N.Y., 1916).
Baughlin, William A., 'The Development of Nativism in Cincinnati', *Bulletin of the Cincinnati Historical Society,* XXII (Oct. 1964), 240-55.
Beard, Charles A., *The Economic Origins of Jeffersonian Democracy* (N.Y., 1915).
Benson, Lee, *The Concept of Jacksonian Democracy* (Princeton, 1970).
Bergeron, Paul, 'The Jackson Party on Trial: Presidential Politics in Tennessee, 1836-1856' (Ph.D. thesis, Vanderbilt, 1965).
Berthoff, Rowland, 'The American Social Order: A Conservative Hypothesis', *A.H.R.,* LXV (April 1960), 495-614.
Billington, Ray A., *The Protestant Crusade* (N.Y., 1938).
Binkley, Wilfred E., *American Political Parties, Their Natural History* (N.Y., 1945).
Binney, Charles C., *Life of Horace Binney* (Phil., 1903)
Boucher, Chauncey S., 'Sectionalism, Representation and the Electoral Question in Ante-Bellum South Carolina', *Washington University Studies* IV (Oct. 1916), 3-62.
Boyet, Gene W,. 'The Whigs of Arkansas, 1836-1865' (Ph.D. thesis, Louisiana State University, 1972).
Brauer, Kinley J., *Cotton versus Conscience: Massachusetts Whig*

298

Politics and South Western Expansion, 1843-1848 (Lexington, 1967).

Brewer, Paul W., 'The Rise of the Second Party System: Missouri, 1815-1845' (Ph.D. thesis, Washington University, St Louis, 1974).

Brock, William R., *The Evolution of American Democracy* (N.Y., 1970).

_____ *Conflict and Transformation: the United States 1844-1877* (London, 1977).

Brown, Delva P., 'The Economic Views of Illinois Democrats, 1836-1861' (Ph.D. thesis, Boston University, 1970).

Brown, Norman D., *Daniel Webster and the Politics of Availability* (Athens, Ga., 1969).

Brown, Richard H., ' "Southern Planters and Plain Republicans of the North": Martin Van Buren's Formula for National Politics' (Ph.D. thesis, Yale, 1955).

Brownson, Henry F., *Orestes A. Brownson's Early Life From 1803 to 1844* (Detroit, 1898).

Bulkley, Robert D. Jr., 'Robert Rantoul, Jr., 1805-1852: Politics and Reform in Ante-Bellum Massachusetts' (Ph.D. thesis, Princeton, 1971).

Byrne, Frank L., *Prophet of Prohibition: Neal Dow and his Crusade* (Madison, Wisc., 1961).

Carey, Robert L., *Daniel Webster as an Economist* (N.Y., 1929).

Carleton, William G., 'Political Aspects of the Van Buren Era', *S.A.Q.*, L (April 1951), 167-85.

Carr, John W., 'The Manhood Suffrage Movement in North Carolina', *Trinity College Historical Society Historical Papers*, Series XI (1915), 47-78.

Carroll, E. Malcolm, *Origins of the Whig Party* (Durham, N.C., 1925).

Catterall, Ralph C.H., *The Second Bank of the United States* (Chicago, 1903).

Cave, Alfred A., *Jacksonian Democracy and the Historians* (Gainesville, Fl., 1964).

_____ *An American Conservative in the Age of Jackson: The Political and Social Thought of Calvin Colton* (Fort Worth, 1969)

Cawelti, John G., *Apostles of the Self-Made Man* (Chicago, 1965).

Chadbourne, Walter W., *A History of Banking in Maine* (Orono, Me., 1936).

Chambers, William N., *Old Bullion Benton, Senator from the New West: Thomas Hart Benton, 1782-1858* (Boston, 1956).

Chambers, William N. and Burnham, Walter D. (eds.), *The American Party Systems* (N.Y., 1967).

299

Ciaburn, Robert L., 'The Dorr Rebellion in Rhode Island: The Moderate Phase', *R.I.H.*, XXVI (July 1967), 73-87.
Clapp, Margaret A., *Forgotten First Citizen: John Bigelow* (Boston, 1947).
Cochran, Thomas C., 'The Business Revolution', *A.H.R.*, LXXIX (Dec. 1974), 1449-66.
Cole, Arthur C., *The Whig Party in the South* (Washington, D.C., 1913).
Cole. Donald B., *Jacksonian Democracy in New Hampshire* (Camb., Mass., 1970).
Coleman, Peter J., *The Transformation of Rhode Island 1790-1860* (Providence, 1963).
Collins, Bruce, 'The Ideology of the Ante-Bellum Northern Democrats', *J.A.S.*, XI (April 1977), 103-121.
Conley, Patrick T., 'Rhode Island Constitutional Development, 1636-1841: Prologue to the Dorr Rebellion' (Ph.D. thesis, Notre Dame University, 1970).
Connelley, William E. and Coulter, E.M., *A History of Kentucky* 5 vols. (Chicago, 1922).
Conrad, Henry C., *History of the State of Delaware* 3 vols. (Wilmington, 1908).
Cooper, William J., *The South and the Politics of Slavery 1828-1856* (Baton Rouge, 1978).
Coulter, Ellis M., *William G. Brownlow: Fighting Parson of the Southern Highlands* (Knoxville, 1973).
Crockett, Walter H., *Vermount, The Green Mountain State* 4 vols. (N.Y., 1921).
Cross, Whitney R., *The Burned-over District: The Social and Intellectual History of Enthusiastic Religion in Western New York, 1800-1850* (Ithaca, 1950).
Crouthamel, James L., *James Watson Webb, A Biography* (Middletown, Conn., 1969).
Current, Richard C., *Daniel Webster and the Rise of National Conservatism* (Boston, 1955).
Curtis, James C., *The Fox at Bay: Martin Van Buren and the Presidency, 1837-1841* (Lexington, 1970).
Darling, Arthur B., *Political Changes in Massachusetts* (New Haven, 1968).
_____ 'Jacksonian Democracy in Massachusetts, 1824-1848', *A.H.R.*, XXIX (Jan. 1924), 271-87.
Davis, David B., 'Some Themes of Counter-Subversion: An Analysis of Anti-Masonic, Anti-Catholic, and Anti-Mormon Literature', *M.V.H.R.*, XLVII (Sept. 1960), 205-24.
Davis, Harold, 'The Economic Basis of Ohio Politics, 1820-1840',

300

O.S.A.H.Q., XLVII (Oct. 1938), 288-318.
Davis, Rodney O., 'Illinois Legislators and Jacksonian Democracy, 1834-1841' (Ph.D. thesis, University of Iowa, 1966).
Debats, Donald A., 'Elites and Masses: Political Structure, Communication and Behavior in Ante-Bellum Georgia' (Ph.D. thesis, University of Wisconsin, 1973).
Degler, Carl N., 'The Loco Focos: Urban Agrarians', *J.E.H.*, XVI (Sept. 1956), 322-33.
Dent, Lynwood M. Jr., 'The Virginian Democratic Party, 1824-1847' 2 vols. (Ph.D. thesis, Louisiana State University, 1974).
Dingledine, Raymond C. Jr., 'The Political Career of William Cabell Rives' (Ph.D. thesis, University of Virginia, 1947).
Doherty, Herbert J. Jr., *The Whigs of Florida 1845-1854* (Gainesville, 1959).
Donovan, Herbert A., *The Barnburners: A Study of the Internal Movements in the Political History of New York State 1830-1852* (N.Y., 1946).
Dorfman, Joseph, *The Economic Mind In American Civilisation, 1606-1865* 2 vols. (N.Y., 1925).
_____ 'The Jackson Wage-Earner Thesis', *A.H.R.*, LIV (Jan. 1949), 296-306.
Duckett, Alvin L., *John Forsyth, Political Tactician* (Athens, 1962).
Eaton, Clement, *Henry Clay and the Art of American Politics* (Boston, 1957).
Elliott, Robert N., *The 'Raleigh Register', 1799-1863* (Chapel Hill, 1955).
Ellis, Richard E., *The Jeffersonian Crisis: Courts and Politics in the Young Republic* (N.Y., 1971).
Emerson, Donald E., *Richard Hildreth* (Baltimore, 1946).
Erikson, Erling A., 'Banks and Politics before the Civil War: The Case of Iowa, 1836-1865' (Ph.D. thesis, University of Iowa, 1967).
Ershkowitz, Herbert and Shade, William G., 'Consensus or Conflict? Political Behavior in the State Legislatures during the Jacksonian Era', *J.A.H.*, LVIII (Dec. 1971), 591-621.
Fallow, Walter R., 'The Rise of the Whig Party in New Jersey' (Ph.D thesis, Princeton, 1966).
Farry, Joseph P., 'Themes of Continuity and Change in the Political Philosophy of Orestes Brownson: A Comparative Study' (Ph.D. thesis, Fordham University, 1968).
Fehrenbacher, Donald E., *Chicago Giant, A Biography of 'Long John' Wentworth* (Madison, Wisc., 1957).
Feuss, Claude M., *Daniel Webster* 2 vols. (Boston, 1930).
Fischer, David H., *The Revolution of American Conservatism*

(N.Y., 1965).

Flatt, Donald E., 'Historians view Jacksonian Democracy: A Historiographical Study' (Ph.D. thesis, University of Kentucky, 1974).

Foner, Eric, *Free soil, Free Labour, Free Men: The Ideology of the Republican Party before the Civil War* (N.Y., 1970).

Forderhase, Rudolph E., 'Jacksonianism in Missouri, From Prediliction to Party' (Ph.D. thesis, University of Missouri, 1968).

Formisano, Ronald P., *The Birth of Mass Parties: Michigan 1827-1861* (Princeton, 1971).

————— 'Toward a Reorientation of Jacksonian Politics: A Review of the Literature, 1959-1975', *J.A.H.*, LXIII (June 1976), 42-65.

Fournier, Sister Theresa, 'The Political Career of Azariah Cutting Flagg: 1823-1847' (Ph.D. thesis, Middle Tennessee State University, 1975).

Fox, Dixon, R., *The Decline of Aristocracy in the Politics of New York* (N.Y., 1919).

Freehling, William W., *Prelude to Civil War: The Nullification Controversy in South Carolina, 1816-1836* (N.Y., 1965).

Freidel, Frank, *Francis Lieber, Nineteenth-Century Liberal* (Baton Rouge, 1947).

Fulsom, Burton W. III, 'The Politics of Elites: Prominence and Party in Davidson County, Tennessee, 1835-1861', *J.S.H.*, XXIX (Aug. 1973), 359-78.

Gappleburg, Leonard I., 'M.M. Noah and the *Evening Star:* Whig Journalism 1833-1840' (Ph.D. thesis, Yeshiva University, 1970).

Garraty, John A., *Silas Wright* (N.Y., 1949).

Gatell, Frank O., 'Sober Second Thoughts on Van Buren, the Albany Regency and the Wall Street Conspiracy', *J.A.H.*, LIII (June 1966), 19-40.

————— 'Money and Party in Jacksonian America: A Quantitative Look at New York City's Men of Quality', *P.S.Q.*, LXXXII (June 1967), 235-52.

————— 'Beyond Jacksonian Consensus', in Herbert J. Bass (ed.), *The State of American History* (Chicago, 1970), 350-61.

Gates, Paul, W., *The Farmer's Age, 1815-1860* (N.Y., 1960).

Gettleman, Marvin E., *The Dorr Rebellion, A Study in American Radicalism: 1833-1848* (N.Y., 1973).

Gillet, Ransom H., *The Life and Times of Silas Wright* 2 vols. (Albany, 1874).

Ginsberg, Judah B., 'The Tangled Web: The New York Democratic Party and The Slavery Controversy, 1844-1860' (Ph.D. thesis, University of Wisconsin, 1974).

Goldstein, Kalman, 'The Albany Regency: The Failure of Practical

302

Politics' (Ph.D. thesis, Columbia, 1969).

Govan, Thomas P., *Nicholas Biddle: Nationalist and Public Banker, 1786-1844* (Chicago, 1959).

―――― 'Banking and the Credit System in Georgia, 1810-1860', *J.S.H.*, IV (May 1938), 164-84.

―――― ' "Agrarian" and "Agrarianism": A Study in the Use and Abuse of Words', *J.S.H.*, XXX (Feb. 1964), 35-47.

Grant, Philip A., 'The Antimasons Retain Control of the Green Mountain State', *VtH.*, XXXIV (July 1966), 169-87.

Gresham, L. Paul, 'The Public Career of Hugh Lawson White', *T.H.Q.*, III (Dec. 1944), 291-318.

Griffin, Clifford, S., *Their Brothers' Keepers, Moral Stewardship in the United States 1800-1865* (New Brunswick, N.J., 1960).

Gunderson, Robert E., *The Log Cabin Campaign* (Lexington, 1957).

Hamilton, J.G. de Roulhac, 'Party Politics in North Carolina, 1835-1860' *J.S.H.P.*, vol. XV (Durham, N.C., 1916).

Hammond, Bray, *Banks and Politics in America from the Revolution to the Civil War* (Princeton, 1957).

Handlin, Oscar and Flug, Mary, *Commonwealth: A Study of the Role of Government in the American Economy: Massachusetts, 1774-1861* (N.Y., 1947).

Hans, Robert J., 'Massachusetts Whigs, 1833-1854' (Ph.D. thesis, University of Nebraska, 1973).

Harkness, Donald, 'Crosscurrents; American Anti-democracy from Jackson to the Civil War (1820-1860)' (Ph.D. thesis, University of Minnesota, 1955).

Harris, Sheldon H., 'The Public Career of John Louis O'Sullivan' (Ph.D. thesis, Columbia, 1958).

Hartz, Louis, *The Liberal Tradition in America* (N.Y., 1955).

―――― 'Seth Luther, the Story of a Working Class Rebel', *N.E.Q.*, XIII (Sept., 1940), 401-18.

Hatch, Louis C., *Maine: A History* 4 vols. (N.Y., 1919).

Heale, Michael J., *The Making of American Politics, 1750-1850* (London, 1977).

―――― 'Harbingers of Progressivism: Responses to the Urban Crisis in New York City, 1845-1860', *J.A.S.*, X (April 1976), 17-36.

―――― 'From City Fathers to Social Critics: Humanitarianism and Government in New York, 1790-1860', *J.A.H.*, LXIII (June 1976), 21-41.

Heath, Milton S., *Constructive Liberalism: The Role of the State in Economic Development in Georgia* (Cambridge, Mass., 1954).

Hershkowitz, Leo, 'New York City, 1834-1840, A Study in Local Politics' (Ph.D. thesis, New York University, 1960).

_____ 'The Native American Democratic Association in New York City, 1835-1836', *N. Y. H. S. Q.*, XLVI (Jan. 1962), 40-60.

Hibbard, Benjamin, *A History of the Public Land Policies* (N.Y., 1939).

Higham, John, 'Hanging Together: Divergent Unities in American History', *J.A.H.*, LXI (June 1974), 5-28.

Hoffmann, William, S., 'Andrew Jackson and North Carolina Politics', *J.S.H.P.*, vol. XL (Chapel Hill, 1958).

Hofstadter, Richard, *The American Political Tradition* (N.Y., 1959).

_____ *The Idea of a Party System: The Rise of a Legitimate Opposition in the United States, 1780-1840* (Berkeley, 1969).

_____ 'William Leggett, Spokesman of Jacksonian Democracy', *P.S.Q.*, LVIII (Dec. 1943), 581-94.

Holt, Edgar A., 'Party Politics in Ohio, 1840-1850', *O.S.A.H.Q.*, XXXVII (July 1928), 439-591; XXXVIII (Jan. 1929), 41-182, (April 1929), 260-402.

Holt, Michael F., *Forging a Majority: The Formation of the Republican Party in Pittsburgh 1848-1860* (New Haven, 1969).

_____ *The Political Crisis of the 1850s* (N.Y., 1977).

Horton, John T., *James Kent, A Study in Conservatism, 1763-1847* (N.Y., 1939).

Horvarter, Nancy, 'The Social and Political Views of Orestes Augustus Brownson' (Ph.D. thesis, Ball State University, Ind., 1974).

Hueston, Robert F., 'The Catholic Press and Nativism, 1840-1860' (Ph.D. thesis, Notre Dame University, Ind., 1972).

Huggins, Walter E., *Jacksonian Democracy and the Working Class: A Study of the New York Workingmen's Movement 1829-1837* (Stanford, 1960).

Hunt, Henry D., *Hannibal Hamlin of Maine, Lincoln's First Vice-President* (Syracuse, N.Y., 1969).

Isely, Jeter A., *Horace Greeley and the Republican Party, 1853-1861* (Princeton, 1947).

Jack, Theodore H., *Sectionalism and Party Politics in Alabama, 1819-1842* (Menasha, Wisc., 1919).

Jackson, Carlton, L., 'A History of the Whig Party in Alabama, 1828-1860' (Ph.D. thesis, University of Georgia, 1962).

James, Marquis, *Andres Jackson: The Border Captain* (Indianapolis, 1933).

Johnson, Zachary T., *The Political Policies of Howell Cobb* (Nashville, 1929).

Johnston, Richard M. and Browne, William H., *Life of Alexander H. Stephens* (N.Y., 1971).

Kelly, Robert, *The Cultural Pattern in American Politics: The First Century* (N.Y., 1979).
_____ 'Ideology and Political Culture from Jefferson to Nixon', *A.H.R.*, LXXXII (June 1977), 531-62
Kesilman, Sylvan H., 'John Tyler and the Presidency: Old School Republicanism, Partisan Realignment, and Support for his Administration' (Ph.D. thesis, Ohio State University, 1973).
Kirwan, Albert D., *John H. Crittenden, The Struggle for the Union* (Kentucky University, 1962).
Kohn, Hans, *American Nationalism* (N.Y., 1957).
Kousser, J. Morgan, 'The "New Political History": A Methodological Critique', *R.A.H.*, IV (March 1976), 1-14.
Kriedman, Herbert, 'New York's Philip Hone: Businessman – Politician – Patron of Arts and Letters' (Ph.D. thesis, New York University, 1965).
Krout, John A., *The Origins of Prohibition* (N.Y., 1925).
Lannie, Vincent P., *Public Money and Parochial Education: Bishop Hughes, Governor Seward, and the New York School Controversy* (Cleveland, 1968).
Lapati, Americo D., *Orestes Augustus Brownson* (N.Y., 1965).
Latner, Richard B., *The Presidency of Andrew Jackson* (Athens, Ga., 1979).
_____ 'A New Look at Jacksonian Politics', *J.A.H.*, LXI (March 1975), 943-69.
Latner, Richard B. and Levine, Peter D., 'Perspectives on Ante-Bellum Pietistic Politics', *R.A.H.*, IV (March 1976), 15-24.
Lebowitz, Michael A., 'The Significance of Claptrap in American History', *S.L.*, III (Winter 1963), 79-94.
_____ 'The Jacksonians: Paradox Lost?' in Barton J. Bernstein (ed.), *Towards a New Past: Dissenting Essays in American History* (N.Y., 1969), 65-89.
Lefler, Hugh T. and Newsome, Albert R., *North Carolina, The History of a Southern State* (Chapel Hill, 1954).
Leonard, Adam A., 'Personal Politics in Indiana 1816-1840', *Ind. M.H.*, XIX (March 1923), 2-56, (June 1923), 132-168, (Sept. 1923), 241-81.
Leonard, Ira M., 'New York City Politics, 1841-1844: Nativism and Reform' (Ph.D. thesis, New York University, 1965).
Leopold, Richard W., *Robert Dale Owen, A Biography* (N.Y., 1969).
Levine, Peter D., 'Party-in-the-Legislature: New Jersey, 1829-1844' (Ph.D. thesis, Rutgers, 1971).
Lichterman, Martin, 'John Adams Dix, 1798-1879' (Ph.D. thesis, Columbia, 1952).

Lipsky, George A., *John Quincy Adams: His Theory and Ideas* (N.Y., 1950).
Liston, Ann E., 'W.C. Rives, Diplomat and Politician, 1829-1853' (Ph..D. thesis, Ohio State University, 1972).
Loudon, Herbert I., 'The Nativist Movement in the American Republican Party in New York City during the Period 1843-1847' (Ph.D. thesis, New York Univeristy, 1966).
Lucey, William C., *Edward Kavanagh: Catholic, Statesman, Diplomat from Maine* (Francestown, N.H., 1946).
Marshall, Hugh, *Orestes Brownson and the American Republic* (Washington, D.C., 1971).
Marshall, Lynn L., 'The Strange Stillbirth of the Whig Party', *A.H.R.,* LXXVII (Jan. 1967), 445-68.
Mathews, J.V., ' "Whig History": The New England Whigs and a Useable Past', *N.E.Q.,* LI (March 1978), 193-208.
Maynard, Theodore, *Orestes Brownson, Yankee, Radical, Catholic* (N.Y., 1971).
Mayo, Edward L., 'The *National Intelligencer* and Jacksonian Democracy' (Ph.D. thesis, Claremont Graduate School, 1969).
McCarthy, Charles, 'The Antimasonic Party: A Study in Political Antimasonry in the United States, 1827-1840', *Annual Report of the American Historical Association for the Year 1902* 2 vols. (Washington, D.C., 1928).
McClure, Clarence H., *Opposition in Missouri to Thomas Hart Benton* (Nashville., 1927).
McConville, Sister Mary St Patrick, *Political Nativism in the State of Maryland, 1830-1860* (Washington, D.C., 1928).
McCormick, Richard L., 'Ethno-Cultural Interpretations of Nineteenth-Century American Voting Behavior', *P.S.Q.,* LXXXIX (June 1974), 351-77.
_____ 'The Party Period and Public Policy: An Exploratory Hypothesis', *J.A.H.,* LXVI (Sept. 1979), 279-98.
McCormick, Richard P., *The Second American Party System* (Chapel Hill, 1966).
McFaul, John M., *The Politics of Jacksonian Finance* (Ithaca, 1972).
_____ 'Expediency *versus* Morality: Jacksonian Politics and Slavery', *J.A.H.,* LXII (June 1975), 24-39.
McGee, Patricia E., 'Issues and Factions: New York States Politics from the Panic of 1837 to the Election of 1848' (Ph.D. thesis, St. John's University, 1969).
McGrane, Reginald C., *William Allen, A Study in Western Democracy* (Columbus, Ohio, 1925).
McLean, Robert C., *George Tucker, Moral Philosopher and Man of*

306

Letters (Chapel Hill, 1961)
MacLeod, Duncan J., *Slavery, Race and the American Revolution* (Cambridge, 1974).
Meek, Melinda, 'The Life of Archibald Yell', *Ark. H.Q.,* XXVI (Spring 1967), 11-23, (Summer 1967), 162-84, (Autumn 1967), 226-43, (Winter 1967), 353-78.
Mering, John V., *The Whig Party in Missouri* (Columbia, Mo., 1967).
Meyers, Marvin, *The Jacksonian Persuasion: Politics and Belief* (Stanford, 1957).
Miller, Douglas T., *Jacksonian Aristocracy: Class and Democracy in New York, 1830-1860* (N.Y., 1941).
Mims, Edward, *The Majority of the People* (N.Y., 1941).
Mims, Helen S., 'Early American Democratic Theory and Orestes Brownson', *S.S.,* III (Spring 1938), 166-98.
Mitchell, Stewart, *Horatio Seymour of New York* (Camb., Mass., 1938).
Moffit, Robert E., 'Metaphysics and Constitutionalism: The Political Theory of Orestes Brownson' (Ph.D. thesis, University of Arizona, 1975).
Morantz, Regina A.M. ' " Democracy" and "Republic" in American Ideology, 1787-1840' (Ph.D. thesis, Columbia, 1971).
Morris, John D., 'The New York State Whigs, 1834-1842, A Study of Political Organization' (Ph.D. thesis, University of Rochester, 1970).
Morse, Jarvis M., *A Neglected Period of Connecticut's History* (New Haven, 1933).
Mowry, Arthur M., *The Dorr War or the Constitutional Struggle in Rhode Island* (Providence, 1901).
Mueller, Henry R., *The Whig Party in Pennsylvania* (N.Y., 1922).
Muller, Ernest P., 'Preston King: A Political Biography' (Ph.D. thesis, Columbia, 1957).
Murdoch, James M., 'Charles Hammond, Egalitarian Whig' (Ph.D. thesis, North Western University, 1971).
Murray, Paul, 'The Whig Party in Georgia', *J.S.H.P.,* vol. XXIX (Chapel Hill, 1948).
Nagel, Paul, *This Sacred Trust: American Nationality 1798-1898* (N.Y., 1971).
―――― *One Nation Indivisible: The Union in American Thought, 1776-1861* (N.Y., 1964).
Nathans, Sydney, *Daniel Webster and Jacksonian Democracy* (Baltimore, 1973).
Newhard, Leota, 'The Beginning of the Whig Party in Missouri, 1824-1840', *Mo.H.R.,* XXV (Jan. 1931), 254-80.

Nichols, Roy F., *Franklin Pierce: Young Hickory of the Granite Hills* (Phil., 1958).

Noonan, Carroll J., *Nativism in Connecticut, 1829-1869* (Washington, D.C., 1938).

North, Douglass C., *The Economic Growth of the United States 1790-1860 (Englewood Cliffs, 1966).*

_____ *Growth and Welfare in the American Past* (Englewood Cliffs, 1966).

Norton, Clarence C., 'The Democratic Party in Ante-Bellum North Carolina', *J.S.H.P.*, vol. XXI (Chapel Hill, 1930).

Nye, Russel B., *George Bancroft, Brahmin Rebel* (N.Y., 1944).

O'Connor, Thomas H., *Lords of the Loom, the Cotton Whigs and the Coming of the Civil War* (N.Y., 1968).

Parish, John C. (ed.) 'The Autobiography of John Chambers', *I.J.H.P.*, VI (April 1908), 247-86.

Parish, Peter J., 'Daniel Webster, New England, and the West', *J.A.H.*, LIV (Dec. 1967), 524-49.

Parkes, Norman L., 'The Career of John Bell as Congressman from Tennessee, 1827-1841', *T.H.Q.*, I (Sept. 1942), 229-49.

Parmet, Robert D., 'The Know-Nothings in Connecticut' (Ph.D. thesis, Columbia 1966).

Parrington, Vernon L., *Main Currents in American Thought* 3 vols. (N.Y., 1930).

Parry, Stanley J., 'The Premises of Brownson's Political Theory', *R.P.*, XVI (April 1954), 194-211.

Parsons, Lynn H., 'The Hamiltonian Tradition in the United States, 1804-1912' (Ph.D. thesis, Johns Hopkins, 1967).

Pease, Theodore C., *The Frontier State 1818-1848* (Springfield, Ill., 1918).

Pelzer, Louis, 'The History and Principles of the Democratic Party of the Territory of Iowa', *I.J.H.P.*, VI (Jan. 1908), 3-54.

_____ 'The History and Principles of the Whigs of the Territory of Iowa, *I.J.H.P.*, V (Jan. 1907), 46-90.

_____ 'The History and Principles of the Democratic Party of Iowa, 1846-1857', *I.J.H.P.*, VI (April 1908), 163-246.

Penney, Sharon H., 'Daniel Dewey Barnard: Patrician in Politics', (Ph.D. thesis, State University of New York at Albany, 1972).

Perkins, Dexter, 'William H. Seward', *N.Y.H.*, XV (April 1934), 160-74.

Pessen, Edward, *Most Uncommon Jacksonians, The Radical Leaders of The Early Labor Movement* (Albany, 1967).

_____ *Jacksonian America: Society, Personality and Politics* rev. ed. (Homewood, Ill., 1978).

_____ *Riches, Class and Power before the Civil War* (Lexington,

308

1973).
Peterson, Merrill D., *The Jefferson Image in the American Mind* (N.Y., 1962).
Phillips, Ulrich B., 'The Southern Whigs, 1834-1854', in *Essays in American History dedicated to Frederick Jackson Turner* (N.Y., 1951), 203-29.
Poage, George R., *Henry Clay and the Whig Party* (Chapel Hill, 1936).
Ratcliffe, Donald J., 'Politics in Jacksonian Ohio: Reflections on the Ethnocultural Interpretation', *O.H.*, LXXXVIII (Winter 1979), 5-36.
Reed, Henry C. (ed), *Delaware, A History of the First State* 3 vols. (N.Y., 1947).
Reed, John J., 'The Emergence of the Whig Party in the North: Massachusetts, New York, Pennsylvania and Ohio' (Ph.D. thesis, University of Pennsylvania, 1953).
Remini, Robert V., *Andrew Jackson* (N.Y., 1966).
Rezneck, Samual, 'Social History of an American Depression, 1837-1843', *A.H.R.*, XL (July 1935), 662-87.
Rich, Robert S., 'Politics and Pedigrees: The Wealthy Men of Boston, 1798-1852' (Ph.D. thesis, U.C.L.A., 1975).
Robbins, Roy M., *Our Landed Heritage: The Public Domain 1776-1936* (Princeton, 1942).
Roemer, Lawrence D., *Brownson on Democracy and the Trend Towards Socialism* (N.Y., 1953).
Rossiter, Clinton, *Conservatism in America* (N.Y., 1955).
Rothman, David J., *The Discovery of the Asylum: Social Order and Disorder in the Early Republic* (Boston, 1971).
Rozett, John M., 'The Social Bases of Party Conflict in the Age of Jackson: Individual Voting Behavior in Greene County, Illinois, 1838-1848' (Ph.D. thesis, University of Michigan, 1974).
Rumbarger, John J., 'The Social Origins and Functions of the Political Temperance Movement in the Reconstruction of American Society, 1825-1917' (Ph.D. thesis, University of Pennsylvania, 1968).
Russo, David J., *The Major Political Issues of the Jacksonian Period and the Development of Party Loyalty in Congress, 1830-1840* (Phil., 1972).
Ryan, Thomas R., *The Sailor's Snug Harbor, Studies in Brownson's Thought* (Westminster, My. 1952).
Scharf, John T., *History of Delaware, 1609-1888* 2 vols. (Phil., 1888).
Schelin, Robert C., 'Millard Fillmore, Anti-Mason to Know-Nothing: A Moderate in Politics' (Ph.D. thesis, State University of New

York at Binghampton, 1975).
Schlesinger, Arthur M. Jr., *The Age of Jackson* (Boston, 1945).
_____ *Orestes A. Brownson, A Pilgrim's Progress* (N.Y., 1963).
Schugg, Roger W., *The Origins of Class Struggle in Louisiana* (Baton Rouge, 1968).
Sellers, Charles G. Jr., *James K. Polk, Jacksonian* (Princeton, 1957).
_____ *James, K. Polk, Continentalist* (Princeton, 1966).
_____ 'Who were the Southern Whigs?', *A.H.R.,* LIX (Jan 1954), 335- 46.
_____ 'Andrew Jackson *versus* the Historians', *M.V.H.R.,* XLIV (March 1958), 615-34.
Sewell, Richard H., *John P. Hale and the Politics of Abolition* (Camb., Mass., 1965).
Shade, William G., *Banks or no Banks: The Money Issue in Western Politics, 1832-1865* (Detroit, 1972).
Sharp, James R., *The Jacksonians versus the Banks: Politics in the States after the Panic of 1837* (N.Y., 1970).
Shortridge, Ray M., 'Voting Patterns in the American Midwest, 1840-1872' (Ph.D. thesis, University of Michigan, 1974).
Silbey, Joel H., *The Shrine of Party: Congressional Voting Behavior, 1841-1852* (Pittsburgh, 1967).
Simms, Henry F., *The Rise of the Whigs in Virginia* (Richmond, 1929).
Smith, Alfred G., Jr., *Economic Readjustment of an Old Cotton State, South Carolina, 1820-1860* (Columbia, S.C. 1958).
Smith, Henry Nash, *Virgin Land: The American West as Symbol and Myth* (Camb., Mass., 1950).
Smith, William E., *The Francis Preston Blair Family in Politics* 2 vols. (N.Y., 1933).
Snyder, Charles M., *The Jacksonian Heritage: Pennsylvania Politics 1833-1848* (Harrisburg, 1958).
Somit, Albert, *'Andrew Jackson as Political Theorist',* T.H.Q., VIII (June 1949), 99-126.
Somkin, Fred, *Unquiet Eagle: Memory and Desire in the Idea of American Freedom* (Ithaca, 1967).
Spencer, Ivor D., *The Victor and the Spoils: A Life of William L. Marcy* (Providence, 1959).
Stanwood, Edward, *American Tariff Controversies in the Nineteenth Century* 2 vols. (Boston, 1930).
Stephenson, George M., *The Political History of the Public Lands from 1840-1862 – from Pre-Emption to Homestead* (Boston, 1917).
Sternscher, Bernard, *Consensus, Conflict and American Historians*

(Bloomington, Ind., 1975).
Streeter, Floyd B., *Political Parties in Michigan, 1837-1860* (Lansing, 1918).
Sweet, Edward F., 'The Origin of the Democratic Party in Rhode Island 1824-1836' (Ph.D. thesis, Fordham University, 1971).
Tabachnik, Leonard, 'Origins of the Know-Nothing Party: A Study of the Native American Party in Philadelphia, 1844-1852' (Ph.D. thesis, Columbia, 1973).
Taylor, George R., *The Transportation Revolution, 1815-1860* (N.Y., 1951).
Temin, Peter, *The Jacksonian Economy* (N.Y., 1969).
Thompson, Arthur W., *Jacksonian Democracy on the Florida Frontier* (Gainesville, 1961).
Thompson, Charles M., *The Illinois Whigs before 1846* (Urbana, Ill., 1915).
Thompson, William Y., *Robert Toombs of Georgia* (Baton Rouge, 1966).
Thornton, Jonathan M., III, *Politics and Power in a Slave Society: Alabama 1806-1860* (Baton Rouge, 1978).
Tomlinson, Robert H., 'The Origins and Editorial Politics of the *Richmond Whig and Public Advertiser,* 1824-1865' (Ph.D. thesis, Michigan State University, 1921).
Tregle, Joseph G., Jr., 'Louisiana in the Age of Jackson: A Study in Ego Politics' (Ph.D. thesis, University of Pennsylvania, 1954).
Trimble, William, 'Diverging Tendencies in the New York Democracy in the Period of the Loco Focos', *A.H.R.,* XXIV (April 1919), 396-421.
_____ 'The Social Philosophy of the Loco Foco Democracy', *A.J.S.,* XXVI (May 1921), 705-15.
Turner, Frederick J., *The United States, 1830-1850* (N.Y., 1935).
Tutorow, Norman E., 'Whigs of the old Northwest and Texas Annexation, 1836 - April 1844', *Ind. M.H.,* (March 1970), 56-60.
Tyrell, Ian R., 'Drink and the Process of Social Reform: From Temperance to Prohibition in Ante-Bellum America, 1813-1860' (Ph.D. thesis, Duke University, 1974).
Van Deusen, Glyndon G., *The Life of Henry Clay* (Boston, 1935).
_____ *Thurlow Weed: Wizard of the Lobby* (Boston, 1947).
_____ *Horace Greeley, Nineteenth Century Crusader* (Phil., 1953).
_____ *The Jacksonian Era* (N.Y., 1963).
_____ *William Henry Seward* (N.Y., 1967).
_____ *The Rise and Decline of Jacksonian Democracy* (N.Y., 1970).
_____ 'Some Aspects of Whig Thought and Theory in the

Jacksonian Period', *A. H. R.*, LXIII (Jan. 1958), 305-22.

Van Zandt, Roland, *The Metaphysical Foundations of American History* (The Hague, 1959).

Vigilante, Emil C., 'The Temperance Reform in New York State, 1829-1857' (Ph.D. thesis, New York University, 1964).

Wagstaff, Henry M., *State Rights and Political Parties in North Carolina, 1776-1861* (Baltimore, 1906).

Wallace, Michael L., 'Ideologies of Party in the Ante-Bellum Republic (Ph.D. thesis, Columbia, 1973).

Walton, Brian G., 'The Second Party System in Arkansas, 1836-1848', *Ark. H. Q.*, XXVIII (Summer 1969), 120-155.

Ward, John W., *Andrew Jackson – Symbol for an Age* (N.Y., 1955).

_____ 'The Age of the Common Man', in John Higham (ed.), *The Reconstruction of American History* (N.Y., 1962). 82-97.

_____ 'Jacksonian Democratic Thought: A Natural Charter of Privilege', in Stanley Coben and Lorman Ratner (eds.), *The Development of an American Culture* (Englewood Cliffs, 1970), 44-63.

Warner, Lee H., 'The Silver Greys: New York State Conservative Whigs 1846-1856' (Ph.D. thesis, University of Wisconsin, 1971).

Weisenburger, Francis P., *The Passing of the Frontier, 1825-1850* (Columbus, Ohio, 1941).

Wellinton, Raynor M., *The Political and Sectional Influence of the Public Lands, 1828-1842* (Camb., Mass., 1914).

Welter, Rush *The Mind of America, 1820-1860* (N.Y., 1975).

Westcott, Richard R., 'A History of Maine Politics 1840-1856: The Formation of the Republican Party' (Ph.D. thesis, University of Maine, 1966).

Whalen, Doran, *Granite for God's House: The Life of Orestes Brownson* (N.Y., 1941).

Wheaton, Philip D., 'Levi Woodbury, Jacksonian Financier' (Ph.D. thesis, University of Maryland, 1955).

White, Laura M., *Robert Barnwell Rhett: Father of Secession* (N.Y., 1931).

White, Leonard D., *The Jacksonians: A Study in Administrative History 1829-1861* (N.Y., 1954).

Williams, William A., *The Contours of American History* (London, 1961).

Williamson, Chilton, *American Suffrage from Property to Democracy, 1760-1860* (Princeton, 1960).

Wilson, Major L., *Space, Time and Freedom* (London, 1979).

_____ 'Liberty and Union: An Analysis of Three Concepts Involved in the Nullification Controversy', *J.S.H.*, XXXIII

312
(Aug. 1967), 331-55.

_____ 'The Concept of Time and the Political Dialogue in the United States, 1828-1848', *A.Q.*, XIX (Winter 1967), 619-44.

Wilson, Samuel W., *A History of Kentucky* 4 vols. (Chicago, 1928).

Wiltse, Charles M., *John C. Calhoun* 3 vols. (Indianapolis, 1944-51).

_____ *The Jeffersonian Tradition in American Democracy* (Chapel Hill, 1935).

Wire, Richard A., 'John M. Clayton and the Search for Order: A Study in Whig Politics and Diplomacy' (Ph.D. thesis, University of Maryland, 1971).

Wood, Gordon, *The Creation of the American Republic* (N.Y., 1972)

Worton, Stanley N., 'William Leggett, Political Journalist (1800-1839): A Study in Democratic Thought' (Ph.D. thesis, Columbia, 1954).

Wright, James E., 'The Ethnocultural Model of Voting: A Behavioral and Historical Critique', *A.B.S.*, XVI (May/June 1973), 653-74.

Wyatt-Brown, Bertram, 'Prelude to Abolitionism: Sabbatarian Politics and the Rise of the Second Party System', *J.A.H.*, LVIII (Sept. 1971), 316-41.

Wyllie, Irvin G., *The Self Made Man in America, the Myth of Rags to Riches* (New Brunswick, N.J., 1954).

Young, David N., 'The Mississippi Whigs 1834-1860' (Ph.D. thesis, University of Alabama, 1968).

Zahler, Helene S., *Eastern Workingmen and National Land Policy, 1829-1862* (N.Y., 1941).

INDEX